SELECT WORKS OF EDMUND BURKE

VOLUME 2

Select Works of Edmund Burke

A NEW IMPRINT OF THE PAYNE EDITION

VOLUME 1

Thoughts on the Cause of the Present Discontents

The Two Speeches on America

VOLUME 2

Reflections on the Revolution in France

VOLUME 3

Letters on a Regicide Peace

Miscellaneous Writings

EDMUND BURKE

SELECT WORKS OF EDMUND BURKE

A NEW IMPRINT OF THE PAYNE EDITION

Foreword by Francis Canavan

VOLUME 2

REFLECTIONS ON THE REVOLUTION IN FRANCE

LIBERTY FUND

This book is published by Liberty Fund, Inc., a foundation established to encourage study of the ideal of a society of free and responsible individuals.

𒂼𒄄

Frontispiece is of the statue of Edmund Burke by John Henry Foley that stands at the Front Gate of Trinity College Dublin. By permission of the Board of Trinity College Dublin.

09 21 22 23 24 C 6 5 4 3 2
24 25 26 27 28 P 10 9 8 7 6

Library of Congress Cataloging-in-Publication Data
Burke, Edmund, 1729–1797.
  [Selections. 1999]
  Select works of Edmund Burke : a new imprint of the Payne edition / foreword and biographical note by Francis Canavan.
    p.   cm.
  Vols. 1–3 originally published: Oxford : Clarendon Press, 1874–1878.
  Includes bibliographical references.
  Contents: v. 1. Thoughts on the cause of the present discontents. The two speeches on America—v. 2. Reflections on the revolution in France—v. 3. Letters on a regicide peace—[4] Miscellaneous writings.
  ISBN 0-86597-162-5 (v. 1 : hc : alk. paper).—ISBN 0-86597-163-3 (v. 1 : pb : alk. paper)
  1. Great Britain—Politics and government—18th century. 2. Great Britain—Colonies—America. 3. France—History—Revolution, 1789–1799. 4. Great Britain—Relations—France. I. Canavan, Francis, 1917–   . II. Payne, Edward John, 1844–1904. III. Title.
  JC176.B826   1999
  320.9'033—dc21   97-34325

    ISBN-13: 978-0-86597-165-3 (v. 2 : pb : alk. paper)
    ISBN-13: 978-0-86597-254-4 (set : pb : alk. paper)

LIBERTY FUND, INC.
11301 North Meridian Street
Carmel, Indiana 46032
libertyfund.org

CONTENTS

EDITOR'S FOREWORD

Edmund Burke's *Reflections on the Revolution in France* is his most famous work, endlessly reprinted and read by thousands of students and general readers as well as by professional scholars. After it appeared on November 1, 1790, it was rapidly answered by a flood of pamphlets and books. E. J. Payne, writing in 1875, said that none of them "is now held in any account" except Sir James Mackintosh's *Vindiciae Gallicae*.[1] In fact, however, Thomas Paine's *The Rights of Man*, Part 1, although not the best reply to Burke, was and remains to this day by far the most popular one. It is still in print.

Burke scorned to answer Paine directly, but in 1791 he published a sequel to his *Reflections* under the title *An Appeal from the New to the Old Whigs*.[2] In it, he quoted several pages from Paine's book without acknowledging their source, and took them as representative of the views of all the British sympathizers with the French Revolution. Paine came back with *The Rights of Man*, Part 2. Burke ignored it, so in fact there was no debate between him and Paine. The two men talked past each other in appeals to the British public.

THE RADICAL
DEMOCRATIC IDEOLOGY

Burke had been personally acquainted with Paine, but it is unlikely that he had him in mind when he wrote the *Reflections*. He already knew the radical democratic ideology that

1. P. 77.

2. This document is included in *Further Reflections on the Revolution in France* (Indianapolis: Liberty Fund, 1992), edited by Daniel E. Ritchie.

inspired part of the demand for expanding the people's right to vote for members of the House of Commons. Typically but wrongly, he attributed that ideology to most of the parliamentary reformers, as he did in his *Speech on the Reform of the Representation of the Commons in Parliament* in 1782.[3]

The premise of the radical ideology was that men by nature are individuals endowed with natural rights but not, as Aristotle had thought, political animals designed by nature to live in organized political societies. In the prepolitical "state of nature," there was no government and every man was a naturally sovereign individual with an absolute right to govern himself. Only he could transfer that right to a government, and even he could not transfer it totally. The only civil society that he could legitimately enter was one in which his natural right to govern himself became the natural right to take part on equal terms with every other man in the government of civil society.

This view translates into the principles of political equality and majority rule. Civil society is a purely artificial institution created by independent individuals who contract with one another to set up a government whose primary purpose is to protect them in the exercise of their natural rights. Its basic structural principles are dictated by the nature of man as a sovereign individual. In this theory, natural rights are prior to social obligations.

BURKE'S REACTION TO THE FRENCH REVOLUTION

Burke encountered this theory also in *A Discourse on the Love of Our Country*, a speech which a Dissenting minister, Dr. Richard Price, delivered on November 4, 1789, to the Revolution Society, a group that met annually to celebrate

---

3. This speech is included in *Miscellaneous Writings,* companion to this set of volumes.

the English Revolution of 1688. This speech (which Burke did not read until January) was delivered two days after the French National Assembly confiscated the estates of the Catholic Church in France. Burke's reaction to the French Revolution had been slow in forming, but events in France in the fall of 1789, such as the confiscation of Church property, opened his eyes to how radical the Revolution there was. Dr. Price's speech awakened a fear in Burke of a similar ideology's bringing about a similar revolution in Great Britain.

On February 9, 1790, he gave a speech in the Commons on the Army Estimates that marked the beginning of his eventual complete break with his political party, the Whigs, now led by Charles James Fox, who admired the French Revolution. In the meantime, Burke was working on what was to become *Reflections on the Revolution in France*. It had begun with a letter, written in November 1789, to Charles-Jean-François Depont.[4] Depont, a young Frenchman who had visited the Burke family in 1785, now wrote to ask Burke to assure him that the French were worthy of the liberty that their Revolution was bringing them. Burke's reply was a calm and cool analysis of the Revolution. When Dr. Price spurred him to respond to his praise of the French Revolution, Burke couched his reply in the form of another letter to Depont. But it grew into a book addressed in reality to the British public in a highly rhetorical style.

Yet there is more, much more, to the *Reflections* than rhetoric. E. J. Payne, the editor of this set of volumes, who was very English and very much a man of the nineteenth century's Victorian age, could say, "No student of history by this time needs to be told that the French Revolution was, in a more or less extended sense, a very good thing."[5] (When the bicentenary of the Revolution was celebrated in 1989, schol-

4. This letter is included in Ritchie, ed., *Further Reflections on the Revolution in France.*

5. P. 11.

ars were no longer quite so sure about that.)[6] Payne also, like most students of Burke who were educated in the British Isles, reflects the empiricism and positivism that are so strong a strain in English thought and make it difficult for British students of Burke to perceive that there is a genuine philosophy wrapped in the gorgeous rhetoric of the *Reflections.*

It is not that Burke was or claimed to be a philosopher. Nor is his book a detached philosophical reflection on a great historical event. It is designed not merely to explain the event, but to persuade a reading public that the French Revolution is a menace to the civilization of Europe, and of Britain in particular. Yet, since the Revolution was built upon a political theory, Burke found himself obliged for the first time to organize his own previous beliefs about God, man, and society into a coherent political countertheory.

BURKE'S CONSTITUTIONAL THEORY

The *Reflections* begins with an attack on Dr. Price and his speech.[7] According to Dr. Price, as quoted by Burke, George III was "almost the *only* lawful king in the world, because the *only* one who owes his crown to *the choice of his people.*"[8] Popular choice, then, was the criterion of legitimacy. This followed from what Dr. Price said was a basic principle established by the Revolution of 1688, namely, the right of the people of England "1. 'To choose our own governors.' 2. 'To cashier them for misconduct.' 3. 'To frame a government

6. See, for example, Simon Schama, *Citizens: A Chronicle of the French Revolution* (New York: Alfred A. Knopf, 1989).

7. The pages that follow are taken, with the permission of the publisher, from my *Edmund Burke: Prescription and Providence* (Durham, N.C.: Carolina Academic Press; Claremont, Calif.: Claremont Institute for the Study of Statesmanship and Political Philosophy, 1987). All page references from this point on, unless otherwise specified, are to the text of the *Reflections* in this volume.

8. P. 99.

for ourselves.'"⁹ Burke read this declaration of the right of the people as an assertion of the doctrine of popular sovereignty, and he denounced it as unknown to and incompatible with the British constitution.

Certainly, he said, it was unknown to the leaders of the Revolution in 1688. He admitted that it would be "difficult, perhaps impossible, to give limits to the mere *abstract* competence of the supreme power, such as was exercised by parliament at that time." But there was no doubt in the minds of the revolutionary leaders or in Burke's about the limits of what they were *morally* competent to do:

The house of lords, for instance, is not morally competent to dissolve the house of commons; no, nor even to dissolve itself, nor to abdicate, if it would, its portion in the legislature of the kingdom. Though a king may abdicate for his own person, he cannot abdicate for the monarchy. By as strong, or by a stronger reason, the house of commons cannot renounce its share of authority. The engagement and pact of society, which generally goes by the name of the constitution, forbids such invasion and such surrender. The constituent parts of a state are obliged to hold their public faith with each other, and with all those who derive any serious interest under their engagements, as much as the whole state is bound to keep its faith with separate communities.¹⁰

THE PRINCIPLE
OF INHERITANCE

For this reason, Burke continued, "the succession of the crown has always been what it now is, an hereditary succession by law." Originally, succession was defined by common law; after the Revolution, by statute. "Both these descriptions of law are of the same force," however, "and are derived from an equal authority, emanating from the common agreement and original compact of the state, *communi sponsione reipublicae,* and as such are equally binding on king, and people

9. P. 102.   10. Pp. 107–8.

too, as long as the terms are observed, and they continue the same body politic."[11]

The operative moral principle, it will be noticed, is that the terms of the constitution, once set, must be observed. But the reason for accepting hereditary government as a *constitutional* principle is a practical one: "No experience has taught us, that in any other course or method than that of an *hereditary crown,* our liberties can be regularly perpetuated and preserved sacred as our *hereditary right.*"[12] It was this consideration that made Burke a monarchist, not devotion to any abstract principles of royal right parallel to abstract principles of popular right. Burke explicitly rejected the notions that "hereditary royalty was the only lawful government in the world," that "monarchy had more of a divine sanction than any other mode of government," or that "a right to govern by inheritance [was] in strictness *indefeasible* in every person, who should be found in the succession to a throne, and under every circumstance."[13] But he considered hereditary monarchy justified as an integral part of a constitution that was wholly based on the principle of inheritance and historically had served the people well.

"We have," he said, "an inheritable crown; an inheritable peerage; and a house of commons and a people inheriting privileges, franchises, and liberties, from a long line of ancestors." Indeed, "it has been the uniform policy of our constitution to claim and assert our liberties, as an *entailed inheritance* derived to us from our forefathers, and to be transmitted to our posterity; as an estate specially belonging to the people of this kingdom without any reference whatever to any other more general or prior right."[14]

This passage may seem to imply that there is no standard of natural right anterior and superior to the constitution.

---

11. P. 108.   12. P. 112.

13. P. 114.   14. P. 121.

But it will be noticed that Burke is speaking here, not of the objective moral order, but of "the uniform policy of our constitution," and that he praises this policy, not as a statement of ultimate moral principles, but as a manifestation of practical wisdom "working after the pattern of nature."[15]

It will be further noticed that throughout this passage Burke contrasts inherited rights, not with natural rights (to which he could and did appeal on other occasions), but with "the rights of men," which are the original rights of men in the state of nature. Dr. Price and others presume that it is possible to appeal to those rights in order to determine what rights men ought to have now, in an old and long-established civil society. It is this appeal that Burke says English statesmen of the past rejected in favor of the historic rights of Englishmen.

These statesmen wisely "preferred this positive, recorded, *hereditary* title to all which can be dear to the man and the citizen, to that vague speculative right, which exposed their sure inheritance to be scrambled for and torn to pieces by every wild litigious spirit."[16] It is advisable, therefore, to have some viable definition of what men's rights are. Positive and recorded rights are better than original rights, in Burke's view, because they have been defined, nuanced, and given sure modes of protection through long historical experience. Original rights, which are objects of speculation rather than of experience, can give rise to conflicting absolute claims that can tear a society apart.

THE TRUE RIGHTS OF MAN

Furthermore, it is to misunderstand the social condition to think that men's claims on society and one another can be reduced to rights which they enjoyed in abstract and unquali-

15. Pp. 121–22.   16. P. 120.

fied forms before civil society came into being. Burke never denied that there had been a state of nature, that men had original rights in it, or that civil society had been formed by a compact. Either he accepted these beliefs as one tends to accept the commonplaces of his age or he knew that others accepted them so generally that to deny them would be to lose the argument at the outset. For whatever reason, he restricted himself to arguing that the original rights of men were not unreal, but irrelevant to civil society. The change they underwent in the civil state was so profound that they no longer furnished a standard for judging the rights of "civil social man."[17] In Burke's own words:

These metaphysic rights entering into common life, like rays of light which pierce into a dense medium, are, by the laws of nature, refracted from their straight line. Indeed in the gross and complicated mass of human passions and concerns, the primitive rights of men undergo such a variety of refractions and reflections, that it becomes absurd to talk of them as if they continued in the simplicity of their original direction. The nature of man is intricate; the objects of society are of the greatest possible complexity; and therefore no simple disposition or direction of power can be suitable either to man's nature, or to the quality of his affairs.[18]

We must think, then, of men's rights in society in another way:

If civil society be made for the advantage of man, all the advantages for which it is made become his right. It is an institution of beneficence; and law itself is only beneficence acting by a rule. Men have a right to live by that rule; they have a right to do justice; as between their fellows, whether their fellows are in politic function or in ordinary occupation. They have a right to the fruits of their industry; and to the means of making their industry fruitful. They have a right to the acquisitions of their parents; to the nourishment and improvement of their offspring; to instruction in life, and to consolation

17. P. 151.   18. P. 153.

in death. Whatever each man can separately do, without trespassing upon others, he has a right to do for himself; and he has a right to a fair portion of all which society, with all its combinations of skill and force, can do in his favour.[19]

Civil society is "an institution of beneficence"; its purpose is to do good to its members, and the good that it can do for them becomes their right or legitimate claim upon it. But their civil rights are not merely the legal form taken, after the social compact, by their original natural rights. Nor is government derived from every man's original right to act according to his own will and judgment.

The purposes of government are specified by the natural wants of men, understood not as their desires, but as their real needs. "Government," according to Burke, "is a contrivance of human wisdom to provide for human *wants*. Men have a right that these wants should be provided for by this wisdom."[20] But among these wants is the education of men to virtue through legal as well as moral restraints upon their passions. "In this sense the restraints on men as well as their liberties, are to be reckoned among their rights." Burke, one sees, is moving toward rational moral ends as the legitimating principle of government, and away from original rights and their corollary, consent. But his immediate concern in this passage is to point out that, "as the liberties and the restrictions vary with times and circumstances, and admit of infinite modifications, they cannot be settled upon any abstract rule; and nothing is so foolish as to discuss them upon that principle."[21]

Rather, one must say: "The rights of men are in a sort of *middle*, incapable of definition, but not impossible to be discerned. The rights of men in governments are their advantages; and these are often in balances between differences

19. P. 150.   20. P. 151.

21. P. 152.

of good; in compromises sometimes between good and evil, and sometimes between evil and evil."[22] To clarify what Burke is getting at, let us agree by way of example that it is not good for human beings to be starved, beaten, humiliated, deprived of human affections, or intellectually stultified. There are conceivable circumstances in which any of these, in a limited degree and for a limited time, might do someone more good than harm. But they could be justified only as a means to good ends, for these things are not in themselves human goods. Therefore, they cannot constitute the ends of life or the purposes of society. On the other hand, one can name human needs that do specify, in a general way, what civil society is for, and Burke did name some of them.

THE GOALS OF CIVIL SOCIETY

Civil society exists to guarantee to men justice, the fruits of their industry, the acquisitions of their parents, the nourishment and improvement of their offspring, instruction in life, and consolation in death. These are among the advantages that civil society exists to provide for men. But it is impossible to define antecedently, in the abstract and for all possible circumstances, the concrete forms in which these advantages are to be acquired and safeguarded. That must be left to social experience and the gradual development of custom and law.

The end of civil society, then, in global terms, is to promote what is good for human beings. Human goods are "not impossible to be discerned"—Burke was not a radical cultural relativist—and they can serve as the general goals that guide law and public policy. They will therefore set the outer limits of what government may do to people and define what it may not do to them. Burke was not inconsistent when he

22. P. 154.

denounced the Protestant Ascendancy in Ireland and Warren Hastings in India for violating natural law by their treatment of the populations subject to their power. To deny that natural law is an abstract code of rights is not to say that it forbids nothing.

But when it comes to specifying in the concrete the claims on society that its goals confer on people, it becomes evident that the rights of men "are in a sort of *middle,* incapable of definition." They cannot be defined, that is, in the abstract and in advance. Human goods must be limited and trimmed in order to be simultaneously attainable in society. Not only that, but evils, which are negations of good, must be tolerated, sometimes even protected, in order that any good at all may be attained. A society ruthlessly purged of all injustice might turn out to be a vast prison. So, for that matter, might a society single-mindedly devoted to the individual's liberty.

THE RIGHT TO GOVERN

These considerations are particularly relevant to the right that was fundamentally at issue between Burke and his opponents. They held that every man in the state of nature had a sovereign right to govern himself and for that reason had a right to an equal share in the government of civil society. Burke held that what was important in the civil state was not that every man's will should be registered in the process of government, but that his real interests (advantages, goods) should be achieved.

By entering civil society, Burke insisted, man "abdicates all right to be his own governor." [23] Hence, "as to the share of power, authority, and direction which each individual ought to have in the management of the state, that I must deny to be amongst the direct original rights of man in civil society."

23. P. 151.

On the contrary, "it is a thing to be settled by convention."[24] "The moment you abate any thing from the full rights of men, each to govern himself, and suffer any artificial positive limitation upon those rights, from that moment the whole organization of government becomes a consideration of convenience." But to organize a government and distribute its powers "requires a deep knowledge of human nature and human necessities, and of the things which facilitate or obstruct the various ends which are to be pursued by the mechanism of civil institutions."[25] The allocation of power in the state, in other words, ought to be made by a prudent judgment about that structure of government which will best achieve the goals of civil society, not merely in general, but in *this* historically existing society. But this implies that purpose, rather than original rights and individual consent, is the organizing and legitimizing principle of a constitution.

A further conclusion about the nature of political theory follows: "The science of constructing a commonwealth, or renovating it, or reforming it, is, like every other experimental science, not to be taught a priori. Nor is it a short experience that can instruct us in that practical science."[26] Moral and political theory may enlighten us on the ultimate ends of social life, but the means thereunto are the object of a practical science that relies on experience.

Who, then, shall make the practical judgments of politics? The question cannot be answered by appealing to the rights of men. "Men have no right to what is not reasonable, and to what is not for their benefit."[27] But as to what is for their benefit, Burke said: "The will of the many, and their interest, must very often differ."[28] The first duty of statesmen, indeed, is to "provide for the *multitude;* because it is the *multitude;* and

24. P. 151.   25. P. 152.
26. Pp. 152–53.   27. P. 154.
28. P. 142.

is therefore, as such, the first object . . . in all institutions." [29]
But the object is the good of the people, not the performance
of their will. The duties of statesmen, in consequence, do not
belong by right to those whom the many have chosen, but
ought to be performed by those qualified by "virtue and wisdom, actual or presumptive," [30] for the task of government.

BURKE'S VIEW OF DEMOCRACY

Burke was undoubtedly what today is called an elitist and,
in his own terminology, an aristocrat in principle. He had a
very low estimation of the political capacity of the mass of
the population, and when he agreed that the people had a
role in government, he meant only a fairly well-educated and
prosperous segment of the people. But the main object of his
attack on the democratic theory of his day was not so much
the idea that the populace at large was capable of exercising
political power as the principle that it had an inherent right
to do its own will.

He certainly rejected the notion "that a pure democracy
is the only tolerable form into which human society can be
thrown." [31] But it could be an acceptable one, though not
often:

I reprobate no form of government merely upon abstract principles.
There may be situations in which the purely democratic form will become necessary. There may be some (very few, and very particularly
circumstanced) where it would be clearly desirable. This I do not take
to be the case of France, or of any other great country. [32]

Democracy as a mere form of government, then, would
be sometimes, if only rarely, acceptable to Burke. What would
never be acceptable was that the people "should act as if they

29. P. 198.   30. P. 140.
31. P. 224.   32. Pp. 224–25.

were the entire masters."[33] Burke explained his objection to this conception of popular sovereignty in the course of his defense of the principle of a state establishment of religion. Under a "mixed and tempered government"[34] such as that of Great Britain, "free citizens . . . in order to secure their freedom, . . . must enjoy some determinate portion of power." But "all persons possessing any portion of power ought to be strongly and awfully impressed with an idea that they act in trust; and that they are to account for their conduct in that trust to the one great master, author and founder of society."[35]

AUTHORITY AND
THE ORDER OF CREATION

This sense that authority is a trust given by God is all the more necessary "where popular authority is absolute and unrestrained." No one can and no one should punish a whole people, Burke said, but this conclusion followed: "A perfect democracy is therefore the most shameless thing in the world." It is essential, then, that the people "should not be suffered to imagine that their will, any more than that of kings, is the standard of right and wrong." To exercise political power or any part of it, the people must empty themselves "of all the lust of selfish will, which without religion it is utterly impossible they ever should." They must become "conscious that they exercise, and exercise perhaps in a higher link of the order of delegation, the power, which to be legitimate must be according to that external immutable law, in which will and reason are the same."[36]

The phrase concerning the place of the people in the order of delegation is interesting because it may refer to a

33. P. 191.   34. P. 224.
35. P. 188.   36. Pp. 189–90.

theory of the origin of political authority which was generally accepted in Late Scholasticism and was most elaborately presented by the sixteenth-century Jesuit Francisco Suarez. In this theory, all political authority comes from God, not by any special divine act, but simply as a consequence of God's having made man a political animal by nature. This authority consequently inheres in the first instance in the body politic or whole community. But the community can and, for its own common good, normally will transfer its authority to a king or a body of men smaller than the whole.[37]

In any case, God plays a larger role in Burke's political theory than in Paine's. For Paine, once God had given man his original rights at the creation, His work was done. Men then were able to create political authority out of their own wills. But for Burke, the authority of even the people was a trust held from God. They were accountable to Him for their conduct in it, and they must perform it in accordance with "that eternal immutable law, in which will and reason are the same." In Burke's thought, arbitrary will was never legitimate, because will was never superior to reason, not even in the sovereign Lord of the Universe. In God, however, will is always rational because His will is identical with His reason. The people, for their part, must make their will rational by keeping it in subordination to and conformity with the law of God.

THE MORAL ORDER OF CREATION

The law of God that Burke has in mind is not only or primarily His revealed law but the natural moral law, because it is a law that follows from the nature of man as created by God. The Creator is

---

37. That Burke was acquainted with Suarez's writings is indicated by his quoting Suarez at some length in his *Tracts relating to Popery Laws*, in *The Writings and Speeches of Edmund Burke*, ed. Paul Langford (Oxford: Oxford University Press, Clarendon Press, 1981–), 9:457–58.

the institutor, and author and protector of civil society; without which civil society man could not by any possibility arrive at the perfection of which his nature is capable, nor even make a remote and faint approach to it. . . . He who gave our nature to be perfected by our virtue, willed also the necessary means of its perfection—He willed therefore the state—He willed its connection with the source and original archetype of all perfection.[38]

There is an entire metaphysics implicit in this passage. God, as Creator, is the source of all being. The infinite fullness of His being, therefore, is the archetype of all finite being and becoming. All created beings reflect the goodness of their primary cause and tend toward their own full development or perfection by approaching His perfection, each in its own mode and within the limits of its potentialities. The state, as the necessary means of human perfection, must be connected to that original archetype. In Burke's philosophy, there can be no merely secular society, because there is no merely secular world.

The end of the state, for Burke, is divinely set and in its highest reach is nothing less than the perfection of human nature by its virtue. (According to Burke, "in a Christian Commonwealth the Church and the State are one and the same thing, being different integral parts of the same whole."[39] He thus found it easy to attribute to the state, or commonwealth, or civil society, the totality of men's social goals, whereas we today should be inclined to divide them between the political and religious spheres.)

Hence Burke could say, "Society is indeed a contract,"[40] but with a difference. The constitution of civil society was a convention whose shape and form was not a necessary con-

38. Pp. 194–95.

39. *Speech on the Petition of the Unitarians*, in *The Works of the Rt. Hon. Edmund Burke* (London: Rivington, 1812), 10:44.

40. P. 192.

clusion drawn from principles of natural law. Nonetheless, society was natural in the sense of being the necessary and divinely willed means to achieve the perfection of human nature. If one equates the natural with the primitive, one will say that it is more natural to live in a cave than in a house; that is what is usually implied in the phrase "back to nature." But if one equates the natural with the mature perfection of any species of being, one will say that it is more natural for human beings to live in houses than in caves. Houses are undeniably artificial works of human hands, but they are a natural habitat for men because they more adequately satisfy the needs of human nature than caves can do. Similarly — and this was Burke's meaning — civil society is artificial, conventional, even, if you will, contractual. But it is natural to man because "he is never perfectly in his natural state, but when he is placed where reason may be best cultivated, and most predominates.[41] The Aristotelian teleology of this remark seems obvious.

THE SOCIAL CONTRACT

Society, then, is indeed a contract, but not one to be regarded in the same light as a commercial contract that is entered into for a limited and self-interested purpose and can be dissolved at the will of the contracting parties. Paine could look upon human society as rather like a vast commercial concern, potentially worldwide in scope, that was held together by reciprocal interest and mutual consent. Burke could not share this utilitarian view of society:

It is to be looked on with other reverence; because it is not a partnership in things subservient only to the gross animal existence of a tem-

41. *An Appeal From the New to the Old Whigs,* in Ritchie, ed., *Further Reflections on the Revolution in France,* pp. 168–69.

porary and perishable nature. It is a partnership in all science; a partnership in all art; a partnership in every virtue, and in all perfection.[42]

Because of the nature of its purposes, the contract of society has a character and a binding force that are different from those of ordinary contracts. "As the ends of such a partnership cannot be obtained in many generations, it becomes a partnership not only between those who are living, but between those who are living, those who are dead, and those who are to be born."[43] This sentence offended Paine's commonsense mind and led him to ask what possible obligation can exist between those who are dead and gone, and those who are not yet born and arrived in the world; a fortiori, how could either of them impose obligations on the living? In a literal sense he was, of course, quite right. But if one turns one's attention from contracting wills to the rational moral ends which those wills are bound to serve, one may conclude that, in the light of those ends, obligations descend upon the present generation from the past, and there are obligations in regard to generations yet unborn.

Men achieve their natural social goals only in history. The structures inherited from the past, if they have served and still serve those goals, are binding upon those who are born into them. These persons are not morally free to dismantle the structures at pleasure and to begin anew from the foundations. For the goals in question are not those alone of the collection of individuals now present on earth, but also those of human nature and of God.

The constitution of a society, conventional and historically conditioned though it is, becomes a part of the natural moral order because of the ends that it serves. This is the thought that lies behind Burke's rhetorical language in the next part of the passage on the contract of society:

42. P. 193.   43. Ibid.

Each contract of each particular state is but a clause in the great pri-maeval contract of eternal society, linking the lower with the higher natures, connecting the visible and invisible world, according to a fixed compact sanctioned by the inviolable oath which holds all physi-cal and all moral natures, each in their appointed place. This law is not subject to the will of those, who by an obligation above them, and infinitely superior, are bound to submit their will to that law.[44]

The "great primaeval contract" and the "inviolable oath" are, of course, the moral order of the world as established by God. That moral order furnishes a law to which civil societies as well as individuals are obliged to conform.

WHEN REVOLUTION IS JUSTIFIED

But are people never free to change the constitution and their government? Burke does not quite say that. "The municipal corporations of that universal kingdom are not morally at liberty at their pleasure, and on their speculations of a contingent improvement, wholly to separate and tear asunder the bands of their subordinate community, and to dissolve it into an unsocial, uncivil, unconnected chaos of ele-mentary principles."[45] The key phrase in this statement is "at their pleasure." There is also the unspoken assumption, char-acteristic of Burke, that a political revolution would be tan-tamount to a dissolution of society as such. Underlying that assumption was a conception of the constitution which one writer has well described in these words: "Burke . . . under-stood 'constitution' to mean the entire social structure of En-gland and not only the formal governmental structure. . . . In-cluded in his concept of constitution was the whole corporate society to which he was devoted."[46] No people, Burke said,

44. Ibid.

45. Ibid.

46. R. B. Ripley, "Adams, Burke, and Eighteenth-Century Conservatism," *Political Science Quarterly* 80 (1965): 228.

had the right to overturn such a structure at pleasure and on a speculation that by so doing they might make things better.

Nonetheless, he could not and did not deny that a revolution was sometimes necessary. He only insisted that it could not be justified but by reasons that were so obvious and so compelling that they were themselves part of the moral order:

> It is the first and supreme necessity only, a necessity that is not chosen but chooses, a necessity paramount to deliberation, that admits no discussion, and demands no evidence, which alone can justify a resort to anarchy. This necessity is no exception to the rule; because this necessity itself is a part too of that moral and physical disposition of things to which man must be obedient by consent or force. But if that which is only submission to necessity should be made the object of choice, the law is broken, nature is disobeyed, and the rebellious are outlawed, cast forth, and exiled, from this world of reason, and order, and peace, and virtue, and fruitful penitence, into the antagonist world of madness, discord, vice, confusion, and unavailing sorrow.[47]

One may think that here Burke has gone beyond rhetoric into rhapsody. Yet the lines of his argument are clear enough. In *An Appeal from the New to the Old Whigs*, he made them more explicit and clearer still. It is difficult, therefore, to understand why Frank O'Gorman says: "The present writer has always found it strange that Burke rarely refers, either explicitly or even implicitly, to the principles that are supposed to have been the foundations of his thought. Burke was, indeed, uninterested in the workings of the Divine power."[48] It seems obvious to this writer that, particularly in the *Reflections* and *An Appeal,* Burke not only refers to but also elaborates in detail the principles that are the foundation of his theory of civil society and political authority. He was, it is true, a practicing politician, not a philosopher, and in these two works he wrote

47. Pp. 193–94.

48. *Edmund Burke: His Political Philosophy* (Bloomington and London: Indiana University Press, 1973), p. 13, n. 5.

a polemic, not a dispassionate treatise on political theory. But his polemic included the presentation of a countertheory to the theory he was attacking. The countertheory depended in turn on explicitly stated premises of a moral and metaphysical nature. The premises are expounded, one must admit, in rhetorical language, especially in the *Reflections*. But they are, to borrow Burke's words, not impossible to be discerned.

BASIC PREMISES OF BURKE'S THOUGHT

Briefly, the ultimate premises of Burke's political thought are provided by the metaphysics of a created universe. They assume the superiority of reason or intellect to will in both God and man. Part of this universe is the natural moral order based on the nature of man as created by God. Man's nature is oriented by creation toward ends that may be globally described as its natural perfection. Since civil society is necessary to the attainment of that perfection, it too is natural and willed by God.

The authority of the state derives from the rational and moral ends that it is intended by nature to serve. Consent plays a role in the formation of the state and the conferral of its authority on government, since both involve human acts of choice. But the obligation to form a civil society is prior to consent, and, for those born under a constitution, consent to the constitution is commanded by the previous obligation to obey a government that is adequately serving the natural goals of society. Rights also play a part in Burke's political theory. But the basic political right is the right to be governed well, not the right to govern oneself. In Burke's thought, purpose and obligations are more fundamental than rights and consent.

FRANCIS CANAVAN
Fordham University

EDITOR'S NOTE

In this volume, the pagination of E. J. Payne's edition is indicated by bracketed page numbers embedded in the text. Cross references have been changed to reflect the pagination of the current edition. Burke's and Payne's spellings, capitalizations, and use of italics have been retained, strange as they may seem to modern eyes. The use of double punctuation (e.g., ,—) has been eliminated except in quoted material. We have corrected Payne's occasional confusion of Charles-Jean-François Depont to whom the *Reflections on the Revolution in France* were addressed and Pierre-Gaëton Dupont who translated the *Reflections* into French.

All references to Burke's *Correspondence* are to the 1844 edition.

Chronology

1729 Burke born in Dublin, January 12.

1735–40 Lives with mother's relatives in countryside of County Cork.

1741–44 Attends Abraham Shackleton's Quaker school in Kildare.

1744–48 Attends Trinity College, Dublin, and graduates A.B.

1750 Moves to London to study law in Inns of Court, abandons it for a literary career.

1756 Publishes *A Vindication of Natural Society,* a satire on Enlightenment political and religious reasoning.

1757 Publishes *A Philosophical Enquiry into the Origin of Our Ideas of the Sublime and Beautiful,* an essay in aesthetics.

Marries Miss Jane Nugent.

1758 Richard Burke, Jr., born.

Becomes editor of *The Annual Register.*

1761 Returns to Ireland as secretary to William Gerard Hamilton, Chief Secretary to the Lord Lieutenant.

Begins but never finishes *Tracts Relative to the Laws Against Popery in Ireland.*

1764 Returns to London, has bitter break with Hamilton.

Becomes a charter member, along with Johnson, Reynolds, Goldsmith, and others, of The Literary Club.

1765 Becomes private secretary to the Marquis of Rockingham.

George III reluctantly appoints Rockingham Prime Minister.

Burke elected to House of Commons from borough of Wendover.

1766 Rockingham dismissed as Prime Minister after achieving repeal of Stamp Act that inflamed the American colonies.

1768 Burke buys an estate in Buckinghamshire.

1770 Publishes *Thoughts on the Cause of the Present Discontents*, the political creed of the Rockingham Whigs.

1771 Becomes parliamentary agent for the colony of New York.

1773 Visits France.

1774 Elected Member of Parliament for city of Bristol, delivers classic speech on the independence of a representative.

Delivers *Speech on American Taxation*, criticizing British policy of taxing the colonies.

1775 Delivers *Speech on Conciliation with the Colonies*.

1780 Because of opposition, withdraws from election at Bristol. Is elected M.P. from borough of Malton through Rockingham's influence.

Speech on the Economical Reform advocates Whig policy of reducing the king's influence on Parliament.

1782 Rockingham again appointed Prime Minister to end the American War.

Burke becomes Paymaster of the Forces.

Rockingham dies in office.

1783 Rockingham Whigs under Charles James Fox form a government in coalition with Lord North.

Burke, again Paymaster, delivers *Speech on Fox's East India Bill*, attacking East India Company's government of India.

Coalition falls from power and is replaced by William Pitt the Younger's Tory ministry, leaving the Whigs out of power for rest of Burke's life.

1786 Burke moves the impeachment of Warren Hastings, the Company's Governor-General of Bengal.

1788 Trial of Hastings begins, led by Burke.

1789 French Revolution begins.

1790 In November, publishes *Reflections on the Revolution in France*.

CHRONOLOGY

1791 Breaks with Fox, leader of the former Rockingham Whigs, over the French Revolution.

A Letter to a Member of the National Assembly [of France], *An Appeal from the New to the Old Whigs,* and *Thoughts on French Affairs.*

1793 War breaks out between Great Britain and France.

Burke criticizes failure to prosecute the war vigorously in *Observations on the Conduct of the Ministry* and *Remarks on the Policy of the Allies.*

1794 Prosecution of Hastings ends; Burke retires from Parliament.

Burke's son dies.

1795 Hastings is acquitted.

Thoughts and Details on Scarcity.

1796 Burke defends his public life in *A Letter to a Noble Lord.*

1796–97 *Letters on a Regicide Peace* protest British willingness to make peace with Revolutionary France.

1797 Burke dies, July 9.

SELECT WORKS OF EDMUND BURKE

VOLUME 2

REFLECTIONS ON THE
REVOLUTION IN FRANCE

INTRODUCTION

BY E. J. PAYNE

THE FAMOUS LETTER OR PAMPHLET contained in this volume represents the workings of an extraordinary mind at an extraordinary crisis: and can therefore be compared with few things that have ever been spoken or written. Composed in a literary age, it scarcely belongs to literature; yet it is one of the greatest of literary masterpieces. It embodies nothing of history save fragments which have mostly lost their interest, yet no book in the world has more historical significance. It scorns and defies philosophy, but it discloses a compact and unique system of its own. It tramples on logic, yet carries home to the most logical reader a conviction that its ill-reasoning is substantially correct. No one would think of agreeing with it in the mass, yet there are parts to which every candid mind will assent. Its many true and wise sayings are mixed up with extravagant and barefaced sophistry: its argument, with every semblance of legal exactness, is disturbed by hasty gusts of anger, and broken by chasms which yawn in the face of the least observant reader. It is an intellectual puzzle, not too abstruse for solution: and hence few books are better adapted to stimulate the attention and judgment, and to generate the invaluable habit of mental vigilance. To discover its defects is easy enough. No book in the world yields itself an easier prey to hostile criticism: there are thousands of school-boys, "with liberal notions under their caps," to whom the greatest intellect of our nation since Milton,[1] represented

---

1. So Macaulay has styled Burke.

3

by the best known parts of the present work, might well seem little better than a fool. After a time, this impression disappears; eloquence and deep conviction have done their work, and the wisdom of a few pages, mostly dealing in generalities, is constructively extended to the whole. But the reader now vacillates again: and this perpetual alternation of judgment on the part of a reader not thoroughly in earnest constitutes a main part of that fascination which Burke universally exercises. It is like the [vi] fascination of jugglery: now you believe your eyes, now you distrust them: the brilliancy of the spectacle first dazzles, and then satisfies: and you care little for what lies behind. This is what the author intended: the critical faculty is disarmed, the imagination is enthralled.

What did Burke propose to himself when he sat down to write this book? The letter to Depont is obviously a mere peg upon which to hang his argument: the book is written for the British public. He believed himself to foresee whither the revolutionary movement in France was tending: he saw one party in England regarding it with favour, the other with indifference: he saw clear revolutionary tendencies on all sides among the people: and not a single arm was as yet raised to avert the impending catastrophe. Burke aimed at recalling the English nation to its ancient principles, and at showing the folly and imprudence of the French political movement. Burke's independence led him even to the extent of revolting from his own party. The great historical Whig party, the party of Somers, of Walpole, and of Chatham, was slowly passing through a painful transformation, which many observers mistook for dissolution. Burke found himself constrained to desert it, and that upon an occasion which afforded an opportunity of rendering it material support. From that time forward he became a marked man. Even for Burke the act of thinking for himself was stigmatised as a crime. While the events of the French Revolution commended themselves to the leaders of his party, he ought not to have allowed

---

it to be seen that they aroused in him nothing but anger and scorn; nor ought he to have appealed to the nation at large to support him in his opposition. Such an appeal to the general public was characteristic of definite change of allegiance. Hence the obloquy which overwhelmed the last years of his life, raised by those who had been his associates during a career of a quarter of a century. Hence his counter-denunciation of them as "New Whigs," as renegades from the principles of the English Revolution, by virtue of the countenance they gave to the political changes which were taking place in France.

Are Burke's opinions in the present work consistent with those contained in the first volume? Notwithstanding that fundamental unity which may be justly claimed for Burke's opinions, [vii] it would be idle to deny that the present treatise, like his subsequent writings, contains, on comparison with his earlier ones, certain very great discrepancies. They are, however, but few; they are obvious, and lie upon the surface. It is hard for those who live a hundred years after the time to say whether such discrepancies were or were not justifiable. Scrutiny will discover that they turn mainly upon words. The House of Lords, for instance, in the first volume of these Select Works, is asserted to be a form of popular representation; in the present, the Peers are said to hold their share in the government by original and indefeasible right. Twenty years before, Burke had said that the tithes were merely a portion of the taxation, set apart by the national will for the support of a national institution. In the present work, he argues that Church property possesses the qualities of private property. In the former volume it is asserted that all governments depend on public opinion: in the present, Burke urges that public opinion acts within much narrower limits. On the strength of such differences, it has been supposed that Burke had now either completely abandoned the political principles which had guided him through a career of twenty-five years, or else that he really was, what a Tory writer has called him, "the most double-minded man that ever lived." But a man who is not thus far double-minded can never be a politician, though he may be a hero and a martyr. Abstract truths, when embodied in the form of popular opinion, sometimes prove to be moral falsehoods. And popular opinion in the majority of cases proves to be a deceptive and variable force. Institutions stand or fall by their material strength and cohesion; and though these are by no means unconnected with the arguments which are advanced for or against them, the names and qualities with which they are invested in argument are altogether a secondary consideration. The position of the Church, for instance, or the Peerage, has not been materially influenced by either way of regarding them. They have stood, as they continue to stand, because they are connected by many ties which are strong, though subtle and complicated, with the national being. They stand, in some degree, because it is probable that the stronger half of the nation would fight for them. "National taxation" and "private property," "descendible right" and "popular representation," are, in point of fact, little more than ornamental antitheses.

[viii] It is not to such obvious discrepancies that we owe the fact that the connexion between the present treatise and those contained in the former volume is less easily traced by points of resemblance than by points of contrast. The differencing causes lie deeper and spread wider. In the first place, Burke in the present volume is appealing to a larger public. He is appealing directly to the whole English Nation, and indirectly to every citizen of the civilised world.

In his early denunciations of the French Revolution, Burke stood almost alone. At first sight he appeared to have the most cherished of English traditions against him. If there was one word which for a century had been sacred to Englishmen, it was the word Revolution. Those to whom it was an offence were almost wholly extinct: and a hundred years' prescription had sanctified the English Revolution even in the eyes of the bitterest adversaries of Whiggism. The King, around whom the discontented Whigs and the remnant of the Tories had rallied, was himself the creature of the Revolution. Now the party of Fox recognised a lawful relation between the Revolution of 1688, and that which was entering daily on some new stage of its mighty development in France. There was really but little connexion between the two. Burke never said a truer thing than that the Revolution of 1688 was "a revolution not made, but prevented." The vast convulsions of 1789 and the following years were ill-understood by the Foxite Whigs. Pent in their own narrow circle, they could form no idea of a political movement on a bigger scale than a coalition: to them the French Revolution seemed merely an ordinary Whiggish rearrangement of affairs which would soon settle down into their places, the King, as in England, accepting a position subordinate to his ministers. Nor were Pitt and his party, with the strength of Parliament and the nation at their back, disposed to censure it. There was a double reason for favouring it, on the part of the English Premier. On the one hand, it was a surprise and a satisfaction to see the terrible monarchy of France collapse without a blow, and England's hereditary foe deprived, to all appearance, of all power of injury or retaliation. On the other, Mr. Pitt conceived that the new Government would naturally be favourable to those liberal principles of commercial intercourse which he had with so much difficulty forced on the old one. Neither side saw, as [ix] Burke saw it, the real magnitude of the political movement in France, and how deep and extensive were the interests it involved. Burke, in the unfavourable impression which he conceived of the Revolution, was outside of both parties. He could find no audience in the House of Commons, where leading politicians had long looked askance upon him. They laughed, not altogether without reason, when he told them that he looked upon France as "not politically existing." Discouraged in the atmosphere of Parliament, Burke resolved to appeal to the whole nation. He had in his portfolio the commencement of a letter to a young Frenchman who had solicited from him an expression of opinion, and this letter he resolved to enlarge and give to the world. He thus appealed from the narrow tribunal of the House of Commons to the Nation at large. It was the first important instance of the recognition, on the part of a great statesman, of the power of public opinion in England in its modern form. Burke here addresses his arguments to a much wider public than of old. He recognises, what is now obvious enough, that English policy rests on the opinion of a reasonable democracy.

The reader, in comparing the two volumes, will notice this difference in the tribunal to which the appeal is made. Public opinion in the last twenty years had gone through rapid changes. The difference between the condition of public opinion in 1770 and in 1790 was greater than between 1790 and 1874. In 1770 it was necessary to rouse it into life: in 1790 it was already living, watching, and speaking for itself. The immorality of the politicians of the day had awakened the distrust of the people: and the people and the King were united in supporting a popular minister. There was more activity, more public spirit, and more organisation. In England, as in France, communication with the capital from the remotest parts of the kingdom had become frequent and regular. London had in 1790 no less than fourteen daily newspapers; and many others appeared once or twice a week. No one can look over the files of these newspapers without perceiving the magnitude of the space which France at this time occupied in the eye of the English world. The rivalry of the two nations was already at its height. The Bourbon kingdoms summed up, for the Englishman, the idea of foreign Powers: and disturbances in France told on England [x] with much greater effect than now. In England there prevailed a deceptive tranquillity. Burke and many others knew that the England of 1790 was not the England of 1770. The results of the American War were slowly convincing people that something more was possible than had hitherto been practised in modern English policy. Democracy had grown from a possibility into a power. Whiggism, as a principle, had long been distrusted and discredited. With its decline had begun the discredit of all that it had idolised. The English Constitution, against which in 1770 hardly a breath had been raised, was in the succeeding twenty years exposed to general ridicule. Under a minister who proclaimed himself a Reformer, the newly awakened sentiment for political change was extending in all directions. Seats in Parliament had always been bought and sold; but, owing to the increased wealth of the community, prices had now undergone a preposterous advance. Five thousand pounds was the average figure at which a wealthy merchant or rising lawyer had to purchase his seat from the patron of a borough. The disgraceful history of the Coalition made people call for reform in the Executive as well as the Legislative. Montesquieu had said that England must perish as soon as the Legislative power became more corrupt than the Executive; but it now seemed as if both branches of the government were competing in a race for degradation. Corrupt as the Legislative was in its making, its material, drawn from the body of the nation, and not from a corps of professed intriguers, saved it from the moral disgrace which attended the Executive. Many were in favour of restoring soundness to the Executive as a preliminary reform; and many were the schemes proposed for effecting it. One very shrewd thinker, who sat in the House, proposed an annual Ministry, chosen by lot. Others proposed an elective Ministry: others wished to develop the House of Lords into something like the Grand Council of Venice. No political scheme was too absurd to lack an advocate. Universal suffrage, annual parliaments, and electoral districts were loudly demanded, and Dukes were counted among their warmest supporters. The people, as in the times of Charles I, called for the "ancient Saxon constitution." What it was, and what right they had to it, or how it was to be adapted to modern requirements, they did not very well know, but the lawyers were able to tell them. The [xi] lawyers demonstrated how greatly the liberties of the nation had fallen off, and how grossly their nature was misunderstood. They proved it to be the duty of the People to reclaim them, and that no obstacle stood in the way. In this cry many Whigs and Tories, members of both Houses of Parliament, were found to join.

This liberal movement was not confined to England. It spread, in a greater or less degree, all over Europe, even to St. Petersburg and Constantinople. In England, Reform was rather a cry than a political movement; but in France and Austria it was a movement as well as a cry. In the latter country, indeed, the Reform was supplied before the demand, and the Emperor Joseph was forced by an ignorant people to reverse projects in which he had vainly tried to precede his age. But the demands abroad were for organic reforms, such as had long been effected in England. England, after the reign of Charles II, is a completely modern nation; society is reorganised on the basis which still subsists. But France and Germany in 1789 were still what they had been in the Middle Ages. The icy fetters which England had long ago broken up had on the Continent hardened until nothing would break them up but a convulsion. In France this had been demonstrated by the failures of Turgot. The body of oppressive interests which time and usage had legalised was too strong to give way to a moderate pressure. A convulsion, a mighty shock, a disturbance of normal forces, was necessary: and the French people had long been collecting themselves for the task. Forty years a Revolution had been foreseen, and ten years at least it had been despaired of. But it came at last, and came unexpectedly; the Revolution shook down the feudalism of France, and the great general of the Revolution trampled to dust the tottering relics of it in the rest of Western Europe. Conspicuous among the agencies which effected it was the new power of public opinion, which wrought an obvious effect, by means of the Gazettes of Paris, throughout the western world. Burke saw this, and to public opinion he appealed against the movement, and so far as this country was concerned, successfully. It was he whose "shrilling trumpet" sounded the first alarm of the twenty years' European war against the French Revolution.

It was hard, at such a crisis, to sever general ideas from the [xii] immediate occasion. Burke tells us less about the French Revolution than about English thought and feeling on the subject of Revolutions in general. On the applicability of these general views to the occasion of their enunciation, it is not necessary for the reader to form any definite judgment. Properly speaking, indeed, the question depends only in a small degree on grounds which demand or justify such a mode of treatment. To condemn all Revolutions is monstrous. To say categorically that the French Revolution was absolutely a good thing or a bad thing conveys no useful idea. Either may be said with some degree of truth, but neither can be said without qualifications which almost neutralise the primary thesis. No student of history by this time needs to be told that the French Revolution was, in a more or less extended sense, a very good thing. Consequently, the student is not advised to assent, further than is necessary to gain an idea of Burke's standpoint, to the summary and ignominious condemnation with which the Revolution is treated by Burke. But it must be remembered that whatever may have been its good side, it was not Burke's business to exhibit it. No one was better qualified than Burke to compose an apologetic for the final appeal of a people against tyranny: but *nunc non erat his locus.* Burke's business was not to cool the pot, but to make it boil: to raise a strong counter-cry, and make the most of the bad side of the Revolution. Burke appears here in the character of an advocate: like all advocates, he says less than he knows. It was his cue to represent the Revolution as a piece of voluntary and malicious folly; he could not well admit that it was the result of deep-seated and irresistible causes. Not that the Revolution could not have been avoided—every one knew that it might; but it could only have been avoided by an equally sweeping Revolution from above. In default of this there came to pass a Revolution from below. Though the Revolution brought with it mistakes in policy, crimes, and injuries, it involved no more of each than the fair average of human affairs will allow, if we consider its character and magnitude; and we must pay less than usual heed to Burke when he insists that these were produced wholly by the ignorance and wickedness of the Revolutionary leaders. The sufferers in a large measure brought them on themselves by ill-timed resistance and vacillating counsels.

[xiii] From the present work the student will learn little of the history of the Revolution. It had barely begun: only two incidents of importance, the capture of the Bastille and the transportation from Versailles to Paris, had taken place: of that coalition of hostile elements which first gave the Revolution force and self-consciousness, there was as yet not a trace. It was not only in its beginnings, but even these beginnings were imperfectly understood. School-boys now know more of the facts of the matter than was known to Burke, and thanks to the pen of De Tocqueville, most persons of moderate literary pretensions can claim a closer familiarity with its fundamental nature. Wherein, then, consists the value of the book? what are the merits which won for it the emphatic commendation of Dumont, the disciple and populariser of Bentham—that it was probably the "salvation of Europe"? How came this virulent and intemperate attack to have the wide and beneficial effect which attended it? What was the

nature of its potent magic, which disarmed the Revolutionists of England, and exorcised from the thinking classes of
Europe the mischievous desire of political change?

It was obvious that the movement in France was accompanied by a general distrust of the existing framework of society.
Something of the same kind was prevalent in England; but
it belonged to a narrower class, with narrower motives and
meaner ends. From his earliest years Burke had been familiar with the idea of a nation of human savages rising in revolt
against law, religion, and social order, and he believed the
impulse to such a revolt to exist in human nature as a specific
moral disease. The thing which he greatly feared now seemed
to have come suddenly upon him. Burke manifestly erred in
representing such an element as the sole aliment and motive
force of the French Revolution. Distrust of society was widely
disseminated in England, though less widely than Burke believed, and far less widely than in France; but Burke had
no means of verifying his bodings. Jacobinism had prevailed
in France, and a Revolution had followed—it was coming
to prevail in England, and a Revolution might be expected.
England had in France the highest reputation for political
progress, liberty, and good government. England's liberty
was bound up with the fact of her having passed through a
Revolution, which, after the lapse of a century, was considered [xiv] a worthy object of commemoration. It was represented in France that the French Revolution was proceeding on English principles. It was further understood that
England sympathised with and intended to benefit by the
broader and more enlightened Revolution which was being
accomplished in France. This Burke takes all pains to refute.
He shows that this famous English Revolution was, in truth,
a Revolution not made, but prevented. He aims to prove by
conclusive evidence that English policy, though not averse
from reform, is stubbornly opposed to revolution. He shows
that the main body of the British nation, from its historical

traditions, from the opinions and doctrines transmitted to it from the earliest times, from its constitution and essence, was utterly hostile to these dangerous novelties, and bound to eschew and reprobate them. Though mainly sound and homogeneous, the body politic had rotten members, and it is the utterances of these, by which the intelligent Frenchman might otherwise be pardonably misled, that Burke in the first instance applies himself to confute.

The earliest title of the work (see Notes, p. 369) indicates that it was occasioned proximately not by the events in France, but by events of much less importance in England. Knowing little of Europe in general, by comparison with his intimate knowledge of England, Burke can have been little disposed or prepared to rush into print, in the midst of absorbing state business at home, with a general discussion of the changes which had taken place in a foreign nation. This was not the habit of the time. In our day a man must be able to sustain an argument on the internal politics of all nations of the earth: in that day, Englishmen chiefly regarded their own business. Had the Revolution been completely isolated, it would never have occupied Burke's pen. But the Revolutionists had aiders and abettors on this side of the Channel, and they openly avowed their purpose of bringing about a catastrophe similar to that which had been brought about in France. Finally, some of these English "sympathisers" were persons long politically hateful to Burke and his party. Hence that strong tincture of party virulence which is perceptible throughout the work. Burke writes not as a Hallam—not as a philosophical critic or a temperate judge, but in his accustomed character as an impassioned advocate and an angry debater. Indeed anything like a reserved and observant [xv] attitude, on the part of his countrymen, irritates him to fury. He bitterly attacks all who, with the steady temper of Addison's Portius,

Can look on guilt, rebellion, fraud, and Caesar,
In the calm lights of mild philosophy.

His real aim is less to attack the French than the English
Revolutionists: not so much to asperse Sieyes and Mirabeau,
as Dr. Price and Lord Stanhope.

The work, then, professes to be a general statement, con-
fessedly hasty and fragmentary, of the political doctrines and
sentiments of the English people. It was, on the whole, recognised as true. The body of the nation agreed in this fierce
and eloquent denunciation. The Jacobins steadily went down
in public estimation from the day of its publication. Burke's
fiery philippic seemed to dry up their strength, as the sun
dries up the dew. Nothing could stand, in public opinion,
against Burke's imperious dilemmas. But it is the moral power
of the argument, and the brilliancy with which it is enforced,
which give the work its value. The topics themselves are of
slighter significance. Half awed by the tones of the preacher,
half by his evident earnestness and self-conviction, we are
predisposed to submit to his general doctrines, although we
cannot feel sure of their applicability to the occasion. Un-
fair as this denunciation was to France, we sympathise in its
effects on the malcontents in England. The tone of the book
was well suited to the occasion. A loud and bitter cry was to be
raised—the revolutionary propaganda was to be stayed—and
to this end all that could be said against it was to be clearly,
sharply, emphatically, and uncompromisingly put forth. With
Hannibal at the gates, it was no time for half-opinions, for
qualification, and for temporisation. No wise man could hesitate to do his best to discredit the Jacobins, without any very
scrupulous regard to absolute justice. They were unjust and
unscrupulous, and it was perhaps pardonable to attack them
with their own weapons. From all this we deduce the critical canon, that properly to understand Burke's book we must

INTRODUCTION

look on him not as a critic, but as an advocate. The book is not history, nor philosophy, but a polemic. It is a polemic against Jacobinism, particularly English Jacobinism.

What is, or rather was, Jacobinism? In the usage of the day, [xvi] it was a vituperative term applied summarily to all opposition to the dominant party. He who doubted Mr. Pitt was set down as a Jacobin, much as he who doubted the Bishops was set down as an infidel. But the Jacobin proper is the revolter against the established order of society. What those who stood by this established order understood by the term is roughly expressed in Burke's phrase of *Treason against property*. "You have too much, I have too little—you have privileges, I have none—your liberties are essentially an encroachment upon mine, or those which ought to be mine." These formulas constitute the creed of Jacobinism in its simplest and rudest form, the sentimental antagonism of poverty against wealth.

Well, whiles I am a beggar, I will rail,
And say, There is no sin but to be rich:
And being rich, my virtue then shall be
To say, There is no vice but beggary.[1]

This creed will never lack exponents. It is founded on an ancient tale, and in a certain sense, a tale of wrong; but whilst the human species maintains its vantage above the lower animals, it is a wrong that will never be completely righted. In Burke's view, it is of the nature and essence of property to be unequal. The degrees of social prosperity must always exhibit many shades of disparity, "Take but degree away, untune that string," and you destroy most things which set man above the brutes. Degree is inseparable from the maintenance of the artificial structure of civilisation. The last phrase leads us to note the fundamental fallacy of the doctrine in its next stage

---

1. Shakespeare, King John, Act II.

of philosophical or *speculative* Jacobinism. Civilisation, social happiness, the comfortable arts of life, are no gift of nature to man. They are, in the strictest sense, artificial. The French philosophers, by a gross assumption, took them to be natural, and therefore a matter of common right to all.

We notice here a fundamental antagonism alleged by Burke to exist between the Revolutionists and the English school of politicians. The former base their claims upon Right; Burke, following the traditions of English statesmanship, claims to base his upon Law. It is not that Law has no basis in natural Right: it is rather that Law, having occupied as a basis a portion of [xvii] the space naturally covered by Right, all outside it ceases to be right in the same sense in which it was so before. In other words, realised Right, in the shape of tangible and enforceable Law, is understood to be so material an advance upon abstract Right, that your acceptance of the former amounts to a renunciation of the latter. You cannot have both at once. Now Jacobinism may be regarded as the sentiment which leads man to repudiate Law and take his stand upon natural Right. The difficulty is that in so doing he limits himself, and seeks to reduce his fellow-men, to the right of the naked savage, for natural right cannot extend beyond the state of nature. As Jacobinism is the repudiation of Law, Burke takes his stand upon the Law; and one of the defects of the present work is that he carries this too far. It has been said of his attitude in this work that he begins like a pettifogger and ends like a statesman. The argument of the first thirty-eight pages of this volume, by which he claims to prove that Englishmen have irrevocably bargained away their liberties for ever, is unquestionably one of the weakest passages in the whole of Burke's writings. Hallam has proved it untenable at many points: and the refutation may, it is believed, be completely made out by reference to the notes at the end of this volume. A British statesman may, however, plead a closer relation between law and liberty than is usual in most countries, and claim to be leniently criticised for defending himself on the standpoint of the lawyer.

Men of the law were the statesmen under whom the British Constitution grew into shape. Men of the law defended it from Papal aggression, a circumstance to which Burke complacently alludes (p. 183): and one of his main ideas is the thoroughly lawyer-like one that liberty can only proceed "from precedent to precedent." This onward progress he admitted as far as the epoch of the Revolution, but there, in a way characteristic of him, he resolved to take his stand. Magna Charta, the Petition of Right, the Bill of Rights, and the Act of Settlement, were his undoubted chain of English constitutional securities, and he declined to admit any further modification of them. So far he was in harmony with popular ideas. When he went beyond this, and declared that the Act of Settlement bound the English nation for ever, his reasoning was obviously false. The whole procedure of Burke throughout this book is, as has been observed, [xviii] avowedly that of an advocate. In his apology called the "Appeal from the New to the Old Whigs," he states as the reason that when any one of the members of a vast and balanced whole is endangered, he is the true friend to them all who supports the part attacked, "with all the power of stating, of argument, and of colouring, which he happens to possess, and which the case demands. He is not to embarrass the minds of his hearers, or to incumber or overlay his speech, by bringing into view at once (as if he were reading an academic lecture) all that may and ought, when a just occasion presents itself, be said in favour of the other members. At that time they are out of court; there is no question concerning them. Whilst he opposes his defence on the part where the attack is made, he presumes that for his regard to the just rights of all the rest, he has credit in every candid mind." Burke's overstrained reverence for the Act of Settlement may be partly due to the general feeling of uncertainty which, during his own century, prevailed as to party principle. As early as Swift's time, parties and their creeds had become thoroughly confused and undistinguishable. But Burke demanded something positive— something to which men could bind themselves by covenant. Casting a glance back upon the history of parties from Burke's time, the Revolution is the first trustworthy landmark that we meet with. In the apology from which we have just quoted, he proclaims the speeches of the managers of the impeachment of Sacheverel, as representing those who brought about the English Revolution, to be the fountains of true constitutional doctrine. After this epoch he seems to have distrusted all political creeds. There is hardly one notable political work of the day immediately preceding him to which he makes allusion, and then only in terms of censure.

As an illustration at once of Burke's instinctive retreat to the shelter of legal orthodoxy, and of the charm which his pen could throw over the driest statement of first principles, let us observe how he has worked up a well-known passage of a well-known legal classic.

"The design of entering into society being the protection of our persons and security of our property, men in civil society have a right, and indeed are [xix] obliged to apply to the public for redress when they are injured; for were they allowed to be their own carvers, or to make reprisals, which they might do in a state of nature, such permission would introduce all that inconvenience which the state of nature did endure, and which government was at first invented to prevent; hence therefore they are obliged to submit to the public the measure of their damages,

"One of the first motives to civil society, and which becomes one of its fundamental rules, is *that no man should be judge in his own cause.* By this each person has at once divested himself of the fundamental right of uncovenanted man, that is, to judge for himself, and to assert his own cause. He abdicates all right to be his own governor. He inclusively, in a great measure, abandons the right of self-defence, the first law of nature. Men cannot enjoy the rights of an uncivil and of a civil state together. That he may obtain justice he gives up his right of determining what and to have recourse to the law and the courts of justice, which are appointed to give them redress and ease in their affairs." (Bacon's Abridgment, art. Actions in General.)

it is, in points the most essential to him. That he may secure some liberty, he makes a surrender in trust of the whole of it." (Page 151.)

The practical jurisprudence of England in Burke's time stood sadly in need of Reform. That of France was in a still worse case. Burke fully recognised the necessity of removing the "defects, redundancies, and errors" of the law (p. 191), though he still maintained it to be the "collected reason of ages," and the "pride of the human intellect." Whether in France "the old independent judicature of the Parliaments" was worth preserving, in a reformed condition, as Burke so strongly insists, admits of doubt. Scandalous as were the delays, the useless and cumbrous processes, and the exaction which attended the management of the English law, those who administered it were at least able men, and men who had honestly risen to their places, in virtue of their native and acquired qualifications. It was not so in France. In France judges purchased their places and suitors purchased justice. In cases where this may not be absolutely true, justice at the hands of the "sworn guardians of property" was a doubtful commodity, and few will now deny that the Assembly were justified in making a clean sweep of it (see p. 222). As to the common law which they administered, its condition will be best gathered from the articles on the subject contained in the Encyclopédie. It is enough to say of it that it exhibited the worst characteristics of English law before the time of [xx] Richard II. The general system of English law he thought entitled a qualified commendation. His views on the subject were however very different from those of his contemporary, Lord Eldon. He did not systematically discountenance all enquiry, and scout all proposed reform. He had taken the lead in 1780, in advocating reforms dealing with the Royal

---

property, which have since been carried out with general approval. He had commenced, early in his career, a treatise advocating that reform of the Irish Penal Laws which, when carried through by his friends Savile and Dunning, produced the awful riots of 1780. His judgment on the question of how far reform was admissible, and at what point it degenerated into innovation, coincides with that of Bacon and Hale, rather than with that of Coke and Eldon.

Conceiving the English nation as a four-square fabric supported on the four bases of the Church, the Crown, the Nobility, and the People, it is natural to find the author insisting most on the excellences of those elements which were then assailed in France. The People, of course, needed no defence, nor was the Crown as yet overthrown. The dream of the moment was a constitutional monarchy, based on elements similar to those of the English Constitution.[1] Only the Church and the Aristocracy were as yet threatened: and, next to the defence of the Church, the best known section of the present treatise is that which relates to the Nobility. On this subject, independently of constitutional law and of theory, Burke cherished prejudices early formed and never shaken. He had lived on terms of intimacy with, and was bound by ties of mutual obligation to some of the worthiest members of the British aristocracy. It is mainly to them personally that his panegyric is applicable. Nobility, however, possessed claims which he was as eager to recognise, as an important establishment of the common law of the country, and as justified by universal analogy and supported by the best general theories of society. "To be honoured, and even privileged, by the laws, opinions, and inveterate usages of our country," was with him not only a noble prize to the person who attained it, but a politic institution for the community which conferred it. Why? Because it operated as an instinct to secure property,

1. See vol. i. Introduction, p. 21.

[xxi] and to preserve communities in a settled state (p. 241). But Burke's reasoning is vitiated by a cardinal fault. It is pervaded by his own conception of an aristocracy, derived from his own personal friends and fellow-workers. The aristocracy of France differed from that of England as substance differs from shadow. In England, nobility had long implied privileges which are merely honorary; in France it implied privileges substantial in themselves, and grievous to those who were excluded from them. Practically, though Burke in the duties of his advocacy denies the fact, the nobility were untaxed. To use a sufficiently accurate expression, the *feudal system* was still in operation in France. If not aggravated by natural growth during successive centuries, it exhibited a growing incompatibility with what surrounded it. In England it had practically been extinct for two centuries, and it was now absolutely out of mind. Barons and Commons had long made up but one People; the old families were mostly extinct, and the existing Peers were chiefly commoners with coronets on their coats of arms. At the present moment not a single seat in the House of Peers is occupied in virtue of tenure,[1] and the Peerage, saving heraldic vanities and some legal and social courtesies, practically confers nothing but a descendible personal magistracy, exercised at considerable expense and inconvenience. The status of a Peer generally involves, in addition, the maintenance of the bulk of a fortune not always large in the least remunerative of investments. The qualification for a Peerage has long been limited to a long-continued course of service to the State. Every one of these conditions was reversed in France. The nobleman was a member of a decaying privileged class, who clung to their unjust and oppressive privileges with the most obstinate tenacity. It was the idle noble who spent the hard earnings of the peasant. Taxation

1. In one or two recent instances a claim to sit by tenure has been advanced and rejected.

in England fell lightly in the extreme upon the poorer classes; in France they bore almost the whole burden of the national expenses. Society in France thus rested on a tottering and artificial frame: while in England the frame had gradually and safely accommodated itself to the change of social force.

But in the method of Burke every argument in favour of a [xxii] particular element of the State, based upon the special excellence of that element, is subordinate to his general doctrine of the nature of the State as a grand working machine. A machine, he thought, to attain the end for which it was devised, must be allowed to work fairly and continuously. To be perpetually stopping its system for the purpose of trying experiments, was an error venial only in a child. To destroy it, in order to use its parts in the construction of some other ideal machine, which might never be got to work at all, was criminal madness. The strictures of Burke with reference to this great and central point in his political philosophy are only partially applicable to the French Reformers of his day; nor are they at any time unexceptionably appropriate. Yet they constitute a profound and necessary substructure in every intelligent conception of civil matters, and as such they will never cease to be worthy of the remembrance of the most practised statesmen, as well as an indispensable part of the education of the beginner in politics. Every student must begin, if he does not end, with Conservatism; and every Reformer must bear in mind that without a certain established base, secured by a large degree of this often-forgotten principle, his best devised scheme cannot fail to fall to the ground. The present work is the best text-book of Conservatism which has ever appeared.

Burke claims for his views the support of the English nation. Political events and the popularity of his book alike proved that this was no idle boast: but it necessarily indicated nothing more than that the party of progress was in England in the minority, while in France it was in the ascendant. Burke's claim, however, involves far more. It asserts that the doctrines of the revolution had long been well known in England: that the belief in the "rights of man" had long been exploded, and its consequences dismissed as pernicious fallacies: and that in this condemnation the best minds in England had concurred. To examine the justice of this claim would involve the whole political and religious history of the stirring century between the Spanish Armada and the Revolution of 1688. This is far beyond our present purpose, which may be equally well served on ground merely literary. Taking English literature as our guide, we shall find that, two hundred years before, conclusions very similar to those of Burke were formed in the minds of philosophical [xxiii] observers. The significance of those conclusions is not impaired by the historical results of the contest. They throw no shade upon the glorious victories of the spirit of English liberty. They rather illustrate and complement them. They rather tend to justify the partial adoption, by sober and reasonable men, when the substance of English liberty began to be attacked under the Scotch kings, of ideas which were previously limited to intemperate and half-educated minds. But these ideas never penetrated the mass of English contemporary thinkers. Milton, in his proposed organisation of the republic, followed Italian, not English ideas: and the honour due to Milton will not prevent our recognising the beauty and propriety of doctrines from which, under other circumstances, even he might have drawn his practical deductions.

That Conservatism is compatible with philosophical statesmanship can be illustrated in a remarkable degree from the great work of Hooker. Hooker and Grotius allow a view of the general rights and obligations of civil society, which goes far beyond what Burke, in the present work, will admit.[1] But the great English divine, while discerning the necessity of forsaking the narrow political theories of the middle ages,

1. Hooker, Book i. ch. 10; Grotius, Book i. c. 3. § 8. par. 2, &c.

fortified himself in his enlarged position by a clear definition of the limits of political change. In the state, Hooker
saw distinctly reflected the order and discipline which he believed to have been impressed upon the natural face of the
universe by an all-wise and beneficent Creator. The reign of
law on earth reflected the reign of law in heaven. Hooker
ridicules the turbulent wits of old, to whom, in the words
of the Roman historian, *quieta movere magna merces videbatur.*
"They thought the very disturbance of things established an
hire sufficient to set them on work." The reader of Hooker
can hardly fail to be struck by his coincidence with Burke's
mode of thought and argument. Both point out the value of
what the English nation regards as an everlasting possession;
both lay bare the deep foundations of law, order, and temporal polity; and seek, by the united force of truth and reason,
to display and vindicate in the eye of the world the gradations, the dignities, and the majesty of a well-balanced state.
The limits of the application of general principles in politics
are [xxiv] admirably sketched out by Hooker. Following Aristotle, he remarks the fallacies which occur from disregarding
the nature of the stuff which the politician has to work upon.

These varieties [the phases of human will and sentiment] are
not known but by much experience, from whence to draw the true
bounds of all principles, to discern how far forth they take effect, to
see where and why they fail, to apprehend by what degrees and means
they lead to the practice of things in shew, though not indeed repugnant and contrary one to another, requireth more sharpness of wit,
more intricate circuitions of discourse, more industry and depth of
judgment than common opinion doth yield. So that general rules, till
their limits be fully known (especially in matter of public and ecclesiastical affairs), are by reason of the manifold secret exceptions which
lie hidden in them, no other, to the eye of man's understanding, than
cloudy mists cast before the eye of common sense. They that walk in
darkness, know not whither they go.—Book v. ch. 9.

Such conceptions are naturally generated in a comprehensive mind, as soon as the world is stirred by the impulse

to shake off old evils. Wisdom consists in no inconsiderable degree, says Burke, in knowing what amount of evil is to be tolerated. "Il ne faut pas tout corriger," says Montesquieu. "Both in civil and in ecclesiastical polity," says Hooker, "there are, and will be always, evils which no art of man can cure, breaches and leaks more than man's art hath hands to stop." This may be: but it is certain that breaches and leaks which one age has regarded as incurable have been stopped in another. The science of politics, unlike most other sciences, is too often regarded as having reached its final stage: many a specious conclusion is vitiated by this assumption. The defect of such aphorisms as that of Montesquieu obviously lies in their extreme liability to abuse: and Burke cannot be absolved from the charge of abusing the principle which the aphorism embodies. But it cannot be denied that Hooker and many another Englishman whose authority English people held in high respect, had done the same thing before him. The following passage of Hooker strikingly reminds the reader of a mode of argument frequently employed by Burke:

For first, the ground whereupon they build, is not certainly their own, but with special limitations. Few things are so restrained to any one end or purpose, that the same being extinct [xxv] they should forthwith utterly become frustrate. Wisdom may have framed one and the same thing to serve commodiously for divers ends, and of those ends any one be sufficient cause for continuance, though the rest have ceased, even as the tongue, which nature hath given us for an instrument of speech, is not idle in dumb persons, because it also serveth for taste. Again, if time have worn out, or any other mean altogether taken away, what was first intended, uses not thought upon before may afterwards spring up, and be reasonable causes of retaining that which other considerations did formerly procure to be instituted. And it cometh sometime to pass, that a thing unnecessary in itself as touching the whole direct purpose whereto it was meant or can be applied, doth notwithstanding appear convenient to be still held even without use, lest by reason of that coherence which it hath with somewhat more necessary, the removal of the one should indamage the other; and therefore men which have clean lost the possibility of sight, keep still their eyes nevertheless in the place where nature set them. — Book v. ch. 42.

The ground of this philosophical or rational conservatism mainly consists in seeking to contemplate things with reference to their dependency on an entire system, and to have regard to the coherence and significance of the system. It is liable to abuse: and many may think that the whole conception belongs to the domain of poetry rather than to that of philosophy. The poetry of the time, indeed, reflects it in more than one place. The idea is clearly traceable in Spenser's Cantos of Mutability, the "hardy Titaness," who, seduced by "some vain error," dared

To see that mortal eyes have never seen.

The poet foreshadows a calamitous break-up of the established order of things, a mischievous contortion of the "world's fair frame, which none yet durst of gods or men to alter or misguide," and a reversal of the laws of nature, justice, and policy. It reminds us something of the bodings of the Greek chorus, when they sing that the founts of the sacred rivers are turned backward, and that justice and the universe are suffering a revolution. Such notions are unquestionably more than the over-wrought dreams of poets. They have their key in the defective moral tone of their age: but it by no means follows that the moral defect which this implies covers the whole ground to which they extend. Slumber seems natural to certain stages of human history: and a slumbering nation always resents the first signs of [xxvi] its awakenment. We may trace a similar vein of feeling, stimulated by the same revolutionary agencies, though in a later stage, in the poems of the philosophical and "well-languaged" Daniel. The faculty of looking on an institution on many sides enabled Daniel to point out

How pow'rs are thought to wrong, that wrongs debar.

Daniel had trained himself in an instructive school, in the preparation and composition of his History of the Civil Wars. Like Burke, he was of opinion that political wisdom was not to be obtained *à priori*. The statesman must study

The sure records of books, in which we find
The tenure of our state, how it was held
By all our ancestors, and in what kind
We hold the same, and likewise how in th' end
This frail possession of felicity
Shall to our late posterity descend
By the same patent of like destiny.
In them we find that nothing can accrue
To man, and his condition, that is new.[1]

It is an apt illustration of Burke's vehement contention that Englishmen will never consent to abandon the sense of national continuity. The English nation is emphatically an *old* nation: it proceeds on the assumption that there is nothing new under the sun. It is always disposed to criticise severely any one who labours, as Warburton says, under that epidemic distemper of idle men, the idea of instructing and informing the world. The heart of men, and the greater heart of associated bodies of men, has been radically the same in all ages. In the laws of life we cannot hope for much additional illumination: new lights in general turn out to be old illusions. There is no unexplored *terra australis,* whether of morality or political science. The great principles of government and the ideas of liberty "were understood long before we were born, altogether as well as they will be after the grave has heaped

---

1. Dedication of Philotas.

---

its mould upon our presumption, and the silent tomb shall have imposed its law upon our pert loquacity."[1] In a literary and scientific age, it is impossible that [xxvii] this dogmatism can pass unchallenged: but Burke is right in asserting an antagonism between the beliefs of the best minds of England, as represented in a great historic literary past, and those of the existing literary generation in France. Englishmen have in all times affected a taste for public matters and for scholarship: and this affectation is not ill exemplified in one who was a man of letters, with the superadded qualities of the philosopher and the politician. Curious illustrations of a normal antagonism between these elements may be derived from Daniel's Dialogue entitled "Musophilus." Musophilus is the man of letters, Philocosmus the man of the world. Philocosmus taunts Musophilus with his empty and purposeless pursuits, to which Musophilus replies by a spirited defence of learning. Philocosmus changes his ground, and lays to the charge of the professors of learning, who overswarm and infest the English world, a general spirit of discontent, amounting to sedition.

Do you not see these pamphlets, libels, rhimes,
These strange compressed tumults of the mind,
Are grown to be the sickness of the times,
The great disease inflicted on mankind?
Your virtues, by your follies made your crimes,
Have issue with your indiscretion joined.

Burke insists on identifying the "literary cabal" as the chief element in the ferment of Revolution: "Men of letters, fond of distinguishing themselves, are rarely averse to innovation" (p. 208). See how a retired observer in the time of the first Stuart anticipates the effects of the same misplaced activity.

1. Page 181.

For when the greater wits cannot attain
Th' expected good which they account their right,
And yet perceive others to reap that gain
Of far inferior virtues in their sight;
They present, with the sharp of envy, strain
To wound them with reproaches and despite.

. . . .

Hence discontented sects and schisms arise;
Hence interwounding controversies spring,
That feed the simple, and offend the wise.

Action, Philocosmus goes on to say, differs materially from
what is read of in books:

[xxviii] The world's affairs require in managing
More arts than those wherein you clerks proceed.

Men of letters, in the indulgence of the tastes which their
pursuits have fostered, lose those faculties which are necessary to the conduct of affairs.

The skill wherewith you have so cunning been
Unsinews all your powers, unmans you quite.
Public society and commerce of men
Require another grace, another port.

Beware of the philosopher who pretends to statesmanship.
The Scholar replies, that the Statesman, with all his boasted
skill, cannot anticipate the perils of the time, or see

how soon this rolling world can take
Advantage for her dissolution,
Fain to get loose from this withholding stake
Of civil science and discretion;
How glad it would run wild, that it might make
One formless form of one confusion.

The mysteries of State, the "Norman subtleties," says the
Scholar, are now vulgarised and common. Giddy innovations
would overthrow the whole fabric of society. But what is the

remedy? To "pull back the onrunning state of things"? This might end in bringing men more astray, and destroy the faith in the unity and continuity of civil life, which is

> that close-kept palladium
> Which once remov'd, brings ruin evermore.

Investigation would discover much the same vein of thought in many of Daniel's contemporaries. Compare, for instance, Fletcher's portraiture of Dichostasis, or Sedition,

That wont but in the factious court to dwell,
But now to shepherd swains close linked is.
. . . .
A subtle craftsman fram'd him seemly arms,
Forg'd in the shop of wrangling sophistry;
And wrought with curious arts, and mighty charms,
Temper'd with lies, and false philosophy.

> The Purple Island, Canto vii.

[xxix] Among Shakspere's most obvious characteristics is that which is often called his objectiveness. He does not task his characters to utter his private sentiments and convictions. His characters are realities, not masks. But no one who has endeavoured to penetrate the mind of Shakspere as reflected in his whole works will deny to him a full participation in Burke's doctrine of faith in the order of society. To borrow the words of Hartley Coleridge,[1] Shakspere, as manifested in his writings, is one of those "who build the commonweal, not on the shifting shoals of expedience, or the incalculable tides of popular will, but on the sure foundations of the divine purpose, demonstrated by the great and glorious ends of rational being; who deduce the rights and duties of men, not from the animal nature, in which neither right nor duty can inhere, not from a state of nature which never existed, nor from an arbitrary contract which never took place in the memory of

1. Essays, vol. i. p. 134.

man nor angels, but from the demands of the complex life of the soul and the body, defined by reason and conscience, expounded and ratified by revelation." So exact is the application, one might think he was speaking of Burke. A book might be made up by illustrating the political conceptions of Shakspere out of his plays: but it will be enough for our purpose to consider one or two specimens. The following extract from the speech in which Ulysses demonstrates the ills arising from the feuds of the Greek champions is alike remarkable for the compass of its thought and for the accuracy with which it reflects a feeling which has always been common among Englishmen. A narrower conception of the same argument is summed up in a famous epigram of Pope commencing "Order is heaven's first law."

The heavens themselves, the planets and this centre,
Observe degree, priority, and place,
Insisture, course, proportion, season, form,
Office and custom, in all line of order:
And therefore is the glorious planet, Sol,
In noble eminence enthroned and sphered
Amidst the other: whose med'cinable eye
Corrects the ill aspects of planets evil,
And posts, like the commandment of a king,
Sans check, to good and bad. But when the planets
[xxx] In evil mixture to disorder wander,
What plagues and what portents! what mutiny!
What raging of the sea! shaking of earth!
Commotion in the winds! frights, changes, horrors,
Divert and crack, rend and deracinate
The unity and married calm of states
Quite from their fixture! O, when degree is shak'd,
Which is the ladder of all high designs,
The enterprise is sick! How could communities,
Degrees in schools, and brotherhoods in cities,
Peaceful commerce from dividable shores,
The primogenitive and due of birth,
Prerogative of age, crowns, sceptres, laurels,

INTRODUCTION

But by degree, stand in authentic place?
Take but degree away, untune that string,
And, hark! what discord follows! Each thing meets
In mere oppugnancy: the bounded waters
Should lift their bosoms higher than the shores,
And make a sop of all this solid globe:
Strength should be lord of imbecility,
And the rude son should strike his father dead:
Force should be right: or rather, right and wrong,
(Between whose endless jar justice resides)
Should lose their names, and so should justice too.
Then everything includes itself in power,
Power into will, will into appetite:
And appetite, an universal wolf,
So doubly seconded with will and power,
Must make perforce an universal prey,
And, last, eat up himself. Great Agamemnon,
This chaos, when degree is suffocate,
Follows the choking.

Troilus and Cressida, Act i. Sc. 3.

No passage in literature reflects more faithfully the general spirit of the present work. The grave tone of mingled doctrine and portent, and the two contrasted moral effects, are in each exactly similar.

Jack Cade and his rout, and the mob in Coriolanus, will doubtless occur to the student as instances of sharp satire against Democracy. Shakspere always conceives political action, especially in England, as proceeding from a lawful monarch, wielding [xxxi] real power under the guidance of wise counsellors: and this does not differ greatly from the Whig theory to which Burke always adhered.

Quitting the Elizabethan period, it would be easy to continue the historical vindication of Burke's claim. The popular party of the Commonwealth and the Revolution were the true conservatives of their age. They fought, as Burke had pointed out in a previous work, for a liberty that had been consecrated by long usage and tradition; and outside this memorable strife the greatest of English minds, with a few exceptions, surrendered themselves to the general tide of anti-revolutionary opinion. Dryden, always a favourite authority with Burke, is an obvious instance. One passage from his prose works may be adduced to show that the worst arguments employed by Burke in the present treatise do not lack the authority of great and popular English names:

> Neither does it follow that an unalterable succession supposes England to be the king's estate, and the people his goods and chattels on it. For the preservation of his right destroys not our propriety, but maintains us in it. He has tied himself by law not to invade our possessions, and we have obliged ourselves as subjects to him and all his lawful successors: by which irrevocable act of ours, both for ourselves and our posterity, we can no more exclude the successor than we can depose the present king. The estate of England is indeed the king's, and I may safely grant their supposition, as to the *government* of England: but it follows not that the people are his goods and chattels on it, for then he might sell, alienate, or destroy them as he pleas'd; from all which he has tied himself by the liberties and privileges which he has granted us by laws. — Vindication of the Duke of Guise, p. 53.

It may be truly objected that the course of English political events destroys the authority of these Tory formulas. But it is well known that the Whig policy of England since the Revolution had not been supported by a majority of the English people. The majority of English people, told by the head, would down to the beginning of the reign of George III have been found to be Tory: and Burke was in a strong position when he averred that such was the disposition of the English nation as a whole. Among Dryden's poems, the famous "Absalom and Achitophel" will illustrate the Tory feeling which the English people [xxxii] cherished: but it will be found in its most compendious form in the pendant of "Absalom," the matchless satire called "The Medal." The lines following the portraiture of Shaftesbury, and bitterly ridiculing the appeal to the people as a test of truth, sum up in a masterly form the historical and philosophical topics commonly urged in this belief:

He preaches to the crowd that power is *lent,*
But not *conveyed,* to royal government:
That claims successive bear no binding force:
That coronation oaths are things of course:
Maintains the multitude can never err:
And sets the people in the papal chair.
The reason's obvious: Interest never lies,
The most have still their interest in their eyes,
The power is always theirs, and power is ever wise.
Almighty crowd! thou shortenest all dispute,
Power is thy essence, wit thy attribute:
Nor faith nor reason make thee at a stay:
Thou leap'st o'er all eternal truths in thy Pindaric way!

Phocion and Socrates are satirically instanced as examples of popular justice. Then follows a remarkable forecast of an opinion first elaborated and given to the world by the French philosophers in the next century:

The common cry is even religion's test,
The Turk's is at Constantinople best,
Idols in India, Popery at Rome,
And our own worship only true at home.
.   .   .   .
A tempting doctrine, plausible and new:
What fools our fathers were, if this be true!
Who, to destroy the seeds of civil war,
Inherent right in monarchs did declare:
And, that a lawful power might never cease,
Secured succession, to secure our peace.
Thus property and sovereign sway at last
In equal balances were justly cast:
But this new Jehu spurs the hot-mouthed horse,
Instructs the beast to know his native force,
To take the bit between his teeth, and fly
To the next headlong steep of anarchy.

INTRODUCTION

[xxxiii] In the conclusion of the "Medal" the poet fore-shadows what is called the "bursting of the floodgates"; the inevitable strife of the "cut-throat sword and clamorous gown," the abolition of "Peerage and Property," and the supremacy of a popular military commander. Such vaticinations had in Burke's time been familiar to the world for a century: and he now imagined that he saw them about to be fulfilled in France.[1]

It would be easy to pursue the same track in Butler and Swift, in the vast field of the Essayists, and in English theological and historical writers, among whom most of the popular names will be found on the same side. The Whigs and Tories of the century, if we except a few clerical politicians, alike avoid professing extremes. The popular poets of Burke's own generation kept up the idea of a grand historical past closely connected with the existing political establishment. English poetry, from Spenser and Drayton to Scott and Tennyson, has in fact always been largely pervaded by this idea, and a retrospective tendency, tinged with something of pride and admiration, has generally accompanied literary taste in the Englishman. Milton and Spenser revelled in the antique fables which then formed the bulk of what was called the History of England. Shakespeare dramatised the history of the ages preceding his own, with even more felicity than the remote legends of Lear and Cymbeline. Little of this is to be noticed in the taste of any foreign nation, and the literature of France has always been eminently the offspring of the moment. French minds have never dwelt with the interest derived from a sense of identity upon the events or products of the past. Continental critics have, as might be expected, traced the love of the English for the English past to a narrow insularity. They ought also to point out how intense was the contrast, down to the French Revolution, of insular and

1. Burke himself quotes "our political poet" Denham (p. 216).

INTRODUCTION

continental institutions. In Burke's time, religious and political liberty were to Frenchmen entirely foreign ideas. National greatness was a conception common to both the Englishman and the Frenchman: but England had of late repeatedly humbled that of France, and the Frenchman was just beginning to enquire into the causes which had given the smaller country its superiority. There was a contrast, and a [xxxiv] disposition to enquire into it: the English and French people, during the eighteenth century, observed the social and political tendencies of their neighbours with curious watchfulness. The antagonism was heightened by the commencement of social intercourse between them in the intervals of war. We may learn something of the contrast which was believed to subsist between the normal tendencies of the English and the French mind from the criticism of a thoroughly English man of letters upon De Vertot, whose works during the last century were so eagerly read by the French people.[1] Warburton,[2] himself an early friend of Burke, marks out among the cheats adopted to catch the popular ear, that "entirely new species of historical writing" which deals with the revolutions of a country. De Vertot had put together in a popular style the story of those violent changes which had taken place in ancient Rome, and in modern Sweden and Portugal. His sensationalism had secured him an extraordinary success. Warburton, indignant at "the present fondness for the cheat, and its yet unsuspected importance," proves the system false in itself, "injurious to the country it dismembers," and destructive to all just history.

That this form should wonderfully allure common readers, is no way strange. The busy active catastrophe of revolutions gives a tumultuous kind of pleasure to those vulgar minds that remain unaffected

1. See note, p. 367.

2. Tracts by Warburton and a Warburtonian, p. 99.

with the calm scenes that the still and steady advances of a well-balanced state, to secure its peace, power, and durability, present before them. Add to this that the revolution part is the great repository of all the stores for admiration, whose power and fascination on the fancy we have at large examined; whereas the steady part affords entertainment only for the understanding, by its sober lessons on public utility.

It is not only passively useless; it tends to disgust us with the system of society altogether; "to think irreverently of it, and in time to drop all concern for its interests." But, it may be objected, this kind of history best discovers the nature and genius of a people. "Ridiculous!" says the critic, "as if one should measure the benefits of the Trent, the Severn, or the Thames, by the casual overflowing of a summer inundation." He goes on to complain of the injustice inflicted on Englishmen [xxxv] by this "historical method." We, "the best natured people upon earth," are branded by these charlatans, on the score of our struggles to preserve our inherited liberties, "with the title of savage, restless, turbulent revolutionists." It is easy to trace here the argument of Burke. For fifty years and more, when Burke was writing, the French people had been coming to believe in Revolutions, and to look to their neighbours on the other side of the water for authentic revolutionary methods. The facts on which this belief was based were ill selected and ill understood. But the craving for change had developed into a social necessity. The Frenchman still turned in his desperation to England, and the Englishman at once repulsed him as an enemy and despised him as a slave. In Warburton's time, the "Anglomania" of which this was but one form was a novelty. Innovation is always jealous of rivalry: and this circumstance no doubt helped to attract Warburton's wrath. But that which was a novelty in 1727 had become inveterate in 1789. The sense of historical and political truth had become more and more obscured, and the morbid demand for change had grown little by little into a madness. Practical political life, the soul and school of true political doctrine, was extinct. The old fabric of the state was decayed, and none knew how to repair it. But this, fact as it was, was hardly within the comprehension of Englishmen.

To this day it may be said that the mutual criticisms which Englishmen and Frenchmen have bandied at each other are generally based on some misunderstanding. It was far more so a century ago. In more than one topic of the present work Burke transfers to French matters ideas which were really only proper to England. In Burke's famous delineation of European society, at its best, as he believed, in this country, there was little or nothing to interest or instruct the Frenchman. Those parts of the work which are best calculated to their end are the arguments which are to be found scattered up and down the book which deduce from English society the higher laws which ought to govern civil life in general. On this ground we have Burke at his strongest.

To the cherished tradition of the English philosophy of the State, the incidents of the French Revolution administered an unexpected and powerful impulse. Burke conceived the English [xxxvi] political creed to be threatened and misunderstood: his ready intellect at once traced this creed to its most imposing deductions, and his fiery and poetical fancy moulded it into new and more striking forms. We have in the present work, for the first time, a deliberate retrospect of what European society in its old-fashioned and normal shape has done for the human race, heightened by all that passion and rhetoric can do to recommend it. Burke had caught inspiration from his opponents. Just as the Revolutionist in his dogmatism displays all the bitterness and the intractability of an ecclesiastic, so Burke communicates to his philosophy of society something of the depth and fervour of religion. The state, according to his solemn figure, which reflects alike the mode of thought of the great statesman and philosopher of

Rome, and of our English philosophical divines, is an emanation of the Divine Will.[1]

The political philosophy of Burke, though in itself systematic and complete, makes no pretence to the character of what is understood by a *scientific theory*. It rests on ignorance, and, in technical language, may be described as sceptical. The best formula afforded by the present work to express it is that which describes the human race as a "great mysterious incorporation."[2] Society, though a changeable and destructible system, is not like a machine which can at will be taken to pieces, regulated, and reconstructed. Its motive force is as incomprehensible as that of the individual man. All analysis is evaded by those ties which bind together the obligations and affections of the individual into an intelligible and operative whole; and it is exactly so with those which bind together the system of the State. Society, to repeat a trite formula, is an organism, not a mechanism. As life itself is an insoluble mystery, so is the life of that invisible entity which is understood by the term "society." The attempt to defy this mystery is as fatuous and presumptuous as would be, in the mechanical world, the attempt to animate a mass of dead parts. Society is not made, it grows; and by ways as dark and mysterious as those which from its earliest germ conduct and limit the destination of life in the individual. Φύσει πολιτικὸν ζῷον ἄνθρωπος. The elementary nature expressed in each word of this profound expression of Aristotle, is involved in an equal degree [xxxvii] of obscurity. Neither *Man* nor the *State* can escape from the character of original mystery impressed upon them by the *life* and the *nature* in and by which they are generated. Frankly admitting this, and drawing our conclusions only from the positive character which the moral and political man in his several aspects actually reveals, we shall be

1. Page 194.

2. Page 122.

safe; but in the fruitless effort to lift the veil we cannot but err. The true method of politics, as of all branches of practical knowledge, is that of experiment. Examine the face of society. Observe, as Newton did in the planetary system, the strong gravitating forces which draw its particles into congruous living shapes; but with the wisdom of Newton, discard all tempting hypotheses, and penetrate no further. Trust and cherish whatever you find to be a motive power, or a cementing principle, knowing that, like the wind that blows as it lists, it is a power over which you have no control, save to regulate and to correct. Deal reverently, as one that has learnt to fear himself,[1] and to love and respect his kind, even with the errors, the prejudices, the unreasoned habits, that are mixed in those powers and principles. You cannot understand them, you cannot disregard or defy them; you cannot get rid of them. You must take the frame of man and of society as a Power above you has made them. To guide you in dealing with them, you have the experience of many who have gone before you, presumably not your inferiors in qualifications for the task, and who may have been free from special difficulties which stand in your own way.

Burke's doctrine on the origin of society corresponds to this view of its nature and foundation. More than one of the uses which help to keep society together have in theory been adopted as its possible origin, but these uses all germinate from the instinct of congregation. Aristotle and Cicero had each in their time maintained, against contemporary theorists, that in this instinct is to be traced the true germ of social organisation; and their view was revived, at the revival of letters, in the remarkable tract of Buchanan, *De Jure Regni*. According to this view, the uses and advantages of social life are entirely an aftergrowth upon the results of the unreasoned tendency, operating through the rude channels of

1. Page 275.

the feelings, of individual human animals to [xxxviii] gravi-
tate together. "Ea est quaedam naturae vis, non hominibus
modo, sed mansuetioribus etiam aliorum animantium in-
dita . . . congregandorum hominum caussa longe antiquior,
et communitatis eorum inter ipsos multo prius et sanctius
vinculum." It is this law of nature (pp. 121, 122) which true
political philosophy ever follows: the varied utilities of life
grow out of nature, as out of a living stock. The State then,
says Buchanan, is no device of the orator or the lawyer, but
an immediate emanation of the Divine Power and Goodness:
and he proceeds to cite the beautiful sentiment of Cicero,
quoted in these pages of Burke, "nihil eorum quae quidem
fiant in terris acceptius quam concilia et coetus hominum
jure sociati quae civitates appellantur." The same belief, that
society rests on the developement of a mysterious instinct
under the guidance of divine law, colours Burke's view of the
duties of the statesman. In his mind these duties invested him
with something of the character of a religious teacher, and it
was natural that this conception should be heightened by his
belief that the theorists whom he was opposing were principled atheists. The great principles of faith and duty were in
Burke's imagination equally threatened, and he boldly takes
his stand upon both for the defence of both. It is enough for
us to observe that this theory of the State, though reflecting
in a great degree doctrines which seem to belong chiefly to
theology, is neither inconsistent nor improbable. While he
despises, as Buchanan had done, the beggarly theory which
would make society exclusively dependent upon the utilities
which attend it, and rests it upon the simpler and higher
basis of nature, he does not go beyond the lines of evidence
and of legitimate presumption, and he makes the domain of
political philosophy a wider and a more interesting field.

In Burke's philosophy, God, Nature, and Society are conceived as three inseparable entities. Burke thus followed the
pagan philosopher Cicero in fortifying his political creed by

---

reference to that religious sentiment which is so nearly akin to it. Religion, according to Burke, is a necessary buttress to the social fabric. It is more than this: it pervades and cements the whole. It is the basis of education: it attends the citizen in every act of life from the cradle to the grave. Religion is part of man's rights. The exact form of religion which the State should authorise was believed by Burke to be an entirely secondary matter. [xxxix] It is probable that he would have had the Roman Catholic Church established in Ireland, as the Anglican Church was established in England. In common with many English churchmen of his age he had thus entirely abandoned the position of a century ago. For religion in some positive form Burke always argued strongly, in opposition to the contrary opinion which was then fast spreading both in France and England. Philosopher though he was, the arguments of the Freethinkers were to him entirely inconclusive. It is no solid objection, in Burke's method, to any element of doctrine that it rests more or less upon what is artificial, or upon what cannot be wholly sustained by reference to scientific laws. When we find any more or less dubious doctrine tenaciously cherished by reasonable and civilised men, it will mark us for true politicians, perhaps for true philosophers, not uselessly to denounce it as a ridiculous fancy, but to treat the apparent error, to borrow a beautiful expression of Coleridge, as the uncertain reflection of some truth that has not yet risen above the horizon. It should be enough to secure our respect, if not our total approval and our sincere enthusiasm, that any element has so inwrought and domesticated itself in the human mind, as to become an inseparable part of the heritage of successive generations. Something of this kind, uniting our civil and social instincts with a faith in some Divine order of things, can certainly be recognised in the highest as well as in the lowest order of minds. At any rate, the explanation of the "obstinate questionings" of nature obtained by this way of looking at them was good enough for Aristotle and for Bacon, for Milton and for Newton, for Cicero and for Burke, and it is good enough for ordinary people. How it enters into the present argument may be summarily expressed in the words of Hooker, as taken down by an anecdotist from the mouth of Burke himself.[1] "The reason why first we do admire those things which are greatest, and second those things which are ancientest, is because the one are least distant from the infinite substance, the other from the infinite continuance, of God." It is the germ of political theory contained in the present volume. A man asked Grotius what was the best book on Politics. The best, [xl] said Grotius, is a blank book. Look around you, and write what you see. The first thing which a man sees is, that men do not in general reason upon Politics. Their reason seems to exhaust itself upon other subjects. Their best reasoned conclusions are often forced to give way to instincts and sentiments for which they have no rational account to give. Even so it is with reason and instinct in matters of religion. It is a paradox, but when we speak of things above ourselves, what is not paradox?

Resolved into their elements, the mainspring both of rational religion and of rational politics seems to be the sentiment of *dependence*. The effect traceable to this no other theory of life or of society will account for. The sum-total of rational metaphysics has been held to consist of but two propositions. The first, which is involved in the *Cogito, ergo sum*, of Descartes, may be expressed as "Here I am." The second as "I did not put myself here." To cut ourselves off, even in thought, from our dependence on our surroundings, is to commit moral suicide. But our dependence on what is outside us, is not limited to our contemporaries. It passes on from generation to generation: it binds us to the past and to

1. In an interesting breakfast-conversation with Burke, a year or two before the Revolution, detailed in an anonymous "Beauties of Burke," 2 vols. 1798. The quotation is from Book v. ch. 69.

INTRODUCTION

the future. Society, says Burke, in his grand Socratic expo-
sure of the imbecile logic which confounded two meanings
of one word,[1] is a partnership in all science, in all art, in every
virtue, and in all perfection: a partnership not only between
those who are living, but between those who are living, those
who are dead, and those who are to be born. There is, says a
poet who had fed upon this sublime thought,

One great society alone on earth,
The noble living and the noble dead.

The fair mansion of civilisation which we enjoy was not
built with our hands, and our hands must refrain from pollut-
ing it. Being mere life-tenants, we have no business to cut off
the entail, or to commit waste on the inheritance.[2] On both
sides of us extends a vast array of obligations. Millions as we
may be, we stand as a small and insignificant band between
the incalculable mass of those who have gone before us, and
the infinite army of those who follow us, and are even now
treading on our heels. Our relation to the great structure in
which we are privileged to [xli] occupy a niche for a while,
is as that of the worm and the mollusc to the mysterious and
infinite totality of universal life. We stand there as the undertakers of an awful trust. Like the torch-players in the stadium,
it is our business to transmit the precious fire which we bear,
unquenched and undimmed, to those who succeed us. This
is what Burke explains as "one of the first and most leading
principles on which the commonwealth and the laws are consecrated." To deny it is to reduce men to the condition of the
"flies of a summer" (p. 191).

It is an observation of Hume that one generation does
not go off the stage at once, and another succeed, as is the
case with silkworms and butterflies. There is a perpetually

1. "Société," meaning both *society* and *partnership* (pp. 192–93).

2. Page 191.

varying margin, into which the men of one age and those
of that which succeed are blended. In this everlasting continuity, which secures that the human race shall never be
wholly old or wholly new, lies the guarantee for the existence
of civilisation. No break in this continuity is possible without
the lapse of mankind into its primitive grossness. Imagine for
a moment such an intermission. The shortest blank would be
enough to ensure the disappearance of every pillar, buttress,
and vault, which helps to sustain the lofty and intricate structure of civilised society. We can hardly figure to ourselves the
horrible drama of a new generation of utter savages succeeding to the ruins of all that we enjoy. Yet so soon as the work
of moral and political education flags, this result is immediately hazarded. In the imagination of Burke, France was well
on the highroad to this awful situation: to a solution of moral
continuity as disastrous in its effects as a geological catastrophe. All the facts of history prove that civilisation is destructible. It is an essence that is ever tending to evaporate: and
though the appreciation of all that is precious in the world
depends on the feeling of its perishability, it is seldom that
this fact is realised. We come to regard our social life as a perpetual and indestructible possession, destined, like the earth
on which we move, to devolve, without any trouble or care on
our part, upon our posterity. But the whole tenour of history
is against us. The Greeks little dreamed of the day when their
broken relics, once more understood, would repair a decayed
world, and to those who come after us, things which to us
are almost as valuable, and quite as little valued as the air we
breathe, may be the [xlii] objects of curious conjecture, or
of contemptuous neglect. Regard our inheritance in its true
light, as a precious thing that we should fear to lose, and we
begin to estimate it at its true value. Regard our own title to
it as a solemn trust for the benefit of our descendants, and
we shall understand how foolishly and immorally we act in
tampering with it. How such anticipations as Burke's wrought

INTRODUCTION

on kindred minds, might be aptly illustrated from Words-worth's well-known Dream of the Arab,[1] who, forewarned by prophecy, is hastening to bury, for preservation from the approaching deluge, the precious talisman that

Had voices more than all the winds, with power
To exhilarate the spirit, and to soothe,
Through every clime, the heart of human kind.

This conception of great intersecular duties devolving upon humanity, generation after generation, reflects on a large scale an instinct which has undoubtedly been strong in the English people. The disposition rather to recur in thought upon the value of the social life and social character which we inherit, than to strain discontentedly for some imaginary ideal, has largely entered into the temperament of those races which have been chiefly instrumental in super-inducing civilised society over the face of the earth. "Moribus antiquis res stat Romana, virisque," says Ennius. So says Burke, in effect, of the civilised life which the English race have now spread over the four quarters of the globe. With the English race have universally gone the old English ideas on religion, on politics, and on education; America and the rest of the new world have taken them from us and are giving them a new and fruitful development. After the lapse of nearly a century, America and England still exhibit on the whole the highest political and social ideals. The English type, during the present century, has been more widely imitated than the Greek or the Roman at the height of their fame. Our social ideas, poor as they may be by comparison with the creations of ingenious speculation, clearly have some very remarkable value of their own. One element of this value is that effect upon the individual which is attributed to them by Burke. They tend to, or at any rate favour the develop-

1. Prelude, Book v.

ment of a certain "native plainness and directness of character." They keep a man face to face with life [xliii] and reality.
They include a moral code which fits all times and seasons,
all ranks and conditions of life; which hardens a man where
it is good that he should be hardened, and softens him where
it is good that he should be softened. The same may perhaps
be said, in a less degree, of some moral codes of the ancient
world; but it certainly cannot be said of those of modern
paganism. The lives of some of the best and most earnest of
modern Englishmen may not be fairly comparable with that
of Socrates; but we may justly boast of a standard far tran-
scending that of Rousseau and of Goethe. A high standard
of character cannot be independent of some corresponding
standard of politics; and every name which keeps the name
of England respected throughout the world, will be found,
in a greater or less degree, to confirm that aspect of English
character, private and public, which Burke puts forward.

Burke is at his best when enlarging thus on the general
philosophy of society: he breaks down when he proceeds to
its application. There are few topics in the present volume of
which this is not true: and, as has been already noticed, it is
conspicuously true of the opening argument on the British
Constitution. Pitiful as it is to see the fine mind of Burke self-
devoted to the drudgery of Tory casuistry, it is even more so
to find his usually ready and generous sympathies, as the work
advances, remorselessly denied to the cause of the French
people. It was not for any liberal-minded Englishman, rich in
the inheritance of constitutional wisdom and liberty, to greet
the dawn of representative institutions in France with nothing but a burst of contempt and sarcasm. Least of all was this
attitude towards the National Assembly becoming to Burke.
His opening address to the French politicians[1] is more than
ungenerous: it is unjust. It seems incredible that any one

---

1. Pages 123–24.

should have been found to declare that the path of reform in France was "a smooth and easy career of felicity and glory," which had been recklessly abandoned.[2] To [xliv] do Burke

2. In the opinion that France possessed all the elements of a good constitution, which only required to be cleared of rust and obstructions and put in working condition, Burke erred with many intelligent and patriotic Frenchmen. We can now see that such was not the case, and further that France was not at that time in a condition to adopt any political system of the kind which was then meant by the term constitutional. The boasted English constitution of Burke's time was a notorious sham. It has now been exploded; England, as every one knows, is a democracy ruled by the delegates of the Commons. But it was that very pasteboard show of interdependent powers which was fast losing its credit in England, which Burke wished to see imitated in France. Montesquieu was more clear-sighted. Intensely as he affected to admire the political system of England, his doctrine was that France ought to be left alone. "Leave us as we are," is the constant theme of that hypothetical speaker by whom Montesquieu (De l'Esprit des Lois, Liv. xix. ch. 5–8) expresses his own opinions. "Nature compensates for everything." Many smiled contemptuously when they heard people talk of liberty and a constitution. Montesquieu had said that a free nation only could have a liberator, an enslaved nation could only have another oppressor. He little knew the terrible awakening which was reserved for the French nation: but he was probably right in counselling that such an awakening should not be anticipated by a false political reformation. The reform which France wanted was a social one: the need penetrated to the very roots of the nation's life. The selfishness and cruelty of whole classes had to be exorcised: a slumbering nation had to be aroused to a sense of political duty. It is hard in the present day to imagine how completely public spirit had vanished from the mass of the French nation, and how utterly void the French were at that time of political knowledge or experience. Turgot was as solitary a being in France as if his lot had been cast in the Sandwich islands. Except a few men of the type of Sieyes, probably few French politicians cared for politics otherwise than as an amusement, or a path to distinction. The Frenchman was repelled by what Burke calls the "severe brow of moral freedom." Voltaire at Ferney looked on the political affairs of Geneva merely as a matter for satire and ridicule. "It is impossible," said a Frenchman to Groenfelt, in 1789, "for a Frenchman to be serious: we must amuse ourselves, and in pursuit of our amusements we continually change our object, but those very changes prove us always the same. . . . Our nation is naturally gay. Political liberty requires a degree of seriousness, which is not in our character: we shall soon grow sick of politics." (Letters on the Revolution, p. 4.) This gay incuriosity is still the characteristic of the vast majority; and hence France has ever since been, though in a diminishing degree, the prey of petty and interested factions.

justice, he quickly saw how falsely he had judged in discerning no effect of the Revolution upon France save mutilation and disaster. Two years more, and we hear nothing about the "fresh ruins of France," and the French nation "not politically existing." Under that guidance which at first appeared so contemptible, France speedily acquired a power far more formidable than had been known in the most vigorous period of the monarchy. Burke then ceased to call the leaders of the Revolution fools, and declared them to be fiends.

Burke's contemptuous parallel of the representatives of the [xlv] *Tiers Etat* with the English House of Commons[1] is typical of the whole argument. This herd of country clowns and pettifoggers, as he declares it to have been, certainly forms an effective contrast by the side of the British Parliament in the days of Pitt and Fox. We trace here the beginning of a secondary thread of sentiment which runs quite through the book. A sense of triumphant hostility to the French as a nation had been produced by a century of international relations: and Burke could hardly avoid displaying it on the present occasion. His purpose was not merely to instruct the French nation, but to humiliate, if not to insult it. Englishmen had long looked on the French as a nation of slaves: he now strove to show that a nation of slaves could produce nothing worthy of the serious attention or sympathy of a nation of freemen. Burke might have taken the opportunity of exhibiting that keen sympathy for freedom by which most of his political career, as he himself declares in a moment of compunction,[2] had been guided. He knew that France was peopled by a race as oppressed and down-trodden as Ireland or India. Was freedom to be the monopoly of England? Had Burke no sympathy for any sufferings but those of royalty? Here we touch another point of some interest. Popular instinct at once seized on Burke's famous description of the

1. Page 134.   2. Page 364.

transportation to Paris of the 6th of October[1] as the key to the whole work. That picturesque incident had inspired the jubilations of Dr. Price:[2] and Burke naturally invested it at once with the very opposite character. But his description was borrowed from prejudiced witnesses. The people still trusted the King, however much they may have distrusted the Queen: and there was nothing extraordinary in their insisting on the abandonment of Versailles. Burke frankly admits that this gloomy foretaste of the change in the royal fortunes coloured his whole conception. Endowed with the imagination and sensibility of the poet, this melodramatic spectacle sank deeply into his mind; and the consciousness that it yet remained undenounced was too much for one ever swayed, as Burke was, by

> . . . stormy pity, and the cherished lure
> Of pomp, and proud precipitance of soul.[3]

[xlvi] Philip Francis at once declared this exhibition of sympathy for the Queen to be mere affectation, or in his own phrase, "foppery." He knew Burke well; better, perhaps, than any contemporary: but this particular charge Burke declared to be false. He averred that in writing this famous passage tears actually dropped from his eyes, and wetted the paper. It is likely enough. Burke carried the strong feelings which were natural to him into most things that he did: and his tears for Marie Antoinette were as much part of the inspiration of the moment as his triumphant declaration, when his own lawful sovereign was stricken down by the saddest of maladies, that "the Almighty had hurled him from his throne." Burke's persistency exposed him to a keen repartee from Francis. "No tears," wrote the latter, "are shed for nations." This was altogether unjust, and Francis knew it, for he had long been

1. Pages 164–65. 2. Page 158.

3. Coleridge.

associated with Burke in the gigantic effort that was being
made to ameliorate the condition of the oppressed millions
of India by the prosecution of Warren Hastings. But it was
in vain to beguile Burke from his chosen attitude. There was
the tyranny of the despot, and the tyranny of the mob: and
he declared that it was his business to denounce the one as
well as the other. If the champion of Ireland and of India
had to choose between the French people and the French
queen, he would choose the latter: and he declared that history would confirm his decision.[1] It has not been so: history
has transferred the world's sympathies, engaged for a while
on the opposite side by the eloquence of Burke, to the suffering people. Nor can it be said that history has confirmed
Burke's judgment on a political question which he treats at
some length, and which concerned England far less than it
concerned France. The Church question, which in different
shapes has ever since the French Revolution vexed the whole
Christian world, had been suddenly raised from the level of
speculation to that of policy by the attempted reforms of
Joseph in Austria. It needed no great sagacity to foresee the
impending storm, when the ancient principle of ecclesiastical
establishments was repudiated in its very stronghold. Burke
here carries to the extreme his principle of saying all that
could be said in favour of whichever side of a doubtful question is most in need of support. Burke's vindication of Church
establishments, [xlvii] echoed, as it has been, by two generations of obscurantists, is based on half a dozen bad arguments
adroitly wrought into the semblance of one good one. But
no logical mystification could avert the impending ruin: and
Burke committed a mistake in parading before an English
public arguments which were so little likely to impose upon
it. A cotton-mill, in the eyes of a French economical theo-
rist, might be an institution as unproductive to the state as a

1. Page 164.

monastery:[1] but no Englishman could treat such an argument with respect. Devoted pupils of the school of Bossuet might rejoice to hear Burke's fervid eulogy of a state consecrated, in all its members and functions, by a National Church: but no candid Englishman could aver that Church and State were ideas inseparable to the English mind. The French ecclesiastic might fairly claim as private property the estates on which his order had thriven unchallenged ever since France had been a nation: no reader of Selden could think the argument applicable to the Church of England. "When once the Commonwealth," says Burke, "has established the estates of the Church as property, it can, consistently, hear nothing of the more or the less." Such has been the claim of the clerical party in every country of the Western world: and there is not one in which it has been accepted. There is not one in which lawfulness of the secularization of Church property has not by this time been practically admitted. Burke's argument is confuted by each successive step of that long series of unwillingly enforced reforms which has enabled the English Church to stand its ground. In reading Burke's account of the Church of England, we must bear in mind the peculiar circumstances of his education. Burke was the son of an Irish Catholic and an Irish Protestant. He was educated by a Quaker: and by trustworthy testimony[2] he valued no Christian sect above another, and believed in his heart that no one then existing represented Christianity in its normal or final shape. Stoutly as he had opposed the famous Latitudinarian petition a few years before, Burke was in all religious matters liberal to a degree which trespassed on what would now be called rationalism. His picture of the Church is really painted from the outside: and, though a country squire of a quarter of a century's standing, it is from the outside that he conducts his defence of the Establishment.

1. Page 266.   2. That of his schoolfellow Shackleton.

[xlviii] It would be impossible to follow Burke's impatient and stormy career over the whole broad field of his "Reflections." A minute criticism of such books defeats its own object. Burke is here an advocate and a rhetorician. Though an attitude of discursiveness and informality, admitting of striking and rapid change, is of the essence of his method, there are many isolated passages in which this is less apparent than usual, and these passages have historical value. Armed with the twofold knowledge of history and of human nature, it was impossible for Burke not to hit the mark in many of his minor observations on the course of events in France. His description of the growth of the monied interest, of the hostility of the Paris literary cabal to the Church, and of the coalition of these two elements for its destruction,[1] stands forth as a bold and accurate outline of an actual process. His retrospect of the past glories of France[2] is no mere exercise in declamation: and his observations on the government of Louis XVI[3] prove that he had studied antecedent events perhaps as accurately as to an Englishman was possible. Those observations are illustrated by the circumstances which attended the Revolutions of 1830 and 1848. A mild and constitutional régime, as Burke concluded, predisposes to revolution: if this régime is rudely interrupted, or its sincerity rendered doubtful, a revolution is certain. No monarch has a harder part to play than a king of France. Under Louis XVI, Charles X, Louis Philippe, and Louis Napoleon, the French people have abundantly proved themselves to be the same. But few would now draw from the fact the conclusion which was drawn by Burke. An unusual show of "patriotism," such as Burke praised in the government of Louis, affords unusual matter of suspicion: and the causes of a restless jealousy for liberty, which Burke had exposed so admirably in his speech on American

1. Page 207.   2. Page 231.

3. Pages 176, 232.

INTRODUCTION

Conciliation, operated as surely in the nascent freedom of France as in the ripe liberty of America. Burke was equally correct in auguring an alteration in the internal balance of power in France from the changes introduced into the army. The substitution of a popular for a merely mercenary force has always been a measure necessary to secure great political reforms: and it leads, as Burke pointed out, to the ascendancy of popular generals. There is nothing astonishing in this. When the old bonds of loyalty are [xlix] as thoroughly worn out as they have proved to be in France, military genius, allied with civil prudence, necessarily becomes the head of all authority: and the rise of Bonaparte proved the truth of Burke's surmise.[1] Burke applied his knowledge of France and French policy with good effect in turning from domestic to colonial policy.[2] The history of Hayti amply verified all that he foretold would follow on the assertion of the rights of men in the French colonies. Hayti asserted its right to a constitution and free trade: and as the colonists rose against the Government, the negroes rose on the colonists. Ten years later, and Burke might have written a telling conclusion to the tale which he sketched out: for when Republican France had defeated the whole of Europe, she was herself beaten by the despised negroes of the plantations. Such were the consequences of what Burke called "attempting to limit logic by despotism." Among Burke's historical forecasts none is more remarkable than that which relates to the organisation throughout Europe of secret political societies.[3] Contemporary critics laughed the argument to scorn; but its accuracy is testified by the history of liberal movements all over Catholic Europe and America. Thirty years more, and the world rang with the alarm. It was by the aid of these secret organisations that Mexico and South America threw off the yoke of the

1. Page 332. 2. Page 335.

3. Page 260.

priesthood. We know the history of similar clubs in Spain, Italy, and Switzerland between 1815 and 1848: and the great power for attack provided by these means justifies the hostility with which the Catholic Church still regards all secret organisations.

Perhaps the great merit of Burke's view of the changes in France consisted in his perception of their actual magnitude, and of the new character which they were likely to impress upon French policy. He was right in supposing that revolutionised France would become the centre of a revolutionary propaganda, and that success would transform the representatives of French liberty into the tyrants of Europe. Burke knew well how often vanity and ambition become leading motives in national action. He rightly guessed that their appetite would not be satiated by mere internal successes, and that the conquest of France by its own ambitious citizens would be only the first [1] in a series of revolutionary triumphs. Burke rightly judged that the spirits of the old despotism and of the new liberty were quite capable of coalescing. Under the Revolution and the Empire, France was as much a prey to the lust of empire as in the days of Louis the Fourteenth. The illusions of the days of the Grand Monarque have subsisted indeed down to our own times, not only undiminished, but vastly heightened by the events of the period which was just opening. France has not increased in physical resources so fast as her neighbours: and her comparative weight in Europe has therefore been diminishing. In proportion as this fact has been made plain, the French people have resented it: and until very recently the mass of the people probably believed themselves to be a nation as powerful in the world for good or evil as in the days of the First Empire. In England, the country of all the world, whatever else may be alleged against it, where illusions are fewest, this attitude on the part of her near neighbour has always been conspicuous.

Introduction

On the general question of the great political principle involved in the present volume the reader may safely take it for
granted that it was neither true in itself nor natural to Burke,
who was employing it merely for purposes of what he believed
to be legitimate advocacy. Burke's real belief is contained in
the following passage from his "Address to the King" (1776):
"The revolution is a departure from the antient course of
descent of the monarchy. *The people, at that time, entered into
their original rights;* and it was not because a positive law authorized what was then done, but because the freedom and
safety of the subject, the origin and cause of all laws, required
a proceeding paramount and superior to them. At that ever
remarkable and instructive period, the letter of the law was
suspended in favour of the substance of liberty. . . . *Those statutes have not given us our liberties; our liberties have produced them.*"
Coleridge says that on a comparison of Burke's writings on
the American War with those on the French Revolution, the
principles and the deductions will be found the same, though
the practical inferences are opposite; yet in both equally
legitimate, and in both equally confirmed by results.[1] This
estimate is coloured by the natural sympathy of political par-
tisanship. Burke was always Conservative in his instincts: [li]
but it is undeniable that he thought the present a legitimate
occasion for shifting his ground. The historical value of the
"Reflections" is thus unequal in the different parts. In charac-
terising English political instinct and doctrine, it falls back on
a vanishing past; it repudiates that which possessed life and
growth. It represents the sentimental rather than the intellectual side of its author's character: and hence it will be used by
posterity less as an historical document than as a great literary model. Burke, in a higher degree than any other Englishman, transferred to his writings the force and vigour which

---

1. Biog. Lit. ch. x: Friend, Sect. i. Ess. 4.

properly belong to speeches; and there is scarcely a single rhetorical device which may not be learned from his pages. The art of language had been wrought by thirty years of incessant practice into Burke's very soul: and the mere voluntary effort of expression acted upon his powers like touching the spring of a machine. Burke wrote as he talked, and as he spoke in the senate: we have here the man himself accurately reflected, with all his excellencies and all his imperfections. Burke's was not only a mind large and spacious, but endowed with an extraordinary degree of sensibility, and these qualities were well adapted to produce a vast convulsion of feeling at the contemplation of incidents and prospects so strange and portentous as those which now presented themselves to view. Burke's was a mind in which those objects sank most deeply, found the readiest reception, and were perceived in their widest extent. We cannot wonder at the keenness and profusion of the sentiments which they first generated and then forced out trumpet-tongued to the world.

From what has been said it will be gathered that Burke's book is by no means what is called a scientific book. Its roots touch the springs of the theology, of the jurisprudence, of the morals, of the history, and of the poetry of his age: and in this way it acquires an historical value resembling in some measure that of the famous "Republic" of Plato. Few books reflect more completely the picture of European thought as it existed a century ago. Nor is there any in which the literary expression of the age is better exemplified. Burke is careful to maintain a mode of expression which is untechnical. It is even occasionally indefinite. The essential antithesis in thought between science and poetry is curiously reflected in his habitual language. In employing words, he does not, like the man of science, keep in [lii] mind, in connection with them, any certain and invariable connotation. Like the poet, he rather takes pleasure in placing old words in new combinations, and in applying them with a changed or reinforced meaning.

INTRODUCTION

Dixeris egregie, notum si callida verbum
Reddiderit junctura novum.

To think with the wise, and to speak with the vulgar, to
give in common and popular phrase the results of uncommon and studious thought, has always been counted among
the rarest of rare accomplishments. A critic has observed
that the main difference between our older and our modern
literature, is that in the former we get uncommon ideas vul-
garly expressed, and in the latter obvious and commonplace
thoughts furnished forth with false ornament, and inspired
with false refinement. Now as Burke often conveys his most
admirable lessons under the guise of trite and vulgar topics,
so does he clothe his most cogent arguments with the plain-
est language, and support them by the most familiar illustrations. But he continually surprises us by bursts of rhetorical
appeal, by sudden allusions to some historical incident, by
keen sarcasm, by a quotation which recalls a train of associations. Macaulay has characterised the contents of Burke's
mind as a treasure at once rich, massy, and various. Burke's
mature style reflects the rich contents of his mature mind,
as displayed in daily conversation. Burke, who was, by the
testimony of Johnson, the greatest master of conversation in
his time, wrote as he talked, because he talked as the greatest master of writing need not be ashamed to write. He is
a standing example of that fundamental axiom of style, too
often forgotten by writers, that its excellence chiefly depends
on the closeness with which it reflects the excellences of the
vox viva. A "good passage" is simply one which, if delivered
by the speaker to an attentive listener, would easily, certainly,
and lastingly convey to the latter the meaning of the former.
Men in general are neither scientific nor political: they are
simply open to be impressed by clear statement, fair argument, and common sense. In the practice of the best masters
what seem to be the ornaments of style are really its necessi-

ties. Figures and images do not belong to poetry, but to language—especially to the economy of language. It is possible to be lavish and [liii] fertile in the development and illustration of an argument, with great poverty of resources; but he who would be brief must be wealthy in words. Those who have tasted the enjoyment of fine conversation, know how nearly Burke reflects its essential manner. What is meant may be illustrated by saying that the great master of conversation avoids, *tanquam scopulum*, the odious vice which is commonly described as "talking like a book"; whereas the great master of the pen does in fact employ in turn all the methods and devices which a versatile mind and a practised tongue employ in conversation.

English and French literature have generally aimed at this character. When we pass to the yard-long sentences, the tangled notions, and the flat expression of an ordinary German book, we recognise the normal opposite. How is this? In the latter case the book has probably been written by a man of silent habits in the retirement of his cabinet; and there is consequently no habitual subordination, in the practice of the writer, to the conditions of convenient and intelligent reception on the part of the reader. Why are chapters, paragraphs, sentences, and phrases measured by a certain average of length? Simply on the principle which regulates how much a man can or ought to be eating or drinking at one time. The habits of Reception (or as the Scotch philosophers call it, Attention) and Assimilation proceed by *morceaux* or portions. It can make no difference whether the material is conveyed through the voice of another, or in a way at once more complex and more compendious, through the eye of the recipient. Burke's age, like Cicero's, was eminently an age of Conversation. A glance at Boswell is enough to prove its high range as a fine art, and to show how much it had assumed a palaestral character. Literary fame was distributed by a few men, who habitually weighed merit in a commonsense balance: and the atmosphere of the study thus came to be neglected for that of the club. The influence of academical models had long ago begun to yield to that of keen living criticism: and in the age of Johnson the change was well-nigh complete. The conditions of the best literary age of Greece, including a cultivated and watchful auditory leading the opinion of the general public, were thus nearly reproduced.

Writing is false and poor in proportion as those conditions are [liv] forgotten. Moreover, as composition is built upon spoken language, so the decline of the art of conversation has been accompanied by the decline of style. A century has produced vast changes in both. Every one who knows how perfect a harmony subsists between or among the two or more people who engage in true intellectual converse — how unconsciously and how delicately each responds to the touches of the other, knows also how exceedingly rare is the habit which produces it. The coarse deluge with which the pretentious sophist, whom in the person of Thrasymachus Socrates compares to a *bathing-man,* still overwhelms his hearers — the jar and wrangle proper to the Bar, and the prating of the foolish, conspire to thrust it from society. So is it of the harmony which ought to subsist between writers and their probable readers: and the social defect is reflected in the literary. Literature has become divorced from life, and the very term "literary" comes to connote something dull, dry, and undesirable. If we wish to see how life and letters can nevertheless go together, we have to refer to the De Oratore of Cicero, the Table Talk of Selden, and Boswell's Life of Johnson.

The model of a letter, the form into which the present work, like nearly all Burke's best compositions, is cast, gives the writer some valuable advantages. It represents a convenient medium between the looseness of common talk and the set phrases of deliberate composition. It enables him to preserve an even key through the body of his observations, while he may, with perfect propriety, descend to familiar and pointed phraseology, or mount at will into the region of rhetoric. Such a variety at once preserves that impression of a close relation between the reader and the writer which is necessary to secure attention, and enables the writer to make the best use of his opportunities. Where he fancies the reader yielding to a plain forcible piece of common sense, he can press on. He can repeat the approved thesis in some more studied phrase, approaching the philosophical style, and finally enforce it by a bold appeal to the feelings. He can gradually season and mingle his rhetoric with the gall of irony, or he can abruptly drop into that stimulating vein at a moment's notice. Probably the greatest impression of power in the mind of the reader is produced by the ability to preserve an even balance of moderate discourse, ever and anon varied by these [lv] occasional diversions. Perpetual familiarities, perpetual didactics, or perpetual declamation would equally disgust and fatigue. The great artist so mingles them that each shall mutually relieve and enhance the effect of the other.

In the study of particular passages, it must be remarked that there is no mastering the secrets of style by the eye alone. The student must read aloud, repeat to himself, and transcribe. The fact is so much testimony to our canon that the standard of writing is the *vox viva*. It is necessary to make a strong effort of imagination, to force one's-self into the author's own place, and to construct over again his phrases and periods, if we would view his work in its full beauty and propriety.

Let us examine, as an example of Burke's method, his remarks on the New Year's Address presented to Louis XVI. They conclude with the following paragraph:

A man is fallen indeed, when he is thus flattered. The anodyne draught of oblivion, thus drugged, is well calculated to preserve a galling wakefulness, and to feed the living ulcer of a corroding memory.

Thus to administer the opiate potion of amnesty, powdered with all the ingredients of scorn and contempt, is to hold to his lips, instead of "the balm of hurt minds," the cup of human misery full to the brim, and to force him to drink it to the dregs. (p. 164.)

The exceeding strength and fulness of these lines depend on the fact that every word in them, saving mere auxiliaries, represents a distinct image. When we apply to them Burke's well-known canon that the master sentence of every paragraph should involve, firstly, a thought, secondly, an image, and thirdly, a sentiment, we see how all such canons fail. The thought and the sentiment are clear enough, but they are completely enveloped in this congeries of images. Turning back, however, we shall see how it is prepared for in the preceding pages. The Address is introduced at the end of a previous paragraph (p. 163), as the climax of a sustained rhetorical *arsis*. Pausing to give this striking feature its due effect, the writer then drops suddenly in a fresh paragraph into a vein of irony, bitter and elaborate, but not strongly coloured. In fact, both the beginning and the end of this paragraph are relieved by something approaching very nearly to a quaint equivocation. It is slightly prosaic, diffuse, and familiar. We have another pause, and another change. The writer gathers [lvi] himself up for a strong effort, and pours out, in these half-a-dozen lines, a series of images coloured with all the depth which words can give, destined to unite with and deepen the effect of the preceding periods. The three paragraphs are, as it were, in three keys of colour, one over the other, the deepest, the most vigorous, and at the same time the most sparingly applied, coming last. Burke does not in general severely tax the memory. He may expect you to carry your vision through a dozen pages, but he lends you every assistance that art can give. He puts his most striking images last, that the reader may pause upon them, and see how they sum up and illustrate his previous argument. If this volume is opened at p. 191, the three terminations of the paragraphs, though in each case he ends with an image, will curiously illustrate the variety of his resources.

Let us see again how an image is varied, another is grafted upon it, and it disappears in the vein of pure irony to which it is intended to conduct:

> "The ears of the people of England are distinguishing. They hear these men speak broad. Their tongue betrays them.[1] Their language is in the patois of fraud; in the cant and gibberish of hypocrisy. The people of England must think so, when these praters affect to carry back the clergy to that primitive evangelic poverty," &c. (p. 201.)

Burke excels in this preparation of transitions: and it always distinguishes the master. The passage on the Queen (p. 169), which is perhaps the most famous in the book, is intended in this way. It fitly concludes the reflections on the sufferings of the Royal Family, and prepares the way for the animated contrast which follows of ancient and modern modes of social and political feeling. In these pages (170–72) we observe Burke's happiest manner, that progressive and self-developing method which distinguishes him among prose writers, as it does Dryden among poets. "His thesis grows in the very act of unfolding it."[2] Each sentence seems, by a kind of scintillation, to suggest the image contained in the next; and this again instantly flames and germinates into a crowd of others. There is no loss, however, of the ultimate aim, and the rich fancy never gets, so to speak, out of hand [lvii] or seems to burst into mere wanton coruscations. The boldest strokes come in exactly in the right places, and we acquiesce in the judgment with which the strain on our imagination is duly relaxed, and we are allowed to relapse into the strain of plain statement and direct argument. "Burke," says Hazlitt, "is really one of the severest of writers." Even in his half-

---

1. Cp. vol. i. p. 248, l. 33.

2. De Quincey.

prophetic mood we never miss a certain understood calmness, and a background of self-restraint and coolness: there is always a principle of restoration in the opposite direction. "In the very whirlwind of his passion he begets a temperance." To this effect his habit of repetition very much contributes. He produces the same thought, first expanded and illustrated with all his imagery, then contracted and weighed with all his sententiousness. Fulness and brevity, ardour and philosophical calm, light and shade, are ever alternating.

In style, as in everything else, the nature of things is best seen in their smallest proportions. The best writers are immediately discernible by their mere phrases, by the ability and the happiness with which they conjoin the simple elements of substantive and verb, adjective or participle. It is not that words are coerced into a strange collocation, or that the writer "will for a tricksy phrase defy the matter"; but that expressions are constructed which seem natural, without being common or obvious. Notwithstanding the depth and rapidity of the current of Burke's ideas, it flows in general as clear as if it were the shallowest of rills. Still, the freedom with which he employs his extraordinary *copia verborum* occasionally leads him into obscurity. One passage has been often marked as an instance. It occurs near the end of the book (pp. 361–62), where it is remarked that the little arts and devices of popularity are not to be condemned:

> They facilitate the carrying of many points of moment; they keep the people together; they refresh the mind in its exertions; and they diffuse occasional gaiety over the severe brow of moral freedom.

The last sentence has been confidently pronounced to be nonsense in the strict acceptance of the word—that is, to have no meaning, and to be neither true nor false. The obscurity lies in the involution, in an abbreviated form, of a statement which occurs at page 126, that all nations but France had [lviii] begun political reformation in a serious and even severe temper. "All other people have laid the foundations of civil freedom in severer manners, and a system of more austere and masculine morality." France, on the other hand, doubled the licence of her ferocious dissoluteness in manners. The contrast, in the passage criticised, is between the political licence of the demagogues of France, and the occasional condescension of the more austere English patriot to the humours of his constituents.[1] It is not denied that Burke wrote, in the first instance, hastily, and that there are occasional blemishes in this book; but most of them disappeared before it issued from the press. Pages 149–50, for instance, were amended after the first edition, and might have been amended somewhat more. Burke was, however, averse from making any important alterations, and he refused to correct some palpable errors, on the ground of their non-importance. He himself considered that he had elaborated the work with even more than his habitual carefulness of composition; and it is known that large portions of it were recomposed, and the whole subjected to a never-satisfied revision, which excited the remonstrances of his printer. "The fragments of his manuscripts which remain," says Dr. Croly,[2] "show that not words but things were the objects of his revision. At every fresh return some fine idea found enlargement; some strong feeling was invigorated; some masculine moral was aggrandised into universal application, and coloured into poetic beauty." The blemishes

---

1. Bristle, in his dialogue with Sir Edward Courtly, describes the old practice in less plausible terms: "I think, Sir, that it's very civil of you to come and spend fifteen hundred or two thousand pounds, besides being obliged to keep company with a parcel of dirty, drunken, ill-mannered fellows for two or three months together, without any other design but *serving your country*." The Craftsman, No. 58. "Drunkenness, rioting, and insolence, on the one side, abject flattery, cringing and preposterous adulation on the other," was the true meaning of the "little arts and devices of popularity."

2. Memoir of Burke, vol. i. p. 292.

which are still left are partially shielded by the extraordinary *compass* of Burke's writing. His great art and originality in putting together his phrases and sentences makes even his negligence seem less than it really is. We are often tempted to think that his most heedless combinations are rather studied than spontaneous. It cannot, however, escape notice, that the workmanship of the treatise is [lix] very unequal. Burke always relied much upon correction, and extensively pruned and altered his first draughts. On the strength of many marks of carelessness which this process has left on the face of the work, it has, from the merely literary point of view, been undervalued. Francis (Junius) wrote to Burke,[1] "Why will you not learn that polish is material to preservation? . . . I wish you would let me teach you to write English!" Such expressions from Francis were mere impudence. It has been well remarked that compared to the athletic march of the writings of Burke, the best letters of Junius remind us irresistibly of the strut of a *petit-maître*. It is the ramp of the lion by the side of the mordacious snarl of the cur. Of literature, in the highest sense, Francis knew next to nothing. He represented, however, in some measure those current canons of literary taste which Burke recklessly broke through. But let it be remembered that Burke was not writing as an aspirant for literary or any other fame. It was not for this that day after day saw him dashing off these pages in his gloomy room in gloomy Gerard Street. The objects of earlier years had sunk below his horizon, and the fame of his book came as a mere corollary. What he wrote was the result of a mental convulsion, vast, though spontaneous. He alludes to it in his correspondence as "deeply occupying and agitating him." His nerves were strung up to the pitch of the highest human sympathies. Tears, he averred, dropped from his eyes and wetted his paper as he wrote the passage on the Queen, which Mack-

1. Correspondence of Burke, vol. iii. p. 164.

intosh called "stuff," and Francis "foppery." Burke was a man of strong passions, and these passions mingled fiercely in all his pursuits.

Anger is said to "make dull men witty."[1] In excess, it far more frequently paralyses the intellect, or drives a man into mere verbal excesses.

Some fierce thing, replete with too much rage,
Whose strength's abundance weakens his own heart.[2]

If Burke's wrath sometimes lost him personal respect, and occasionally hurried him into grossness of metaphor, it gave such [lx] terrible fire to his expression, that the gain was greater than the loss. It scathed like lightning the men, the systems, or the sentiments which were the objects of his moral indignation, and marked indelibly those who had incurred his personal resentment. The tension and force gained from anger seemed often to sustain his style long after his direct invective had ceased. Though high-tempered, he seems to have been free from the sort of ill-nature which indeed belongs to colder temperaments, noticeable in Swift and Junius. Even in the case of political opponents, he was almost universally a lenient and generous judge. His anger towards those who had excited it, if not absolutely just, was felt to be the result of his own full conviction, and so carried with him the sympathy of his hearers and readers, instead of exciting them, as is usually the case, to seek excuses for his victims. It is rare for so much force to produce so little reaction. Burke sways the mass of intelligent and cultivated readers with almost as little resistance as a demagogue experiences from a mob.[3]

1. Bacon records this as a repartee of Queen Elizabeth to an insolent courtier. She sarcastically added—"but it keeps them poor."

2. Shakespeare, Sonnet xxiii.

3. For this paragraph, for that which commences at the tenth line of page 78, and for many of the Notes at the end of the volume, the Editor is indebted to the accomplished pen of John Frederick Boyes, Esq. It may be added that

Introduction

Burke suffers no sense of literary formality to veil and to break the force of his thoughts. He strives to stand face to face with the reader, as he would stand before a circle of listening friends, or on the floor of the House of Commons. To repeat a previous observation, Burke wrote as he talked. "Burke's talk," Johnson used to say, "is the ebullition of his mind; he does not talk from a desire of distinction, but because his mind is full." As a mark of his style, this naturally has the effect of investing his chief writings with something of a *dramatic* character. They possess something of what we mean when we ascribe to works of art a general dramatic unity. The statesman and the man are so finely blended in the contexture of his thought that it is difficult [lxi] to distinguish between warp and woof. This character is reflected not obscurely in his diction. In discussions upon literary matters, he was fond of pointing out the dramatic writer as the true model, instancing Plautus, Terence, and the fragments of Publius Syrus as among the best examples. The hint was the more applicable in an age when the theatre was still a great school of style and of manners. Junius, as is well known, modelled his letters on the pointed dialogue of Congreve. Burke was familiar with the lessons of a higher school. Humble, from the aesthetic point of view, as is the work of a political writer, there is often an almost Shakespearian freshness and originality about the mintage of Burke's phrases, and the design of his paragraphs. In reading him we are less than usually conscious of the mere literary element. Burke, in fact, though commonly understood to be one of the greatest masters of English prose, does not fall naturally into a place in

---

Burke was deeply offended at the neglect his views from the first met with in the English political world. "Pique," says Sir G. Savile, in a letter to the Marquis of Rockingham, "is one of the strongest motives in the human mind. Fear is strong, but transient. Interest is more lasting, perhaps, and steady, but infinitely weaker; I will ever back pique against them both. It is the spur the Devil rides the noblest tempers with, and will do more work with them in a week, than with other poor jades in a twelve-month."

any historical series of the masters of the art. The Spectator seems to have been his early model, the Treatise on the Sublime and Beautiful being evidently suggested by Addison's beautiful and original essays on the Pleasures of the Imagination. But he soon deserted the school of polite prose. Hume, on the other hand, is an instance of an accomplished writer, who throughout his long labours never cast the slough of his first style. Wholly disregarding the models of the strict, polished, and academic writers of his day, Burke fell back upon a free and expansive method, which reminds us of the great poet and dramatist, Dryden. The fact that no student of literature now thinks of consulting Temple or Sprat, while such prose as that of Dryden and Cowley still retains a large measure of popularity, is some testimony to the correctness of his taste. The father of modern criticism had not been neglected by Burke, and the freedom and copiousness of Dryden's pen cannot have escaped his notice. He still remains the great master of good pedestrian prose; and for the best specimens of the somewhat more elevated key of political reasoning, we are still obliged to recur to Bolingbroke, another of Burke's models. In both Bolingbroke and Burke the habit of public speaking moulded and transformed their literary style: and we can scarcely point to any other writer who, though at once accurate, polished, and striking, reflects Burke's disregard of the set literary manner. Addison must have proceeded to compose [lxii] a Spectator much as he was wont to set about making a copy of his inimitable Latin verses; and something of the same kind never forsook Johnson, and other great essayists. Burke has nothing of this. He goes back, though not consciously, over the heads of his contemporaries. He writes with the tone of authoritative speech. He employs alternately the profound, stately, philosophical manner of Hooker,[1] the

---

1. In a debate after the riots of 1780, Burke adverted to his early education at the school of Mr. Shackleton. "Under his eye I have read the Bible,

imaginative declamation of Taylor, the wise sarcasm of South, and the copious and picturesque facility of Dryden. We need not maintain that elements so multifarious never suffer in his hands. Burke lived in a time when literary ideals had degenerated. Both Hooker and Bacon—the former with his vast cycle of reasoning and his unapproachable compass of language, the latter with his dense, serried body of picked thought and his powerful concocting and assimilating style, represent a literary attitude which neither Burke nor any of his contemporaries ever dreamed of assuming. Burke, moreover, in his maturity, cared nothing for literature, except so far as it was useful in its effect on life; nor did he cherish the thought of living in his works.

These pages are intended rather to put many threads of independent study into the hands of the student, and to afford hints for looking at the subject on many sides, than to exhaust any department of it. Burke's works will be found to be at once a canon or measure to guide those who will undertake the pleasurable toil of exploring the inexhaustible field of English prose-writing, and in themselves a rich mine of the most useful practical examples. They strikingly illustrate, among other things, the fact that the works of a great writer of prose, like those of great poets, must, so to speak, drain a large area. He must possess something of the *myriad-mindedness* which has been ascribed, as the sum and substance of his intellectual [lxiii] qualities, to Shakespeare. "The understanding," says Shelley, "grows bright by gazing upon many truths." In like manner the taste is only to be justly regulated by applying it to many and various beauties,

---

morning, noon, and night, and have ever since been the happier and better man for such reading. I afterwards turned my attention to the reading of all the theological publications on all sides, which were written with such wonderful ability in the last and present centuries. But, finding at length that such studies tended to confound and bewilder rather than enlighten, I dropped them, embracing and holding fast a firm faith in the Church of England."

and the judgment is only to be ripened by directing it in succession upon many objects, and in various aspects.

With one additional observation on a point of some moment, these hints on the general intention and style of Burke's book are terminated. It has been said that the best styles are the freest from Latinisms, and it has been laid down that a good writer will never have recourse to a Latinism while a "Saxon" word will serve his purpose. The notion was first carelessly put forth by Sydney Smith. If it were true, Burke would often be liable to severe censure. The fact is, however, that the practice of almost every great master of the English tongue, from Chaucer downwards, makes very small account of any such consideration. Swift and Defoe, who are usually cited in illustration of it, count for little, and their authority on this point cannot be held to be exactly commensurate with the place in literature which their merits have earned them. Their vernacular cast is very much due to the fact that they were among the first political writers who aspired to be widely read among the common people. The same circumstance fostered the racy native English style of Cobbett, and had its effects on journalists like Mr. Fonblanque, and orators like Mr. Bright. But most of our great writers, unreservedly and freely as they use the Latin element in the language, are also thoroughly at home in the exclusive use of the vernacular. Brougham was wrong in saying that Burke excelled in every variety of style except the plain and unadorned. It is not a question of principle, but of art and of propriety. It may be worth while occasionally to study the art of writing in "pure Saxon," but to confine ourselves in practice to this interesting feat, would be as absurd as for a musician to employ habitually and on principle the *tour de force* of playing the pianoforte with one hand. We should lose breadth, power, and richness of combination. The harmony of our language, as we find it in Hooker, Shakespeare, and Milton, is fully established. We must take it as we find it. At any rate it is not until the student is a considerable master in the full compass of our remarkable tongue, that he can venture with safety on the experiment of [lxiv] restricting himself from the use of the most copious and effective of its elements. The inimitable passage from Shakespeare already quoted[1] is enough to prove how much the greatest writers of English have relied on Latinisms: yet Shakespeare was never at a loss for pure Saxon idioms. Burke generally puts the strength of his Saxon element into short, energetic, suggestive sentences, in the body of the paragraph, and concludes it with a few sonorous Latinisms. He often broke out, in the House of Commons, into a strain of farmer-like bluntness. In one of his great Letters on the Peace, in the midst of a complaint of the poverty and insufficiency of the political notions of the French, which he compares to their meagre diet, he suddenly exclaims that English people want "food that will stick to the ribs." So in this volume (p. 314) he declares that a machine like the reformed French monarchy is "not worth the grease of its wheels." We need not multiply examples. The so-called Saxon element is of immense use as a general source of energy; and a great master may employ it with great effect in the pathetic line. Upon its successful manipulation depends very much of the effect of all that is written in our tongue; but we act unwisely in neglecting to make much, if not the most, of our so-called Latinism. The extent of its use must depend mainly upon the ear.

Burke's Tract, as it stands, exceeds the measure of what he intended when it was commenced, and falls short of the great idea which grew upon him as he proceeded with it—of exhibiting fully and fairly to the eye of the world the grand and stable majesty of the civil and social system of England, in contrast with the hasty and incongruous edifice run up by the French Reformers. The analysis which precedes the text

1. Page 32.

in the present edition distinguishes it into two portions, the first including two thirds, the second, one third, of the book. The First Part is occupied with England. It is to this First Part that the foregoing observations chiefly apply. It differs in so many points from the Second Part, which is occupied with the new political system of France, that a critic of the omniscient school might well be excused for attributing it to another hand. Half of the First Part, or one third of the whole work, forms what may be called the Introduction. It answers strictly to the original [lxv] title "Reflections on Certain Proceedings of the Revolution Society."[1] It is sufficiently complete and coherent, and may be advantageously read by itself. The remainder of the First Part consists of several dissertations unequal in length and completeness. The most important is that which has been called Section I (the Church Establishment). It seems to be interrupted at page 223, and resumed at page 241, the intermediate space being occupied with a fragmentary vindication of the French monarchy and nobility. We have here the half-finished components of a greater work, the completion of which was prevented by the urgency of the occasion. The vindication of the English democracy, for Burke's immediate purpose the least important part, but which would have perhaps possessed the highest interest for posterity, is omitted altogether. The "Appeal from the New to the Old Whigs" to some extent supplies its place. But the whole of the middle third of the work is incomplete, and requires to be read with caution. Burke probably wrote the pieces which compose it at different times, during the spring, and laid the work aside altogether during the summer, of 1790.

The Second Part, or Critique of the new French Constitution, was composed, according to appearances, as autumn approached, and the necessity for producing the work for

1. See note, p. 369.

the winter season, then the chief season of the year, whether for business or any other purposes, became apparent. This portion is rather a voucher or *pièce justificative* than a necessary part of the book. It is a piece of vigorous and exhaustive, though rapid and one-sided, criticism. It is a direct and unsparing diatribe on the new French statesmanship, viewing the system it produced wholly by the light of reason and common sense, and leaving out of account all the arguments which are adduced in the First Part of the work. It is, as might be anticipated, not altogether just. We may fairly demur, on the threshold, to the general spirit of Burke's criticism.

> Dart thy skill at me;
> Bruise me with scorn; confound me with a flout;
> Thrust thy sharp wit quite through my ignorance;
> Cut me to pieces with thy keen conceit.

Posterity, however, in the words of Burke himself, written thirty [lxvi] years before, will not accept satire in the place of history. These pages contain more of Burke's personal manner, and have a character less declamatory, more minute, and more to the immediate purpose, than what precedes. They evidently represent a great intellectual effort, and contrast strongly with the previous almost spontaneous ebullition of sentiment and doctrine. Yet they are marked, and by no means sparingly, with striking literary beauties, which the student will do well to search out for himself. The historical value of this part of the work is still considerable, though its interest is diminished by the fact that much of the constitution which it attacks speedily disappeared, and that Burke's knowledge of it was not altogether correct or complete. As an instance we may take the ludicrous error at pp. 279–80, where it is assumed that the Departments and Communes were to be portioned out by straight lines with the aid of the theodolite. Burke was fond of a certain ponderous style of repartee, and something of this is traceable in his endeavours to show that the Liberty boasted by the Assembly was a mere semblance, and that they treated France "exactly like a conquered country." Nothing can be more admirable than his applying to them the saying attributed to Louis XIV, "C'est mon plaisir—c'est pour ma gloire" (p. 214). Burke always had two favourite images, derived from the art of the housebuilder, by which to illustrate the labours of the politician. One of these is the Buttress, the other the Cement, or Cementing principle.[1] Both of these he applies unsparingly in his vigorous condemnation of the details of the novelties of French polity. The buttresses were shams, and the cement had no binding in it. The criticism on the reformed Office of the King, and on the new Judicature, is brief, but to the purpose; but the most remarkable is that which relates to the army, containing as it does a forecast of the condition of a military democracy, and an anticipation of the future despotism of Napoleon (p. 332). Only one Frenchman, Rivarol, appears to have expressed a similar foreboding. The value of the remarks on the financial system, which conclude the work, is clouded by the perturbation of the question which came with the lengthened [lxvii] wars, and the Republic early took care to avoid bankruptcy by enormous contributions levied on the countries which fell under its yoke. The main predictions of Burke, however, were literally fulfilled. "The Assignats, after having poured millions into the coffers of the ruling rebellion, suddenly sank into the value of the paper of which they were made. Thousands and tens of thousands were ruined. The nation was bankrupt, but the Jacobin Government was rich; and the operation had thus all the results it was ever made for."[2] On the appearance of M. Calonne's

---

1. The substantive "cement," by the way, unlike the verb "to cement," should be accented on the first syllable. This trifle is essential to the harmony of more than one of Burke's sentences. See vol. i. p. 287.

2. Croly, Memoir of Burke, vol. ii. p. 134.

work, "De l'Etat de France," Burke considerably altered this Second Part of the work, and the text of the first edition differs, therefore, in many places, from the subsequent ones.

Burke's Tract provoked, in reply, as is well known, a whole literature of its own, no single representative of which is now held in any account, if we except the "Vindiciae Gallicae," the early work of Sir James Mackintosh. It had, of course, its replies in French literature; but its general influence on France is best traced in De Bonald,[1] De Maistre, Chateaubriand, and other *littérateurs* of the reaction. The same kind of influence is traceable in German thought in the works of Goerres, Stolberg, Frederick Schlegel, and others. Burke's true value was early appreciated in Germany, and A. M. von Müller, lecturing at Dresden in 1806, even remarked on the circumstance that Burke only met with his due honours from strangers. "His country but half understands him, and feels only half his glory, considering him chiefly as a brilliant orator, as a partisan, and a patriot. He is acknowledged in Germany as the real and successful mediator between liberty and law, between union and division of power, and between the republican and aristocratic principles." Burke certainly has not been without his effect on the political notions of the non-theological philosophers, as Schelling, Steffens, Reinhold, &c.; and if the student should wish to set by the side of Burke for purposes of contrast the views of a competent professor of scientific theory, he should turn to the pages of Ancillon.[2]

1. The connexion, however, is rather conventional. There was little in common between Burke and De Bonald, who recommended despotism as the primitive and normal form of legislation, and objected to toleration.

2. "Ueber die Staats-wissenschaft, von Friedrich Ancillon. Berlin, 1820." Political theory, like everything else, has its uses as well as its abuses. "The successful progress of reforms depends in a great measure on the political maxims which prevail among governors and governed, and on the advances of political science. False doctrines lead to erratic wishes, destructive misconceptions, and dangerous misinterpretations. Theory must combat and clear away the errors of theories, indicate the general direction of the right way,

He [lxviii] must, however, be prepared to encounter a vast army of desperate commonplaces. Gentz, the translator of Burke, himself a considerable politician, is well imbued with his model; and at home the school of Burke is represented by the names of Coleridge, Wordsworth, Southey, Macaulay, Arnold, and Whately.[1] These few names will suffice to indicate approximately Burke's peculiar place in general literature; but his influence in every way extends far more widely than any line which could be usefully drawn.

Considering that Burke stands unapproachably the first of our political orators, and indeed in the very first rank as a writer and a thinker, it seems strange that so few express and formal tributes have been paid to his memory. Had Burke been a Frenchman, nearly every French critic, great or small, would have tried his hand on such a subject, not in parenthetical allusion, or in a few brief words of ardent praise, but in regular essays and notices without number. Where we have placed a stone, they would have piled a cairn. Thus have the Cousins, Saint-Beuves, Guizots, and Pontmartins taken every opportunity for long disquisition upon their Montaigne, Pascal, Bossuet, Molière, La Fontaine, and the other great authors of France. With us, moreover, the editions of Burke have been few, considering his fame; and his direct praises have been for the most part confined, here to a page, there

---

and establish the true goal; it will thus be easier for practical politics, conducted by experience, to construct every portion of the road with a sure hand and firm footsteps." Ancillon, Preface, p. xxxi.

1. It would be unjust to pass over the name of Mathias, the author of the "Pursuits of Literature," a clever satire, illustrated with instructive and amusing original notes. No one should omit to read it who would comprehend the direct effect of Burke on his own generation. At this distance of time, however, we do not tolerate idle panegyrics. Johnson once said, somewhat pettishly, "Where is all the wonder? Burke is, to be sure, a man of uncommon abilities; with a great quantity of matter in his mind, and a great fluency of language in his mouth; but we are not to be stunned and astonished by him!" Boswell, ed. Croker, p. 681.

to a paragraph. It is necessary for an Englishman to know Burke's writings well if he would be enabled to judge of the extent of his influence on the leading minds of this country. Only know [lxix] Burke, and you will find his thoughts and expressions gleaming like golden threads in the pages of distinguished men of the generations which have succeeded his own. This is the form in which Burke has chiefly received his honours, and exercised his authority.[1]

The art of speaking and of writing in that grand old style, of which Burke was so great a master, is now wellnigh unknown. As in the case of the English dramatists, and of the Italian painters, it is the fault of a broken tradition, of a forgotten training, and of changed habits of life. That which was once the treasure of the few has somewhat suffered in the general diffusion. Arts appear to languish in an atmosphere of contagious mediocrity. There is no one to teach, either by word or by example, the perfect design of Correggio, or the powerful brush-play of Tintoret. When we glance over the treasures of those great English masters of prose, among whom Burke stands almost last, our hearts may well sink within us. We have to study as well as we can, and strive to pick up piece by piece the fragments of a lost mystery. It may be said that we have developed qualities which are more real, more enduring, and more valuable. Cuyp and Hals were doubtless greater masters in certain departments of their art than Rubens; and Hallam presents us with a variety of political method which contrasts in many respects advantageously with that of Burke. It is an interesting task to represent faithfully and minutely the features of a distant scene, to magnify it and artificially to approximate it to the eye of the observer, to blend its shadows carefully and easily with a mild and uniform light, to balance the composition without the appearance of artifice, and so nearly to lose and discard the effects

1. See footnote, p. 68, ante.

of perspective that the picture shall almost assume the proportions of a geometrical elevation. A sense of repose and
of completeness mingles perceptibly with our satisfaction at
these works half of art, half of antiquarianism. Burke is a
Rubens rather than a Cuyp. The objects are distinct and near
at hand: the canvas is large, the composition almost coarse
in its boldness and strength, and the colours are audaciously
contrasted and dashed in with a sort of gallant carelessness.
The human face is exaggerated in its proportions, and we attribute more to the [lxx] quick imagination of the artist than
to the mere influence of the objects which he proposes to
himself to delineate. More than all, however, in the writing
of Burke, is the effect due to a certain firm and uniformly
large method of manipulation. His thoughts run naturally, as
it were, into large type out of the "quick forge and working-
house" of his thought. Profound as they are, they never appear as the forced and unmellowed fruit of study. Objective
as they are, they come nearer to the lively impress of the
man who thinks, than to the mere portraiture of the thing
he is contemplating. We feel that we are in the presence of
une âme à double et triple étage. Such is, in great measure, the
general characteristic of what De Quincey has denominated
the Literature of *Power,* the stimulating, fructifying, and if its
seed should fall on a fit soil, the self-reproducing. On looking at a picture of Velasquez, said Northcote, you almost
lose the powerlessness of the undisciplined and unassisted
hand. "You feel as if you could take up the brush and do
anything." It is in like wise with the fine living and speaking
performances of Cicero and Burke, of Virgil and Dryden. It
is in writers such as these that we find the self-continuing impulse, the lost power of school and tradition, the communication of a precious secret, the touch of the coal from off the
altar. But as in the case of a rapidly-touched work of a great
painter, we see the genius, though we trace little or nothing of the intellectual and manual toil which has developed

it. Let it never be forgotten that the greatest masters have been the most patient, anxious, and assiduous students, and he who aspires to be of their number must be prepared to accept the conditions. The nature and extent of the studies of Cicero and Burke can only be adequately estimated from their writings. They aimed at a close contact with realities, at uniting in themselves literature, philosophy, and a high standard of practical life, at facilitating this happy combination in others, and at justifying their position as statesmen by being the wisest as well as the cleverest men of their day. The conception of such aims is rarely found with power of mind and body to accomplish them, nevertheless; "So toil the workmen that repair a world."

London,
March 11, 1875.

In the Introduction to the previous volume was inserted an inscription, written by Dr. Parr, intended for a national monument to Burke. It may be interesting to add here the equally masterly one inserted by Parr in the Dedication to his edition of Bellendenus.

EDMUNDO.BURKE

VIRO.TUM.OB.DOCTRINAM.MULTIPLICEM.ET.EXQUISITAM

TUM.OB.CELERES.ILLOS.INGENII.MOTUS

QUI.ET.AD.EXCOGITANDUM.ACUTI.ET.AD.EXPLICANDUM

ORNANDUMQUE.UBERES.SUNT

EXIMIO.AC.PRAECLARO

OPTIME.DE.LITTERIS.QUAS.SOLAS.ESSE.OMNIUM.TEMPORUM

OMNIUMQUE.LOCORUM.EXPERTUS.VIDIT

OPTIME.DE.SENATU.CUJUS.PERICLITANTIS

IPSE.DECUS.ET.COLUMEN.FUIT

OPTIME.DE.PATRIA.IN.CIVES

SUI.AMANTISSIMOS.EHEU.INGRATA

NUNQUAM.NON.PROMERITO

LIBRUM.HUNCCE.EA.QUA.PAR.EST.OBSERVANTIA

D.D.D.

A.E.A.O.

Reflections on the Revolution in France, and on the Proceedings in Certain Societies in London Relative to that Event in a Letter Intended to Have Been Sent to a Gentleman in Paris by the Right Honourable Edmund Burke

[Published in October, 1790. Eleventh Edition, Dodsley, 1791.]

[Argument

PART I, pp. 88–269.

The Sentiments and Political Doctrines of Englishmen compared with those of the French Revolutionists

REFLECTIONS ON THE REVOLUTION IN FRANCE

IT MAY NOT BE UNNECESSARY to inform the Reader, that the following Reflections had their origin in a correspondence between the Author and a very young gentleman at Paris, who did him the honour of desiring his opinion upon the important transactions, which then, and ever since, have so much occupied the attention of all men. An answer was written some time in the month of October, 1789; but it was kept back upon prudential considerations. That letter is alluded to in the beginning of the following sheets. It has

REFLECTIONS ON THE REVOLUTION IN FRANCE

been since forwarded to the person to whom it was addressed. The reasons for the delay in sending it were assigned in a short letter to the same gentleman. This produced on his part a new and pressing application for the Author's sentiments.

The Author began a second and more full discussion on the subject. This he had some thoughts of publishing early in the last spring; but the matter gaining upon him, he found that what he had undertaken not only far exceeded the measure of a letter, but that its importance required rather a more detailed consideration than at that time he had any leisure to bestow upon it. However, having thrown down his first thoughts in the form of a letter, and indeed when he sat down to write, having intended it for a private letter, he found it difficult to change the form of address, when his sentiments had grown into a greater extent, and had received another direction. A different plan, he is sensible, might be more favourable to a commodious division and distribution of his matter.

[4] Dear Sir,

You are pleased to call again, and with some earnestness, for my thoughts on the late proceedings in France. I will not give you reason to imagine that I think my sentiments of such value as to wish myself to be solicited about them. They are of too little consequence to be very anxiously either communicated or withheld. It was from attention to you, and to you only, that I hesitated at the time, when you first desired to receive them. In the first letter I had the honour to write to you, and which at length I send, I wrote neither for nor from any description of men; nor shall I in this. My errors, if any, are my own. My reputation alone is to answer for them.

REFLECTIONS ON THE REVOLUTION IN FRANCE

You see, Sir, by the long letter I have transmitted to you, that, though I do most heartily wish that France may be animated by a spirit of rational liberty, and that I think you bound, in all honest policy, to provide a permanent body, in which that spirit may reside, and an effectual organ, by which it may act, it is my misfortune to entertain great doubts concerning several material points in your late transactions.

You imagined, when you wrote last, that I might possibly be reckoned among the approvers of certain proceedings in France, from the solemn public seal of sanction they have received from two clubs of gentlemen in London, called the Constitutional Society, and the Revolution Society.

I certainly have the honour to belong to more clubs than one, in which the constitution of this kingdom and the principles of the glorious Revolution, are held in high reverence: and I reckon myself among the most forward in my zeal for maintaining that constitution and those principles in their utmost purity and vigour. It is because I do so, that I think it necessary for me, that there should be no mistake. Those who cultivate the memory of our revolution, and those who are attached to the constitution of this kingdom, will [5] take good care how they are involved with persons who, under the pretext of zeal towards the Revolution and Constitution, too frequently wander from their true principles; and are ready on every occasion to depart from the firm but cautious and deliberate spirit which produced the one, and which presides in the other. Before I proceed to answer the more material particulars in your letter, I shall beg leave to give you such information as I have been able to obtain of the two clubs which have thought proper, as bodies, to interfere in the concerns of France; first assuring you, that I am not, and that I have never been, a member of either of those societies.

The first, calling itself the Constitutional Society, or Society for Constitutional Information, or by some such title, is, I believe, of seven or eight years standing. The institution of this society appears to be of a charitable, and so far of a laudable, nature: it was intended for the circulation, at the expence of the members, of many books, which few others would be at the expence of buying; and which might lie on the hands of the booksellers, to the great loss of an useful body of men. Whether the books so charitably circulated, were ever as charitably read, is more than I know. Possibly several of them have been exported to France; and, like goods not in request here, may with you have found a market. I have heard much talk of the lights to be drawn from books that are sent from hence. What improvements they have had in their passage (as it is said some liquors are meliorated by crossing the sea) I cannot tell: But I never heard a man of common judgment, or the least degree of information, speak a word in praise of the greater part of the publications circulated by that society; nor have their proceedings been accounted, except by some of themselves, as of any serious consequence.

Your National Assembly seems to entertain much the [6] same opinion that I do of this poor charitable club. As a nation, you reserved the whole stock of your eloquent acknowledgments for the Revolution Society; when their fellows in the Constitutional were, in equity, entitled to some share. Since you have selected the Revolution Society as the great object of your national thanks and praises, you will think me excuseable in making its late conduct the subject of my observations. The National Assembly of France has given importance to these gentlemen by adopting them; and they return the favour, by acting as a committee in England for extending the principles of the National Assembly. Henceforward we must consider them as a kind of privileged persons; as no inconsiderable members in the diplomatic body. This is one among the revolutions which have given splendour to obscurity, and distinction to undiscerned merit. Until very lately I do not recollect to have heard of this club. I am quite sure that it never occupied a moment of my thoughts; nor, I believe, those of any person out of their own set. I find, upon enquiry, that on the anniversary of the Revolution in 1688, a club of dissenters, but of what denomination I know not, have long had the custom of hearing a sermon in one of their churches; and that afterwards they spent the day cheerfully, as other clubs do, at the tavern. But I never heard that any public measure, or political system, much less that the merits of the constitution of any foreign nation, had been the subject of a formal proceeding at their festivals; until, to my inexpressible surprise, I found them in a sort of public capacity, by a congratulatory address, giving an authoritative sanction to the proceedings of the National Assembly in France.

In the antient principles and conduct of the club, so far at least as they were declared, I see nothing to which I could take exception. I think it very probable, that for some purpose, new members may have [7] entered among them; and that some truly christian politicians, who love to dispense benefits, but are careful to conceal the hand which distributes the dole, may have made them the instruments of their pious designs. Whatever I may have reason to suspect concerning private management, I shall speak of nothing as of a certainty, but what is public.

For one, I should be sorry to be thought, directly or indirectly, concerned in their proceedings. I certainly take my full share, along with the rest of the world, in my individual and private capacity, in speculating on what has been done, or is doing, on the public stage; in any place antient or modern; in the republic of Rome, or the republic of Paris: but having no general apostolical mission, being a citizen of a particular state, and being bound up in a considerable degree, by its public will, I should think it, at least improper and irregular, for me to open a formal public correspondence with the actual government of a foreign nation, without the express authority of the government under which I live.

I should be still more unwilling to enter into that correspondence, under anything like an equivocal description, which to many, unacquainted with our usages, might make the address, in which I joined, appear as the act of persons in some sort of corporate capacity, acknowledged by the laws of this kingdom, and authorized to speak the sense of some part of it. On account of the ambiguity and uncertainty of unauthorized general descriptions, and of the deceit which may be practised under them, and not from mere formality, the house of Commons would reject the most sneaking petition for the most trifling object, under that mode of signature to which you have thrown open the folding-doors of your presence chamber, and have ushered into your National Assembly, with as much ceremony and [8] parade, and with as great a bustle of applause, as if you had been visited by the whole representative majesty of the whole English nation. If what this society has thought proper to send forth had been a piece of argument, it would have signified little whose argument it was. It would be neither the more nor the less convincing on account of the party it came from. But this is only a vote and resolution. It stands solely on authority; and in this case it is the mere authority of individuals, few of whom appear. Their signatures ought, in my opinion, to have been annexed to their instrument. The world would then have the means of knowing how many they are; who they are; and of what value their opinions may be, from their personal abilities, from their knowledge, their experience, or their lead and authority in this state. To me, who am but a plain man, the proceeding looks a little too refined, and too ingenious; it has too much the air of a political stratagem, adopted for the sake of giving, under an high-sounding name, an importance to the public declarations of this club, which, when the matter came to be closely inspected, they did not altogether so well deserve. It is a policy that has very much the complexion of a fraud.

I flatter myself that I love a manly, moral, regulated liberty as well as any gentleman of that society, be he who he will; and perhaps I have given as good proofs of my attachment to that cause, in the whole course of my public conduct. I think I envy liberty as little as they do, to any other nation. But I cannot stand forward, and give praise or blame to any thing which relates to human actions, and human concerns, on a simple view of the object as it stands stripped of every relation, in all the nakedness and solitude of metaphysical abstraction. Circumstances (which with some gentlemen pass for nothing) give in reality to every political principle its distinguishing colour, and discriminating effect. The [9] circumstances are what render every civil and political scheme beneficial or noxious to mankind. Abstractedly speaking, government, as well as liberty, is good; yet could I, in common sense, ten years ago, have felicitated France on her enjoyment of a government (for she then had a government) without enquiry what the nature of that government was, or how it was administered? Can I now congratulate the same nation upon its freedom? Is it because liberty in the abstract may be classed amongst the blessings of mankind, that I am seriously to felicitate a madman, who has escaped from the protecting restraint and wholesome darkness of his cell, on his restoration to the enjoyment of light and liberty? Am I to congratulate an highwayman and murderer, who has broke prison, upon the recovery of his natural rights? This would be to act over again the scene of the criminals condemned to the gallies, and their heroic deliverer, the metaphysic Knight of the Sorrowful Countenance.

When I see the spirit of liberty in action, I see a strong principle at work; and this, for a while, is all I can possibly know of it. The wild *gas*, the fixed air, is plainly broke loose: but we ought to suspend our judgment until the first effervescence is a little subsided, till the liquor is cleared, and until we see something deeper than the agitation of a troubled and frothy surface. I must be tolerably sure, before I venture publicly to congratulate men upon a blessing, that they have really received one. Flattery corrupts both the receiver and the giver; and adulation is not of more service to the people than to kings. I should therefore suspend my congratulations on the new liberty of France, until I was informed how it had been combined with government; with public force; with the discipline and obedience of armies; with the collection of an effective and well-distributed revenue; with morality and religion; with the solidity of [10] property; with peace and order; with civil and social manners. All these (in their way) are good things too; and, without them, liberty is not a benefit whilst it lasts, and is not likely to continue long. The effect of liberty to individuals is, that they may do what they please: we ought to see what it will please them to do, before we risque congratulations, which may be soon turned into complaints. Prudence would dictate this in the case of separate insulated private men; but liberty, when men act in bodies, is *power*. Considerate people, before they declare themselves, will observe the use which is made of *power;* and particularly of so trying a thing as *new* power in *new* persons, of whose principles, tempers, and dispositions, they have little or no experience, and in situations where those who appear the most stirring in the scene may possibly not be the real movers.

All these considerations however were below the transcendental dignity of the Revolution Society. Whilst I continued in the country, from whence I had the honour of writing to you, I had but an imperfect idea of their transactions. On my coming to town, I sent for an account of their proceedings, which had been published by their authority, containing a sermon of Dr. Price, with the Duke de Rochefoucault's and the Archbishop of Aix's letter, and several other documents annexed. The whole of that publication, with the manifest design of connecting the affairs of France with those of England, by drawing us into an imitation of the conduct of the National Assembly, gave me a considerable degree of uneasiness. The effect of that conduct upon the power, credit, prosperity, and tranquillity of France, became every day more evident. The form of constitution to be settled, for its future polity, became more clear. We are now in a condition to discern, with tolerable exactness, the true nature of the object held up to our imitation. If the prudence of reserve and decorum dictates silence in some [11] circumstances, in others prudence of an higher order may justify us in speaking our thoughts. The beginnings of confusion with us in England are at present feeble enough; but with you, we have seen an infancy still more feeble, growing by moments into a strength to heap mountains upon mountains, and to wage war with Heaven itself. Whenever our neighbour's house is on fire, it cannot be amiss for the engines to play a little on our own. Better to be despised for too anxious apprehensions, than ruined by too confident a security.

Solicitous chiefly for the peace of my own country, but by no means unconcerned for your's, I wish to communicate more largely, what was at first intended only for your private satisfaction. I shall still keep your affairs in my eye and continue to address myself to you. Indulging myself in the freedom of epistolary intercourse, I beg leave to throw out my thoughts, and express my feelings, just as they arise in my mind, with very little attention to formal method. I set out with the proceedings of the Revolution Society; but I shall not confine myself to them. Is it possible I should? It looks to me as if I were in a great crisis, not of the affairs of France alone, but of all Europe, perhaps of more than Europe. All circumstances taken together, the French revolution is the most astonishing that has hitherto happened in the world. The most wonderful things are brought about in many instances by means the most absurd and ridiculous; in the most ridiculous modes; and apparently, by the most contemptible instruments. Every thing seems out of nature in this strange chaos of levity and ferocity, and of all sorts of crimes jumbled together with all sorts of follies. In viewing this monstrous tragi-comic scene, the most opposite passions necessarily succeed, and sometimes mix with each other in the mind: alternate laughter and tears; alternate scorn and horror.

[12] IT CANNOT HOWEVER BE DENIED, that to some this strange scene appeared in quite another point of view. Into them it inspired no other sentiments than those of exultation and rapture. They saw nothing in what has been done in France, but a firm and temperate exertion of freedom; so consistent, on the whole, with morals and with piety, as to make it deserving not only of the secular applause of dashing Machiavelian politicians, but to render it a fit theme for all the devout effusions of sacred eloquence.

On the forenoon of the 4th of November last, Doctor Richard Price, a non-conforming minister of eminence, preached at the dissenting meeting-house of the Old Jewry, to his club or society, a very extraordinary miscellaneous sermon, in which there are some good moral and religious sentiments, and not ill expressed, mixed up in a sort of porridge of various political opinions and reflections: but the revolution in France is the grand ingredient in the cauldron. I consider the address transmitted by the Revolution Society to the National Assembly, through Earl Stanhope, as originating in the principles of the sermon, and as a corollary from them. It was moved by the preacher of that discourse. It was passed by those who came reeking from the effect of the sermon, without any censure or qualification, expressed or implied. If, however, any of the gentlemen concerned shall wish to separate the sermon from the resolution, they know how to acknowledge the one, and to disavow the other. They may do it: I cannot.

For my part, I looked on that sermon as the public declaration of a man much connected with literary caballers, and intriguing philosophers; with political theologians, and theological politicians, both at home and abroad. I know they set him up as a sort of oracle; because, with the best intentions in the world, he naturally *philippizes,* and chaunts his prophetic song in exact unison with their designs.

[13] That sermon is in a strain which I believe has not been heard in this kingdom, in any of the pulpits which are tolerated or encouraged in it, since the year 1648, when a predecessor of Dr. Price, the Reverend Hugh Peters, made the vault of the king's own chapel at St. James's ring with the honour and privilege of the Saints, who, with the "high praises of God in their mouths, and a *two*-edged sword in their hands, were to execute judgment on the heathen, and punishments upon the *people;* to bind their *kings* with chains, and their *nobles* with fetters of iron."* Few harangues from the pulpit, except in the days of your league in France, or in the days of our solemn league and covenant in England, have ever breathed less of the spirit of moderation than this lecture in the Old Jewry. Supposing, however, that something like moderation were visible in this political sermon; yet politics and the pulpit are terms that have little agreement. No sound ought to be heard in the church but the healing voice of Christian charity. The cause of civil liberty and civil government gains as little as that of religion by this confusion of duties. Those who quit their proper character, to assume what does not belong to them, are, for the greater part, ignorant both of the character they leave, and of the character they assume. Wholly unacquainted with the world in which they are so fond of meddling, and inexperienced in all its affairs, on which they pronounce with so much confidence, they have nothing of politics but the passions they excite. Surely the church is a place where one day's truce ought to be allowed to the dissensions and animosities of mankind.

This pulpit style, revived after so long a discontinuance,

---

*Psalm cxlix.

had to me the air of novelty, and of a novelty not wholly without danger. I do not charge this danger equally to every part of the discourse. The hint given to a noble and [14] reverend lay-divine, who is supposed high in office in one of our universities,* and to other lay-divines "of *rank* and literature," may be proper and seasonable, though somewhat new. If the noble *Seekers* should find nothing to satisfy their pious fancies in the old staple of the national church, or in all the rich variety to be found in the well-assorted warehouses of the dissenting congregations, Dr. Price advises them to improve upon non conformity; and to set up, each of them, a separate meeting-house upon his own particular principles.† It is somewhat remarkable that this reverend divine should be so earnest for setting up new churches, and so perfectly indifferent concerning the doctrine which may be taught in them. His zeal is of a curious character. It is not for the propagation of his own opinions, but of any opinions. It is not for the diffusion of truth, but for the spreading of contradiction. Let the noble teachers but dissent, it is no matter from whom or from what. This great point once secured, it is taken for granted their religion will be rational and manly. I doubt whether religion would reap all the benefits which the calculating divine computes from this "great company of great preachers." It would certainly be a valuable addition of nondescripts to the ample collection of known classes, genera and species, which at present beautify the *hortus siccus* of dissent. A sermon from

---

*Discourse on the Love of our Country, Nov. 4, 1789, by Dr. Richard Price, 3d edition, p. 17 and 18.

†"Those who dislike that mode of worship which is prescribed by public authority ought, if they can find *no* worship *out* of the church which they approve, *to set up a separate worship for themselves;* and by doing this, and giving an example of a rational and manly worship, men of *weight* from their *rank* and literature may do the greatest service to society and the world." P. 18. Dr. Price's Sermon.

a noble duke, or a noble marquis, or a noble earl, or baron bold, would certainly increase and diversify the amusements of this town, which begins to grow satiated with the uniform round of its vapid dissipations. I should only stipulate that [15] these new *Mess-Johns* in robes and coronets should keep some sort of bounds in the democratic and levelling principles which are expected from their titled pulpits. The new evangelists will, I dare say, disappoint the hopes that are conceived of them. They will not become, literally as well as figuratively, polemic divines, nor be disposed so to drill their congregations that they may, as in former blessed times, preach their doctrines to regiments of dragoons, and corps of infantry and artillery. Such arrangements, however favourable to the cause of compulsory freedom, civil and religious, may not be equally conducive to the national tranquillity. These few restrictions I hope are no great stretches of intolerance, no very violent exertions of despotism.

BUT I MAY SAY OF OUR PREACHER, "*utinam nugis tota illa dedisset tempora saevitiae.*" All things in this his fulminating bull are not of so innoxious a tendency. His doctrines affect our constitution in its vital parts. He tells the Revolution Society, in this political sermon, that his majesty "is almost the *only* lawful king in the world, because the *only* one who owes his crown to the *choice of his people.*" As to the kings of *the world,* all of whom (except one) this archpontiff of the *rights of men,* with all the plenitude, and with more than the boldness of the papal deposing power in its meridian fervour of the twelfth century, puts into one sweeping clause of ban and anathema, and proclaims usurpers by circles of longitude and latitude, over the whole globe, it behoves them to consider how they admit into their territories these apostolic missionaries, who are to tell their subjects they are not lawful kings. That is their concern. It is ours, as a domestic interest of some moment, seriously to consider the solidity of the *only* principle upon which these gentlemen acknowledge a king of Great Britain to be entitled to their allegiance.

[16] This doctrine, as applied to the prince now on the British throne, either is nonsense, and therefore neither true nor false, or it affirms a most unfounded, dangerous, illegal, and unconstitutional position. According to this spiritual doctor of politics, if his majesty does not owe his crown to the choice of his people, he is no lawful king. Now nothing can be more untrue than that the crown of this kingdom is so held by his majesty. Therefore if you follow their rule, the king of Great Britain, who most certainly does not owe his high office to any form of popular election, is in no respect better than the rest of the gang of usurpers, who reign, or rather rob, all over the face of this our miserable world, without any sort of right or title to the allegiance of their people. The policy of this general doctrine, so qualified, is evident enough. The propagators of this political gospel are in hopes their abstract principle (their principle that a popular choice is necessary to the legal existence of the sovereign magistracy) would be overlooked whilst the king of Great Britain was not affected by it. In the mean time the ears of their congregations would be gradually habituated to it, as if it were a first principle admitted without dispute. For the present it would only operate as a theory, pickled in the preserving juices of pulpit eloquence, and laid by for future use. *Condo et compono quae mox depromere possim.* By this policy, whilst our government is soothed with a reservation in its favour, to which it has no claim, the security, which it has in common with all governments, so far as opinion is security, is taken away.

Thus these politicians proceed, whilst little notice is taken of their doctrines: but when they come to be examined upon the plain meaning of their words and the direct tendency of their doctrines, then equivocations and slippery constructions come into play. When they say the king [17] owes his crown to the choice of his people, and is therefore the only lawful sovereign in the world, they will perhaps tell us they mean to say no more than that some of the king's predecessors have been called to the throne by some sort of choice; and therefore he owes his crown to the choice of his people. Thus, by a miserable subterfuge, they hope to render their proposition safe, by rendering it nugatory. They are welcome to the asylum they seek for their offence, since they take refuge in their folly. For, if you admit this interpretation, how does their idea of election differ from our idea of inheritance? And how does the settlement of the crown in the Brunswick line derived from James the first, come to legalize our monarchy, rather than that of any of the neighbouring countries? At some time or other, to be sure, all the beginners of dynasties were chosen by those who called them to govern. There is ground enough for the opinion that all the kingdoms of Europe were, at a remote period, elective, with more or fewer limitations in the objects of choice; but whatever kings might have been here or elsewhere, a thousand years ago, or in whatever manner the ruling dynasties of England or France may have begun, the King of Great Britain is at this day king by a fixed rule of succession, according to the laws of his country; and whilst the legal conditions of the compact of sovereignty are performed by him (as they are performed) he holds his crown in contempt of the choice of the Revolution Society, who have not a single vote for a king amongst them, either individually or collectively; though I make no doubt they would soon erect themselves into an electoral college, if things were ripe to give effect to their claim. His majesty's heirs and successors, each in his time and order, will come to the crown with the same contempt of their choice with which his majesty has succeeded to that he wears.

Whatever may be the success of evasion in explaining [18] away the gross error of *fact,* which supposes that his majesty (though he holds it in concurrence with the wishes) owes his crown to the choice of his people, yet nothing can evade their full explicit declaration, concerning the principle of a right in the people to choose, which right is directly maintained, and tenaciously adhered to. All the oblique insinuations concerning election bottom in this proposition, and are referable to it. Lest the foundation of the king's exclusive legal title should pass for a mere rant of adulatory freedom, the political Divine proceeds dogmatically to assert,* that by the principles of the Revolution the people of England have acquired three fundamental rights, all which, with him, compose one system, and lie together in one short sentence; namely, that we have acquired a right

1. "To choose our own governors."
2. "To cashier them for misconduct."
3. "To frame a government for ourselves."

This new, and hitherto unheard-of bill of rights, though made in the name of the whole people, belongs to those gentlemen and their faction only. The body of the people of England have no share in it. They utterly disclaim it. They will resist the practical assertion of it with their lives and fortunes. They are bound to do so by the laws of their country, made at the time of that very Revolution, which is appealed to in favour of the fictitious rights claimed by the society which abuses its name.

THESE GENTLEMEN OF THE OLD JEWRY, in all their reasonings on the Revolution of 1688, have a revolution which happened in England about forty years before, and the late French revolution, so much before their eyes, and in their hearts, that they are constantly confounding all the three together. It is necessary that we should separate what they

*P. 34, Discourse on the Love of our Country, by Dr. Price.

[19] confound. We must recall their erring fancies to the *acts* of the Revolution which we revere, for the discovery of its true *principles*. If the *principles* of the Revolution of 1688 are any where to be found, it is in the statute called the *Declaration of Right*. In that most wise, sober, and considerate declaration, drawn up by great lawyers and great statesmen, and not by warm and inexperienced enthusiasts, not one word is said, nor one suggestion made, of a general right "to choose our own governors; to cashier them for misconduct; and to form a government for ourselves."

This Declaration of Right (the act of the 1st of William and Mary, sess. 2. ch. 2) is the corner-stone of our constitution, as reinforced, explained, improved, and in its fundamental principles for ever settled. It is called "An act for declaring the rights and liberties of the subject, and for *settling* the *succession* of the crown." You will observe, that these rights and this succession are declared in one body, and bound indissolubly together.

A few years after this period, a second opportunity offered for asserting a right of election to the crown. On the prospect of a total failure of issue from King William, and from the Princess, afterwards Queen Anne, the consideration of the settlement of the crown, and of a further security for the liberties of the people, again came before the legislature. Did they this second time make any provision for legalizing the crown on the spurious Revolution principles of the Old Jewry? No. They followed the principles which prevailed in the Declaration of Right; indicating with more precision the persons who were to inherit in the Protestant line. This act also incorporated, by the same policy, our liberties, and an hereditary succession in the same act. Instead of a right to choose our own governors, they declared that the *succession* in that line (the protestant line drawn from James the First) was absolutely necessary "for [20] the peace, quiet, and security of the realm," and that it was equally urgent on them "to maintain a *certainty in the succession* thereof, to which the subjects may safely have recourse for their protection." Both these acts, in which are heard the unerring, unambiguous oracles of Revolution policy, instead of countenancing the delusive, gypsey predictions of a "right to choose our governors," prove to a demonstration how totally adverse the wisdom of the nation was from turning a case of necessity into a rule of law.

Unquestionably there was at the Revolution, in the person of King William, a small and a temporary deviation from the strict order of regular hereditary succession; but it is against all genuine principles of jurisprudence to draw a principle from a law made in a special case, and regarding an individual person. *Privilegium non transit in exemplum.* If ever there was a time favourable for establishing the principle, that a king of popular choice was the only legal king, without all doubt it was at the Revolution. Its not being done at that time is a proof that the nation was of opinion it ought not to be done at any time. There is no person so completely ignorant of our history, as not to know, that the majority in parliament of both parties were so little disposed to any thing resembling that principle, that at first they were determined to place the vacant crown, not on the head of the prince of Orange, but on that of his wife Mary, daughter of King James, the eldest born of the issue of that king, which they acknowledged as undoubtedly his. It would be to repeat a very trite story, to recall to your memory all those circumstances which demonstrated that their accepting king William was not properly a *choice;* but, to all those who did not wish, in effect to recall King James, or to deluge their country in blood, and again to bring their religion, laws, and liberties into the peril they had just [21] escaped, it was an act of *necessity,* in the strictest moral sense in which necessity can be taken.

In the very act, in which for a time, and in a single case, parliament departed from the strict order of inheritance, in favour of a prince, who, though not next, was however very near in the line of succession, it is curious to observe how Lord Somers, who drew the bill called the Declaration of Right, has comported himself on that delicate occasion. It is curious to observe with what address this temporary solution of continuity is kept from the eye; whilst all that could be found in this act of necessity to countenance the idea of an hereditary succession is brought forward, and fostered, and made the most of, by this great man, and by the legislature who followed him. Quitting the dry, imperative style of an act of parliament, he makes the lords and commons fall to a pious, legislative ejaculation, and declare, that they consider it "as a marvellous providence, and merciful goodness of God to this nation, to preserve their said majesties' royal persons most happily to reign over us *on the throne of their ancestors,* for which, from the bottom of their hearts, they return their humblest thanks and praises." The legislature plainly had in view the Act of Recognition of the first of Queen Elizabeth, Chap. 3d, and of that of James the First, Chap. 1st, both acts strongly declaratory of the inheritable nature of the crown; and in many parts they follow, with a nearly literal precision, the words and even the form of thanksgiving, which is found in these old declaratory statutes.

The two houses, in the act of king William, did not thank God that they had found a fair opportunity to assert a right to choose their own governors, much less to make an election the *only lawful* title to the crown. Their having been in a condition to avoid the very appearance of it, as much as possible, was by them considered as a providential [22] escape. They threw a politic, well-wrought veil over every circumstance tending to weaken the rights, which in the meliorated order of succession they meant to perpetuate; or which might furnish a precedent for any future departure from what they had then settled for ever. Accordingly, that they might not relax the nerves of their monarchy, and that they might preserve a close conformity to the practice of their ancestors, as it appeared in the declaratory statutes of Queen Mary* and Queen Elizabeth, in the next clause they vest, by recognition, in their majesties, all the legal prerogatives of the crown, declaring, "that in them they are most fully, rightfully, and intirely invested, incorporated, united, and annexed." In the clause which follows, for preventing questions, by reason of any pretended titles to the crown, they declare (observing also in this the traditionary language, along with the traditionary policy of the nation, and repeating as from a rubric the language of the preceding acts of Elizabeth and James) that on the preserving "a *certainty* in the SUCCESSION thereof, the unity, peace, and tranquillity of this nation doth, under God, wholly depend."

They knew that a doubtful title of succession would but too much resemble an election; and that an election would be utterly destructive of the "unity, peace, and tranquillity of this nation," which they thought to be considerations of some moment. To provide for these objects, and therefore to exclude for ever the Old Jewry doctrine of "a right to choose our own governors," they follow with a clause, containing a most solemn pledge, taken from the preceding act of Queen Elizabeth, as solemn a pledge as ever was or can be given in favour of an hereditary succession, and as solemn a renunciation as could be made of the principles by this society imputed to them. "The lords spiritual and temporal, and commons, do, in the name [23] of all the people aforesaid, most humbly and faithfully submit *themselves, their heirs and posterities for ever;* and do faithfully promise, that they will stand to, maintain, and defend their said majesties, and also the *limitation of the crown,* herein specified and contained, to the utmost of their powers," &c. &c.

So far is it from being true, that we acquired a right by

---

* 1st Mary, Sess. 3. ch. 1.

the Revolution to elect our kings, that if we had possessed it before, the English nation did at that time most solemnly renounce and abdicate it, for themselves and for all their posterity for ever. These gentlemen may value themselves as much as they please on their whig principles; but I never desire to be thought a better whig than Lord Somers; or to understand the principles of the Revolution better than those by whom it was brought about; or to read in the declaration of right any mysteries unknown to those whose penetrating style has engraved in our ordinances, and in our hearts, the words and spirit of that immortal law.

It is true that, aided with the powers derived from force and opportunity, the nation was at that time, in some sense, free to take what course it pleased for filling the throne; but only free to do so upon the same grounds on which they might have wholly abolished their monarchy, and every other part of their constitution. However they did not think such bold changes within their commission. It is indeed difficult, perhaps impossible, to give limits to the mere *abstract* competence of the supreme power, such as was exercised by parliament at that time; but the limits of a *moral* competence, subjecting, even in powers more indisputably sovereign, occasional will to permanent reason, and to the steady maxims of faith, justice, and fixed fundamental policy, are perfectly intelligible, and perfectly binding upon those who exercise any authority, under any name, or under any title, in the state. The house of lords, for instance, is not [24] morally competent to dissolve the house of commons; no, nor even to dissolve itself, nor to abdicate, if it would, its portion in the legislature of the kingdom. Though a king may abdicate for his own person, he cannot abdicate for the monarchy. By as strong, or by a stronger reason, the house of commons cannot renounce its share of authority. The engagement and pact of society, which generally goes by the name of the constitution, forbids such invasion and such surrender. The constituent parts of a state are obliged to hold their public faith with each other, and with all those who derive any serious interest under their engagements, as much as the whole state is bound to keep its faith with separate communities. Otherwise competence and power would soon be confounded, and no law be left but the will of a prevailing force. On this principle the succession of the crown has always been what it now is, an hereditary succession by law: in the old line it was a succession by the common law; in the new, by the statute law, operating on the principles of the common law, not changing the substance, but regulating the mode, and describing the persons. Both these descriptions of law are of the same force, and are derived from an equal authority, emanating from the common agreement and original compact of the state, *communi sponsione reipublicae,* and as such are equally binding on king, and people too, as long as the terms are observed, and they continue the same body politic.

It is far from impossible to reconcile, if we do not suffer ourselves to be entangled in the mazes of metaphysic sophistry, the use both of a fixed rule and an occasional deviation; the sacredness of an hereditary principle of succession in our government, with a power of change in its application in cases of extreme emergency. Even in that extremity (if we take the measure of our rights by our exercise of them at the Revolution) the change is to be confined [25] to the peccant part only: to the part which produced the necessary deviation; and even then it is to be effected without a decomposition of the whole civil and political mass, for the purpose of originating a new civil order out of the first elements of society.

A state without the means of some change is without the means of its conservation. Without such means it might even risque the loss of that part of the constitution which it wished the most religiously to preserve. The two principles of conservation and correction operated strongly at the two critical periods of the Restoration and Revolution, when England found itself without a king. At both those periods the nation had lost the bond of union in their antient edifice; they did not, however, dissolve the whole fabric. On the contrary, in both cases they regenerated the deficient part of the old constitution through the parts which were not impaired. They kept these old parts exactly as they were, that the part recovered might be suited to them. They acted by the ancient organized states in the shape of their old organization, and not by the organic *moleculae* of a disbanded people. At no time, perhaps, did the sovereign legislature manifest a more tender regard to their fundamental principle of British constitutional policy, than at the time of the Revolution, when it deviated from the direct line of hereditary succession. The crown was carried somewhat out of the line in which it had before moved; but the new line was derived from the same stock. It was still a line of hereditary descent; still an hereditary descent in the same blood, though an hereditary descent qualified with protestantism. When the legislature altered the direction, but kept the principle, they shewed that they held it inviolable.

On this principle, the law of inheritance had admitted some amendment in the old time, and long before the aera of the Revolution. Some time after the conquest great [26] questions arose upon the legal principles of hereditary descent. It became a matter of doubt, whether the heir *per capita* or the heir *per stirpes* was to succeed; but whether the heir *per capita* gave way when the heirdom *per stirpes* took place, or the Catholic heir, when the Protestant was preferred, the inheritable principle survived with a sort of immortality through all transmigrations— *multosque per annos stat fortuna domus et avi numerantur avorum.* This is the spirit of our constitution, not only in its settled course, but in all its revolutions. Whoever came in, or however he came in, whether he obtained the crown by law, or by force, the hereditary succession was either continued or adopted.

The gentlemen of the Society for Revolutions see nothing in that of 1688 but the deviation from the constitution; and they take the deviation from the principle for the principle. They have little regard to the obvious consequences of their doctrine, though they must see, that it leaves positive authority in very few of the positive institutions of this country. When such an unwarrantable maxim is once established, that no throne is lawful but the elective, no one act of the princes who preceded the aera of fictitious election can be valid. Do these theorists mean to imitate some of their predecessors, who dragged the bodies of our antient sovereigns out of the quiet of their tombs? Do they mean to attaint and disable backwards all the kings that have reigned before the Revolution, and consequently to stain the throne of England with the blot of a continual usurpation? Do they mean to invalidate, annul, or to call into question, together with the titles of the whole line of our kings, that great body of our statute law which passed under those whom they treat as usurpers? to annul laws of inestimable value to our liberties—of as great value at least as any which have passed at or since the period of the Revolution? If kings, who did not owe their crown [27] to the choice of their people, had no title to make laws, what will become of the statute *de tallagio non concedendo?*—of the *petition of right?*—of the act of *habeas corpus?* Do these new doctors of the rights of men presume to assert, that King James the Second, who came to the crown as next of blood, according to the rules of a then unqualified succession, was not to all intents and purposes a lawful king of England, before he had done any of those acts which were justly construed into an abdication of his crown? If he was not, much trouble in parliament might have been saved at the period these gentlemen commemorate. But King James was a bad king with a good title, and not an usurper. The princes who succeeded according to the act of parliament which settled the crown on the electress Sophia and on her descendants, being Protestants, came in as much by a title of inheritance as King James did. He came in according to the law, as it stood at his accession to the crown; and the princes of the House of Brunswick came to the inheritance of the crown, not by election, but by the law, as it stood at their several accessions of Protestant descent and inheritance, as I hope I have shewn sufficiently.

The law by which this royal family is specifically destined to the succession, is the act of the 12th and 13th of King William. The terms of this act bind "us and our *heirs,* and our *posterity,* to them, their *heirs,* and their *posterity,*" being Protestants, to the end of time, in the same words as the declaration of right had bound us to the heirs of King William and Queen Mary. It therefore secures both an hereditary crown and an hereditary allegiance. On what ground, except the constitutional policy of forming an establishment to secure that kind of succession which is to preclude a choice of the people for ever, could the legislature have fastidiously rejected the fair and abundant [28] choice which our own country presented to them, and searched in strange lands for a foreign princess, from whose womb the line of our future rulers were to derive their title to govern millions of men through a series of ages?

The Princess Sophia was named in the Act of Settlement of the 12th and 13th of King William, for a *stock* and root of *inheritance* to our kings, and not for her merits as a temporary administratrix of a power, which she might not, and in fact did not, herself ever exercise. She was adopted for one reason, and for one only, because, says the act, "the most excellent Princess Sophia, Electress and Dutchess Dowager of Hanover, is *daughter* of the most excellent Princess Elizabeth, late Queen of Bohemia, *daughter* of our late *sovereign lord* King James the First, of happy memory, and is hereby declared to be the next in *succession* in the Protestant line," &c.

&c.; "and the crown shall continue to the *heirs* of her body, being Protestants." This limitation was made by parliament, that through the Princess Sophia an inheritable line, not only was to be continued in future but (what they thought very material) that through her it was to be connected with the old stock of inheritance in King James the First; in order that the monarchy might preserve an unbroken unity through all ages, and might be preserved, with safety to our religion, in the old approved mode by descent, in which, if our liberties had been once endangered, they had often, through all storms and struggles of prerogative and privilege, been preserved. They did well. No experience has taught us, that in any other course or method than that of an *hereditary crown,* our liberties can be regularly perpetuated and preserved sacred as our *hereditary right.* An irregular, convulsive movement may be necessary to throw off an irregular, convulsive disease. But the course of succession is the [29] healthy habit of the British constitution. Was it that the legislature wanted, at the act for the limitation of the crown in the Hanoverian line, drawn through the female descendants of James the First, a due sense of the inconveniencies of having two or three, or possibly more, foreigners in succession to the British throne? No! They had a due sense of the evils which might happen from such foreign rule, and more than a due sense of them. But a more decisive proof cannot be given of the full conviction of the British nation, that the principles of the Revolution did not authorize them to elect kings at their pleasure, and without any attention to the antient fundamental principles of our government, than their continuing to adopt a plan of hereditary Protestant succession in the old line, with all the dangers and all the inconveniencies of its being a foreign line full before their eyes, and operating with the utmost force upon their minds.

A few years ago I should be ashamed to overload a matter, so capable of supporting itself, by the then unnecessary support of any argument; but this seditious, unconstitutional doctrine is now publicly taught, avowed, and printed. The dislike I feel to revolutions, the signals for which have so often been given from pulpits; the spirit of change that is gone abroad; the total contempt which prevails with you, and may come to prevail with us, of all ancient institutions, when set in opposition to a present sense of convenience, or to the bent of a present inclination: all these considerations make it not unadviseable, in my opinion, to call back our attention to the true principles of our own domestic laws; that you, my French friend, should begin to know, and that we should continue to cherish them. We ought not, on either side of the water, to suffer ourselves to be imposed upon by the counterfeit wares which some persons, by a double [30] fraud, export to you in illicit bottoms as raw commodities of British growth, though wholly alien to our soil, in order afterwards to smuggle them back again into this country, manufactured after the newest Paris fashion of an improved liberty.

The people of England will not ape the fashions they have never tried; nor go back to those which they have found mischievous on trial. They look upon the legal hereditary succession of their crown as among their rights, not as among their wrongs; as a benefit, not as a grievance; as a security for their liberty, not as a badge of servitude. They look on the frame of their commonwealth, *such as it stands,* to be of inestimable value; and they conceive the undisturbed succession of the crown to be a pledge of the stability and perpetuity of all the other members of our constitution.

I shall beg leave, before I go any further, to take notice of some paltry artifices, which the abettors of election as the only lawful title to the crown, are ready to employ, in order to render the support of the just principles of our constitution a task somewhat invidious. These sophisters substitute a fictitious cause, and feigned personages, in whose favour they suppose you engaged, whenever you defend the inheritable nature of the crown. It is common with them to dispute as if they were in a conflict with some of those exploded fanatics of slavery, who formerly maintained, what I believe no creature now maintains, "that the crown is held by divine, hereditary, and indefeasible right." These old fanatics of single arbitrary power dogmatized as if hereditary royalty was the only lawful government in the world, just as our new fanatics of popular arbitrary power maintain that a popular election is the sole lawful source of authority. The old prerogative enthusiasts, it is true, did speculate foolishly, and perhaps impiously too, as if monarchy [31] had more of a divine sanction than any other mode of government; and as if a right to govern by in-heritance were in strictness *indefeasible* in every person, who should be found in the succession to a throne, and under every circumstance, which no civil or political right can be. But an absurd opinion concerning the king's hereditary right to the crown does not prejudice one that is rational, and bottomed upon solid principles of law and policy. If all the absurd theories of lawyers and divines were to vitiate the ob-jects in which they are conversant, we should have no law, and no religion, left in the world. But an absurd theory on one side of a question forms no justification for alledging a false fact, or promulgating mischievous maxims, on the other.

THE SECOND CLAIM of the Revolution Society is "a right of cashiering their governors for *misconduct*." Perhaps the apprehensions our ancestors entertained of forming such a precedent as that "of cashiering for misconduct," was the cause that the declaration of the act which implied the ab-dication of King James, was, if it had any fault, rather too guarded, and too circumstantial.* But all this guard, and all

---

* "That King James the second, having endeavoured to *subvert the constitu-tion* of the kingdom, by breaking the *original contract* between king and people, and by the advice of jesuits, and other wicked persons, having violated the *fundamental* laws, and *having withdrawn himself out of the kingdom,* hath *abdicated* the government, and the throne is thereby *vacant.*"

this accumulation of circumstances, serves to shew the spirit of caution which predominated in the national councils, in a situation in which men irritated by oppression, and elevated by a triumph over it, are apt to abandon themselves to violent and extreme courses: it shews the anxiety of the great men who influenced the conduct of affairs at that great event, to make the Revolution a parent of settlement, and not a nursery of future revolutions.

[32] No government could stand a moment, if it could be blown down with anything so loose and indefinite as an opinion of "*misconduct.*" They who led at the Revolution, grounded the virtual abdication of King James upon no such light and uncertain principle. They charged him with nothing less than a design, confirmed by a multitude of illegal overt acts, to *subvert the Protestant church and state,* and their *fundamental,* unquestionable laws and liberties: they charged him with having broken the *original contract* between king and people. This was more than *misconduct.* A grave and overruling necessity obliged them to take the step they took, and took with infinite reluctance, as under that most rigorous of all laws. Their trust for the future preservation of the constitution was not in future revolutions. The grand policy of all their regulations was to render it almost impracticable for any future sovereign to compel the states of the kingdom to have again recourse to those violent remedies. They left the crown what, in the eye and estimation of law, it had ever been, perfectly irresponsible. In order to lighten the crown still further, they aggravated responsibility on ministers of state. By the statute of the 1st of king William, sess. 2nd, called "*the act for declaring the rights and liberties of the subject, and for settling the succession of the crown,*" they enacted, that the ministers should serve the crown on the terms of that declaration. They secured soon after the *frequent meetings of parliament,* by which the whole government would be under the constant inspection and active controul of the popular representative and of the magnates of the kingdom. In the next great constitu-

tional act, that of the 12th and 13th of King William, for the further limitation of the crown, and *better* securing the rights and liberties of the subject, they provided, "that no pardon under the great seal of England should be pleadable to [33] impeachment by the commons in parliament." The rule laid down for government in the Declaration of Right, the constant inspection of parliament, the practical claim of impeachment, they thought infinitely a better security not only for their constitutional liberty, but against the vices of administration, than the reservation of a right so difficult in the practice, so uncertain in the issue, and often so mischievous in the consequences, as that of "cashiering their governors."

Dr. Price, in this sermon,* condemns very properly the practice of gross, adulatory addresses to kings. Instead of this fulsome style, he proposes that his majesty should be told, on occasions of congratulation, that "he is to consider himself as more properly the servant than the sovereign of his people." For a compliment, this new form of address does not seem to be very soothing. Those who are servants, in name, as well as in effect, do not like to be told of their situation, their duty, and their obligations. The slave, in the old play, tells his master, "*Haec commemoratio est quasi exprobratio.*" It is not pleasant as compliment; it is not wholesome as instruction. After all, if the king were to bring himself to echo this new kind of address, to adopt it in terms, and even to take the appellation of Servant of the People as his royal style, how either he or we should be much mended by it, I cannot imagine. I have seen very assuming letters, signed, "Your most obedient, humble servant." The proudest domination that ever was endured on earth took a title of still greater humility than that which is now proposed for sovereigns by the Apostle of Liberty. Kings and nations were trampled upon by the foot of one calling himself "the Servant of Servants"; and mandates for deposing sovereigns were sealed with the signet of "the Fisherman."

*P. 22, 23, 24.

[34] I should have considered all this as no more than a sort of flippant vain discourse, in which, as in an unsavoury fume, several persons suffer the spirit of liberty to evaporate, if it were not plainly in support of the idea, and a part of the scheme, of "cashiering kings for misconduct." In that light it is worth some observation.

Kings, in one sense, are undoubtedly the servants of the people, because their power has no other rational end than that of the general advantage; but it is not true that they are, in the ordinary sense (by our constitution, at least) any thing like servants; the essence of whose situation is to obey the commands of some other, and to be removeable at pleasure. But the king of Great Britain obeys no other person; all other persons are individually, and collectively too, under him, and owe to him a legal obedience. The law, which knows neither to flatter nor to insult, calls this high magistrate, not our servant, as this humble Divine calls him, but *"our sovereign Lord the King"*; and we, on our parts, have learned to speak only the primitive language of the law, and not the confused jargon of their Babylonian pulpits.

As he is not to obey us, but as we are to obey the law in him, our constitution has made no sort of provision towards rendering him, as a servant, in any degree responsible. Our constitution knows nothing of a magistrate like the *Justicia* of Arragon; nor of any court legally appointed, nor of any process legally settled for submitting the king to the responsibility belonging to all servants. In this he is not distinguished from the commons and the lords; who, in their several public capacities, can never be called to an account for their conduct; although the Revolution Society chooses to assert, in direct opposition to one of the wisest and most beautiful parts of our constitution, that "a king is no more than the first servant of the public, created by it, *and responsible to it.*"

[35] Ill would our ancestors at the Revolution have deserved their fame for wisdom, if they had found no security for their freedom, but in rendering their government

feeble in its operations, and precarious in its tenure; if they had been able to contrive no better remedy against arbitrary power than civil confusion. Let these gentlemen state who that *representative* public is to whom they will affirm the king, as a servant, to be responsible. It will be then time enough for me to produce to them the positive statute law which affirms that he is not.

The ceremony of cashiering kings, of which these gentlemen talk so much at their ease, can rarely, if ever, be performed without force. It then becomes a case of war, and not of constitution. Laws are commanded to hold their tongues amongst arms; and tribunals fall to the ground with the peace they are no longer able to uphold. The Revolution of 1688 was obtained by a just war, in the only case in which any war, and much more a civil war, can be just. "Justa bella quibus *necessaria*." The question of dethroning, or, if these gentlemen like the phrase better, "cashiering" kings, will always be, as it has always been, an extraordinary question of state, and wholly out of the law; a question (like all other questions of state) of dispositions, and of means, and of probable consequences, rather than of positive rights. As it was not made for common abuses, so it is not to be agitated by common minds. The speculative line of demarcation, where obedience ought to end, and resistance must begin, is faint, obscure, and not easily definable. It is not a single act, or a single event, which determines it. Governments must be abused and deranged indeed, before it can be thought of; and the prospect of the future must be as bad as the experience of the past. When things are in that lamentable condition, the nature of the disease is to indicate the remedy to those whom nature has qualified to [36] administer in extremities this critical, ambiguous, bitter potion to a distempered state. Times and occasions, and provocations, will teach their own lessons. The wise will determine from the gravity of the case; the irritable from sensibility to oppression; the high-minded from disdain and indignation at abusive power in unworthy hands;

the brave and bold from the love of honourable danger in a generous cause: but, with or without right, a revolution will be the very last resource of the thinking and the good.

THE THIRD HEAD OF RIGHT, asserted by the pulpit of the Old Jewry, namely, the "right to form a government for ourselves," has, at least, as little countenance from any thing done at the Revolution, either in precedent or principle, as the two first of their claims. The Revolution was made to preserve our *antient* indisputable laws and liberties, and that *antient* constitution of government which is our only security for law and liberty. If you are desirous of knowing the spirit of our constitution, and the policy which predominated in that great period which has secured it to this hour, pray look for both in our histories, in our records, in our acts of parliament, and journals of parliament, and not in the sermons of the Old Jewry, and the after-dinner toasts of the Revolution Society. In the former you will find other ideas and another language. Such a claim is as ill-suited to our temper and wishes as it is unsupported by any appearance of authority. The very idea of the fabrication of a new government is enough to fill us with disgust and horror. We wished at the period of the Revolution, and do now wish, to derive all we possess as *an inheritance from our forefathers.* Upon that body and stock of inheritance we have taken care not to inoculate any cyon alien to the nature of the original plant. All the reformations we have hitherto made, have proceeded upon the principle of reference to antiquity; and I hope, nay [37] I am persuaded, that all those which possibly may be made hereafter, will be carefully formed upon analogical precedent, authority, and example.

Our oldest reformation is that of Magna Charta. You will see that Sir Edward Coke, that great oracle of our law, and indeed all the great men who follow him, to Blackstone,* are

---

*See Blackstone's Magna Charta, printed at Oxford, 1759.

industrious to prove the pedigree of our liberties. They endeavour to prove, that the antient charter, the Magna Charta of King John, was connected with another positive charter from Henry I. and that both the one and the other were nothing more than a re-affirmance of the still more antient standing law of the kingdom. In the matter of fact, for the greater part, these authors appear to be in the right; perhaps not always: but if the lawyers mistake in some particulars, it proves my position still the more strongly; because it demonstrates the powerful prepossession towards antiquity, with which the minds of all our lawyers and legislators, and of all the people whom they wish to influence, have been always filled; and the stationary policy of this kingdom in considering their most sacred rights and franchises as an *inheritance.*

In the famous law of the 3rd of Charles I. called the *Petition of Right,* the parliament says to the king, "Your subjects have *inherited* this freedom," claiming their franchises, not on abstract principles as the "rights of men," but as the rights of Englishmen, and as a patrimony derived from their forefathers. Selden, and the other profoundly learned men, who drew this petition of right, were as well acquainted, at least, with all the general theories concerning the "rights of men," as any of the discoursers in our pulpits, or on your tribune; full as well as Dr. Price, or as the Abbé Sieyes. But, for reasons worthy of that practical wisdom which superseded their theoretic science, they preferred this positive, [38] recorded, *hereditary* title to all which can be dear to the man and the citizen, to that vague speculative right, which exposed their sure inheritance to be scrambled for and torn to pieces by every wild litigious spirit.

The same policy pervades all the laws which have since been made for the preservation of our liberties. In the 1st of William and Mary, in the famous statute, called the Declaration of Right, the two houses utter not a syllable of "a right to frame a government for themselves." You will see, that their whole care was to secure the religion, laws, and liberties, that had been long possessed, and had been lately endangered. "Taking* into their most serious consideration the *best* means for making such an establishment, that their religion, laws, and liberties might not be in danger of being again subverted," they auspicate all their proceedings, by stating as some of those *best* means, "in the *first place*" to do "as their *ancestors in like cases have usually* done for vindicating their *antient* rights and liberties, to *declare*"; and then they pray the king and queen, "that it may be *declared* and enacted, that *all and singular* the rights and liberties *asserted and declared* are the true *antient* and indubitable rights and liberties of the people of this kingdom."

You will observe, that from Magna Charta to the Declaration of Right, it has been the uniform policy of our constitution to claim and assert our liberties, as an *entailed inheritance* derived to us from our forefathers, and to be transmitted to our posterity; as an estate specially belonging to the people of this kingdom without any reference whatever to any other more general or prior right. By this means our constitution preserves an unity in so great a diversity of its parts. We have an inheritable crown; an inheritable peerage; and an house of commons and a people inheriting privileges, franchises, and liberties, from a long line of ancestors.

[39] This policy appears to me to be the result of profound reflection; or rather the happy effect of following nature, which is wisdom without reflection, and above it. A spirit of innovation is generally the result of a selfish temper and confined views. People will not look forward to posterity, who never look backward to their ancestors. Besides, the people of England well know, that the idea of inheritance furnishes a sure principle of conservation, and a sure principle of transmission; without at all excluding a principle of

* 1 W. and M.

improvement. It leaves acquisition free; but it secures what it acquires. Whatever advantages are obtained by a state proceeding on these maxims, are locked fast as in a sort of family settlement; grasped as in a kind of mortmain for ever. By a constitutional policy, working after the pattern of nature, we receive, we hold, we transmit our government and our privileges, in the same manner in which we enjoy and transmit our property and our lives. The institutions of policy, the goods of fortune, the gifts of Providence, are handed down, to us and from us, in the same course and order. Our political system is placed in a just correspondence and symmetry with the order of the world, and with the mode of existence decreed to a permanent body composed of transitory parts; wherein, by the disposition of a stupenduous wisdom, moulding together the great mysterious incorporation of the human race, the whole, at one time, is never old, or middle-aged, or young, but in a condition of unchangeable constancy, moves on through the varied tenour of perpetual decay, fall, renovation, and progression. Thus, by preserving the method of nature in the conduct of the state, in what we improve, we are never wholly new; in what we retain we are never wholly obsolete. By adhering in this manner and on those principles to our forefathers, we are guided not by the superstition of antiquarians, but by the spirit of philosophic analogy. In this [40] choice of inheritance we have given to our frame of polity the image of a relation in blood; binding up the constitution of our country with our dearest domestic ties; adopting our fundamental laws into the bosom of our family affections; keeping inseparable, and cherishing with the warmth of all their combined and mutually reflected charities, our state, our hearths, our sepulchres, and our altars.

Through the same plan of a conformity to nature in our artificial institutions, and by calling in the aid of her unerring and powerful instincts, to fortify the fallible and feeble contrivances of our reason, we have derived several other, and those no small benefits, from considering our liberties in the light of an inheritance. Always acting as if in the presence of canonized forefathers, the spirit of freedom, leading in itself to misrule and excess, is tempered with an awful gravity. This idea of a liberal descent inspires us with a sense of habitual native dignity, which prevents that upstart insolence almost inevitably adhering to and disgracing those who are the first acquirers of any distinction. By this means our liberty becomes a noble freedom. It carries an imposing and majestic aspect. It has a pedigree and illustrating ancestors. It has its bearings and its ensigns armorial. It has its gallery of portraits; its monumental inscriptions; its records, evidences, and titles. We procure reverence to our civil institutions on the principle upon which nature teaches us to revere individual men; on account of their age; and on account of those from whom they are descended. All your sophisters cannot produce any thing better adapted to preserve a rational and manly freedom than the course that we have pursued, who have chosen our nature rather than our speculations, our breasts rather than our inventions, for the great conservatories and magazines of our rights and privileges.

[41] You might, if you pleased, have profited of our example, and have given to your recovered freedom a correspondent dignity. Your privileges, though discontinued, were not lost to memory. Your constitution, it is true, whilst you were out of possession, suffered waste and dilapidation; but you possessed in some parts the walls, and in all the foundations, of a noble and venerable castle. You might have repaired those walls; you might have built on those old foundations. Your constitution was suspended before it was perfected; but you had the elements of a constitution very nearly as good as could be wished. In your old states you possessed that variety of parts corresponding with the various descriptions of which your community was happily composed; you had all that combination, and all that opposition of interests,

you had that action and counteraction which, in the natural and in the political world, from the reciprocal struggle of discordant powers, draws out the harmony of the universe. These opposed and conflicting interests, which you considered as so great a blemish in your old and in our present constitution, interpose a salutary check to all precipitate resolutions; they render deliberation a matter not of choice, but of necessity; they make all change a subject of *compromise*, which naturally begets moderation; they produce *temperaments*, preventing the sore evil of harsh, crude, unqualified reformations; and rendering all the headlong exertions of arbitrary power, in the few or in the many, for ever impracticable. Through that diversity of members and interests, general liberty had as many securities as there were separate views in the several orders; whilst by pressing down the whole by the weight of a real monarchy, the separate parts would have been prevented from warping and starting from their allotted places.

You had all these advantages in your antient states; but you chose to act as if you had never been moulded into civil [42] society, and had everything to begin anew. You began ill, because you began by despising everything that belonged to you. You set up your trade without a capital. If the last generations of your country appeared without much lustre in your eyes, you might have passed them by, and derived your claims from a more early race of ancestors. Under a pious predilection for those ancestors, your imaginations would have realized in them a standard of virtue and wisdom, beyond the vulgar practice of the hour: and you would have risen with the example to whose imitation you aspired. Respecting your forefathers, you would have been taught to respect yourselves. You would not have chosen to consider the French as a people of yesterday, as a nation of low-born servile wretches until the emancipating year of 1789. In order to furnish, at the expence of your honour, an excuse to your apologists here for several enormities of yours, you would not have been content to be represented as a gang of Maroon slaves, suddenly broke loose from the house of bondage, and therefore to be pardoned for your abuse of the liberty to which you were not accustomed and ill fitted. Would it not, my worthy friend, have been wiser to have you thought, what I, for one, always thought you, a generous and gallant nation, long misled to your disadvantage by your high and romantic sentiments of fidelity, honour, and loyalty; that events had been unfavourable to you, but that you were not enslaved through any illiberal or servile disposition; that in your most devoted submission, you were actuated by a principle of public spirit, and that it was your country you worshipped, in the person of your king? Had you made it to be understood, that in the delusion of this amiable error you had gone further than your wise ancestors; that you were resolved to resume your ancient privileges, whilst you preserved the spirit of your ancient and your recent loyalty and honour; or, if diffident of yourselves, and [43] not clearly discerning the almost obliterated constitution of your ancestors, you had looked to your neighbours in this land, who had kept alive the ancient principles and models of the old common law of Europe meliorated and adapted to its present state — by following wise examples you would have given new examples of wisdom to the world. You would have rendered the cause of liberty venerable in the eyes of every worthy mind in every nation. You would have shamed despotism from the earth, by showing that freedom was not only reconcileable, but as, when well disciplined it is, auxiliary to law. You would have had an unoppressive but a productive revenue. You would have had a flourishing commerce to feed it. You would have had a free constitution; a potent monarchy; a disciplined army; a reformed and venerated clergy; a mitigated but spirited nobility, to lead your virtue, not to overlay it; you would have had a liberal order of commons, to emulate and to recruit that nobility; you

would have had a protected, satisfied, laborious, and obedient people, taught to seek and to recognize the happiness
that is to be found by virtue in all conditions; in which consists the true moral equality of mankind, and not in that
monstrous fiction, which, by inspiring false ideas and vain expectations into men destined to travel in the obscure walk of
laborious life, serves only to aggravate and imbitter that real
inequality, which it never can remove; and which the order
of civil life establishes as much for the benefit of those whom
it must leave in an humble state, as those whom it is able to
exalt to a condition more splendid, but not more happy. You
had a smooth and easy career of felicity and glory laid open
to you, beyond anything recorded in the history of the world;
but you have shewn that difficulty is good for man.

Compute your gains: see what is got by those extravagant and presumptuous speculations which have taught your
[44] leaders to despise all their predecessors, and all their
contemporaries, and even to despise themselves, until the
moment in which they became truly despicable. By following
those false lights, France has bought undisguised calamities
at a higher price than any nation has purchased the most
unequivocal blessings. France has bought poverty by crime!
France has not sacrificed her virtue to her interest; but she
has abandoned her interest, that she might prostitute her
virtue. All other nations have begun the fabric of a new
government, or the reformation of an old, by establishing
originally, or by enforcing with greater exactness, some rites
or other of religion. All other people have laid the foundations of civil freedom in severer manners, and a system of a
more austere and masculine morality. France, when she let
loose the reins of regal authority, doubled the licence, of a
ferocious dissoluteness in manners, and of an insolent irreligion in opinions and practices; and has extended through all
ranks of life, as if she were communicating some privilege, or
laying open some secluded benefit, all the unhappy corrup-

tions that usually were the disease of wealth and power. This is one of the new principles of equality in France.

France, by the perfidy of her leaders, has utterly disgraced the tone of lenient council in the cabinets of princes, and disarmed it of its most potent topics. She has sanctified the dark suspicious maxims of tyrannous distrust; and taught kings to tremble at (what will hereafter be called) the delusive plausibilities of moral politicians. Sovereigns will consider those who advise them to place an unlimited confidence in their people, as subverters of their thrones; as traitors who aim at their destruction, by leading their easy good-nature, under specious pretences, to admit combinations of bold and faithless men into a participation of their power. This alone, if there were nothing else, is an irreparable calamity to you and to mankind. Remember that [45] your parliament of Paris told your king, that in calling the states together, he had nothing to fear but the prodigal excess of their zeal in providing for the support of the throne. It is right that these men should hide their heads. It is right that they should bear their part in the ruin which their counsel has brought on their sovereign and their country. Such sanguine declarations tend to lull authority asleep; to encourage it rashly to engage in perilous adventures of untried policy; to neglect those provisions, preparations, and precautions, which distinguish benevolence from imbecillity; and without which no man can answer for the salutary effect of any abstract plan of government or of freedom. For want of these, they have seen the medicine of the state corrupted into its poison. They have seen the French rebel against a mild and lawful monarch, with more fury, outrage, and insult, than ever any people has been known to rise against the most illegal usurper, or the most sanguinary tyrant. Their resistance was made to concession; their revolt was from protection; their blow was aimed at an hand holding out graces, favours, and immunities.

This was unnatural. The rest is in order. They have found

their punishment in their success. Laws overturned; tribunals subverted; industry without vigour; commerce expiring; the revenue unpaid, yet the people impoverished; a church pillaged, and a state not relieved; civil and military anarchy made the constitution of the kingdom; every thing human and divine sacrificed to the idol of public credit, and national bankruptcy the consequence; and to crown all, the paper securities of new, precarious, tottering power, the discredited paper securities of impoverished fraud, and beggared rapine, held out as a currency for the support of an empire, in lieu of the two great recognised species that represent the lasting conventional credit of mankind, which disappeared and hid themselves in the earth from whence [46] they came, when the principle of property, whose creatures and representatives they are, was systematically subverted.

Were all these dreadful things necessary? Were they the inevitable results of the desperate struggle of determined patriots, compelled to wade through blood and tumult, to the quiet shore of a tranquil and prosperous liberty? No! nothing like it. The fresh ruins of France, which shock our feelings wherever we can turn our eyes, are not the devastation of civil war; they are the sad but instructive monuments of rash and ignorant counsel in time of profound peace. They are the display of inconsiderate and presumptuous, because unresisted and irresistible authority. The persons who have thus squandered away the precious treasure of their crimes, the persons who have made this prodigal and wild waste of public evils (the last stake reserved for the ultimate ransom of the state) have met in their progress with little, or rather with no opposition at all. Their whole march was more like a triumphal procession than the progress of a war. Their pioneers have gone before them, and demolished and laid every thing level at their feet. Not one drop of *their* blood have they shed in the cause of the country they have ruined. They have made no sacrifices to their projects of greater consequence than their shoebuckles, whilst they were imprisoning their king, murdering their fellow citizens, and bathing in tears, and plunging in poverty and distress, thousands of worthy men and worthy families. Their cruelty has not even been the base result of fear. It has been the effect of their sense of perfect safety, in authorizing treasons, robberies, rapes, assassinations, slaughters, and burnings throughout their harrassed land. But the cause of all was plain from the beginning.

THIS UNFORCED CHOICE, this fond election of evil, would [47] appear perfectly unaccountable, if we did not consider the composition of the National Assembly; I do not mean its formal constitution, which, as it now stands, is exceptionable enough, but the materials of which in a great measure it is composed, which is of ten thousand times greater consequence than all the formalities in the world. If we were to know nothing of this Assembly but by its title and function, no colours could paint to the imagination any thing more venerable. In that light the mind of an enquirer, subdued by such an awful image as that of the virtue and wisdom of a whole people collected into a focus, would pause and hesitate in condemning things even of the very worst aspect. Instead of blameable, they would appear only mysterious. But no name, no power, no function, no artificial institution whatsoever, can make the men of whom any system of authority is composed, any other than God, and nature, and education, and their habits of life have made them. Capacities beyond these the people have not to give. Virtue and wisdom may be the objects of their choice; but their choice confers neither the one nor the other on those upon whom they lay their ordaining hands. They have not the engagement of nature, they have not the promise of revelation for any such powers.

AFTER I HAD READ OVER the list of the persons and descriptions elected into the *Tiers Etat*, nothing which they afterwards did could appear astonishing. Among them, indeed, I saw some of known rank; some of shining talents; but of any practical experience in the state, not one man was to be found. The best were only men of theory. But whatever the distinguished few may have been, it is the substance and mass of the body which constitutes its character, and must finally determine its direction. In all bodies, those who will lead, must also, in a considerable degree, follow. [48] They must conform their propositions to the taste, talent, and disposition of those whom they wish to conduct: therefore, if an Assembly is viciously or feebly composed in a very great part of it, nothing but such a supreme degree of virtue as very rarely appears in the world, and for that reason cannot enter into calculation, will prevent the men of talents disseminated through it from becoming only the expert instruments of absurd projects. If, what is the more likely event, instead of that unusual degree of virtue, they should be actuated by sinister ambition and a lust of meretricious glory, then the feeble part of the Assembly, to whom at first they conform, becomes in its turn the dupe and instrument of their designs. In this political traffick the leaders will be obliged to bow to the ignorance of their followers, and the followers to become subservient to the worst designs of their leaders.

To secure any degree of sobriety in the propositions made by the leaders in any public assembly, they ought to respect, in some degree perhaps to fear, those whom they conduct. To be led any otherwise than blindly, the followers must be qualified, if not for actors, at least for judges; they must also be judges of natural weight and authority. Nothing can secure a steady and moderate conduct in such assemblies, but that the body of them should be respectably composed, in point of condition in life, of permanent property, of education, and of such habits as enlarge and liberalize the understanding.

In the calling of the states general of France, the first thing which struck me, was a great departure from the antient course. I found the representation for the Third Estate composed of six hundred persons. They were equal in number to the representatives of both of the other orders. If the orders were to act separately, the number would not, beyond the consideration of the expence, be of much [49] moment. But when it became apparent that the three orders were to be melted down into one, the policy and necessary effect of this numerous representation became obvious. A very small desertion from either of the other two orders must throw the power of both into the hands of the third. In fact, the whole power of the state was soon resolved into that body. Its due composition became therefore of infinitely the greater importance.

Judge, Sir, of my surprize, when I found that a very great proportion of the Assembly (a majority, I believe, of the members who attended) was composed of practitioners in the law. It was composed not of distinguished magistrates, who had given pledges to their country of their science, prudence, and integrity; not of leading advocates, the glory of the bar; not of renowned professors in universities—but for the far greater part, as it must in such a number, of the inferior, unlearned, mechanical, merely instrumental members of the profession. There were distinguished exceptions; but the general composition was of obscure provincial advocates, of stewards of petty local jurisdictions, country attornies, notaries, and the whole train of the ministers of municipal litigation, the fomenters and conductors of the petty war of village vexation. From the moment I read the list I saw distinctly, and very nearly as it has happened, all that was to follow.

The degree of estimation in which any profession is held becomes the standard of the estimation in which the professors hold themselves. Whatever the personal merits of many individual lawyers might have been, and in many it was undoubtedly very considerable, in that military kingdom, no part of the profession had been much regarded, except the highest of all, who often united to their professional offices great family splendour, and were invested with great power and authority. These certainly were highly respected, and even with no small degree of awe. The next rank was not [50] much esteemed; the mechanical part was in a very low degree of repute.

Whenever the supreme authority is invested in a body so composed, it must evidently produce the consequences of supreme authority placed in the hands of men not taught habitually to respect themselves; who had no previous fortune in character at stake; who could not be expected to bear with moderation, or to conduct with discretion, a power which they themselves, more than any others, must be surprized to find in their hands. Who could flatter himself that these men, suddenly, and, as it were, by enchantment, snatched from the humblest rank of subordination, would not be intoxicated with their unprepared greatness? Who could conceive, that men who are habitually meddling, daring, subtle, active, of litigious dispositions and unquiet minds, would easily fall back into their old condition of obscure contention, and laborious, low, unprofitable chicane? Who could doubt but that, at any expence to the state, of which they understood nothing, they must pursue their private interests, which they understood but too well? It was not an event depending on chance or contingency. It was inevitable; it was necessary; it was planted in the nature of things. They must *join* (if their capacity did not permit them to *lead*) in any project which could procure to them a *litigious constitution;* which could lay open to them those innumerable lucrative jobs which follow in the train of all great convulsions and revolutions in the state, and particularly in all great and violent permutations of property. Was it to be expected that they would attend to the stability of property, whose existence had always depended upon whatever rendered property questionable, ambiguous, and insecure? Their objects would be enlarged with their elevation, but their disposition and habits, and mode of accomplishing their designs, must remain the same.

[51] Well! but these men were to be tempered and restrained by other descriptions, of more sober minds, and more enlarged understandings. Were they then to be awed by the super-eminent authority and awful dignity of an handful of country clowns who have seats in that Assembly, some of whom are said not to be able to read and write? and by not a greater number of traders, who, though somewhat more instructed, and more conspicuous in the order of society, had never known any thing beyond their counting-house? No! both these descriptions were more formed to be overborne and swayed by the intrigues and artifices of lawyers, than to become their counterpoise. With such a dangerous disproportion, the whole must needs be governed by them. To the faculty of law was joined a pretty considerable proportion of the faculty of medicine. This faculty had not, any more than that of the law, possessed in France its just estimation. Its professors therefore must have the qualities of men not habituated to sentiments of dignity. But supposing they had ranked as they ought to do, and as with us they do actually, the sides of sick beds are not the academies for forming statesmen and legislators. Then came the dealers in stocks and funds, who must be eager, at any expence, to change their ideal paper wealth for the more solid substance of land. To these were joined men of other descriptions, from whom as little knowledge of or attention to the interests of a great state was to be expected, and as little regard to the stability of any institution; men formed to be instruments, not controls. Such in general was the composition of the *Tiers Etat* in the National Assembly; in which was scarcely to be perceived the slightest traces of what we call the natural landed interest of the country.

We know that the British house of commons, without shutting its doors to any merit in any class, is, by the sure operation of adequate causes, filled with every thing illustrious [52] in rank, in descent, in hereditary and in acquired opulence, in cultivated talents, in military, civil, naval, and politic distinction, that the country can afford. But supposing, what hardly can be supposed as a case, that the house of commons should be composed in the same manner with the Tiers Etat in France, would this dominion of chicane be borne with patience, or even conceived without horror? God forbid I should insinuate any thing derogatory to that profession, which is another priesthood, administering the rites of sacred justice. But whilst I revere men in the functions which belong to them, and would do as much as one man can do, to prevent their exclusion from any, I cannot, to flatter them, give the lye to nature. They are good and useful in the composition; they must be mischievous if they preponderate so as virtually to become the whole. Their very excellence in their peculiar functions may be far from a qualification for others. It cannot escape observation, that when men are too much confined to professional and faculty habits, and, as it were, inveterate in the recurrent employment of that narrow circle, they are rather disabled than qualified for whatever depends on the knowledge of mankind, on experience in mixed affairs, on a comprehensive connected view of the various complicated external and internal interests which go to the formation of that multifarious thing called a state.

After all, if the house of commons were to have an wholly professional and faculty composition, what is the power of the house of commons, circumscribed and shut in by the immoveable barriers of laws, usages, positive rules of doctrine and practice, counterpoized by the house of lords, and every moment of its existence at the discretion of the crown to continue, prorogue, or dissolve us? The power of the house of commons, direct or indirect, is indeed great; and long may it be able to preserve its greatness, and the spirit belonging [53] to true greatness, at the full; and it will do so, as long as it can keep the breakers of law in India from becoming the makers of law for England. The power, however, of the house of commons, when least diminished, is as a drop of water in the ocean, compared to that residing in a settled majority of your National Assembly. That Assembly, since the destruction of the orders, has no fundamental law, no strict convention, no respected usage to restrain it. Instead of finding themselves obliged to conform to a fixed constitution, they have a power to make a constitution which shall conform to their designs. Nothing in heaven or upon earth can serve as a control on them. What ought to be the heads, the hearts, the dispositions, that are qualified, or that dare, not only to make laws under a fixed constitution, but at one heat to strike out a totally new constitution for a great kingdom, and in every part of it, from the monarch on the throne to the vestry of a parish? But—"*Fools rush in where angels fear to tread.*" In such a state of unbounded power, for undefined and undefinable purposes, the evil of a moral and almost physical inaptitude of the man to the function must be the greatest we can conceive to happen in the management of human affairs.

HAVING CONSIDERED the composition of the third estate as it stood in its original frame, I took a view of the representatives of the clergy. There too it appeared, that full as little regard was had to the general security of property, or to the aptitude of the deputies for their public purposes, in the principles of their election. That election was so contrived as to send a very large proportion of mere country curates to the great and arduous work of new-modelling a state; men who never had seen the state so much as in a picture; men who knew nothing of the world beyond the bounds of an obscure village; who, immersed in hopeless [54] poverty, could regard all property, whether secular or ecclesiastical, with no other eye than that of envy; among whom must be many, who, for the smallest hope of the meanest dividend in plunder, would readily join in any attempts upon a body of wealth, in which they could hardly look to have any share, except in a general scramble. Instead of balancing the power of the active chicaners in the other assembly, these curates must necessarily become the active coadjutors, or at best the passive instruments of those by whom they had been habitually guided in their petty village concerns. They too could hardly be the most conscientious of their kind, who, presuming upon their incompetent understanding, could intrigue for a trust which led them from their natural relation to their flocks, and their natural spheres of action, to undertake the regeneration of kingdoms. This preponderating weight being added to the force of the body of chicane in the Tiers Etat, compleated that momentum of ignorance, rashness, presumption, and lust of plunder, which nothing has been able to resist.

To observing men it must have appeared from the beginning, that the majority of the Third Estate, in conjunction with such a deputation from the clergy as I have described, whilst it pursued the destruction of the nobility, would inevitably become subservient to the worst designs of individuals in that class. In the spoil and humiliation of their own order these individuals would possess a sure fund for the pay of their new followers. To squander away the objects which made the happiness of their fellows, would be to them no sacrifice at all. Turbulent, discontented men of quality, in proportion as they are puffed up with personal pride and arrogance, generally despise their own order. One of the first symptoms they discover of a selfish and mischievous ambition, is a profligate disregard of a dignity which they [55] partake with others. To be attached to the subdivision, to love the little platoon we belong to in society, is the first principle (the germ as it were) of public affections. It is the first link in the series by which we proceed towards a love to our country and to mankind. The interests of that portion of social arrangement is a trust in the hands of all those who compose it; and as none but bad men would justify it in abuse, none but traitors would barter it away for their own personal advantage.

There were, in the time of our civil troubles in England (I do not know whether you have any such in your Assembly in France) several persons, like the then Earl of Holland, who by themselves or their families had brought an odium on the throne, by the prodigal dispensation of its bounties towards them, who afterwards joined in the rebellions arising from the discontents of which they were themselves the cause; men who helped to subvert that throne to which they owed, some of them, their existence, others all that power which they employed to ruin their benefactor. If any bounds are set to the rapacious demands of that sort of people, or that others are permitted to partake in the objects they would engross, revenge and envy soon fill up the craving void that is left in their avarice. Confounded by the complication of distempered passions, their reason is disturbed; their views become vast and perplexed; to others inexplicable; to themselves uncertain. They find, on all sides, bounds to their unprincipled ambition in any fixed order of things. But in the fog and haze of confusion all is enlarged, and appears without any limit.

When men of rank sacrifice all ideas of dignity to an ambition without a distinct object, and work with low instruments and for low ends, the whole composition becomes low and base. Does not something like this now appear in France? Does it not produce something ignoble and [56] inglorious? a kind of meanness in all the prevalent policy? a tendency in all that is done to lower along with individuals all the dignity and importance of the state? Other revolutions have been conducted by persons, who whilst they attempted or effected changes in the commonwealth, sanctified their ambition by advancing the dignity of the people whose peace they troubled. They had long views. They aimed at the rule, not

at the destruction of their country. They were men of great
civil, and great military talents, and if the terror, the ornament of their age. They were not like Jew brokers contending
with each other who could best remedy with fraudulent circulation and depreciated paper the wretchedness and ruin
brought on their country by their degenerate counsels. The
compliment made to one of the great bad men of the old
stamp (Cromwell) by his kinsman, a favourite poet of that
time, shews what it was he proposed, and what indeed to a
great degree he accomplished in the success of his ambition:

Still as *you* rise, the *state*, exalted too,
Finds no distemper whilst 'tis changed by *you;*
Chang'd like the world's great scene, when without noise
The rising sun night's *vulgar* lights destroys.

These disturbers were not so much like men usurping
power, as asserting their natural place in society. Their rising
was to illuminate and beautify the world. Their conquest over
their competitors was by outshining them. The hand that,
like a destroying angel, smote the country, communicated to
it the force and energy under which it suffered. I do not say,
(God forbid)—I do not say, that the virtues of such men were
to be taken as a balance to their crimes; but they were some
corrective to their effects. Such was, as I said, our Cromwell.
Such were your whole race of Guises, Condés, and Colignis.
Such the Richlieus, who in more quiet times acted in the
spirit of a civil war. Such, as better men, and in a less dubious
[57] cause, were your Henry the 4th and your Sully, though
nursed in civil confusions, and not wholly without some of
their taint. It is a thing to be wondered at, to see how very
soon France, when she had a moment to respire, recovered
and emerged from the longest and most dreadful civil war
that ever was known in any nation. Why? Because, among all
their massacres, they had not slain the *mind* in their country.

A conscious dignity, a noble pride, a generous sense of glory and emulation, was not extinguished. On the contrary, it was kindled and inflamed. The organs also of the state, however shattered, existed. All the prizes of honour and virtue, all the rewards, all the distinctions, remained. But your present confusion, like a palsy, has attacked the fountain of life itself. Every person in your country, in a situation to be actuated by a principle of honour, is disgraced and degraded, and can entertain no sensation of life, except in a mortified and humiliated indignation. But this generation will quickly pass away. The next generation of the nobility will resemble the artificers and clowns, and money-jobbers, usurers, and Jews, who will be always their fellows, sometimes their masters. Believe me, Sir, those who attempt to level, never equalize. In all societies, consisting of various descriptions of citizens, some description must be uppermost. The levellers therefore only change and pervert the natural order of things; they load the edifice of society, by setting up in the air what the solidity of the structure requires to be on the ground. The associations of taylors and carpenters, of which the republic (of Paris, for instance) is composed, cannot be equal to the situation, into which, by the worst of usurpations, an usurpation on the prerogatives of nature, you attempt to force them.

The chancellor of France at the opening of the states, [58] said, in a tone of oratorial flourish, that all occupations were honourable. If he meant only, that no honest employment was disgraceful, he would not have gone beyond the truth. But in asserting, that any thing is honourable, we imply some distinction in its favour. The occupation of an hair-dresser, or of a working tallow-chandler, cannot be a matter of honour to any person—to say nothing of a number of other more servile employments. Such descriptions of men ought not to suffer oppression from the state; but the state suffers oppression, if such as they, either individually or collectively, are permitted to rule. In this you think you are combating prejudice, but you are at war with nature.*

I do not, my dear Sir, conceive you to be of that sophistical captious spirit, or of that uncandid dulness, as to require, for every general observation or sentiment, an explicit detail of the correctives and exceptions, which reason will presume to be included in all the general propositions which come from reasonable men. You do not imagine, that I wish to confine power, authority, and distinction to blood, and names, and titles. No, Sir. There is no qualification for government, but virtue and wisdom, actual or presumptive. Wherever they are actually found, [59] they have, in whatever state, condition, profession or trade, the passport of Heaven to human place and honour. Woe to the country which would madly and impiously reject the service of the talents and virtues, civil, military, or religious, that are given to grace and to serve it; and would condemn to obscurity every thing formed to diffuse lustre and glory around a state. Woe to that country too, that passing into the opposite extreme, considers a low education, a mean contracted view of things, a sordid mercenary occupation, as a preferable title to command. Every thing

---

*Ecclesiasticus, chap. xxxviii. verses 24, 25. "The wisdom of a learned man cometh by opportunity of leisure: and he that hath little business shall become wise." "How can he get wisdom that holdeth the plough, and that glorieth in the goad; that driveth oxen; and is occupied in their labours; and whose talk is of bullocks?"

Ver. 27. "So every carpenter and work-master that laboureth night and day." &c.

Ver. 33. "They shall not be sought for in public counsel, nor sit high in the congregation: They shall not sit on the judges seat, nor understand the sentence of judgment: they cannot declare justice and judgment, and they shall not be found where parables are spoken."

Ver. 34. "But they will maintain the state of the world."

I do not determine whether this book be canonical, as the Gallican church (till lately) has considered it, or apocryphal, as here it is taken. I am sure it contains a great deal of sense, and truth.

ought to be open; but not indifferently to every man. No rotation; no appointment by lot; no mode of election operating in the spirit of sortition or rotation, can be generally good in a government conversant in extensive objects. Because they have no tendency, direct or indirect, to select the man with a view to the duty, or to accommodate the one to the other. I do not hesitate to say, that the road to eminence and power, from obscure condition, ought not to be made too easy, nor a thing too much of course. If rare merit be the rarest of all rare things, it ought to pass through some sort of probation. The temple of honour ought to be seated on an eminence. If it be open through virtue, let it be remembered too, that virtue is never tried but by some difficulty, and some struggle.

Nothing is a due and adequate representation of a state, that does not represent its ability, as well as its property. But as ability is a vigorous and active principle, and as property is sluggish, inert, and timid, it never can be safe from the invasions of ability, unless it be, out of all proportion, predominant in the representation. It must be represented too in great masses of accumulation, or it is not rightly protected. The characteristic essence of property, formed out of the combined principles of its acquisition [60] and conservation, is to be *unequal*. The great masses therefore which excite envy, and tempt rapacity, must be put out of the possibility of danger. Then they form a natural rampart about the lesser properties in all their gradations. The same quantity of property, which is by the natural course of things divided among many, has not the same operation. Its defensive power is weakened as it is diffused. In this diffusion each man's portion is less than what, in the eagerness of his desires, he may flatter himself to obtain by dissipating the accumulations of others. The plunder of the few would indeed give but a share inconceivably small in the distribution to the many. But the many are not capable of making this calculation; and those who lead them to rapine, never intend this distribution.

The power of perpetuating our property in our families is one of the most valuable and interesting circumstances belonging to it, and that which tends the most to the perpetuation of society itself. It makes our weakness subservient to our virtue; it grafts benevolence even upon avarice. The possessors of family wealth, and of the distinction which attends hereditary possession (as most concerned in it) are the natural securities for this transmission. With us, the house of peers is formed upon this principle. It is wholly composed of hereditary property and hereditary distinction; and made therefore the third of the legislature; and in the last event, the sole judge of all property in all its subdivisions. The house of commons too, though not necessarily, yet in fact, is always so composed in the far greater part. Let those large proprietors be what they will, and they have their chance of being amongst the best, they are at the very worst, the ballast in the vessel of the commonwealth. For though hereditary wealth, and the rank which goes with it, are too much idolized by creeping sycophants, and the blind abject admirers of power, [61] they are too rashly slighted in shallow speculations of the petulant, assuming, short-sighted coxcombs of philosophy. Some decent regulated pre-eminence, some preference (not exclusive appropriation) given to birth, is neither unnatural, nor unjust, nor impolitic.

It is said, that twenty-four millions ought to prevail over two hundred thousand. True; if the constitution of a kingdom be a problem of arithmetic. This sort of discourse does well enough with the lamp-post for its second: to men who *may* reason calmly, it is ridiculous. The will of the many, and their interest, must very often differ; and great will be the difference when they make an evil choice. A government of five hundred country attornies and obscure curates is not good for twenty-four millions of men, though it were chosen by eight and forty millions; nor is it the better for being guided by a dozen of persons of quality, who have betrayed their trust in order to obtain that power. At present, you seem in everything to have strayed out of the high road of nature. The property of France does not govern it. Of course property is destroyed, and rational liberty has no existence. All you have got for the present is a paper circulation, and a stock-jobbing constitution: and as to the future, do you seriously think that the territory of France, under the republican system of eighty-three independent municipalities, (to say nothing of the parts that compose them) can ever be governed as one body, or can ever be set in motion by the impulse of one mind? When the National Assembly has completed its work, it will have accomplished its ruin. These commonwealths will not long bear a state of subjection to the republic of Paris. They will not bear that this one body should monopolize the captivity of the king, and the dominion over the assembly calling itself National. Each will keep its own portion of the spoil of the church to itself; and it will not suffer either [62] that spoil, or the more just fruits of their industry, or the natural produce of their soil, to be sent to swell the insolence, or pamper the luxury of the mechanics of Paris. In this they will see none of the equality, under the pretence of which they have been tempted to throw off their allegiance to their sovereign, as well as the antient constitution of their country. There can be no capital city in such a constitution as they have lately made. They have forgot, that when they framed democratic governments, they had virtually dismembered their country. The person whom they persevere in calling king, has not power left to him by the hundredth part sufficient to hold together this collection of republics. The republic of Paris will endeavour indeed to compleat the debauchery of the army, and illegally to perpetuate the assembly, without resort to its constituents, as the means of continuing its despotism. It will make efforts, by becoming the heart of a boundless paper circulation, to draw every thing to itself; but in vain. All this policy in the end will appear as feeble as it is now violent.

IF THIS BE YOUR ACTUAL SITUATION, compared to the situation to which you were called, as it were by the voice of God and man, I cannot find it in my heart to congratulate you on the choice you have made, or the success which has attended your endeavours. I can as little recommend to any other nation a conduct grounded on such principles, and productive of such effects. That I must leave to those who can see further into your affairs than I am able to do, and who best know how far your actions are favourable to their designs. The gentlemen of the Revolution Society, who were so early in their congratulations, appear to be strongly of opinion that there is some scheme of politics relative to this country, in which your proceedings may, in some way, be useful. For your Dr. Price, who seems [63] to have speculated himself into no small degree of fervour upon this subject, addresses his auditory in the following very remarkable words: "I cannot conclude without recalling *particularly* to your recollection a consideration which I have *more than once alluded to,* and which probably your thoughts have *been all along anticipating;* a consideration with which my *mind is impressed more than I can express.* I mean the consideration of the *favourableness of the present times to all exertions in the cause of liberty.*"

It is plain that the mind of this political Preacher was at the time big with some extraordinary design; and it is very probable, that the thoughts of his audience, who understood him better than I do, did all along run before him in his reflection, and in the whole train of consequences to which it led.

Before I read that sermon, I really thought I had lived in a free country; and it was an error I cherished, because it gave me a greater liking to the country I lived in. I was indeed aware, that a jealous, ever-waking vigilance, to guard the treasure of our liberty, not only from invasion, but from decay and corruption, was our best wisdom and our first duty. However, I considered that treasure rather as a possession to be secured than as a prize to be contended for. I did not discern how the present time came to be so very favourable to all *exertions* in the cause of freedom. The present time differs from any other only by the circumstance of what is doing in France. If the example of that nation is to have an influence on this, I can easily conceive why some of their proceedings which have an unpleasant aspect, and are not quite reconcileable to humanity, generosity, good faith, and justice, are palliated with so much milky good-nature towards the actors, and borne with so much heroic fortitude towards the sufferers. It is certainly not prudent to discredit the authority of an example we mean [64] to follow. But allowing this, we are led to a very natural question; What is that cause of liberty, and what are those exertions in its favour, to which the example of France is so singularly auspicious? Is our monarchy to be annihilated, with all the laws, all the tribunals, and all the antient corporations of the kingdom? Is every land-mark of the country to be done away in favour of a geometrical and arithmetical constitution? Is the house of lords to be voted useless? Is episcopacy to be abolished? Are the church lands to be sold to Jews and jobbers; or given to bribe new-invented municipal republics into a participation in sacrilege? Are all the taxes to be voted grievances, and the revenue reduced to a patriotic contribution, or patriotic presents? Are silver shoe-buckles to be substituted in the place of the land tax and the malt tax, for the support of the naval strength of this kingdom? Are all orders, ranks, and distinctions, to be confounded, that out of universal anarchy, joined to national bankruptcy, three or four thousand democracies should be formed into eighty-three, and that they may all, by some sort of unknown attractive power, be organized into one? For this great end, is the army to be seduced from its discipline and its fidelity, first, by every kind of debauchery, and then by the terrible precedent of a donative in the encrease of pay? Are the curates to be seduced from their bishops, by holding out to them the delusive hope of a dole out of the spoils of their own order? Are the citizens of London to be drawn from their allegiance, by feeding them at the expence of their fellow-subjects? Is a compulsory paper currency to be substituted in the place of the legal coin of this kingdom? Is what remains of the plundered stock of public revenue to be employed in the wild project of maintaining two armies to watch over and to fight with each other? If these are the ends and means of the Revolution Society, I admit they are [65] well assorted; and France may furnish them for both with precedents in point.

I see that your example is held out to shame us. I know that we are supposed a dull sluggish race, rendered passive by finding our situation tolerable; and prevented by a mediocrity of freedom from ever attaining to its full perfection. Your leaders in France began by affecting to admire, almost to adore, the British constitution; but as they advanced they came to look upon it with a sovereign contempt. The friends of your National Assembly amongst us have full as mean an opinion of what was formerly thought the glory of their country. The Revolution Society has discovered that the English nation is not free. They are convinced that the inequality in our representation is a "defect in our constitution so *gross and palpable*, as to make it excellent chiefly in *form* and *theory*." * That a representation in the legislature of a kingdom is not only the basis of all constitutional liberty in it, but of "*all legitimate government;* that without it a *government* is nothing but an *usurpation*"; that "when the representation is *partial*, the kingdom possesses liberty only *partially;* and if extremely partial it gives only a *semblance;* and if not only extremely par-

* Discourse on the Love of our Country, 3d edit. p. 39.

tial, but corruptly chosen, it becomes a *nuisance.*" Dr. Price considers this inadequacy of representation as our *fundamental grievance;* and though, as to the corruption of this semblance of representation, he hopes it is not yet arrived to its full perfection of depravity; he fears that "nothing will be done towards gaining for us this *essential blessing,* until some *great abuse of power* again provokes our resentment, or some *great calamity* again alarms our fears, or perhaps till the acquisition of a *pure and equal representation by other countries,* whilst we are *mocked* with the *shadow,* kindles our shame." To this he subjoins a note in these words. "A representation, chosen [66] chiefly by the Treasury, and a *few* thousands of the *dregs* of the people, who are generally paid for their votes."

YOU WILL SMILE HERE at the consistency of those democratists, who, when they are not on their guard, treat the humbler part of the community with the greatest contempt, whilst, at the same time, they pretend to make them the depositories of all power. It would require a long discourse to point out to you the many fallacies that lurk in the generality and equivocal nature of the terms "inadequate representation." I shall only say here, in justice to that old-fashioned constitution, under which we have long prospered, that our representation has been found perfectly adequate to all the purposes for which a representation of the people can be desired or devised. I defy the enemies of our constitution to show the contrary. To detail the particulars in which it is found so well to promote its ends, would demand a treatise on our practical constitution. I state here the doctrine of the Revolutionists, only that you and others may see, what an opinion these gentlemen entertain of the constitution of their country, and why they seem to think that some great abuse of power, or some great calamity, as giving a chance for the blessing of a constitution according to their ideas, would be much palliated to their feelings; you see why they are so much enamoured of your fair and equal representation, which being once obtained, the same effects might follow. You see they consider our house of commons as only "a semblance," "a form," "a theory," "a shadow," "a mockery," perhaps "a nuisance."

These gentlemen value themselves on being systematic; and not without reason. They must therefore look on this gross and palpable defect of representation, this fundamental grievance (so they call it), as a thing not only vicious in itself, but as rendering our whole government absolutely *illegitimate*, [67] and not at all better than a downright *usurpation*. Another revolution, to get rid of this illegitimate and usurped government, would of course be perfectly justifiable, if not absolutely necessary. Indeed their principle, if you observe it with any attention, goes much further than to an alteration in the election of the house of commons; for, if popular representation, or choice, is necessary to the *legitimacy* of all government, the house of lords is, at one stroke, bastardized and corrupted in blood. That house is no representative of the people at all, even in "semblance" or in "form." The case of the crown is altogether as bad. In vain the crown may endeavour to screen itself against these gentlemen by the authority of the establishment made on the Revolution. The Revolution which is resorted to for a title, on their system, wants a title itself. The Revolution is built, according to their theory, upon a basis not more solid than our present formalities, as it was made by an house of lords not representing any one but themselves; and by an house of commons exactly such as the present, that is, as they term it, by a mere "shadow and mockery" of representation.

Something they must destroy, or they seem to themselves to exist for no purpose. One set is for destroying the civil power through the ecclesiastical; another for demolishing the ecclesiastick through the civil. They are aware that the worst consequences might happen to the public in accomplishing this double ruin of church and state; but they are so heated with their theories, that they give more than hints, that this ruin, with all the mischiefs that must lead to it and attend it, and which to themselves appear quite certain, would not be unacceptable to them, or very remote from their wishes. A man amongst them of great authority, and certainly of great talents, speaking of a supposed alliance between church and state, says, "perhaps *we must wait for the fall of the civil powers* before this most unnatural alliance [68] be broken. Calamitous no doubt will that time be. But what convulsion in the political world ought to be a subject of lamentation, if it be attended with so desirable an effect?" You see with what a steady eye these gentlemen are prepared to view the greatest calamities which can befall their country!

IT IS NO WONDER THEREFORE, that with these ideas of every thing in their constitution and government at home, either in church or state, as illegitimate and usurped, or, at best as a vain mockery, they look abroad with an eager and passionate enthusiasm. Whilst they are possessed by these notions, it is vain to talk to them of the practice of their ancestors, the fundamental laws of their country, the fixed form of a constitution, whose merits are confirmed by the solid test of long experience, and an increasing public strength and national prosperity. They despise experience as the wisdom of unlettered men; and as for the rest, they have wrought under-ground a mine that will blow up at one grand explosion all examples of antiquity, all precedents, charters, and acts of parliament. They have "the rights of men." Against these there can be no prescription; against these no agreement is binding: these admit no temperament, and no compromise: any thing withheld from their full demand is so much of fraud and injustice. Against these their rights of men let no government look for security in the length of its continuance, or in the justice and lenity of its administration.

The objections of these speculatists, if its forms do not quadrate with their theories, are as valid against such an old and beneficent government as against the most violent tyranny, or the greenest usurpation. They are always at issue with governments, not on a question of abuse, but a question of competency, and a question of title. I have nothing to say to the clumsy subtilty of their political metaphysics. Let them be their amusement in the schools. [69] "Illa *se jactet in aula—Aeolus, et clauso ventorum carcere regnet.*" But let them not break prison to burst like a Levanter, to sweep the earth with their hurricane, and to break up the fountains of the great deep to overwhelm us.

Far am I from denying in theory; full as far is my heart from withholding in practice, (if I were of power to give or to withhold,) the *real* rights of men. In denying their false claims of right, I do not mean to injure those which are real, and are such as their pretended rights would totally destroy. If civil society be made for the advantage of man, all the advantages for which it is made become his right. It is an institution of beneficence; and law itself is only beneficence acting by a rule. Men have a right to live by that rule; they have a right to justice; as between their fellows, whether their fellows are in politic function or in ordinary occupation. They have a right to the fruits of their industry; and to the means of making their industry fruitful. They have a right to the acquisitions of their parents; to the nourishment and improvement of their offspring; to instruction in life, and to consolation in death. Whatever each man can separately do, without trespassing upon others, he has a right to do for himself; and he has a right to a fair portion of all which society, with all its combinations of skill and force, can do in his favour. In this partnership all men have equal rights; but not to equal things. He that has but five shillings in the partnership, has as good a right to it, as he that has five hundred pound has to his larger proportion. But he has not a right to an equal dividend in the product of the joint stock; and as to the share of power, authority, and direction which each individual ought to have in the management of the state, that I must deny to be amongst the direct original rights of man in civil society; for I have in my contemplation the civil social man, and no other. It is a thing to be settled by convention.

[70] If civil society be the offspring of convention, that convention must be its law. That convention must limit and modify all the descriptions of constitution which are formed under it. Every sort of legislative, judicial, or executory power are its creatures. They can have no being in any other state of things; and how can any man claim, under the conventions of civil society, rights which do not so much as suppose its existence? Rights which are absolutely repugnant to it? One of the first motives to civil society, and which becomes one of its fundamental rules, is, *that no man should be judge in his own cause.* By this each person has at once divested himself of the first fundamental right of uncovenanted man, that is, to judge for himself, and to assert his own cause. He abdicates all right to be his own governor. He inclusively, in a great measure, abandons the right of self-defence, the first law of nature. Men cannot enjoy the rights of an uncivil and of a civil state together. That he may obtain justice he gives up his right of determining what it is in points the most essential to him. That he may secure some liberty, he makes a surrender in trust of the whole of it.

GOVERNMENT IS NOT MADE in virtue of natural rights, which may and do exist in total independence of it; and exist in much greater clearness, and in a much greater degree of abstract perfection: but their abstract perfection is their practical defect. By having a right to every thing they want every thing. Government is a contrivance of human wisdom to provide for human *wants.* Men have a right that these wants should be provided for by this wisdom. Among these wants is to be reckoned the want, out of civil society, of a sufficient restraint upon their passions. Society requires not only that the passions of individuals should be subjected, but that even in the mass and body as well as in the [71] individuals, the inclinations of men should frequently be thwarted, their will controlled, and their passions brought into subjection. This can only be done *by a power out of themselves;* and not, in the exercise of its function, subject to that will and to those passions which it is its office to bridle and subdue. In this sense the restraints on men, as well as their liberties, are to be reckoned among their rights. But as the liberties and the restrictions vary with times and circumstances, and admit of infinite modifications, they cannot be settled upon any abstract rule; and nothing is so foolish as to discuss them upon that principle.

The moment you abate any thing from the full rights of men, each to govern himself, and suffer any artificial positive limitation upon those rights, from that moment the whole organization of government becomes a consideration of convenience. This it is which makes the constitution of a state, and the due distribution of its powers, a matter of the most delicate and complicated skill. It requires a deep knowledge of human nature and human necessities, and of the things which facilitate or obstruct the various ends which are to be pursued by the mechanism of civil institutions. The state is to have recruits to its strength, and remedies to its distempers. What is the use of discussing a man's abstract right to food or to medicine? The question is upon the method of procuring and administering them. In that deliberation I shall always advise to call in the aid of the farmer and the physician, rather than the professor of metaphysics.

The science of constructing a commonwealth, or renovating it, or reforming it, is, like every other experimental science, not to be taught *à priori.* Nor is it a short experience that can instruct us in that practical science; because the real effects of moral causes are not always immediate; but that which in the first instance is prejudicial [72] may be excellent in its remoter operation; and its excellence may arise even from the ill effects it produces in the beginning. The reverse also happens; and very plausible schemes, with very pleasing commencements, have often shameful and lamentable conclusions. In states there are often some obscure and almost latent causes, things which appear at first view of little moment, on which a very great part of its prosperity or adversity may most essentially depend. The science of government being therefore so practical in itself, and intended for such practical purposes, a matter which requires experience, and even more experience than any person can gain in his whole life, however sagacious and observing he may be, it is with infinite caution that any man ought to venture upon pulling down an edifice which has answered in any tolerable degree for ages the common purposes of society, or on building it up again, without having models and patterns of approved utility before his eyes.

These metaphysic rights entering into common life, like rays of light which pierce into a dense medium, are, by the laws of nature, refracted from their straight line. Indeed in the gross and complicated mass of human passions and concerns, the primitive rights of men undergo such a variety of refractions and reflections, that it becomes absurd to talk of them as if they continued in the simplicity of their original direction. The nature of man is intricate; the objects of society are of the greatest possible complexity; and therefore no simple disposition or direction of power can be suitable either to man's nature, or to the quality of his affairs. When I hear the simplicity of contrivance aimed at and boasted of in any new political constitutions, I am at no loss to decide that the artificers are grossly ignorant of their trade, or totally negligent of their duty. The simple governments are fundamentally defective, to say no worse of them. If you were to contemplate society in but one point of view, all [73] these simple modes of polity are infinitely captivating. In effect each would answer its single end much more perfectly than the more complex is able to attain all its complex purposes. But it is better that the whole should be imperfectly and anomalously answered, than that, while some parts are provided for with great exactness, others might be totally neglected, or perhaps materially injured, by the overcare of a favourite member.

The pretended rights of these theorists are all extremes; and in proportion as they are metaphysically true, they are morally and politically false. The rights of men are in a sort of *middle*, incapable of definition, but not impossible to be discerned. The rights of men in governments are their advantages; and these are often in balances between differences of good; in compromises sometimes between good and evil, and sometimes, between evil and evil. Political reason is a computing principle; adding, subtracting, multiplying, and dividing, morally and not metaphysically or mathematically, true moral denominations.

By these theorists the right of the people is almost always sophistically confounded with their power. The body of the community, whenever it can come to act, can meet with no effectual resistance; but till power and right are the same, the whole body of them has no right inconsistent with virtue, and the first of all virtues, prudence. Men have no right to what is not reasonable, and to what is not for their benefit; for though a pleasant writer said, *Liceat perire poetis,* when one of them, in cold blood, is said to have leaped into the flames of a volcanic revolution, *Ardentem frigidus Aetnam insiluit,* I consider such a frolic rather as an unjustifiable poetic licence, than as one of the franchises of Parnassus; and whether he were poet, or divine, or politician, that chose to exercise this kind of right, I think that more wise, because more charitable thoughts would urge me rather [74] to save the man, than to preserve his brazen slippers as the monuments of his folly.

THE KIND OF ANNIVERSARY SERMONS, to which a great part of what I write refers, if men are not shamed out of their present course, in commemorating the fact, will cheat many out of the principles, and deprive them of the benefits of the Revolution they commemorate. I confess to you, Sir, I never liked this continual talk of resistance and revolution, or the practice of making the extreme medicine of the constitution its daily bread. It renders the habit of society dangerously valetudinary: it is taking periodical doses of mercury sublimate, and swallowing down repeated provocatives of cantharides to our love of liberty.

This distemper of remedy, grown habitual, relaxes and wears out, by a vulgar and prostituted use, the spring of that spirit which is to be exerted on great occasions. It was in the most patient period of Roman servitude that themes of tyrannicide made the ordinary exercise of boys at school—*cum perimit saevos classis numerosa tyrannos.* In the ordinary state of things, it produces in a country like ours the worst effects, even on the cause of that liberty which it abuses with the dissoluteness of an extravagant speculation. Almost all the high-bred republicans of my time have, after a short space, become the most decided, thorough-paced courtiers; they soon left the business of a tedious, moderate, but practical resistance, to those of us whom, in the pride and intoxication of their theories, they have slighted, as not much better than tories. Hypocrisy, of course, delights in the most sublime speculations; for, never intending to go beyond speculation, it costs nothing to have it magnificent. But even in cases where rather levity than fraud was to be suspected in these ranting speculations, the issue has been much the same. These professors, finding their extreme [75] principles not applicable to cases which call only for a qualified, or, as I may say, civil and legal resistance, in such cases employ no resistance at all. It is with them a war or a revolution, or it is nothing. Finding their schemes of politics not adapted to the state of the world in which they live, they often come to think lightly of all public principle; and are ready, on their part, to abandon for a very trivial interest what they find of very trivial value. Some indeed are of more steady and persevering natures; but these are eager politicians out of parliament, who have little to tempt them to abandon their favourite projects. They have some change in the church or state, or both, constantly in their view. When that is the case, they are always bad citizens, and perfectly unsure connexions. For, considering their speculative designs as of infinite value, and the actual arrangement of the state as of no estimation, they are at best indifferent about it. They see no merit in the good, and no fault in the vicious management of public affairs; they rather rejoice in the latter, as more propitious to revolution. They see no merit or demerit in any man, or any action, or any political principle, any further than as they may forward or retard their design of change: they therefore take up, one day, the most violent and stretched prerogative, and another time the wildest democratic ideas of freedom, and pass from the one to the other without any sort of regard to cause, to person, or to party.

IN FRANCE YOU ARE NOW in the crisis of a revolution, and in the transit from one form of government to another—you cannot see that character of men exactly in the same situation in which we see it in this country. With us it is militant; with you it is triumphant; and you know how it can act when its power is commensurate to its will. I would not be supposed to confine those observations to any description of men, or [76] to comprehend all men of any description within them—No! far from it. I am as incapable of that injustice, as I am of keeping terms with those who profess principles of extremes; and who under the name of religion teach little else than wild and dangerous politics. The worst of these politics of revolution is this; they temper and harden the breast, in order to prepare it for the desperate strokes which are sometimes used in extreme occasions. But as these occasions may never arrive, the mind receives a gratuitous taint; and the moral sentiments suffer not a little, when no political purpose is served by the depravation. This sort of people are so taken up with their theories about the rights of man, that they have totally forgot his nature. Without opening one new avenue to the understanding, they have succeeded in stopping up those that lead to the heart. They have perverted in themselves, and in those that attend to them, all the well-placed sympathies of the human breast.

This famous sermon of the Old Jewry breathes nothing but this spirit through all the political part. Plots, massacres, assassinations, seem to some people a trivial price for obtaining a revolution. A cheap, bloodless reformation, a guiltless liberty, appear flat and vapid to their taste. There must be a great change of scene; there must be a magnificent stage effect; there must be a grand spectacle to rouze the imagination, grown torpid with the lazy enjoyment of sixty years security, and the still unanimating repose of public prosperity. The Preacher found them all in the French revolution. This inspires a juvenile warmth through his whole frame. His enthusiasm kindles as he advances; and when he arrives at his peroration, it is in a full blaze. Then viewing, from the Pisgah of his pulpit, the free, moral, happy, flourishing, and glorious state of France, as in a bird-eye landscape of a promised land, he breaks out into the following rapture:

[77] "What an eventful period is this! I am *thankful* that I have lived to it; I could almost say, *Lord, now lettest thou thy servant depart in peace, for mine eyes have seen thy salvation.* — I have lived to see a *diffusion* of knowledge, which has undermined superstition and error. — I have lived to see *the rights of*

men better understood than ever; and nations panting for liberty which seemed to have lost the idea of it. —I have lived to see *Thirty Millions of People,* indignant and resolute, spurning at slavery, and demanding liberty with an irresistible voice. *Their King led in triumph, and an arbitrary monarch surrendering himself to his subjects.*" *

BEFORE I PROCEED FURTHER, I have to remark, that Dr. Price seems rather to over-value the great acquisitions of light which he has obtained and diffused in this age. The last century appears to me to have been quite as much enlightened. It had, though in a different place, a triumph as memorable as that of Dr. Price; and some of the great preachers of that period partook of it as eagerly as he has done in the triumph of France. On the trial of the Rev. Hugh Peters for high treason, it was deposed, that when King Charles was brought to London for his trial, the Apostle of Liberty in that day conducted the *triumph.* "I saw," says the witness, "his majesty in the coach with six horses, and Peters riding before the king *triumphing.*" Dr. Price, when he talks as if he had made a discovery, only follows a precedent; for, after the commencement of the [78] king's trial, this precursor, the same Dr. Peters, concluding a long prayer at the royal chapel at Whitehall, (he had very triumphantly chosen his place) said, "I have prayed and preached these twenty years; and now I may say with old Simeon, *Lord, now lettest thou thy servant depart in peace, for mine eyes have seen thy salvation.*" † Peters had not the fruits of his prayer; for he neither departed so soon

---

*Another of these reverend gentlemen, who was witness to some of the spectacles which Paris has lately exhibited—expresses himself thus; "*A king dragged in submissive triumph by his conquering subjects* is one of those appearances of grandeur which seldom rise in the prospect of human affairs, and which, during the remainder of my life, I shall think of with wonder and gratification." These gentlemen agree marvellously in their feelings.

† State Trials vol. ii. p. 360, p. 363.

as he wished, nor in peace. He became (what I heartily hope none of his followers may be in this country) himself a sacrifice to the triumph which he led as Pontiff. They dealt at the Restoration, perhaps, too hardly with this poor good man. But we owe it to his memory and his sufferings, that he had as much illumination, and as much zeal, and had as effectually undermined all *the superstition and error* which might impede the great business he was engaged in, as any who follow and repeat after him, in this age, which would assume to itself an exclusive title to the knowledge of the rights of men, and all the glorious consequences of that knowledge.

After this sally of the preacher of the Old Jewry, which differs only in place and time, but agrees perfectly with the spirit and letter of the rapture of 1648, the Revolution Society, the fabricators of governments, the heroic band of cashierers of monarchs, electors of sovereigns, and leaders of kings in triumph, strutting with a proud consciousness of the diffusion of knowledge, of which every member had obtained so large a share in the donative, were in haste to make a generous diffusion of the knowledge they had thus gratuitously received. To make this bountiful communication, they adjourned from the church in the Old Jewry, to the London Tavern; where the famous Dr. Price, in whom the fumes of his oracular tripod were not entirely evaporated, moved and carried the resolution, or address of congratulation, [79] transmitted by Lord Stanhope to the National Assembly of France.

I FIND A PREACHER OF THE GOSPEL prophaning the beautiful and prophetic ejaculation, commonly called "*nunc dimittis*," made on the first presentation of our Saviour in the Temple, and applying it, with an inhuman and unnatural rapture, to the most horrid, atrocious, and afflicting spectacle, that perhaps ever was exhibited to the pity and indignation of mankind. This "*leading in triumph*," a thing in its best form unmanly and irreligious, which fills our Preacher with such unhallowed transports, must shock, I believe, the moral taste of every well-born mind. Several English were the stupified and indignant spectators of that triumph. It was, unless we have been strangely deceived, a spectacle more resembling a procession of American savages, entering into Onondaga, after some of their murders called victories, and leading into hovels hung round with scalps, their captives, overpowered with the scoffs and buffets of women as ferocious as themselves, much more than it resembled the triumphal pomp of a civilized martial nation—if a civilized nation, or any men who had a sense of generosity, were capable of a personal triumph over the fallen and afflicted.

This, my dear Sir, was not the triumph of France. I must believe that, as a nation, it overwhelmed you with shame and horror. I must believe that the National Assembly find themselves in a state of the greatest humiliation, in not being able to punish the authors of this triumph, or the actors in it; and that they are in a situation in which any enquiry they may make upon the subject, must be destitute even of the appearance of liberty or impartiality. The apology of that Assembly is found in their situation; but when we approve what they *must* bear, it is in us the degenerate choice of a vitiated mind.

[80] With a compelled appearance of deliberation, they vote under the dominion of a stern necessity. They sit in the heart, as it were, of a foreign republic: they have their residence in a city whose constitution has emanated neither from the charter of their king, nor from their legislative power. There they are surrounded by an army not raised either by the authority of their crown, or by their command; and which, if they should order to dissolve itself, would instantly dissolve them. There they sit, after a gang of assassins had driven away some hundreds of the members; whilst those who held the same moderate principles with more patience or better hope, continued every day exposed to outrageous insults and murderous threats. There a majority, sometimes

real, sometimes pretended, captive itself, compels a captive king to issue as royal edicts, at third hand, the polluted nonsense of their most licentious and giddy coffee-houses. It is notorious, that all their measures are decided before they are debated. It is beyond doubt, that under the terror of the bayonet, and the lamp-post, and the torch to their houses, they are obliged to adopt all the crude and desperate measures suggested by clubs composed of a monstrous medley of all conditions, tongues, and nations. Among these are found persons, in comparison of whom Catiline would be thought scrupulous, and Cethegus a man of sobriety and moderation. Nor is it in these clubs alone that the publick measures are deformed into monsters. They undergo a previous distortion in academies, intended as so many seminaries for these clubs, which are set up in all the places of publick resort. In these meetings of all sorts, every counsel, in proportion as it is daring, and violent, and perfidious, is taken for the mark of superior genius. Humanity and compassion are ridiculed as the fruits of superstition and ignorance. Tenderness to individuals is considered as treason to the public. Liberty is always to be estimated [81] perfect as property is rendered insecure. Amidst assassination, massacre, and confiscation, perpetrated or meditated, they are forming plans for the good order of future society. Embracing in their arms the carcases of base criminals, and promoting their relations on the title of their offences, they drive hundreds of virtuous persons to the same end, by forcing them to subsist by beggary or by crime.

The Assembly, their organ, acts before them the farce of deliberation with as little decency as liberty. They act like the comedians of a fair before a riotous audience; they act amidst the tumultuous cries of a mixed mob of ferocious men, and of women lost to shame, who, according to their insolent fancies, direct, control, applaud, explode them; and sometimes mix and take their seats amongst them; domineering over them with a strange mixture of servile petulance and proud presumptuous authority. As they have inverted order in all things, the gallery is in the place of the house. This Assembly, which overthrows kings and kingdoms, has not even the physiognomy and aspect of a grave legislative body — *nec color imperii, nec frons erat ulla senatus.* They have a power given to them, like that of the evil principle, to subvert and destroy; but none to construct, except such machines as may be fitted for further subversion and further destruction.

Who is it that admires, and from the heart is attached to national representative assemblies, but must turn with horror and disgust from such a profane burlesque, and abominable perversion of that sacred institute? Lovers of monarchy, lovers of republicks, must alike abhor it. The members of your Assembly must themselves groan under the tyranny of which they have all the shame, none of the direction, and little of the profit. I am sure many of the members who compose even the majority of that body, must feel as I do, notwithstanding the applauses of the Revolution Society. Miserable king! miserable Assembly! How must that assembly [82] be silently scandalized with those of their members, who could call a day which seemed to blot the sun out of Heaven, "*Un beau jour!*"* How must they be inwardly indignant at hearing others, who thought fit to declare to them, "that the vessel of the state would fly forward in her course towards regeneration with more speed than ever," from the stiff gale of treason and murder, which preceded our Preacher's triumph! What must they have felt, whilst with outward patience and inward indignation they heard of the slaughter of innocent gentlemen in their houses, that "the blood spilled was not the most pure?" What must they have felt, when they were besieged by complaints of disorders which shook their country to its foundations, at being compelled coolly to tell the complainants,

* 6th of October, 1789.

that they were under the protection of the law, and that they would address the king (the captive king) to cause the laws to be enforced for their protection; when the enslaved ministers of that captive king had formally notified to them, that there were neither law, nor authority, nor power left to protect? What must they have felt at being obliged, as a felicitation on the present new year, to request their captive king to forget the stormy period of the last, on account of the great good which *he* was likely to produce to his people; to the complete attainment of which good they adjourned the practical demonstrations of their loyalty, assuring him of their obedience, when he should no longer possess any authority to command?

This address was made with much good-nature and affection, to be sure. But among the revolutions in France, must be reckoned a considerable revolution in their ideas of politeness. In England we are said to learn manners at second-hand from your side of the water, and that we dress our behaviour in the frippery of France. If so, we are still in [83] the old cut; and have not so far conformed to the new Parisian mode of good-breeding, as to think it quite in the most refined strain of delicate compliment, whether in condolence or congratulation, to say to the most humiliated creature that crawls upon the earth, that great public benefits are derived from the murder of his servants, the attempted assassination of himself and of his wife, and the mortification, disgrace, and degradation, that he has personally suffered. It is a topic of consolation which our ordinary of Newgate would be too humane to use to a criminal at the foot of the gallows. I should have thought that the hangman of Paris, now that he is liberalized by the vote of the National Assembly, and is allowed his rank and arms in the Herald's College of the rights of men, would be too generous, too gallant a man, too full of the sense of his new dignity, to employ that cutting consolation to any of the persons whom the *leze nation* might bring under the administration of his *executive powers.*

A man is fallen indeed, when he is thus flattered. The anodyne draught of oblivion, thus drugged, is well calculated to
preserve a galling wakefulness, and to feed the living ulcer of
a corroding memory. Thus to administer the opiate potion
of amnesty, powdered with all the ingredients of scorn and
contempt, is to hold to his lips, instead of "the balm of hurt
minds," the cup of human misery full to the brim, and to
force him to drink it to the dregs.

Yielding to reasons at least as forcible as those which were
so delicately urged in the compliment on the new year, the
king of France will probably endeavour to forget these events,
and that compliment. But history, who keeps a durable record of all our acts, and exercises her awful censure over the
proceedings of all sorts of sovereigns, will not forget either
those events or the aera of this liberal refinement in the
intercourse of mankind. History will [84] record, that on the
morning of the 6th of October 1789, the king and queen of
France, after a day of confusion, alarm, dismay, and slaughter, lay down, under the pledged security of public faith, to
indulge nature in a few hours of respite, and troubled melancholy repose. From this sleep the queen was first startled by
the voice of the centinel at her door, who cried out to her, to
save herself by flight—that this was the last proof of fidelity
he could give—that they were upon him, and he was dead.
Instantly he was cut down. A band of cruel ruffians and assassins, reeking with his blood, rushed into the chamber of
the queen, and pierced with an hundred strokes of bayonets
and poniards the bed, from whence this persecuted woman
had but just had time to fly almost naked, and through ways
unknown to the murderers had escaped to seek refuge at the
feet of a king and husband, not secure of his own life for a
moment.

This king, to say no more of him, and this queen, and
their infant children (who once would have been the pride
and hope of a great and generous people) were then forced

to abandon the sanctuary of the most splendid palace in the world, which they left swimming in blood, polluted by massacre, and strewed with scattered limbs and mutilated carcases. Thence they were conducted into the capital of their kingdom. Two had been selected from the unprovoked, unresisted, promiscuous slaughter, which was made of the gentlemen of birth and family who composed the king's body guard. These two gentlemen, with all the parade of an execution of justice, were cruelly and publickly dragged to the block, and beheaded in the great court of the palace. Their heads were stuck upon spears, and led the procession; whilst the royal captives who followed in the train were slowly moved along, amidst the horrid yells, and shrilling screams, and frantic dances, and infamous contumelies, and all the unutterable abominations of the furies [85] of hell, in the abused shape of the vilest of women. After they had been made to taste, drop by drop, more than the bitterness of death, in the slow torture of a journey of twelve miles, pro-tracted to six hours, they were, under a guard, composed of those very soldiers who had thus conducted them through this famous triumph, lodged in one of the old palaces of Paris, now converted into a Bastile for kings.

Is this a triumph to be consecrated at altars? to be com-memorated with grateful thanksgiving? to be offered to the divine humanity with fervent prayer and enthusiastick ejacu-lation? These Theban and Thracian Orgies, acted in France, and applauded only in the Old Jewry, I assure you, kindle prophetic enthusiasm in the minds but of very few people in this kingdom; although a saint and apostle, who may have revelations of his own, and who has so completely vanquished all the mean superstitions of the heart, may incline to think it pious and decorous to compare it with the entrance into the world of the Prince of Peace, proclaimed in an holy temple by a venerable sage, and not long before not worse announced by the voice of angels to the quiet innocence of shepherds.

At first I was at a loss to account for this fit of unguarded transport. I knew, indeed, that the sufferings of monarchs make a delicious repast to some sort of palates. There were re-flexions which might serve to keep this appetite within some bounds of temperance. But when I took one circumstance into my consideration, I was obliged to confess, that much allowance ought to be made for the Society, and that the temptation was too strong for common discretion. I mean, the circumstance of the *Io Paean* of the triumph, the animat-ing cry which called "for all the BISHOPS to be hanged on the lamp-posts,"* might well have brought forth a burst of enthusiasm on the foreseen [86] consequences of this happy day. I allow to so much enthusiasm some little deviation from prudence. I allow this prophet to break forth into hymns of joy and thanksgiving on an event which appears like the pre-cursor of the Millennium, and the projected fifth monarchy, in the destruction of all church establishments. There was, however (as in all human affairs there is) in the midst of this joy something to exercise the patience of these worthy gentle-men, and to try the long-suffering of their faith. The actual murder of the king and queen, and their child, was wanting to the other auspicious circumstances of this *"beautiful day."* The actual murder of the bishops, though called for by so many holy ejaculations, was also wanting. A groupe of regi-cide and sacrilegious slaughter was indeed boldly sketched, but it was only sketched. It unhappily was left unfinished, in this great history-piece of the massacre of innocents. What hardy pencil of a great master, from the school of the rights of men, will finish it, is to be seen hereafter. The age has not yet the compleat benefit of that diffusion of knowledge that has undermined superstition and error; and the king of France wants another object or two, to consign to oblivion, in

*Tous les Évêques à la lanterne.

consideration of all the good which is to arise from his own sufferings, and the patriotic crimes of an enlightened age.*

*It is proper here to refer to a letter written upon this subject by an eye-witness. That eye-witness was one of the most honest, intelligent, and eloquent members of the National Assembly, one of the most active and zealous reformers of the state. He was obliged to secede from the assembly; and he afterwards became a voluntary exile, on account of the horrors of this pious triumph, and the dispositions of men, who, profiting of crimes, if not causing them, have taken the lead in public affairs.

EXTRACT of M. de Lally-Tollendal's Second Letter to a Friend

"Parlons du parti que j'ai pris; il est bien justifié dans ma conscience. Ni cette ville coupable, ni cette assemblée plus coupable encore, ne méritoient que je me justifie; mais j'ai à coeur que vous, et les personnes qui pensent comme vous, ne me condamnent pas. Ma santé, je vous jure, me rendoit mes fonctions impossibles; mais meme en les mettant de côté il a été au-dessus de mes forces de supporter plus long-tems l'horreur que me causoit ce sang, — ces têtes, — cette reine *presque égorgée*, — ce roi, amené *esclave*, entrant à Paris, au milieu de ses assassins, et précédé des têtes de ses malheureux gardes, — ces perfides janissaires, — ces assassins, — ces femmes cannibales, — ce cri de, TOUS LES ÉVÊQUES À LA LANTERNE, dans le moment où le roi entre sa capitale avec deux évêques de son conseil dans sa voiture. Un *coup de fusil*, que j'ai vu tirer dans un des *carosses de la reine*. M. Bailly appellant cela *un beau jour*. L'assemblée ayant déclaré froidement le matin, qu'il n'étoit pas de sa dignité d'aller toute entière environner le roi. M. Mirabeau disant impunément dans cette assemblée, que le vaisseau de l'état, loins d'être arrêté dans sa course, s'élanceroit avec plus de rapidité que jamais vers sa régénération. M. Barnave, riant avec lui, quand des flots de sang couloient autour de nous. Le vertueux Mounier * échappant par miracle à vingt assassins, qui avoient voulu faire de sa tête un trophée de plus.

"Voilà ce qui me fit jurer de ne plus mettre le pied *dans cette caverne d'Anthropophages* [the National Assembly] où je n'avois plus de force d'élever la voix, ou depuis six semaines je l'avois élevée en vain. Moi, Mounier, et tous les honnêtes gens, ont pensé que le dernier effort à faire pour le bien étoit d'en sortir. Aucune idée de crainte ne s'est approchée de moi. Je rougirois de m'en défendre. J'avois encore reçû sur la route de la part de ce peuple, moins coupable que ceux qui l'ont enivré de fureur, des acclamations, et des applaudissements, dont d'autres auroient été flattés, et qui m'ont fait frémir. C'est à l'indignation, c'est à l'horreur, c'est aux convulsions physiques, que le seul aspect du sang me fait éprouver que j'ai cédé. On brave une seule mort; on la brave plusieurs fois, quand elle peut être utile. Mais aucune puissance

REFLECTIONS ON THE REVOLUTION IN FRANCE

[87] Although this work of our new light and knowledge, did not go to the length, that in all probability it was intended it should be carried; yet I must think, that such treatment of any human creatures must be shocking to any but those who are made for accomplishing Revolutions. But I cannot stop here. Influenced by the inborn feelings of my nature, [88] and not being illuminated by a single ray of this new-sprung modern light, I confess to you, Sir, that the exalted rank of the persons suffering, and particularly the sex, the beauty, and the amiable qualities of the descendant of so many kings and emperors, with the tender age of royal infants, insensible only through infancy and innocence of the cruel outrages to which their parents were exposed, instead of being a subject of exultation, adds not a little to my sensibility on that most melancholy occasion.

I hear that the august person, who was the principal object of our preacher's triumph, though he supported himself, felt much on that shameful occasion. As a man, it became him to feel for his wife and his children, and the faithful guards of his person, that were massacred in cold blood about him. As a prince, it became him to feel for the strange and frightful transformation of his civilized subjects, and to be more grieved for them, than solicitous for himself. It dero-

---

sous le ciel, mais aucune opinion publique ou privée n'ont le droit de me condamner à souffrir inutilement mille supplices par minute, et à périr de désespoir, de rage, au milieu des *triomphes*, du crime que je n'ai pu arrêter. Ils me proscriront, il confisqueront mes biens. Je labourerai la terre, et je ne les verrai plus. — Voilà ma justification. Vous pourrez la lire, la montrer, la laisser copier; tant pis pour ceux qui ne la comprendront pas; ce ne sera alors moi qui auroit eu tort de la leur donner."

This military man had not so good nerves as the peaceable gentlemen of the Old Jewry. — See Mons. Mounier's narrative of these transactions; a man also of honour and virtue, and talents, and therefore a fugitive.

---

*N. B. Mr. Mounier was then speaker of the National Assembly. He has since been obliged to live in exile, though one of the firmest assertors of liberty.

gates little from his fortitude, while it adds infinitely to the honour of his humanity. I am very sorry to say it, very sorry indeed, that such personages are in a situation in which it is not unbecoming in us to praise the virtues of the great.

I hear, and I rejoice to hear, that the great lady, the other object of the triumph, has borne that day (one is interested that beings made for suffering should suffer well) and that she bears all the succeeding days, that she bears the imprisonment of her husband, and her own captivity, and the exile of her friends, and the insulting adulation of addresses, and the whole weight of her accumulated wrongs, with a serene patience, in a manner suited to her rank and race, and becoming the offspring of a sovereign distinguished for her piety and her courage; that like her she has lofty sentiments; that she feels with the dignity of a Roman matron; that in the last extremity she will save herself from the last disgrace, and that if she must fall, she will fall by no ignoble hand.

[89] It is now sixteen or seventeen years since I saw the queen of France, then the dauphiness, at Versailles; and surely never lighted on this orb, which she hardly seemed to touch, a more delightful vision. I saw her just above the horizon, decorating and cheering the elevated sphere she just began to move in; glittering like the morning star, full of life, and splendor, and joy. Oh! what a revolution! and what an heart must I have, to contemplate without emotion that elevation and that fall! Little did I dream when she added titles of veneration to those of enthusiastic, distant, respectful love, that she should ever be obliged to carry the sharp antidote against disgrace concealed in that bosom; little did I dream that I should have lived to see such disasters fallen upon her in a nation of gallant men, in a nation of men of honour and of cavaliers. I thought ten thousand swords must have leaped from their scabbards to avenge even a look that threatened her with insult. But the age of chivalry is gone. That of sophisters, oeconomists, and calculators, has succeeded; and

the glory of Europe is extinguished for ever. Never, never more, shall we behold that generous loyalty to rank and sex, that proud submission, that dignified obedience, that sub-ordination of the heart, which kept alive, even in servitude itself, the spirit of an exalted freedom. The unbought grace of life, the cheap defence of nations, the nurse of manly senti-ment and heroic enterprize, is gone! It is gone, that sensibility of principle, that chastity of honour, which felt a stain like a wound, which inspired courage whilst it mitigated ferocity, which ennobled whatever it touched, and under which vice itself lost half its evil, by losing all its grossness.

THIS MIXED SYSTEM of opinion and sentiment had its ori-gin in the antient chivalry; and the principle, though varied in its appearance by the varying state of human [90] affairs, subsisted and influenced through a long succession of gen-erations, even to the time we live in. If it should ever be totally extinguished, the loss I fear will be great. It is this which has given its character to modern Europe. It is this which has distinguished it under all its forms of government, and distin-guished it to its advantage, from the states of Asia, and pos-sibly from those states which flourished in the most brilliant periods of the antique world. It was this, which, without con-founding ranks, had produced a noble equality, and handed it down through all the gradations of social life. It was this opinion which mitigated kings into companions, and raised private men to be fellows with kings. Without force, or oppo-sition, it subdued the fierceness of pride and power; it obliged sovereigns to submit to the soft collar of social esteem, com-pelled stern authority to submit to elegance, and gave a domi-nation vanquisher of laws, to be subdued by manners.

But now all is to be changed. All the pleasing illusions, which made power gentle, and obedience liberal, which har-monized the different shades of life, and which, by a bland assimilation, incorporated into politics the sentiments which beautify and soften private society, are to be dissolved by this new conquering empire of light and reason. All the decent drapery of life is to be rudely torn off. All the superadded ideas, furnished from the wardrobe of a moral imagination, which the heart owns, and the understanding ratifies, as necessary to cover the defects of our naked shivering nature, and to raise it to dignity in our own estimation, are to be exploded as a ridiculous, absurd, and antiquated fashion.

On this scheme of things, a king is but a man; a queen is but a woman; a woman is but an animal; and an animal not of the highest order. All homage paid to the sex in general as such, and without distinct views, is to be regarded [91] as romance and folly. Regicide, and parricide, and sacrilege, are but fictions of superstition, corrupting jurisprudence by destroying its simplicity. The murder of a king, or a queen, or a bishop, or a father, are only common homicide; and if the people are by any chance, or in any way gainers by it, a sort of homicide much the most pardonable, and into which we ought not to make too severe a scrutiny.

On the scheme of this barbarous philosophy, which is the offspring of cold hearts and muddy understandings, and which is as void of solid wisdom, as it is destitute of all taste and elegance, laws are to be supported only by their own terrors, and by the concern which each individual may find in them from his own private speculations, or can spare to them from his own private interests. In the groves of *their* academy, at the end of every visto, you see nothing but the gallows. Nothing is left which engages the affections on the part of the commonwealth. On the principles of this mechanic philosophy, our institutions can never be embodied, if I may use the expression, in persons; so as to create in us love, veneration, admiration, or attachment. But that sort of reason which banishes the affections is incapable of filling their place. These public affections, combined with manners, are required sometimes as supplements, sometimes as correctives, always as aids to law. The precept given by a wise man, as well as a great critic, for the construction of poems, is equally true as to states. *Non satis est pulchra esse poemata, dulcia sunto.* There ought to be a system of manners in every nation which a well-formed mind would be disposed to relish. To make us love our country, our country ought to be lovely.

But power, of some kind or other, will survive the shock in which manners and opinions perish; and it will find other and worse means for its support. The usurpation which, in order to subvert antient institutions, has destroyed antient [92] principles, will hold power by arts similar to those by which it has acquired it. When the old feudal and chivalrous spirit of *Fealty*, which, by freeing kings from fear, freed both kings and subjects from the precautions of tyranny, shall be extinct in the minds of men, plots and assassinations will be anticipated by preventive murder and preventive confiscation, and that long roll of grim and bloody maxims, which form the political code of all power, not standing on its own honour, and the honour of those who are to obey it. Kings will be tyrants from policy when subjects are rebels from principle.

When antient opinions and rules of life are taken away, the loss cannot possibly be estimated. From that moment we have no compass to govern us; nor can we know distinctly to what port we steer. Europe undoubtedly, taken in a mass, was in a flourishing condition the day on which your Revolution was compleated. How much of that prosperous state was owing to the spirit of our old manners and opinions is not easy to say; but as such causes cannot be indifferent in their operation, we must presume, that, on the whole, their operation was beneficial.

We are but too apt to consider things in the state in which we find them, without sufficiently adverting to the causes by which they have been produced, and possibly may be upheld. Nothing is more certain, than that our manners, our civilization, and all the good things which are connected with manners, and with civilization, have, in this European world of ours, depended for ages upon two principles; and were indeed the result of both combined; I mean the spirit of a gentleman, and the spirit of religion. The nobility and the clergy, the one by profession, the other by patronage, kept learning in existence, even in the midst of arms and confusions, and whilst governments were rather in their causes than formed. Learning paid back what it received to [93] nobility and to priesthood; and paid it with usury, by enlarging their ideas, and by furnishing their minds. Happy if they had all continued to know their indissoluble union, and their proper place! Happy if learning, not debauched by ambition, had been satisfied to continue the instructor, and not aspired to be the master! Along with its natural protectors and guardians, learning will be cast into the mire, and trodden down under the hoofs of a swinish multitude.[a]

If, as I suspect, modern letters owe more than they are always willing to own to antient manners, so do other interests which we value full as much as they are worth. Even commerce, and trade, and manufacture, the gods of our oeconomical politicians, are themselves perhaps but creatures; are themselves but effects, which, as first causes, we choose to worship. They certainly grew under the same shade in which learning flourished. They too may decay with their natural protecting principles. With you, for the present at least, they all threaten to disappear together. Where trade and manufactures are wanting to a people, and the spirit of nobility and religion remains, sentiment supplies, and not always ill supplies their place; but if commerce and the arts should be lost in an experiment to try how well a state may stand without these old fundamental principles, what sort of a thing must be a nation of gross, stupid, ferocious, and at the same time,

[a. See the fate of Bailly and Condorcet, supposed to be here particularly alluded to. Compare the circumstances of the trial and execution of the former with this prediction.]

poor and sordid barbarians, destitute of religion, honour, or manly pride, possessing nothing at present, and hoping for nothing hereafter?

I wish you may not be going fast, and by the shortest cut, to that horrible and disgustful situation. Already there appears a poverty of conception, a coarseness and vulgarity in all the proceedings of the assembly and of all their [94] instructors. Their liberty is not liberal. Their science is presumptuous ignorance. Their humanity is savage and brutal.

It is not clear, whether in England we learned those grand and decorous principles, and manners, of which considerable traces yet remain, from you, or whether you took them from us. But to you, I think, we trace them best. You seem to me to be "*gentis incunabula nostrae.*" France has always more or less influenced manners in England; and when your fountain is choaked up and polluted, the stream will not run long, or not run clear with us, or perhaps with any nation. This gives all Europe, in my opinion, but too close and connected a concern in what is done in France. Excuse me, therefore, if I have dwelt too long on the atrocious spectacle of the sixth of October 1789, or have given too much scope to the reflections which have arisen in my mind on occasion of the most important of all revolutions, which may be dated from that day, I mean a revolution in sentiments, manners, and moral opinions. As things now stand, with every thing respectable destroyed without us, and an attempt to destroy within us every principle of respect, one is almost forced to apologize for harbouring the common feelings of men.

Why do I feel so differently from the Reverend Dr. Price, and those of his lay flock, who will choose to adopt the sentiments of his discourse? For this plain reason—because it is *natural* I should; because we are so made as to be affected at such spectacles with melancholy sentiments upon the unstable condition of mortal prosperity, and the tremendous uncertainty of human greatness; because in those natural feelings we learn great lessons; because in events like these our passions instruct our reason; because when kings are hurled from their thrones by the Supreme Director of this great drama, and become the objects of [95] insult to the base, and of pity to the good, we behold such disasters in the moral, as we should behold a miracle in the physical order of things. We are alarmed into reflexion; our minds (as it has long since been observed) are purified by terror and pity; our weak unthinking pride is humbled, under the dispensations of a mysterious wisdom. Some tears might be drawn from me, if such a spectacle were exhibited on the stage. I should be truly ashamed of finding in myself that superficial, theatric sense of painted distress, whilst I could exult over it in real life. With such a perverted mind, I could never venture to shew my face at a tragedy. People would think the tears that Garrick formerly, or that Siddons not long since, have extorted from me, were the tears of hypocrisy; I should know them to be the tears of folly.

Indeed the theatre is a better school of moral sentiments than churches, where the feelings of humanity are thus outraged. Poets, who have to deal with an audience not yet graduated in the school of the rights of men, and who must apply themselves to the moral constitution of the heart, would not dare to produce such a triumph as a matter of exultation. There, where men follow their natural impulses, they would not bear the odious maxims of a Machiavelian policy, whether applied to the attainment of monarchical or democratic tyranny. They would reject them on the modern, as they once did on the antient stage; where they could not bear even the hypothetical proposition of such wickedness in the mouth of a personated tyrant, though suitable to the character he sustained. No theatric audience in Athens would bear what has been borne, in the midst of the real tragedy of this triumphal day; a principal actor weighing, as it were in scales hung in a shop of horrors, so much actual crime against so much contingent advantage, and after putting in and out weights, declaring that the balance was on [96] the side of the advantages. They would not bear to see the crimes of new democracy posted as in a ledger against the crimes of old despotism, and the book-keepers of politics finding democracy still in debt, but by no means unable or unwilling to pay the balance. In the theatre, the first intuitive glance, without any elaborate process of reasoning, would shew, that this method of political computation would justify every extent of crime. They would see, that on these principles, even where the very worst acts were not perpetrated, it was owing rather to the fortune of the conspirators than to their parsimony in the expenditure of treachery and blood. They would soon see, that criminal means once tolerated are soon preferred. They present a shorter cut to the object than through the highway of the moral virtues. Justifying perfidy and murder for public benefit, public benefit would soon become the pretext, and perfidy and murder the end; until rapacity, malice, revenge, and fear more dreadful than revenge, could satiate their insatiable appetites. Such must be the consequences of losing in the splendour of these triumphs of the rights of men, all natural sense of wrong and right.

BUT THE REVEREND PASTOR exults in this "leading in triumph," because, truly, Louis the XVIth was "an arbitrary monarch"; that is, in other words, neither more nor less, than because he was Louis the XVIth, and because he had the misfortune to be born king of France, with the prerogatives of which, a long line of ancestors, and a long acquiescence of the people, without any act of his, had put him in possession. A misfortune it has indeed turned out to him, that he was born king of France. But misfortune is not crime, nor is indiscretion always the greatest guilt. I shall never think that a prince, the acts of whose whole reign were a series of concessions to his subjects, who was willing to [97] relax his authority, to remit his prerogatives, to call his people to a share of freedom, not known, perhaps not desired, by their ancestors; such a prince, though he should be subject to the common frailties attached to men and to princes, though he should have once thought it necessary to provide force against the desperate designs manifestly carrying on against his person, and the remnants of his authority; though all this should be taken into consideration, I shall be led with great difficulty to think he deserves the cruel and insulting triumph of Paris, and of Dr. Price. I tremble for the cause of liberty, from such an example to kings. I tremble for the cause of humanity, in the unpunished outrages of the most wicked of mankind. But there are some people of that low and degenerate fashion of mind, that they look up with a sort of complacent awe and admiration to kings, who know to keep firm in their seat, to hold a strict hand over their subjects, to assert their prerogative, and by the awakened vigilance of a severe despotism, to guard against the very first approaches of freedom. Against such as these they never elevate their voice. Deserters from principle, listed with fortune, they never see any good in suffering virtue, nor any crime in prosperous usurpation.

If it could have been made clear to me, that the king and queen of France (those I mean who were such before the triumph) were inexorable and cruel tyrants, that they had formed a deliberate scheme for massacring the National Assembly (I think I have seen something like the latter insinuated in certain publications) I should think their captivity just. If this be true, much more ought to have been done, but done, in my opinion, in another manner. The punishment of real tyrants is a noble and awful act of justice; and it has with truth been said to be consolatory to the human mind. But if I were to punish a wicked king, I should regard the dignity in avenging the crime. Justice is [98] grave and decorous, and in its punishments rather seems to submit to a necessity, than to make a choice. Had Nero, or Agrippina, or

Louis the Eleventh, or Charles the Ninth, been the subject; if Charles the Twelfth of Sweden, after the murder of Patkul, or his predecessor Christina, after the murder of Monalde-schi, had fallen into your hands, Sir, or into mine, I am sure our conduct would have been different.

If the French King, or King of the French, (or by whatever name he is known in the new vocabulary of your constitution) has in his own person, and that of his Queen, really deserved these unavowed but unavenged murderous attempts, and those subsequent indignities more cruel than murder, such a person would ill deserve even that subordinate executory trust, which I understand is to be placed in him; nor is he fit to be called chief of a nation which he has outraged and oppressed. A worse choice for such an office in a new commonwealth, than that of a deposed tyrant, could not possibly be made. But to degrade and insult a man as the worst of criminals, and afterwards to trust him in your highest concerns, as a faithful, honest, and zealous servant, is not consistent in reasoning, nor prudent in policy, nor safe in practice. Those who could make such an appointment must be guilty of a more flagrant breach of trust than any they have yet committed against the people. As this is the only crime in which your leading politicians could have acted inconsistently, I conclude that there is no sort of ground for these horrid insinuations. I think no better of all the other calumnies.

In England, we give no credit to them. We are generous enemies: we are faithful allies. We spurn from us with disgust and indignation the slanders of those who bring us their anecdotes with the attestation of the flower-de-luce on their shoulder. We have Lord George Gordon fast in Newgate; and neither his being a public proselyte to Judaism, [99] nor his having, in his zeal against Catholic priests and all sort of ecclesiastics, raised a mob (excuse the term, it is still in use here) which pulled down all our prisons, have preserved to him a liberty, of which he did not render himself worthy by a virtuous use of it. We have rebuilt Newgate, and tenanted the mansion. We have prisons almost as strong as the Bastile, for those who dare to libel the queens of France. In this spiritual retreat, let the noble libeller remain. Let him there meditate on his Thalmud, until he learns a conduct more becoming his birth and parts, and not so disgraceful to the antient religion to which he has become a proselyte; or until some persons from your side of the water, to please your new Hebrew brethren, shall ransom him. He may then be enabled to purchase, with the old hoards of the synagogue, and a very small poundage on the long compound interest of the thirty pieces of silver (Dr. Price has shewn us what miracles compound interest will perform in 1790 years) the lands which are lately discovered to have been usurped by the Gallican church. Send us your popish Archbishop of Paris, and we will send you our protestant Rabbin. We shall treat the person you send us in exchange like a gentleman and an honest man, as he is; but pray let him bring with him the fund of his hospitality, bounty, and charity; and, depend upon it, we shall never confiscate a shilling of that honourable and pious fund, nor think of enriching the treasury with the spoils of the poor-box.

TO TELL YOU THE TRUTH, my dear Sir, I think the honour of our nation to be somewhat concerned in the disclaimer of the proceedings of this society of the Old Jewry and the London Tavern. I have no man's proxy. I speak only from myself; when I disclaim, as I do with all possible earnestness, all communion with the actors in that triumph, or with the admirers of it. When I assert anything else, as [100] concerning the people of England, I speak from observation, not from authority; but I speak from the experience I have had in a pretty extensive and mixed communication with the inhabitants of this kingdom, of all descriptions and ranks, and after a course of attentive observation, began early in life, and continued for near forty years. I have often been astonished, considering that we are divided from you but by a slender dyke of about twenty-four miles, and that the mutual intercourse between the two countries has lately been very great, to find how little you seem to know of us. I suspect that this is owing to your forming a judgment of this nation from certain publications, which do very erroneously, if they do at all, represent the opinions and dispositions generally prevalent in England. The vanity, restlessness, petulance, and spirit of intrigue of several petty cabals, who attempt to hide their total want of consequence in bustle and noise, and puffing, and mutual quotation of each other, makes you imagine that our contemptuous neglect of their abilities is a mark of general acquiescence in their opinions. No such thing, I assure you. Because half a dozen grasshoppers under a fern make the field ring with their importunate chink, whilst thousands of great cattle, reposed beneath the shadow of the British oak, chew the cud and are silent, pray do not imagine, that those who make the noise are the only inhabitants of the field; that, of course, they are many in number; or that, after all, they are other than the little shrivelled, meagre, hopping, though loud and troublesome insects of the hour.

I almost venture to affirm, that not one in a hundred amongst us participates in the "triumph" of the Revolution Society. If the king and queen of France, and their children, were to fall into our hands by the chance of war, in the most acrimonious of all hostilities (I deprecate such an event, I deprecate such hostility) they would be treated with [101] another sort of triumphal entry into London. We formerly have had a king of France in that situation; you have read how he was treated by the victor in the field; and in what manner he was afterwards received in England. Four hundred years have gone over us; but I believe we are not materially changed since that period. Thanks to our sullen resistance to innovation, thanks to the cold sluggishness of our national character, we still bear the stamp of our forefathers.

REFLECTIONS ON THE REVOLUTION IN FRANCE

We have not, as I conceive, lost the generosity and dignity of thinking of the fourteenth century; nor as yet have we subtilized ourselves into savages. We are not the converts of Rousseau; we are not the disciples of Voltaire; Helvetius has made no progress amongst us. Atheists are not our preachers; madmen are not our lawgivers. We know that *we* have made no discoveries, and we think that no discoveries are to be made, in morality; nor many in the great principles of government, nor in the ideas of liberty, which were understood long before we were born, altogether as well as they will be after the grave has heaped its mould upon our presumption, and the silent tomb shall have imposed its law on our pert loquacity. In England we have not yet been completely embowelled of our natural entrails; we still feel within us, and we cherish and cultivate, those inbred sentiments which are the faithful guardians, the active monitors of our duty, the true supporters of all liberal and manly morals. We have not been drawn and trussed, in order that we may be filled, like stuffed birds in a museum, with chaff and rags, and paltry blurred shreds of paper about the rights of man. We preserve the whole of our feelings still native and entire, unsophisticated by pedantry and infidelity. We have real hearts of flesh and blood beating in our bosoms. We fear God; we look up with awe to kings; with affection to parliaments; with duty to magistrates; with reverence to priests; and with respect to [102] nobility.* Why? Because when such ideas are brought before our minds, it is *natural* to be so affected; because all other feelings are false and spurious, and tend to corrupt our

---

*The English are, I conceive, misrepresented in a Letter published in one of the papers, by a gentleman thought to be a dissenting minister. When writing to Dr. Price, of the spirit which prevails at Paris, he says, "The spirit of the people in this place has abolished all the proud *distinctions* which the *king* and *nobles* had usurped in their minds; whether they talk of *the king, the noble, or the priest,* their whole language is that of the most *enlightened and liberal amongst the English.*" If this gentleman means to confine the terms *enlightened and liberal* to one set of men in England, it may be true. It is not generally so.

minds, to vitiate our primary morals, to render us unfit for rational liberty; and by teaching us a servile, licentious, and abandoned insolence, to be our low sport for a few holidays, to make us perfectly fit for, and justly deserving of slavery, through the whole course of our lives.

You see, Sir, that in this enlightened age I am bold enough to confess, that we are generally men of untaught feelings; that instead of casting away all our old prejudices, we cherish them to a very considerable degree, and, to take more shame to ourselves, we cherish them because they are prejudices; and the longer they have lasted, and the more generally they have prevailed, the more we cherish them. We are afraid to put men to live and trade each on his own private stock of reason; because we suspect that this stock in each man is small, and that the individuals would do better to avail themselves of the general bank and capital of nations, and of ages. Many of our men of speculation, instead of exploding general prejudices, employ their sagacity to discover the latent wisdom which prevails in them. If they find what they seek, (and they seldom fail) they think it more wise to continue the prejudice, with the reason involved, than to cast away the coat of prejudice, and to leave nothing but the naked reason; because prejudice, with its reason, has a motive to give action to that reason, and an [103] affection which will give it permanence. Prejudice is of ready application in the emergency; it previously engages the mind in a steady course of wisdom and virtue, and does not leave the man hesitating in the moment of decision, sceptical, puzzled, and unresolved. Prejudice renders a man's virtue his habit; and not a series of unconnected acts. Through just prejudice, his duty becomes a part of his nature.

Your literary men, and your politicians, and so do the whole clan of the enlightened among us, essentially differ in these points. They have no respect for the wisdom of others; but they pay it off by a very full measure of confidence in their own. With them it is a sufficient motive to destroy an old scheme of things, because it is an old one. As to the new, they are in no sort of fear with regard to the duration of a building run up in haste; because duration is no object to those who think little or nothing has been done before their time, and who place all their hopes in discovery. They conceive, very systematically, that all things which give perpetuity are mischievous, and therefore they are at inexpiable war with all establishments. They think that government may vary like modes of dress, and with as little ill effect. That there needs no principle of attachment, except a sense of present conveniency, to any constitution of the state. They always speak as if they were of opinion that there is a singular species of compact between them and their magistrates, which binds the magistrate, but which has nothing reciprocal in it, but that the majesty of the people has a right to dissolve it without any reason, but its will. Their attachment to their country itself, is only so far as it agrees with some of their fleeting projects; it begins and ends with that scheme of polity which falls in with their momentary opinion.

These doctrines, or rather sentiments, seem prevalent with [104] your new statesmen. But they are wholly different from those on which we have always acted in this country.

I HEAR IT IS SOMETIMES GIVEN OUT in France, that what is doing among you is after the example of England. I beg leave to affirm, that scarcely any thing done with you has originated from the practice or the prevalent opinions of this people, either in the act or in the spirit of the proceeding. Let me add, that we are as unwilling to learn these lessons from France, as we are sure that we never taught them to that nation. The cabals here who take a sort of share in your transactions as yet consist but of an handful of people. If unfortunately by their intrigues, their sermons, their publications, and by a confidence derived from an expected union with the counsels and forces of the French nation, they should draw considerable numbers into their faction, and in consequence should seriously attempt any thing here in imitation of what has been done with you, the event, I dare venture to prophesy, will be, that, with some trouble to their country, they will soon accomplish their own destruction. This people refused to change their law in remote ages from respect to the infallibility of popes; and they will not now alter it from a pious implicit faith in the dogmatism of philosophers; though the former was armed with the anathema and crusade, and though the latter should act with the libel and the lamp-iron.

Formerly your affairs were your own concern only. We felt for them as men; but we kept aloof from them, because we were not citizens of France. But when we see the model held up to ourselves, we must feel as Englishmen, and feeling, we must provide as Englishmen. Your affairs, in spite of us, are made a part of our interest; so far at least as to keep at a distance your panacea, or your plague. If it be a panacea, we do not want it. We know the consequences [105] of unnecessary physic. If it be a plague, it is such a plague, that the precautions of the most severe quarantine ought to be established against it.

I HEAR ON ALL HANDS that a cabal, calling itself philosophic, receives the glory of many of the late proceedings; and that their opinions and systems are the true actuating spirit of the whole of them. I have heard of no party in England, literary or political, at any time, known by such a description. It is not with you composed of those men, is it? whom the vulgar, in their blunt, homely style, commonly call Atheists and Infidels? If it be, I admit that we too have had writers of that description, who made some noise in their day. At present they repose in lasting oblivion. Who, born within the last forty years, has read one word of Collins, and Toland,

---

and Tindal, and Chubb, and Morgan, and that whole race who called themselves Freethinkers? Who now reads Boling-broke? Who ever read him through? Ask the booksellers of London what is become of all these lights of the world. In as few years their few successors will go to the family vault of "all the Capulets." But whatever they were, or are, with us, they were and are wholly unconnected individuals. With us they kept the common nature of their kind, and were not gregarious. They never acted in corps, nor were known as a faction in the state, nor presumed to influence, in that name or character, or for the purposes of such a faction, on any of our public concerns. Whether they ought so to exist, and so be permitted to act, is another question. As such cabals have not existed in England, so neither has the spirit of them had any influence in establishing the original frame of our consti-tution, or in any one of the several reparations and improve-ments it has undergone. The whole has been done under the auspices, and is confirmed by the sanctions of religion and piety. The whole [106] has emanated from the simplicity of our national character, and from a sort of native plain-ness and directness of understanding, which for a long time characterized those men who have successively obtained au-thority amongst us. This disposition still remains, at least in the great body of the people.

We know, and what is better, we feel inwardly, that reli-gion is the basis of civil society, and the source of all good and of all comfort.* In England we are so convinced of this, that there is no rust of superstition, with which the accu-mulated absurdity of the human mind might have crusted it

---

*Sit igitur hoc ab initio persuasum civibus, dominos esse omnium re-rum ac moderatores, deos; eaque, quae gerantur, eorum geri vi. ditione, ac numine: eosdemque optime de genere hominum mereri; et qualis quisque sit, quid agat, quid in se admittat, qua mente, qua pietate colat religiones intueri; piorum et impiorum habere rationem. His enim rebus imbutae mentes haud sane abhorrebunt ab utili et a vera sententia. Cic. de Legibus, l. 2.

over in the course of ages, that ninety-nine in an hundred of the people of England would not prefer to impiety. We shall never be such fools as to call in an enemy to the substance of any system to remove its corruptions, to supply its defects, or to perfect its construction. If our religious tenets should ever want a further elucidation, we shall not call on atheism to explain them. We shall not light up our temple from that unhallowed fire. It will be illuminated with other lights. It will be perfumed with other incense, than the infectious stuff which is imported by the smugglers of adulterated metaphysics. If our ecclesiastical establishment should want a revision, it is not avarice or rapacity, public or private, that we shall employ for the audit, or receipt, or application, of its consecrated revenue. Violently condemning neither the Greek nor the Armenian, nor, since heats are subsided, the Roman system of religion, we prefer the Protestant; not because we think it has less of the Christian [107] religion in it, but because, in our judgment, it has more. We are protestants, not from indifference, but from zeal.

We know, and it is our pride to know, that man is by his constitution a religious animal; that atheism is against, not only our reason, but our instincts; and that it cannot prevail long. But if, in the moment of riot, and in a drunken delirium from the hot spirit drawn out of the alembick of hell, which in France is now so furiously boiling, we should uncover our nakedness by throwing off that Christian religion which has hitherto been our boast and comfort, and one great source of civilization amongst us, and among many other nations, we are apprehensive (being well aware that the mind will not endure a void) that some uncouth, pernicious, and degrading superstition, might take place of it. For that reason, before we take from our establishment the natural human means of estimation, and give it up to contempt, as you have done, and in doing it have incurred the penalties you well deserve to suffer, we desire that some other may be presented to us in the place of it. We shall then form our judgment.

REFLECTIONS ON THE REVOLUTION IN FRANCE

On these ideas, instead of quarrelling with establishments, as some do, who have made a philosophy and a religion of their hostility to such institutions, we cleave closely
to them. We are resolved to keep an established church,
an established monarchy, an established aristocracy, and an
established democracy, each in the degree it exists, and in no
greater. I shall shew you presently how much of each of these
we possess.

It has been the misfortune, not as these gentlemen think
it, the glory, of this age, that every thing is to be discussed; as
if the constitution of our country were to be always a subject
rather of altercation than enjoyment. For this reason, as well
as for the satisfaction of those among you (if any such you
have among you) who may wish to profit [108] of examples,
I venture to trouble you with a few thoughts upon each of
these establishments. I do not think they were unwise in antient Rome, who, when they wished to new-model their laws,
sent commissioners to examine the best constituted republics within their reach.

FIRST, I BEG LEAVE TO SPEAK of our church establishment, which is the first of our prejudices; not a prejudice
destitute of reason, but involving in it profound and extensive wisdom. I speak of it first. It is first, and last, and midst
in our minds. For, taking ground on that religious system,
of which we are now in possession, we continue to act on
the early received and uniformly continued sense of mankind. That sense not only, like a wise architect, hath built
up the august fabric of states, but like a provident proprietor, to preserve the structure from prophanation and ruin,
as a sacred temple, purged from all the impurities of fraud,
and violence, and injustice, and tyranny, hath solemnly and
for ever consecrated the commonwealth, and all that officiate in it. This consecration is made, that all who administer
in the government of men, in which they stand in the person of God himself, should have high and worthy notions of

their function and destination; that their hope should be full of immortality; that they should not look to the paltry pelf of the moment, nor to the temporary and transient praise of the vulgar, but to a solid, permanent existence, in the permanent part of their nature, and to a permanent fame and glory, in the example they leave as a rich inheritance to the world.

Such sublime principles ought to be infused into persons of exalted situations; and religious establishments provided, that may continually revive and enforce them. Every sort of moral, every sort of civil, every sort of politic institution, aiding the rational and natural ties that connect the human [109] understanding and affections to the divine, are not more than necessary, in order to build up that wonderful structure, Man; whose prerogative it is, to be in a great degree a creature of his own making; and who when made as he ought to be made, is destined to hold no trivial place in the creation. But whenever man is put over men, as the better nature ought ever to preside, in that case more particularly, he should as nearly as possible be approximated to his perfection.

This consecration of the state, by a state religious establishment, is necessary also to operate with an wholesome awe upon free citizens; because, in order to secure their freedom, they must enjoy some determinate portion of power. To them therefore a religion connected with the state, and with their duty towards it, becomes even more necessary than in such societies, where the people by the terms of their subjection are confined to private sentiments, and the management of their own family concerns. All persons possessing any portion of power ought to be strongly and awefully impressed with an idea that they act in trust; and that they are to account for their conduct in that trust to the one great master, author and founder of society.

This principle ought even to be more strongly impressed upon the minds of those who compose the collective sovreignty than upon those of single princes. Without instruments, these princes can do nothing. Whoever uses instruments, in finding helps, finds also impediments. Their power is therefore by no means compleat; nor are they safe in extreme abuse. Such persons, however elevated by flattery, arrogance, and self-opinion, must be sensible that, whether covered or not by positive law, in some way or other they are accountable even here for the abuse of their trust. If they are not cut off by a rebellion of their people, they may be strangled by the very Janissaries kept [110] for their security against all other rebellion. Thus we have seen the king of France sold by his soldiers for an encrease of pay. But where popular authority is absolute and unrestrained, the people have an infinitely greater, because a far better founded confidence in their own power. They are themselves, in a great measure, their own instruments. They are nearer to their objects. Besides, they are less under responsibility to one of the greatest controlling powers on earth, the sense of fame and estimation. The share of infamy that is likely to fall to the lot of each individual in public acts, is small indeed; the operation of opinion being in the inverse ratio to the number of those who abuse power. Their own approbation of their own acts has to them the appearance of a public judgment in their favour. A perfect democracy is therefore the most shameless thing in the world. As it is the most shameless, it is also the most fearless. No man apprehends in his person he can be made subject to punishment. Certainly the people at large never ought: for as all punishments are for example towards the conservation of the people at large, the people at large can never become the subject of punishment by any human hand.* It is therefore of infinite importance that they should not be suffered to imagine that their will, any more than that of kings, is the standard of right and wrong. They

---

*Quicquid multis peccatur inultum.

ought to be persuaded that they are full as little entitled, and far less qualified, with safety to themselves, to use any arbitrary power whatsoever; that therefore they are not, under a false shew of liberty, but, in truth, to exercise an unnatural inverted domination, tyrannically to exact, from those who officiate in the state, not an entire devotion to their interest, which is their right, but an abject submission to their occasional will; extinguishing thereby, in all those who serve them, all moral principle, all sense [111] of dignity, all use of judgment, and all consistency of character, whilst by the very same process they give themselves up a proper, a suitable, but a most contemptible prey to the servile ambition of popular sycophants or courtly flatterers.

When the people have emptied themselves of all the lust of selfish will, which without religion it is utterly impossible they ever should, when they are conscious that they exercise, and exercise perhaps in an higher link of the order of delegation, the power, which to be legitimate must be according to that eternal immutable law, in which will and reason are the same, they will be more careful how they place power in base and incapable hands. In their nomination to office, they will not appoint to the exercise of authority, as to a pitiful job, but as to an holy function; not according to their sordid selfish interest, nor to their wanton caprice, nor to their arbitrary will; but they will confer that power (which any man may well tremble to give or to receive) on those only, in whom they may discern that predominant proportion of active virtue and wisdom, taken together and fitted to the charge, such, as in the great and inevitable mixed mass of human imperfections and infirmities, is to be found.

When they are habitually convinced that no evil can be acceptable, either in the act or the permission, to him whose essence is good, they will be better able to extirpate out of the minds of all magistrates, civil, ecclesiastical, or military, any thing that bears the least resemblance to a proud and lawless domination.

But one of the first and most leading principles on which the commonwealth and the laws are consecrated, is lest the temporary possessors and life-renters in it, unmindful of what they have received from their ancestors, or of what is [112] due to their posterity, should act as if they were the entire masters; that they should not think it amongst their rights to cut off the entail, or commit waste on the inheritance, by destroying at their pleasure the whole original fabric of their society; hazarding to leave to those who come after them, a ruin instead of an habitation, and teaching these successors as little to respect their contrivances, as they had themselves respected the institutions of their forefathers. By this unprincipled facility of changing the state as often, and as much, and in as many ways, as there are floating fancies or fashions, the whole chain and continuity of the commonwealth would be broken. No one generation could link with the other. Men would become little better than the flies of a summer.

And first of all, the science of jurisprudence, the pride of the human intellect, which, with all its defects, redundancies, and errors, is the collected reason of ages, combining the principles of original justice with the infinite variety of human concerns, as a heap of old exploded errors, would be no longer studied. Personal self-sufficiency and arrogance, the certain attendants upon all those who have never experienced a wisdom greater than their own, would usurp the tribunal. Of course, no certain laws, establishing invariable grounds of hope and fear, would keep the actions of men in a certain course, or direct them to a certain end. Nothing stable in the modes of holding property, or exercising function, could form a solid ground on which any parent could speculate in the education of his offspring, or in a choice for their future establishment in the world. No principles would be early worked into the habits. As soon as the most able instructor had completed his laborious course of institution, instead of sending forth his pupil, accomplished in a virtuous discipline, fitted to procure him attention and respect, in his place in society, he would find everything altered; and that he had turned out a poor creature to the contempt and derision [113] of the world, ignorant of the true grounds of estimation. Who would insure a tender and delicate sense of honour to beat almost with the first pulses of the heart, when no man could know what would be the test of honour in a nation, continually varying the standard of its coin? No part of life would retain its acquisitions. Barbarism with regard to science and literature, unskilfulness with regard to arts and manufactures, would infallibly succeed to the want of a steady education and settled principle; and thus the commonwealth itself would, in a few generations, crumble away, be disconnected into the dust and powder of individuality, and at length dispersed to all the winds of heaven.

To avoid therefore the evils of inconstancy and versatility, ten thousand times worse than those of obstinacy and the blindest prejudice, we have *consecrated* the state; that no man should approach to look into its defects or corruptions but with due caution; that he should never dream of beginning its reformation by its subversion; that he should approach to the faults of the state as to the wounds of a father, with pious awe and trembling solicitude. By this wise prejudice we are taught to look with horror on those children of their country who are prompt rashly to hack that aged parent in pieces, and put him into the kettle of magicians, in hopes that by their poisonous weeds, and wild incantations, they may regenerate the paternal constitution, and renovate their father's life.

SOCIETY IS INDEED A CONTRACT. Subordinate contracts, for objects of mere occasional interest, may be dissolved at pleasure; but the state ought not to be considered as nothing better than a partnership agreement in a trade of pepper and coffee, callico or tobacco, or some other such low concern, to be taken up for a little temporary interest, [114] and to be dissolved by the fancy of the parties. It is to be looked on with other reverence; because it is not a partnership in things subservient only to the gross animal existence of a temporary and perishable nature. It is a partnership in all science; a partnership in all art; a partnership in every virtue, and in all perfection. As the ends of such a partnership cannot be obtained in many generations, it becomes a partnership not only between those who are living, but between those who are living, those who are dead, and those who are to be born. Each contract of each particular state is but a clause in the great primaeval contract of eternal society, linking the lower with the higher natures, connecting the visible and invisible world, according to a fixed compact sanctioned by the inviolable oath which holds all physical and all moral natures, each in their appointed place. This law is not subject to the will of those, who by an obligation above them, and infinitely superior, are bound to submit their will to that law. The municipal corporations of that universal kingdom are not morally at liberty at their pleasure, and on their speculations of a contingent improvement, wholly to separate and tear asunder the bands of their subordinate community, and to dissolve it into an unsocial, uncivil, unconnected chaos of elementary principles. It is the first and supreme necessity only, a necessity that is not chosen but chooses, a necessity paramount to deliberation, that admits no discussion, and demands no evidence, which alone can justify a resort to anarchy. This necessity is no exception to the rule; because this necessity itself is a part too of that moral and physical disposition of things to which man must be obedient by consent or force. But if that which is only submission to necessity should be made the object of choice, the law is broken; nature is disobeyed; and the rebellious are outlawed, cast forth, and exiled, from this world of reason, and order, and peace, and virtue, and fruitful penitence, [115] into the antagonist world of madness, discord, vice, confusion, and unavailing sorrow.

THESE, MY DEAR SIR, are, were, and I think long will be the sentiments of not the least learned and reflecting part of this kingdom. They who are included in this description form their opinions on such grounds as such persons ought to form them. The less enquiring receive them from an authority which those whom Providence dooms to live on trust need not be ashamed to rely on. These two sorts of men move in the same direction, tho' in a different place. They both move with the order of the universe. They all know or feel this great antient truth: "Quod illi principi et praepotenti Deo qui omnem hunc mundum regit, nihil eorum quae quidem fiant in terris acceptius quam concilia et coetus hominum jure sociati quae civitates appellantur." They take this tenet of the head and heart, not from the great name which it immediately bears, nor from the greater from whence it is derived; but from that which alone can give true weight and sanction to any learned opinion, the common nature and common relation of men. Persuaded that all things ought to be done with reference, and referring all to the point of reference to which all should be directed, they think themselves bound, not only as individuals in the sanctuary of the heart, or as congregated in that personal capacity, to renew the memory of their high origin and cast; but also in their corporate character to perform their national homage to the institutor, and author and protector of civil society; without which civil society man could not by any possibility arrive at the perfection of which his nature is capable, nor even make a remote and faint approach to it. They conceive that He who gave our nature to be perfected by our virtue, willed also the necessary means of its perfection. He willed therefore the state; He willed its connexion [116] with the source and original archetype of all perfection. They who are convinced of this his will, which is the law of laws and the sovereign of sovereigns, cannot think it reprehensible, that this our corporate fealty and homage, that this our recognition of a seigniory paramount, I had almost said this oblation of the state itself, as a worthy offering on the high altar of universal praise, should be performed, as all publick solemn acts are performed, in buildings, in musick, in decoration, in speech, in the dignity of persons, according to the customs of mankind, taught by their nature; that is, with modest splendour, with unassuming state, with mild majesty and sober pomp. For those purposes they think some part of the wealth of the country is as usefully employed, as it can be in fomenting the luxury of individuals. It is the publick ornament. It is the publick consolation. It nourishes the publick hope. The poorest man finds his own importance and dignity in it, whilst the wealth and pride of individuals at every moment makes the man of humble rank and fortune sensible of his inferiority, and degrades and vilifies his condition. It is for the man in humble life, and to raise his nature, and to put him in mind of a state in which the privileges of opulence will cease, when he will be equal by nature, and may be more than equal by virtue—that this portion of the general wealth of his country is employed and sanctified.

I assure you I do not aim at singularity. I give you opinions which have been accepted amongst us, from very early times to this moment, with a continued and general approbation; and which indeed are so worked into my mind, that I am unable to distinguish what I have learned from others from the results of my own meditation.

It is on some such principles that the majority of the people of England, far from thinking a religious national establishment unlawful, hardly think it lawful to be without one. In France you are wholly mistaken if you do not [117] believe us above all other things attached to it, and beyond all other nations; and when this people has acted unwisely and unjustifiably in its favour (as in some instances they have done most certainly) in their very errors you will at least discover their zeal.

This principle runs through the whole system of their polity. They do not consider their church establishment as convenient, but as essential to their state; not as a thing heterogeneous and separable; something added for accommodation; what they may either keep up or lay aside, according to their temporary ideas of convenience. They consider it as the foundation of their whole constitution, with which, and with every part of which, it holds an indissoluble union. Church and state are ideas inseparable in their minds, and scarcely is the one ever mentioned without mentioning the other.

OUR EDUCATION IS SO FORMED as to confirm and fix this impression. Our education is in a manner wholly in the hands of ecclesiastics, and in all stages from infancy to manhood. Even when our youth, leaving schools and universities, enter that most important period of life which begins to link experience and study together, and when with that view they visit other countries, instead of old domestics whom we have seen as governors to principal men from other parts, threefourths of those who go abroad with our young nobility and gentlemen are ecclesiastics; not as austere masters, nor as mere followers; but as friends and companions of a graver character, and not seldom persons as well born as themselves. With them, as relations, they most commonly keep up a close connexion through life. By this connexion we conceive that we attach our gentlemen to the church; and we liberalize the church by an intercourse with the leading characters of the country.

[118] So tenacious are we of the old ecclesiastical modes and fashions of institution, that very little alteration has been made in them since the fourteenth or fifteenth century; ad-

hering in this particular, as in all things else, to our old settled maxim, never entirely nor at once to depart from antiquity. We found these old institutions, on the whole, favourable to morality and discipline; and we thought they were susceptible of amendment, without altering the ground. We thought that they were capable of receiving and meliorating, and above all of preserving, the accessions of science and literature, as the order of Providence should successively produce them. And after all, with this Gothic and monkish education (for such it is in the ground-work) we may put in our claim to as ample and as early a share in all the improvements in science, in arts, and in literature, which have illuminated and adorned the modern world, as any other nation in Europe; we think one main cause of this improvement was our not despising the patrimony of knowledge which was left us by our forefathers.

It is from our attachment to a church establishment that the English nation did not think it wise to entrust that great fundamental interest of the whole to what they trust no part of their civil or military public service, that is, to the unsteady and precarious contribution of individuals. They go further. They certainly never have suffered and never will suffer the fixed estate of the church to be converted into a pension, to depend on the treasury, and to be delayed, withheld, or perhaps to be extinguished by fiscal difficulties; which difficulties may sometimes be pretended for political purposes, and are in fact often brought on by the extravagance, negligence, and rapacity of politicians. The people of England think that they have constitutional motives, as well as religious, against any project of turning their independent clergy into ecclesiastical pensioners of state. They tremble [119] for their liberty, from the influence of a clergy dependent on the crown; they tremble for the public tranquillity from the disorders of a factious clergy, if it were made to depend upon any other than the crown. They therefore made their church, like their king and their nobility, independent.

From the united considerations of religion and constitutional policy, from their opinion of a duty to make a sure provision for the consolation of the feeble and the instruction of the ignorant, they have incorporated and identified the estate of the church with the mass of *private property*, of which the state is not the proprietor, either for use or dominion, but the guardian only and the regulator. They have ordained that the provision of this establishment might be as stable as the earth on which it stands, and should not fluctuate with the Euripus of funds and actions.

THE MEN OF ENGLAND, the men, I mean, of light and leading in England, whose wisdom (if they have any) is open and direct, would be ashamed, as of a silly deceitful trick, to profess any religion in name, which by their proceedings they appeared to contemn. If by their conduct (the only language that rarely lies) they seemed to regard the great ruling principle of the moral and the natural world, as a mere invention to keep the vulgar in obedience, they apprehend that by such a conduct they would defeat the politic purpose they have in view. They would find it difficult to make others to believe in a system to which they manifestly gave no credit themselves. The Christian statesmen of this land would indeed first provide for the *multitude;* because it is the *multitude;* and is therefore, as such, the first object in the ecclesiastical institution, and in all institutions. They have been taught that the circumstance of the gospel's being preached to the poor was one of the great tests of its true mission. They think, therefore, that those do not believe it, [120] who do not take care it should be preached to the poor. But as they know that charity is not confined to any one description, but ought to apply itself to all men who have wants, they are not deprived of a due and anxious sensation of pity to the distresses of the miserable great. They are not repelled through a fastidious delicacy, at the stench of their arrogance and presumption, from a medicinal attention to their mental blotches and running sores. They are sensible, that religious instruction is of more consequence to them than to any others; from the greatness of the temptation to which they are exposed; from the important consequences that attend their faults; from the contagion of their ill example; from the necessity of bowing down the stubborn neck of their pride and ambition to the yoke of moderation and virtue; from a consideration of the fat stupidity and gross ignorance concerning what imports men most to know, which prevails at courts, and at the head of armies, and in senates, as much as at the loom and in the field.

The English people are satisfied, that to the great the consolations of religion are as necessary as its instructions. They too are among the unhappy. They feel personal pain and domestic sorrow. In these they have no privilege, but are subject to pay their full contingent to the contributions levied on mortality. They want this sovereign balm under their gnawing cares and anxieties, which being less conversant about the limited wants of animal life, range without limit, and are diversified by infinite combinations in the wild and unbounded regions of imagination. Some charitable dole is wanting to these, our often very unhappy brethren, to fill the gloomy void that reigns in minds which have nothing on earth to hope or fear; something to relieve in the killing languor and over-laboured lassitude of those who have nothing to do; something to excite an appetite to existence in the palled satiety which attends on all pleasures [121] which may be bought, where nature is not left to her own process, where even desire is anticipated, and therefore fruition defeated by meditated schemes and contrivances of delight; and no interval, no obstacle, is interposed between the wish and the accomplishment.

The people of England know how little influence the teachers of religion are likely to have with the wealthy and powerful of long standing, and how much less with the newly fortunate, if they appear in a manner no way assorted to those with whom they must associate, and over whom they must even exercise, in some cases, something like an authority. What must they think of that body of teachers, if they see it in no part above the establishment of their domestic servants? If the poverty were voluntary, there might be some difference. Strong instances of self-denial operate powerfully on our minds; and a man who has no wants has obtained great freedom and firmness, and even dignity. But as the mass of any description of men are but men, and their poverty cannot be voluntary, that disrespect which attends upon all lay poverty, will not depart from the ecclesiastical. Our provident constitution has therefore taken care that those who are to instruct presumptuous ignorance, those who are to be censors over insolent vice, should neither incur their contempt, nor live upon their alms; nor will it tempt the rich to a neglect of the true medicine of their minds. For these reasons, whilst we provide first for the poor, and with a parental solicitude, we have not relegated religion, like something we were ashamed to shew, to obscure municipalities or rustic villages. No! We will have her to exalt her mitred front in courts and parliaments. We will have her mixed throughout the whole mass of life, and blended with all the classes of society. The people of England will shew to the haughty potentates of the world, and to their talking sophisters, that a free, a generous, an [122] informed nation, honours the high magistrates of its church; that it will not suffer the insolence of wealth and titles, or any other species of proud pretension, to look down with scorn upon what they look up to with reverence; nor presume to trample on that acquired personal nobility, which they intend always to be, and which often is the fruit, not the reward, (for what can be the reward?) of learning, piety, and virtue. They can see, without pain or grudging, an Archbishop precede a Duke. They can see a Bishop of Durham, or a Bishop of Winchester, in possession of ten thousand pounds a year;

and cannot conceive why it is in worse hands than estates to the like amount in the hands of this Earl, or that Squire; although it may be true, that so many dogs and horses are not kept by the former, and fed with the victuals which ought to nourish the children of the people. It is true, the whole church revenue is not always employed, and to every shilling, in charity; nor perhaps ought it; but something is generally so employed. It is better to cherish virtue and humanity, by leaving much to free will, even with some loss to the object, than to attempt to make men mere machines and instruments of a political benevolence. The world on the whole will gain by a liberty, without which virtue cannot exist.

WHEN ONCE THE COMMONWEALTH has established the estates of the church as property, it can, consistently, hear nothing of the more or the less. Too much and too little are treason against property. What evil can arise from the quantity in any hand, whilst the supreme authority has the full, sovereign superintendance over this, as over all property, to prevent every species of abuse; and, whenever it notably deviates, to give to it a direction agreeable to the purposes of its institution?

In England most of us conceive that it is envy and [123] malignity towards those who are often the beginners of their own fortune, and not a love of the self-denial and mortification of the antient church, that makes some look askance at the distinctions, and honours, and revenues, which, taken from no person, are set apart for virtue. The ears of the people of England are distinguishing. They hear these men speak broad. Their tongue betrays them. Their language is in the *patois* of fraud; in the cant and gibberish of hypocrisy. The people of England must think so, when these praters affect to carry back the clergy to that primitive evangelic poverty which, in the spirit, ought always to exist in them, (and in us too, however we may like it) but in the thing must be varied, when the relation of that body to the state is altered; when manners, when modes of life, when indeed the whole order of human affairs has undergone a total revolution. We shall believe those reformers to be then honest enthusiasts, not as now we think them, cheats and deceivers, when we see them throwing their own goods into common, and submitting their own persons to the austere discipline of the early church.

With these ideas rooted in their minds, the commons of Great Britain, in the national emergencies, will never seek their resource from the confiscation of the estates of the church and poor. Sacrilege and proscription are not among the ways and means in our committee of supply. The Jews in Change Alley have not yet dared to hint their hopes of a mortgage on the revenues belonging to the see of Canterbury. I am not afraid that I shall be disavowed, when I assure you that there is not *one* public man in this kingdom, whom you would wish to quote; no not one of any party or description, who does not reprobate the dishonest, perfidious, and cruel confiscation which the national assembly has been compelled to make of that property which it was their first duty to protect.

[124] It is with the exultation of a little national pride I tell you, that those amongst us who have wished to pledge the societies of Paris in the cup of their abominations, have been disappointed. The robbery of your church has proved a security to the possessions of ours. It has roused the people. They see with horror and alarm that enormous and shameless act of proscription. It has opened, and will more and more open their eyes upon the selfish enlargement of mind, and the narrow liberality of sentiment of insidious men, which commencing in close hypocrisy and fraud have ended in open violence and rapine. At home we behold similar beginnings. We are on our guard against similar conclusions.

I hope we shall never be so totally lost to all sense of the duties imposed upon us by the law of social union, as, upon any pretext of public service, to confiscate the goods of a single unoffending citizen. Who but a tyrant (a name expressive of every thing which can vitiate and degrade human nature) could think of seizing on the property of men, unaccused, unheard, untried, by whole descriptions, by hundreds and thousands together? who that had not lost every trace of humanity could think of casting down men of exalted rank and sacred function, some of them of an age to call at once for reverence and compassion—of casting them down from the highest situation in the commonwealth, wherein they were maintained by their own landed property, to a state of indigence, depression and contempt?

The confiscators truly have made some allowance to their victims from the scraps and fragments of their own tables from which they have been so harshly driven, and which have been so bountifully spread for a feast to the harpies of usury. But to drive men from independence to live on alms is itself great cruelty. That which might be a tolerable condition to men in one state of life, and not habituated to other things, may, when all these circumstances are altered, [125] be a dreadful revolution; and one to which a virtuous mind would feel pain in condemning any guilt except that which would demand the life of the offender. But to many minds this punishment of degradation and infamy is worse than death. Undoubtedly it is an infinite aggravation of this cruel suffering, that the persons who were taught a double prejudice in favour of religion, by education and by the place they held in the administration of its functions, are to receive the remnants of their property as alms from the profane and impious hands of those who had plundered them of all the rest; to receive (if they are at all to receive) not from the charitable contributions of the faithful, but from the insolent tenderness of known and avowed Atheism, the maintenance of religion, measured out to them on the standard of the contempt in which it is held; and for the purpose of rendering those who receive the allowance vile and of no estimation in the eyes of mankind.

But this act of seizure of property, it seems, is a judgment in law, and not a confiscation. They have, it seems, found out in the academies of the *Palais Royal,* and the *Jacobins,* that certain men had no right to the possessions which they held under law, usage, the decisions of courts, and the accumulated prescription of a thousand years. They say that ecclesiastics are fictitious persons, creatures of the state; whom at pleasure they may destroy, and of course limit and modify in every particular; that the goods they possess are not properly theirs, but belong to the state which created the fiction; and we are therefore not to trouble ourselves with what they may suffer in their natural feelings and natural persons, on account of what is done towards them in this their constructive character. Of what import is it, under what names you injure men, and deprive them of the just emoluments of a profession, in which they were not only permitted but encouraged by the state to engage; and [126] upon the supposed certainty of which emoluments they had formed the plan of their lives, contracted debts, and led multitudes to an entire dependence upon them?

You do not imagine, Sir, that I am going to compliment this miserable distinction of persons with any long discussion. The arguments of tyranny are as contemptible as its force is dreadful. Had not your confiscators by their early crimes obtained a power which secures indemnity to all the crimes of which they have since been guilty, or that they can commit, it is not the syllogism of the logician, but the lash of the executioner, that would have refuted a sophistry which becomes an accomplice of theft and murder. The sophistick tyrants of Paris are loud in their declamations against the departed regal tyrants who in former ages have vexed the world. They are thus bold, because they are safe from the dungeons and iron cages of their old masters. Shall we be more tender of the tyrants of our own time, when we see them acting worse tragedies under our eyes? Shall we not use the same liberty that they do, when we can use it with the same safety? when to speak honest truth only requires a contempt of the opinions of those whose actions we abhor?

THIS OUTRAGE ON ALL THE RIGHTS of property was at first covered with what, on the system of their conduct, was the most astonishing of all pretexts—a regard to national faith. The enemies to property at first pretended a most tender, delicate, and scrupulous anxiety for keeping the king's engagements with the public creditor. These professors of the rights of men are so busy in teaching others, that they have not leisure to learn any thing themselves; otherwise they would have known that it is to the property of the citizen, and not to the demands of the creditor of the state, that the first and original faith of civil society is pledged. The claim of the citizen is prior in time, paramount in title, [127] superior in equity. The fortunes of individuals, whether possessed by acquisition, or by descent, or in virtue of a participation in the goods of some community, were no part of the creditor's security, expressed or implied. They never so much as entered into his head when he made his bargain. He well knew that the public, whether represented by a monarch, or by a senate, can pledge nothing but the public estate; and it can have no public estate, except in what it derives from a just and proportioned imposition upon the citizens at large. This was engaged, and nothing else could be engaged, to the public creditor. No man can mortgage his injustice as a pawn for his fidelity.

It is impossible to avoid some observation on the contradictions caused by the extreme rigour and the extreme laxity of the new public faith which influenced in this transaction, and which influenced not according to the nature of the obligation, but to the description of the persons to whom it was engaged. No acts of the old government of the kings of France are held valid in the National Assembly, except its pecuniary engagements; acts of all others of the most ambiguous legality. The rest of the acts of that royal government are considered in so odious a light, that to have a claim under its authority is looked on as a sort of crime. A pension, given as a reward for service to the state, is surely as good a ground of property as any security for money advanced to the state. It is a better; for money is paid, and well paid, to obtain that service. We have however seen multitudes of people under this description in France, who never had been deprived of their allowances by the most arbitrary ministers in the most arbitrary times, by this assembly of the rights of men robbed without mercy. They were told, in answer to their claim to the bread earned with their blood, that their services had not been rendered to the country that now exists.

[128] This laxity of public faith is not confined to those unfortunate persons. The assembly (with perfect consistency it must be owned) is engaged in a respectable deliberation how far it is bound by the treaties made with other nations under the former government, and their Committee is to report which of them they ought to ratify, and which not. By this means they have put the external fidelity of this virgin state on a par with its internal.

It is not easy to conceive upon what rational principle the royal government should not, of the two, rather have possessed the power of rewarding service, and making treaties, in virtue of its prerogative, than that of pledging to creditors the revenue of the state actual and possible. The treasure of the nation, of all things, has been the least allowed to the prerogative of the king of France, or to the prerogative of any king in Europe. To mortgage the public revenue implies the sovereign dominion, in the fullest sense, over the public purse. It goes far beyond the trust even of a temporary

and occasional taxation. The acts however of that dangerous
power (the distinctive mark of a boundless despotism) have
been alone held sacred. Whence arose this preference given
by a democratic assembly to a body of property deriving its
title from the most critical and obnoxious of all the exertions
of monarchical authority? Reason can furnish nothing to reconcile inconsistency; nor can partial favour be accounted for
upon equitable principles. But the contradiction and partiality which admit no justification, are not the less without
an adequate cause; and that cause I do not think it difficult
to discover.

BY THE VAST DEBT OF FRANCE a great monied interest
had insensibly grown up, and with it a great power. By the
antient usages which prevailed in that kingdom, the general
circulation of property, and in particular the mutual convert-
ibility [129] of land into money, and of money into land, had
always been a matter of difficulty. Family settlements, rather
more general and more strict than they are in England; the
jus retractus; the great mass of landed property held by the
crown, and by a maxim of the French law held unalienably;
the vast estates of the ecclesiastic corporations; all these
had kept the landed and monied interests more separated
in France, less miscible, and the owners of the two distinct
species of property not so well disposed to each other as they
are in this country.

The monied property was long looked on with rather an
evil eye by the people. They saw it connected with their distresses, and aggravating them. It was no less envied by the
old landed interests, partly for the same reasons that rendered it obnoxious to the people, but much more so as it
eclipsed, by the splendour of an ostentatious luxury, the un-
endowed pedigrees and naked titles of several among the
nobility. Even when the nobility, which represented the more
permanent landed interest, united themselves by marriage

(which sometimes was the case) with the other description, the wealth which saved the family from ruin, was supposed to contaminate and degrade it. Thus the enmities and heart-burnings of these parties were encreased even by the usual means by which discord is made to cease, and quarrels are turned into friendship. In the mean time, the pride of the wealthy men, not noble or newly noble, encreased with its cause. They felt with resentment an inferiority, the grounds of which they did not acknowledge. There was no measure to which they were not willing to lend themselves, in order to be revenged of the outrages of this rival pride, and to exalt their wealth to what they considered as its natural rank and estimation. They struck at the nobility through the crown and the church. They attacked them particularly on the side on which they thought them the most vulnerable, [130] that is, the possessions of the church, which, through the patron-age of the crown, generally devolved upon the nobility. The bishopricks, and the great commendatory abbies, were, with few exceptions, held by that order.

In this state of real, though not always perceived war-fare between the noble antient landed interest, and the new monied interest, the greatest because the most applicable strength was in the hands of the latter. The monied interest is in its nature more ready for any adventure; and its posses-sors more disposed to new enterprizes of any kind. Being of a recent acquisition, it falls in more naturally with any novel-ties. It is therefore the kind of wealth which will be resorted to by all who wish for change.

ALONG WITH THE MONIED INTEREST, a new description of men had grown up, with whom that interest soon formed a close and marked union; I mean the political Men of Let-ters. Men of Letters, fond of distinguishing themselves, are rarely averse to innovation. Since the decline of the life and greatness of Lewis the XIVth, they were not so much cultivated either by him, or by the regent, or the successors to the crown; nor were they engaged to the court by favours and emoluments so systematically as during the splendid period of that ostentatious and not impolitic reign. What they lost in the old court protection, they endeavoured to make up by joining in a sort of incorporation of their own; to which the two academies of France, and afterwards the vast undertaking of the Encyclopaedia, carried on by a society of these gentlemen, did not a little contribute.

The literary cabal had some years ago formed something like a regular plan for the destruction of the Christian religion. This object they pursued with a degree of zeal which hitherto had been discovered only in the propagators of some system of piety. They were possessed with a spirit [131] of proselytism in the most fanatical degree; and from thence by an easy progress, with the spirit of persecution according to their means.[b] What was not to be done towards their great end by any direct or immediate act, might be wrought by a longer process through the medium of opinion. To command that opinion, the first step is to establish a dominion over those who direct it. They contrived to possess themselves, with great method and perseverance, of all the avenues to literary fame. Many of them indeed stood high in the ranks of literature and science. The world had done them justice; and in favour of general talents forgave the evil tendency of their peculiar principles. This was true liberality; which they returned by endeavouring to confine the reputation of sense, learning, and taste to themselves or their followers. I will venture to say that this narrow, exclusive spirit has not been less prejudicial to literature and to taste, than to morals and true philosophy. These Atheistical fathers have a bigotry of their own; and they have learnt to talk against monks with

[b. *This, down to the end of the first sentence in the next paragraph, and some other parts here and there, were inserted, on his reading the manuscript by my lost Son.*]

the spirit of a monk. But in some things they are men of the world. The resources of intrigue are called in to supply the defects of argument and wit. To this system of literary monopoly was joined an unremitting industry to blacken and discredit in every way, and by every means, all those who did not hold to their faction. To those who have observed the spirit of their conduct, it has long been clear that nothing was wanted but the power of carrying the intolerance of the tongue and of the pen into a persecution which would strike at property, liberty, and life.

The desultory and faint persecution carried on against them, more from compliance with form and decency than with serious resentment, neither weakened their strength, nor [132] relaxed their efforts. The issue of the whole was, that what with opposition, and what with success, a violent and malignant zeal, of a kind hitherto unknown in the world, had taken an entire possession of their minds, and rendered their whole conversation, which otherwise would have been pleasing and instructive, perfectly disgusting. A spirit of cabal, intrigue, and proselytism, pervaded all their thoughts, words, and actions. And, as controversial zeal soon turns its thoughts on force, they began to insinuate themselves into a correspondence with foreign princes; in hopes, through their authority, which at first they flattered, they might bring about the changes they had in view. To them it was indifferent whether these changes were to be accomplished by the thunderbolt of despotism, or by the earthquake of popular commotion. The correspondence between this cabal, and the late king of Prussia, will throw no small light upon the spirit of all their proceedings.* For the same purpose for which they intrigued with princes, they cultivated, in a distinguished manner, the monied interest of France; and partly

---

*I do not chuse to shock the feeling of the moral reader with any quotation of their vulgar, base, and profane language.

through the means furnished by those whose peculiar offices gave them the most extensive and certain means of communication, they carefully occupied all the avenues to opinion.

Writers, especially when they act in a body, and with one direction, have great influence on the publick mind; the alliance therefore of these writers with the monied interest [c] had no small effect in removing the popular odium and envy which attended that species of wealth. These writers, like the propagators of all novelties, pretended to a great zeal for the poor, and the lower orders, whilst in their satires they rendered hateful, by every exaggeration, the faults of courts, of nobility, and of priesthood. They became a sort of demagogues. [133] They served as a link to unite, in favour of one object, obnoxious wealth to restless and desperate poverty.

As these two kinds of men appear principal leaders in all the late transactions, their junction and politics will serve to account, not upon any principles of law or of policy, but as a *cause,* for the general fury with which all the landed property of ecclesiastical corporations has been attacked; and the great care which, contrary to their pretended principles, has been taken, of a monied interest originating from the authority of the crown. All the envy against wealth and power, was artificially directed against other descriptions of riches. On what other principle than that which I have stated can we account for an appearance so extraordinary and unnatural as that of the ecclesiastical possessions, which had stood so many successions of ages and shocks of civil violences, and were guarded at once by justice, and by prejudice, being applied to the payment of debts, comparatively recent, invidious, and contracted by a decried and subverted government?

Was the public estate a sufficient stake for the publick debts? Assume that it was not, and that a loss *must* be in-

[c. *Their connexion with Turgot and almost all the people of the finance.*]

curred somewhere — When the only estate lawfully possessed, and which the contracting parties had in contemplation at the time in which their bargain was made, happens to fail, who, according to the principles of natural and legal equity, ought to be the sufferer? Certainly it ought to be either the party who trusted; or the party who persuaded him to trust; or both; and not third parties who had no concern with the transaction. Upon any insolvency they ought to suffer who were weak enough to lend upon bad security, or they who fraudulently held out a security that was not valid. Laws are acquainted with no other rules of decision. But by the new institute of the rights of men, the [134] only persons, who in equity ought to suffer, are the only persons who are to be saved harmless: those are to answer the debt who neither were lenders or borrowers, mortgagers or mortgagees.

What had the clergy to do with these transactions? What had they to do with any publick engagement further than the extent of their own debt? To that, to be sure, their estates were bound to the last acre. Nothing can lead more to the true spirit of the assembly, which sits for publick confiscation, with its new equity and its new morality, than an attention to their proceeding with regard to this debt of the clergy. The body of confiscators, true to that monied interest for which they were false to every other, have found the clergy competent to incur a legal debt. Of course they declared them legally entitled to the property which their power of incurring the debt and mortgaging the estate implied; recognising the rights of those persecuted citizens, in the very act in which they were thus grossly violated.

If, as I said, any persons are to make good deficiencies to the publick creditor, besides the publick at large, they must be those who managed the agreement. Why therefore are not the estates of all the comptrollers general confiscated? [d]

[d. *All have been confiscated, in their turn.*]

REFLECTIONS ON THE REVOLUTION IN FRANCE

Why not those of the long succession of ministers, financiers, and bankers who have been enriched whilst the nation was impoverished by their dealings and their counsels? Why is not the estate of Mr. Laborde declared forfeited rather than of the archbishop of Paris, who has had nothing to do in the creation or in the jobbing of the publick funds? Or, if you must confiscate old landed estates in favour of the money-jobbers, why is the penalty confined to one description? I do not know whether the expences of the duke de Choiseul have left any thing of the infinite sums which he had derived from the bounty of his master, during the transactions of a [135] reign which contributed largely, by every species of prodigality in war and peace, to the present debt of France. If any such remains, why is not this confiscated? I remember to have been in Paris during the time of the old government. I was there just after the duke d'Aiguillon had been snatched (as it was generally thought) from the block by the hand of a protecting despotism. He was a minister, and had some concern in the affairs of that prodigal period. Why do I not see his estate delivered up to the municipalities in which it is situated? The noble family of Noailles have long been servants (meritorious servants I admit) to the crown of France, and have had of course some share in its bounties. Why do I hear nothing of the application of their estates to the publick debt? Why is the estate of the duke de Rochefoucault more sacred than that of the cardinal de Rochefoucault? The former is, I doubt not, a worthy person; and (if it were not a sort of profaneness to talk of the use, as affecting the title to property) he makes a good use of his revenues; but it is no disrespect to him to say, what authentic information well warrants me in saying, that the use made of a property equally valid, by his brother [ᵉ] the cardinal archbishop of Rouen, was far more

[e. *Not his brother, nor any near relation; but this mistake does not affect the argument.*]

laudable and far more publick-spirited. Can one hear of the proscription of such persons, and the confiscation of their effects, without indignation and horror? He is not a man who does not feel such emotions on such occasions. He does not deserve the name of a free man who will not express them.

FEW BARBAROUS CONQUERORS have ever made so terrible a revolution in property. None of the heads of the Roman factions, when they established "*crudelem illam hastam*" in all their auctions of rapine, have ever set up to sale the [136] goods of the conquered citizen to such an enormous amount. It must be allowed in favour of those tyrants of antiquity, that what was done by them could hardly be said to be done in cold blood. Their passions were inflamed, their tempers soured, their understandings confused, with the spirit of revenge, with the innumerable reciprocated and recent inflictions and retaliations of blood and rapine. They were driven beyond all bounds of moderation by the apprehension of the return to power with the return of property to the families of those they had injured beyond all hope of forgiveness.

These Roman confiscators, who were yet only in the elements of tyranny, and were not instructed in the rights of men to exercise all sorts of cruelties on each other without provocation, thought it necessary to spread a sort of colour over their injustice. They considered the vanquished party as composed of traitors who had borne arms, or otherwise had acted with hostility against the commonwealth. They regarded them as persons who had forfeited their property by their crimes. With you, in your improved state of the human mind, there was no such formality. You seized upon five millions sterling of annual rent, and turned forty or fifty thousand human creatures out of their houses, because "such was your pleasure." The tyrant, Harry the Eighth of England, as he was not better enlightened than the Roman Marius's and

Sylla's, and had not studied in your new schools, did not know what an effectual instrument of despotism was to be found in that grand magazine of offensive weapons, the rights of men. When he resolved to rob the abbies, as the club of the Jacobins have robbed all the ecclesiastics, he began by setting on foot a commission to examine into the crimes and abuses which prevailed in those communities. As it might be expected, his commission reported truths, exaggerations, and falsehoods. But, truly or [137] falsely, it reported abuses and offences. However, as abuses might be corrected, as every crime of persons does not infer a forfeiture with regard to communities, and as property, in that dark age, was not discovered to be a creature of prejudice, all those abuses (and there were enough of them) were hardly thought sufficient ground for such a confiscation as it was for his purposes to make. He therefore procured the formal surrender of these estates. All these operose proceedings were adopted by one of the most decided tyrants in the rolls of history, as necessary preliminaries, before he could venture, by bribing the members of his two servile houses with a share of the spoil, and holding out to them an eternal immunity from taxation, to demand a confirmation of his iniquitous proceedings by an act of parliament. Had fate reserved him to our times, four technical terms would have done his business, and saved him all this trouble; he needed nothing more than one short form of incantation — "*Philosophy, Light, Liberality, the Rights of Men.*"

I can say nothing in praise of those acts of tyranny, which no voice has hitherto ever commended under any of their false colours; yet in these false colours an homage was paid by despotism to justice. The power which was above all fear and all remorse was not set above all shame. Whilst Shame keeps its watch, Virtue is not wholly extinguished in the heart; nor will Moderation be utterly exiled from the minds of tyrants.

I believe every honest man sympathizes in his reflections

with our political poet on that occasion, and will pray to avert the omen whenever these acts of rapacious despotism present themselves to his view or his imagination:

———————— May no such storm
Fall on our times, where ruin must reform.
Tell me (my muse) what monstrous, dire offence,
What crimes could any Christian king incense
To such a rage? Was't luxury or lust?
[138] Was *he* so temperate, so chaste, so just?
Were these their crimes? they were his own much more;
But wealth is crime enough to him that's poor.*

> *The rest of the passage is this—
> Who having spent the treasures of his crown,
> Condemns their luxury to feed his own.
> And yet this act, to varnish o'er the shame
> Of sacrilege, must bear Devotion's name.
> No crime so bold, but would be understood
> A real, or at least a seeming good,
> Who fears not to do ill, yet fears the name;
> And, free from conscience, is a slave to fame.
> Thus he the church at once protects, and spoils:
> But princes' swords are sharper than their styles.
> And thus to th' ages past he makes amends,
> Their charity destroys, their faith defends.
> Then did Religion in a lazy cell,
> In empty aëry contemplations dwell;
> And, like the block, unmoved lay: but ours,
> As much too active, like the stork devours.
> Is there no temprate region can be known,
> Betwixt their frigid, and our torrid zone?
> Could we not wake from that lethargic dream,
> But to be restless in a worse extreme?
> And for that lethargy was there no cure,
> But to be cast into a calenture?
> Can knowledge have no bound, but must advance
> So far, to make us wish for ignorance?
> And rather in the dark to grope our way,
> Than, led by a false guide, to err by day?
> Who sees these dismal heaps, but would demand,
> What barbarous invader sack'd the land?
> But when he hears, no Goth, no Turk did bring
> This desolation, but a Christian king;
> When nothing, but the name of zeal, appears

REFLECTIONS ON THE REVOLUTION IN FRANCE

THIS SAME WEALTH, which is at all times treason and *lese nation* to indigent and rapacious despotism, under all modes of polity, was your temptation to violate property, law, and religion, united in one object. But was the state of France so wretched and undone, that no other resource but rapine remained to preserve its existence? On this point I wish to [139] receive some information. When the states met, was the condition of the finances of France such, that, after oeconomising on principles of justice and mercy through all departments, no fair repartition of burthens upon all the orders could possibly restore them? If such an equal imposition would have been sufficient, you well know it might easily have been made. Mr. Necker, in the budget which he laid before the Orders assembled at Versailles, made a detailed exposition of the state of the French nation.*

If we give credit to him, it was not necessary to have recourse to any new impositions whatsoever, to put the receipts of France on a balance with its expences. He stated the permanent charges of all descriptions, including the interest of a new loan of four hundred millions, at 531,444,000 livres; the fixed revenue at 475,294,000, making the deficiency 56,150,000, or short of 2,200,000 sterling. But to balance it, he brought forward savings and improvements of revenue (considered as entirely certain) to rather more than the amount of that deficiency; and he concludes with these emphatical words (p. 39) "Quel pays, Messieurs, que celui, ou, *sans impôts* et avec de simples objêts *inapperçus,* on peut faire disparoître un deficit qui a fait tant de bruit en Europe." As to the reimbursement, the sinking of debt, and the other great

---

'Twixt our best actions, and the worst of theirs,
What does he think our sacrilege would spare,
When such th' effects of our devotion are?
COOPER'S HILL, by Sir JOHN DENHAM

*Rapport de Mons. le Directeur-général des finances, fait par ordre du Roi à Versailles. Mai 5, 1789.

objects of public credit and political arrangement indicated in Mons. Necker's speech, no doubt could be entertained, but that a very moderate and proportioned assessment on the citizens without distinction would have provided for all of them to the fullest extent of their demand.

If this representation of Mons. Necker was false, then the assembly are in the highest degree culpable for having forced the king to accept as his minister, and since the king's [140] deposition, for having employed as *their* minister, a man who had been capable of abusing so notoriously the confidence of his master and their own; in a matter too of the highest moment, and directly appertaining to his particular office. But if the representation was exact (as, having always, along with you, conceived a high degree of respect for Mr. Necker, I make no doubt it was) then what can be said in favour of those, who, instead of moderate, reasonable, and general contribution, have in cold blood, and impelled by no necessity, had recourse to a partial and cruel confiscation?

Was that contribution refused on a pretext of privilege, either on the part of the clergy or on that of the nobility? No certainly. As to the clergy, they even ran before the wishes of the third order. Previous to the meeting of the states, they had in all their instructions expressly directed their deputies to renounce every immunity, which put them upon a footing distinct from the condition of their fellow-subjects. In this renunciation the clergy were even more explicit than the nobility.

But let us suppose that the deficiency had remained at the 56 millions, (or £2,200,000 sterling) as at first stated by Mr. Necker. Let us allow that all the resources he opposed to that deficiency were impudent and groundless fictions; and that the assembly (or their lords of articles* at the Jacobins)

---

*In the constitution of Scotland during the Stuart reigns, a committee sat for preparing bills; and none could pass but those previously approved by them. This committee was called lords of articles.

were from thence justified in laying the whole burthen of that deficiency on the clergy—yet allowing all this, a necessity of £2,200,000 sterling will not support a confiscation to the amount of five millions. The imposition of £2,200,000 on the clergy, as partial, would have been oppressive and unjust, but it would not have been altogether [141] ruinous to those on whom it was imposed; and therefore it would not have answered the real purpose of the managers.

Perhaps persons, unacquainted with the state of France, on hearing the clergy and the noblesse were privileged in point of taxation, may be led to imagine, that previous to the revolution these bodies had contributed nothing to the state. This is a great mistake. They certainly did not contribute equally with each other, nor either of them equally with the commons. They both however contributed largely. Neither nobility nor clergy enjoyed any exemption from the excise on consumable commodities, from duties of custom, or from any of the other numerous *indirect* impositions, which in France as well as here, make so very large a proportion of all payments to the public. The noblesse paid the capitation. They paid also a land-tax, called the twentieth penny, to the height sometimes of three, sometimes of four shillings in the pound; both of them *direct* impositions of no light nature, and no trivial produce. The clergy of the provinces annexed by conquest to France, which in extent make about an eighth part of the whole, but in wealth a much larger proportion, paid likewise to the capitation and the twentieth penny, at the rate paid by the nobility. The clergy in the old provinces did not pay the capitation; but they had redeemed themselves at the expence of about 24 millions, or a little more than a million sterling. They were exempted from the twentieths; but then they made free gifts; they contracted debts for the state; and they were subject to some other charges, the whole computed at about a thirteenth part of their clear income. They ought to have paid annually about forty thousand pounds more, to put them on a par with the contribution of the nobility.

When the terrors of this tremendous proscription hung over the clergy, they made an offer of a contribution, through the archbishop of Aix, which, for its extravagance, ought [142] not to have been accepted. But it was evidently and obviously more advantageous to the public creditor, than any thing which could rationally be promised by the confiscation. Why was it not accepted? The reason is plain—There was no desire that the church should be brought to serve the state. The service of the state was made a pretext to destroy the church. In their way to the destruction of the church they would not scruple to destroy their country: and they have destroyed it. One great end in the project would have been defeated, if the plan of extortion had been adopted in lieu of the scheme of confiscation. The new landed interest connected with the new republic, and connected with it for its very being, could not have been created. This was among the reasons why that extravagant ransom was not accepted.

THE MADNESS OF THE PROJECT of confiscation, on the plan that was first pretended, soon became apparent. To bring this unwieldly mass of landed property, enlarged by the confiscation of all the vast landed domain of the crown, at once into market, was obviously to defeat the profits proposed by the confiscation, by depreciating the value of those lands, and indeed of all the landed estates throughout France. Such a sudden diversion of all its circulating money from trade to land, must be an additional mischief. What step was taken? Did the assembly, on becoming sensible of the inevitable ill effects of their projected sale, revert to the offers of the clergy? No distress could oblige them to travel in a course which was disgraced by any appearance of justice. Giving over all hopes from a general immediate sale, another project seems to have succeeded. They proposed to take stock in exchange for the church lands. In that project great difficulties arose in equalizing the objects to be exchanged. Other obstacles also presented themselves, which

[143] threw them back again upon some project of sale. The municipalities had taken an alarm. They would not hear of transferring the whole plunder of the kingdom to the stockholders in Paris. Many of those municipalities had been upon system reduced to the most deplorable indigence. Money was no where to be seen. They were therefore led to the point that was so ardently desired. They panted for a currency of any kind which might revive their perishing industry. The municipalities were then to be admitted to a share in the spoil, which evidently rendered the first scheme, if ever it had been seriously entertained, altogether impracticable. Publick exigencies pressed upon all sides. The minister of finance reiterated his call for supply with a most urgent, anxious, and boding voice. Thus pressed on all sides instead of the first plan of converting their bankers into bishops and abbots, instead of paying the old debt, they contracted a new debt, at 3 per cent., creating a new paper currency, founded on an eventual sale of the church lands. They issued this paper currency to satisfy in the first instance chiefly the demands made upon them by the *Bank of discount,* the great machine, or paper-mill, of their fictitious wealth.

The spoil of the church was now become the only resource of all their operations in finance; the vital principle of all their politics; the sole security for the existence of their power. It was necessary by all, even the most violent means, to put every individual on the same bottom, and to bind the nation in one guilty interest to uphold this act, and the authority of those by whom it was done. In order to force the most reluctant into a participation of their pillage, they rendered their paper circulation compulsory in all payments. Those who consider the general tendency of their schemes to this one object as a centre; and a centre from which afterwards all their measures radiate, will not [144] think that I dwell too long upon this part of the proceedings of the national assembly.

To cut off all appearance of connection between the

crown and publick justice, and to bring the whole under implicit obedience to the dictators in Paris, the old independent judicature of the parliaments, with all its merits, and all its faults, was wholly abolished. Whilst the parliaments existed, it was evident that the people might some time or other come to resort to them, and rally under the standard of their antient laws. It became however a matter of consideration that the magistrates and officers, in the courts now abolished, *had purchased their places* at a very high rate, for which, as well as for the duty they performed, they received but a very low return of interest. Simple confiscation is a boon only for the clergy; to the lawyers some appearances of equity are to be observed; and they are to receive compensation to an immense amount. Their compensation becomes part of the national debt, for the liquidation of which there is the one exhaustless fund. The lawyers are to obtain their compensation in the new church paper, which is to march with the new principles of judicature and legislature. The dismissed magistrates are to take their share of martyrdom with the ecclesiastics, or to receive their own property from such a fund and in such a manner, as all those, who have been seasoned with the antient principles of jurisprudence, and had been the sworn guardians of property, must look upon with horror. Even the clergy are to receive their miserable allowance out of the depreciated paper which is stamped with the indelible character of sacrilege, and with the symbols of their own ruin, or they must starve. So violent an outrage upon credit, property, and liberty, as this compulsory paper currency, has seldom been exhibited by the alliance of bankruptcy and tyranny, at any time, or in any nation.

[145] In the course of all these operations, at length comes out the grand *arcanum;* that in reality, and in a fair sense, the lands of the church, so far as any thing certain can be gathered from their proceedings, are not to be sold at all. By the late resolutions of the national assembly, they

are indeed to be delivered to the highest bidder. But it is to be observed, that *a certain portion only of the purchase money is to be laid down.* A period of twelve years is to be given for the payment of the rest. The philosophic purchasers are therefore, on payment of a sort of fine, to be put instantly into possession of the estate. It becomes in some respects a sort of gift to them; to be held on the feudal tenure of zeal to the new establishment. This project is evidently to let in a body of purchasers without money. The consequence will be, that these purchasers, or rather grantees, will pay, not only from the rents as they accrue, which might as well be received by the state, but from the spoil of the materials of buildings, from waste in woods, and from whatever money, by hands habituated to the gripings of usury, they can wring from the miserable peasant. He is to be delivered over to the mercenary and arbitrary discretion of men, who will be stimulated to every species of extortion by the growing demands on the growing profits of an estate held under the precarious settlement of a new political system.

WHEN ALL THE FRAUDS, impostures, violences, rapines, burnings, murders, confiscations, compulsory paper currencies, and every description of tyranny and cruelty employed to bring about and to uphold this revolution, have their natural effect, that is, to shock the moral sentiments of all virtuous and sober minds, the abettors of this philosophic system immediately strain their throats in a declamation against the old monarchical government of France. When they have rendered that deposed power sufficiently black, they then [146] proceed in argument, as if all those who disapprove of their new abuses, must of course be partizans of the old; that those who reprobate their crude and violent schemes of liberty ought to be treated as advocates for servitude. I admit that their necessities do compel them to this base and contemptible fraud. Nothing can reconcile men to their proceedings and projects but the supposition that there is no third option between them, and some tyranny as odious as can be furnished by the records of history, or by the invention of poets. This prattling of theirs hardly deserves the name of sophistry. It is nothing but plain impudence. Have these gentlemen never heard, in the whole circle of the worlds of theory and practice, of any thing between the despotism of the monarch and the despotism of the multitude? Have they never heard of a monarchy directed by laws, controlled and balanced by the great hereditary wealth and hereditary dignity of a nation; and both again controlled by a judicious check from the reason and feeling of the people at large acting by a suitable and permanent organ? Is it then impossible that a man may be found who, without criminal ill intention, or pitiable absurdity, shall prefer such a mixed and tempered government to either of the extremes; and who may repute that nation to be destitute of all wisdom and of all virtue, which, having in its choice to obtain such a government with ease, *or rather to confirm it when actually possessed,* thought proper to commit a thousand crimes, and to subject their country to a thousand evils, in order to avoid it? Is it then a truth so universally acknowledged, that a pure democracy is the only tolerable form into which human society can be thrown, that a man is not permitted to hesitate about its merits, without the suspicion of being a friend to tyranny, that is, of being a foe to mankind?

I do not know under what description to class the present ruling authority in France. It affects to be a pure democracy, [147] though I think it in a direct train of becoming shortly a mischievous and ignoble oligarchy. But for the present I admit it to be a contrivance of the nature and effect of what it pretends to. I reprobate no form of government merely upon abstract principles. There may be situations in which the purely democratic form will become necessary. There may be some (very few, and very particularly circumstanced) where it would be clearly desireable. This I do not take to be the case of France, or of any other great country. Until now, we have seen no examples of considerable democracies. The antients were better acquainted with them. Not being wholly unread in the authors, who had seen the most of those constitutions, and who best understood them, I cannot help concurring with their opinion, that an absolute democracy, no more than absolute monarchy, is to be reckoned among the legitimate forms of government. They think it rather the corruption and degeneracy, than the sound constitution of a republic. If I recollect rightly, Aristotle observes, that a democracy has many striking points of resemblance with a tyranny.* Of this I am certain, that in a democracy, the majority of the citizens is capable of exercising the most cruel oppressions upon the minority, whenever strong divisions prevail in that kind of polity, as they often must; and [148] that oppression of the minority will extend to far greater numbers, and will be carried on with much greater fury, than can almost ever be apprehended from the dominion of a single sceptre. In such a popular persecution, individual sufferers are in a much more deplorable condition than in any other. Under a cruel prince they have the balmy compassion of mankind to assuage the smart of their wounds; they have the plaudits of

---

*When I wrote this I quoted from memory, after many years had elapsed from my reading the passage. A learned friend has found it, and it is as follows:

Τὸ ἦθος τὸ αὐτὸ, καὶ ἄμφω δεσποτικὰ τῶν βελτιόνων, καὶ τὰ ψηφίσματα, ὥσπερ ἐκεῖ τὰ ἐπιτάγματα· καὶ ὁ δημαγωγὸς καὶ ὁ κόλαξ, οἱ αὐτοὶ καὶ ἀνάλογον· καὶ μάλιστα ἑκάτεροι παρ' ἑκατέροις ἰσχύουσιν, οἱ μὲν κόλακες παρὰ τυράννοις, οἱ δὲ δημαγωγοὶ παρὰ τοῖς δήμοις τοῖς τοιούτοις.

"The ethical character is the same; both exercise despotism over the better class of citizens; and decrees are in the one, what ordinances and arrêts are in the other: the demagogue too, and the court favourite, are not unfrequently the same identical men, and always bear a close analogy; and these have the principal power, each in their respective forms of government, favourites with the absolute monarch, and demagogues with a people such as I have described." Arist. Politic. lib. iv. cap. 4.

the people to animate their generous constancy under their sufferings: but those who are subjected to wrong under multitudes, are deprived of all external consolation. They seem deserted by mankind; overpowered by a conspiracy of their whole species.

But admitting democracy not to have that inevitable tendency to party tyranny, which I suppose it to have, and admitting it to possess as much good in it when unmixed, as I am sure it possesses when compounded with other forms; does monarchy, on its part, contain nothing at all to recommend it? I do not often quote Bolingbroke, nor have his works in general, left any permanent impression on my mind. He is a presumptuous and a superficial writer. But he has one observation, which, in my opinion, is not without depth and solidity. He says, that he prefers a monarchy to other governments; because you can better ingraft any description of republic on a monarchy than any thing of monarchy upon the republican forms. I think him perfectly in the right. The fact is so historically; and it agrees well with the speculation.

I know how easy a topic it is to dwell on the faults of departed greatness. By a revolution in the state, the fawning sycophant of yesterday is converted into the austere critic of the present hour. But steady independant minds, when they have an object of so serious a concern to mankind as government, under their contemplation, will disdain to assume the part of satirists and declaimers. They will judge of human institutions as they do of human characters. They will sort [149] out the good from the evil, which is mixed in mortal institutions as it is in mortal men.

Your government in France, though usually, and I think justly, reputed the best of the unqualified or ill-qualified monarchies, was still full of abuses. These abuses accumulated in a length of time, as they must accumulate in every monarchy not under the constant inspection of a popular representative. I am no stranger to the faults and defects of the subverted government of France; and I think I am not inclined by nature or policy to make a panegyric upon any thing which is a just and natural object of censure. But the question is not now of the vices of that monarchy, but of its existence. Is it then true, that the French government was such as to be incapable or undeserving of reform; so that it was of absolute necessity the whole fabric should be at once pulled down, and the area cleared for the erection of a theoretic experimental edifice in its place? All France was of a different opinion in the beginning of the year 1789. The instructions to the representatives to the states-general, from every district in that kingdom, were filled with projects for the reformation of that government, without the remotest suggestion of a design to destroy it. Had such a design been then even insinuated, I believe there would have been but one voice, and that voice for rejecting it with scorn and horror. Men have been sometimes led by degrees, sometimes hurried into things, of which, if they could have seen the whole together, they never would have permitted the most remote approach. When those instructions were given, there was no question but that abuses existed, and that they demanded a reform; nor is there now. In the interval between the instructions and the revolution, things changed their shape; and in consequence of that change, the true question at present is, Whether those who would have reformed, or those who have destroyed, are in the right?

[150] To hear some men speak of the late monarchy of France, you would imagine that they were talking of Persia bleeding under the ferocious sword of Taehmas Kouli Khân; or at least describing the barbarous anarchic despotism of Turkey, where the finest countries in the most genial climates in the world are wasted by peace more than any countries have been worried by war; where arts are unknown, where manufactures languish, where science is extinguished, where agriculture decays, where the human race itself melts away

and perishes under the eye of the observer. Was this the case of France? I have no way of determining the question but by a reference to facts. Facts do not support this resemblance. Along with much evil, there is some good in monarchy itself; and some corrective to its evil, from religion, from laws, from manners, from opinions, the French monarchy must have received; which rendered it (though by no means a free, and therefore by no means a good constitution) a despotism rather in appearance than in reality.

Among the standards upon which the effects of government on any country are to be estimated, I must consider the state of its population as not the least certain. No country in which population flourishes, and is in progressive improvement, can be under a *very* mischievous government. About sixty years ago, the Intendants of the generalities of France made, with other matters, a report of the population of their several districts. I have not the books, which are very voluminous, by me, nor do I know where to procure them (I am obliged to speak by memory, and therefore the less positively) but I think the population of France was by them, even at that period, estimated at twenty-two millions of souls. At the end of the last century it had been generally calculated at eighteen. On either of these estimations France was not ill-peopled. Mr. Necker, who is an authority for his own time at least equal to the Intendants for theirs, [151] reckons, and upon apparently sure principles, the people of France, in the year 1780, at twenty-four millions six hundred and seventy thousand. But was this the probable ultimate term under the old establishment? Dr. Price is of opinion, that the growth of population in France was by no means at its *acmé* in that year. I certainly defer to Dr. Price's authority a good deal more in these speculations, than I do in his general politics. This gentleman, taking ground on Mr. Necker's data, is very confident, that since the period of that minister's calculation, the French population has encreased rapidly; so rapidly that in the year 1789 he will not consent to rate the people of that kingdom at a lower number than thirty millions. After abating much (and much I think ought to be abated) from the sanguine calculation of Dr. Price, I have no doubt that the population of France did encrease considerably during this later period: but supposing that it encreased to nothing more than will be sufficient to compleat the 24,670,000 to 25 millions, still a population of 25 millions, and that in an encreasing progress, on a space of about twenty-seven thousand square leagues, is immense. It is, for instance, a good deal more than the proportional population of this island, or even than that of England, the best-peopled part of the united kingdom.

It is not universally true, that France is a fertile country. Considerable tracts of it are barren, and labour under other natural disadvantages. In the portions of that territory, where things are more favourable, as far as I am able to discover, the numbers of the people correspond to the indulgence of nature.* The Generality of Lisle (this I admit is the strongest example) upon an extent of 404½ leagues, about ten years ago, contained 734,600 souls, which [152] is 1772 inhabitants to each square league. The middle term for the rest of France is about 900 inhabitants to the same admeasurement.

I do not attribute this population to the deposed government; because I do not like to compliment the contrivances of men, with what is due in a great degree to the bounty of Providence. But that decried government could not have obstructed, most probably it favoured, the operation of those causes (whatever they were) whether of nature in the soil, or in habits of industry among the people, which has produced so large a number of the species throughout that whole kingdom, and exhibited in some particular places such prodigies

* De l'Administration des Finances de la France, par Mons. Necker, vol. i. p. 288.

of population. I never will suppose that fabrick of a state to be the worst of all political institutions, which, by experience, is found to contain a principle favourable (however latent it may be) to the encrease of mankind.

THE WEALTH OF A COUNTRY is another, and no contemptible standard, by which we may judge whether, on the whole, a government be protecting or destructive. France far exceeds England in the multitude of her people; but I apprehend that her comparative wealth is much inferior to ours; that it is not so equal in the distribution, nor so ready in the circulation. I believe the difference in the form of the two governments to be amongst the causes of this advantage on the side of England. I speak of England, not of the whole British dominions; which, if compared with those of France, will, in some degree, weaken the comparative rate of wealth upon our side. But that wealth, which will not endure a comparison with the riches of England, may constitute a very respectable degree of opulence. Mr. Necker's book published in 1785,* contains an accurate [153] and interesting collection of facts relative to public oeconomy and to political arithmetic; and his speculations on the subject are in general wise and liberal. In that work he gives an idea of the state of France, very remote from the portrait of a country whose government was a perfect grievance, an absolute evil, admitting no cure but through the violent and uncertain remedy of a total revolution. He affirms, that from the year 1726 to the year 1784, there was coined at the mint of France, in the species of gold and silver, to the amount of about one hundred millions of pounds sterling.†

It is impossible that Mr. Necker should be mistaken in the amount of the bullion which has been coined in the mint.

---

*De l'Administration des Finances de la France, par M. Necker.

†Vol. iii. chap. 8. and chap. 9.

It is a matter of official record. The reasonings of this able financier, concerning the quantity of gold and silver which remained for circulation, when he wrote in 1785, that is about four years before the deposition and imprisonment of the French King, are not of equal certainty; but they are laid on grounds so apparently solid, that it is not easy to refuse a considerable degree of assent to his calculation. He calculates the *numéraire,* or what we call *specie,* then actually existing in France, at about eighty-eight millions of the same English money. A great accumulation of wealth for one country, large as that country is! Mr. Necker was so far from considering this influx of wealth as likely to cease, when he wrote in 1785, that he presumes upon a future annual increase of two per cent. upon the money brought into France during the periods from which he computed.

Some adequate cause must have originally introduced all the money coined at its mint into that kingdom; and some cause as operative must have kept at home, or returned into its bosom, such a vast flood of treasure as Mr. Necker calculates to remain for domestic circulation. Suppose any [154] reasonable deductions from Mr. Necker's computation: the remainder must still amount to an immense sum. Causes thus powerful to acquire and to retain, cannot be found in discouraged industry, insecure property, and a positively destructive government. Indeed, when I consider the face of the kingdom of France; the multitude and opulence of her cities; the useful magnificence of her spacious high roads and bridges; the opportunity of her artificial canals and navigations opening the conveniences of maritime communication through a solid continent of so immense an extent; when I turn my eyes to the stupendous works of her ports and harbours, and to her whole naval apparatus, whether for war or trade; when I bring before my view the number of her fortifications, constructed with so bold and masterly a skill, and made and maintained at so prodigious a charge, present-

ing an armed front and impenetrable barrier to her enemies
upon every side; when I recollect how very small a part of
that extensive region is without cultivation, and to what complete perfection the culture of many of the best productions
of the earth have been brought in France; when I reflect
on the excellence of her manufactures and fabrics, second
to none but ours, and in some particulars not second; when
I contemplate the grand foundations of charity, public and
private; when I survey the state of all the arts that beautify
and polish life; when I reckon the men she has bred for extending her fame in war, her able statesmen, the multitude of
her profound lawyers and theologians, her philosophers, her
critics, her historians and antiquaries, her poets, and her orators sacred and profane, I behold in all this something which
awes and commands the imagination, which checks the mind
on the brink of precipitate and indiscriminate censure, and
which demands, that we should very seriously examine, what
and how great are the latent vices that could authorise us at
once to level so spacious a fabric [155] with the ground. I do
not recognize, in this view of things, the despotism of Turkey. Nor do I discern the character of a government, that has
been, on the whole, so oppressive, or so corrupt, or so negligent, as to be utterly unfit *for all reformation*. I must think such
a government well deserved to have its excellencies heightened; its faults corrected; and its capacities improved into a
British constitution.

WHOEVER HAS EXAMINED into the proceedings of that
deposed government for several years back, cannot fail to
have observed, amidst the inconstancy and fluctuation natural to courts, an earnest endeavour towards the prosperity
and improvement of the country; he must admit, that it had
long been employed, in some instances, wholly to remove,
in many considerably to correct, the abusive practices and
usages that had prevailed in the state; and that even the un-

---

limited power of the sovereign over the persons of his subjects, inconsistent, as undoubtedly it was, with law and liberty, had yet been every day growing more mitigated in the exercise. So far from refusing itself to reformation, that government was open, with a censurable degree of facility, to all sorts of projects and projectors on the subject. Rather too much countenance was given to the spirit of innovation, which soon was turned against those who fostered it, and ended in their ruin. It is but cold, and no very flattering justice to that fallen monarchy, to say, that, for many years, it trespassed more by levity and want of judgment in several of its schemes, than from any defect in diligence or in public spirit. To compare the government of France for the last fifteen or sixteen years with wise and well-constituted establishments, during that, or during any period, is not to act with fairness. But if in point of prodigality in the expenditure of money, or in point of rigour in the exercise of power, it be compared with any of the former reigns, I [156] believe candid judges will give little credit to the good intentions of those who dwell perpetually on the donations to favourites, or on the expences of the court, or on the horrors of the Bastile in the reign of Louis the XVIth.*

Whether the system, if it deserves such a name, now built on the ruins of that antient monarchy, will be able to give a better account of the population and wealth of the country, which it has taken under its care, is a matter very doubtful. Instead of improving by the change, I apprehend that a long series of years must be told before it can recover in any degree the effects of this philosophic revolution, and before the nation can be replaced on its former footing. If Dr. Price should think fit, a few years hence, to favour us with an esti-

---

*The world is obliged to M. de Calonne for the pains he has taken to refute the scandalous exaggerations relative to some of the royal expences, and to detect the fallacious account given of pensions, for the wicked purpose of provoking the populace to all sorts of crimes.

REFLECTIONS ON THE REVOLUTION IN FRANCE

mate of the population of France, he will hardly be able to make up his tale of thirty millions of souls, as computed in 1789, or the assembly's computation of twenty-six millions of that year; or even Mr. Necker's twenty-five millions in 1780. I hear that there are considerable emigrations from France; and that many, quitting that voluptuous climate, and that seductive *Circean* liberty, have taken refuge in the frozen regions, and under the British despotism, of Canada.

In the present disappearance of coin, no person could think it the same country, in which the present minister of the finances has been able to discover fourscore millions sterling in specie. From its general aspect one would conclude that it had been for some time past under the special direction of the learned academicians of Laputa and Balnibarbi.* Already the population of Paris has so declined, that Mr. Necker stated to the national assembly the provision [157] to be made for its subsistence at a fifth less than what had formerly been found requisite.† It is said (and I have never heard it contradicted) that an hundred thousand people are out of employment in that city, though it is become the seat of the imprisoned court and national assembly. Nothing, I am credibly informed, can exceed the shocking and disgusting spectacle of mendicancy displayed in that capital. Indeed, the votes of the national assembly leave no doubt of the fact. They have lately appointed a standing committee of mendicancy. They are contriving at once a vigorous police on this subject, and, for the first time, the imposition of a tax to maintain the poor, for whose present relief great sums appear on the face of the public accounts of the year.‡ In the mean time, the

---

* See Gulliver's Travels for the idea of countries governed by philosophers.

† M. de Calonne states the falling off of the population of Paris as far more considerable; and it may be so, since the period of Mr. Necker's calculation.

‡ Travaux de charité pour

subvenir au manque de travail	Liv.		£	s.	d.
à Paris et dans les provinces	3,866,920	St^g	161,121	13	4

leaders of the legislative clubs and [158] coffee-houses are intoxicated with admiration at their own wisdom and ability. They speak with the most sovereign contempt of the rest of the world. They tell the people, to comfort them in the rags with which they have cloathed them, that they are a nation of philosophers; and, sometimes, by all the arts of quackish parade, by shew, tumult, and bustle, sometimes by the alarms of plots and invasions, they attempt to drown the cries of indigence, and to divert the eyes of the observer from the ruin and wretchedness of the state. A brave people will certainly prefer liberty, accompanied with a virtuous poverty, to a depraved and wealthy servitude. But before the price of comfort and opulence is paid, one ought to be pretty sure it is real liberty which is purchased, and that she is to be purchased at no other price. I shall always, however, consider that liberty as very equivocal in her appearance, which has

	Liv.		£	s.	d.
Destruction de vagabondage et de la mendicité	1,671,417		69,642	7	6
Primes pour l'importation de grains	5,671,907		236,329	9	2
Dépenses relatives aux subsistances, deduction fait des récouvremens qui ont eu lieu	39,871,790		1,661,324	11	8
Total Liv.	51,082,034	St^g	2,128,418	1	8

When I sent this book to the press I entertained some doubt concerning the nature and extent of the last article in the above accounts, which is only under a general head, without any detail. Since then I have seen M. de Calonne's work. I must think it a great loss to me that I had not that advantage earlier. M. de Calonne thinks this article to be on account of general subsistence: but as he is not able to comprehend how so great a loss as upwards of £1,661,000 sterling could be sustained on the difference between the price and the sale of grain, he seems to attribute the enormous head of charge to secret expences of the revolution. I cannot say any thing positively on that subject. The reader is capable of judging, by the aggregate of these immense charges, on the state and condition of France; and the system of publick oeconomy adopted in that nation. These articles of account produced no enquiry or discussion in the National Assembly.

not wisdom and justice for her companions; and does not lead prosperity and plenty in her train.

THE ADVOCATES FOR THIS REVOLUTION, not satisfied with exaggerating the vices of their antient government, strike at the fame of their country itself, by painting almost all that could have attracted the attention of strangers, I mean their nobility and their clergy, as objects of horror. If this were only a libel, there had not been much in it. But it has practical consequences. Had your nobility and gentry, who formed the great body of your landed men, and the whole of your military officers, resembled those of Germany, at the period when the Hanse-towns were necessitated to confederate against the nobles in defence of their property—had they been like the *Orsini* and *Vitelli* in Italy, who used to sally from their fortified dens to rob the trader and traveller—had they been such as the *Mamalukes* in Egypt, or the *Nayres* on the coast of Malabar, I do admit, that too critical an enquiry [159] might not be adviseable into the means of freeing the world from such a nuisance. The statues of Equity and Mercy might be veiled for a moment. The tenderest minds, confounded with the dreadful exigence in which morality submits to the suspension of its own rules in favour of its own principles, might turn aside whilst fraud and violence were accomplishing the destruction of a pretended nobility which disgraced whilst it persecuted human nature. The persons most abhorrent from blood, and treason, and arbitrary confiscation, might remain silent spectators of this civil war between the vices.

But did the privileged nobility who met under the king's precept at Versailles, in 1789, or their constituents, deserve to be looked on as the *Nayres* or *Mamalukes* of this age, or as the *Orsini* and *Vitelli* of antient times? If I had then asked the question, I should have passed for a madman. What have they since done that they were to be driven into exile, that their persons should be hunted about, mangled, and tortured, their families dispersed, their houses laid in ashes, that their order should be abolished, and the memory of it, if possible, extinguished, by ordaining them to change the very names by which they were usually known? Read their instructions to their representatives. They breathe the spirit of liberty as warmly, and they recommend reformation as strongly, as any other order. Their privileges relative to contribution were voluntarily surrendered; as the king, from the beginning, surrendered all pretence to a right of taxation. Upon a free constitution there was but one opinion in France. The absolute monarchy was at an end. It breathed its last, without a groan, without struggle, without convulsion. All the struggle, all the dissension arose afterwards upon the preference of a despotic democracy to a government of reciprocal controul. The triumph of the victorious party was over the principles of a British constitution.

[160] I have observed the affectation, which, for many years past, has prevailed in Paris even to a degree perfectly childish, of idolizing the memory of your Henry the Fourth. If any thing could put one out of humour with that ornament to the kingly character, it would be this overdone style of insidious panegyric. The persons who have worked this engine the most busily, are those who have ended their panegyrics in dethroning his successor and descendant; a man, as good-natured at the least, as Henry the Fourth; altogether as fond of his people; and who has done infinitely more to correct the antient vices of the state than that great monarch did, or we are sure he never meant to do. Well it is for his panegyrists that they have not him to deal with. For Henry of Navarre was a resolute, active, and politic prince. He possessed indeed great humanity and mildness; but an humanity and mildness that never stood in the way of his interests. He never sought to be loved without putting himself first in a condition to be feared. He used soft language with determined conduct. He

asserted and maintained his authority in the gross, and distributed his acts of concession only in the detail. He spent the income of his prerogatives nobly; but he took care not to break in upon the capital; never abandoning for a moment any of the claims, which he made under the fundamental laws, nor sparing to shed the blood of those who opposed him, often in the field, sometimes upon the scaffold. Because he knew how to make his virtues respected by the ungrateful, he has merited the praises of those whom, if they had lived in his time, he would have shut up in the Bastile, and brought to punishment along with the regicides whom he hanged after he had famished Paris into a surrender.

If these panegyrists are in earnest in their admiration of Henry the Fourth, they must remember, that they cannot think more highly of him, than he did of the noblesse of [161] France; whose virtue, honour, courage, patriotism, and loyalty were his constant theme.

But the nobility of France are degenerated since the days of Henry the Fourth. This is possible. But it is more than I can believe to be true in any great degree. I do not pretend to know France as correctly as some others; but I have endeavoured through my whole life to make myself acquainted with human nature: otherwise I should be unfit to take even my humble part in the service of mankind. In that study I could not pass by a vast portion of our nature, as it appeared modified in a country but twenty-four miles from the shore of this island. On my best observation, compared with my best enquiries, I found your nobility for the greater part composed of men of an high spirit, and of a delicate sense of honour, both with regard to themselves individually, and with regard to their whole corps, over whom they kept, beyond what is common in other countries, a censorial eye. They were tolerably well bred; very officious, humane, and hospitable; in their conversation frank and open; with a good military tone; and reasonably tinctured with literature, particularly of the authors in their own language. Many had pretensions far above this description. I speak of those who were generally met with.

As to their behaviour to the inferior classes, they appeared to me to comport themselves towards them with good-nature, and with something more nearly approaching to familiarity, than is generally practised with us in the intercourse between the higher and lower ranks of life. To strike any person, even in the most abject condition, was a thing in a manner unknown, and would be highly disgraceful. Instances of other ill-treatment of the humble part of the community were rare; and as to attacks made upon the property or the personal liberty of the commons, I never [162] heard of any whatsoever from *them;* nor, whilst the laws were in vigour under the antient government, would such tyranny in subjects have been permitted. As men of landed estates, I had no fault to find with their conduct, though much to reprehend, and much to wish changed, in many of the old tenures. Where the letting of their land was by rent, I could not discover that their agreements with their farmers were oppressive; nor when they were in partnership with the farmer, as often was the case, have I heard that they had taken the lion's share. The proportions seemed not inequitable. There might be exceptions; but certainly they were exceptions only. I have no reason to believe that in these respects the landed noblesse of France were worse than the landed gentry of this country; certainly in no respect more vexatious than the landholders, not noble, of their own nation. In cities the nobility had no manner of power; in the country very little. You know, Sir, that much of the civil government, and the police in the most essential parts, was not in the hands of that nobility which presents itself first to our consideration. The revenue, the system and collection of which were the most grievous parts of the French Government, was not administered by the men of the sword; nor were they answerable for the vices of its principle, or the vexations, where any such existed, in its management.

Denying, as I am well warranted to do, that the nobility had any considerable share in the oppression of the people, in cases in which real oppression existed, I am ready to admit that they were not without considerable faults and errors. A foolish imitation of the worst part of the manners of England, which impaired their natural character without substituting in its place what perhaps they meant to copy, has certainly rendered them worse than formerly they were. Habitual dissoluteness of manners continued beyond the [163] pardonable period of life, was more common amongst them than it is with us; and it reigned with the less hope of remedy, though possibly with something of less mischief, by being covered with more exterior decorum. They countenanced too much that licentious philosophy which has helped to bring on their ruin. There was another error amongst them more fatal. Those of the commons, who approached to or exceeded many of the nobility in point of wealth, were not fully admitted to the rank and estimation which wealth, in reason and good policy, ought to bestow in every country; though I think not equally with that of other nobility. The two kinds of aristocracy were too punctiliously kept asunder; less so, however, than in Germany and some other nations.

This separation, as I have already taken the liberty of suggesting to you, I conceive to be one principal cause of the destruction of the old nobility. The military, particularly, was too exclusively reserved for men of family. But after all, this was an error of opinion, which a conflicting opinion would have rectified. A permanent assembly, in which the commons had their share of power, would soon abolish whatever was too invidious and insulting in these distinctions; and even the faults in the morals of the nobility would have been probably corrected by the greater varieties of occupation and pursuit to which a constitution by orders would have given rise.

All this violent cry against the nobility I take to be a mere work of art. To be honoured and even privileged by the laws, opinions, and inveterate usages of our country, growing out of the prejudice of ages, has nothing to provoke horror and indignation in any man. Even to be too tenacious of those privileges, is not absolutely a crime. The strong struggle in every individual to preserve possession of what he has found to belong to him and to distinguish [164] him, is one of the securities against injustice and despotism implanted in our nature. It operates as an instinct to secure property, and to preserve communities in a settled state. What is there to shock in this? Nobility is a graceful ornament to the civil order. It is the Corinthian capital of polished society. *Omnes boni nobilitati semper favemus,* was the saying of a wise and good man. It is indeed one sign of a liberal and benevolent mind to incline to it with some sort of partial propensity. He feels no ennobling principle in his own heart who wishes to level all the artificial institutions which have been adopted for giving a body to opinion, and permanence to fugitive esteem. It is a sour, malignant, envious disposition, without taste for the reality, or for any image or representation of virtue, that sees with joy the unmerited fall of what had long flourished in splendour and in honour. I do not like to see any thing destroyed; any void produced in society; any ruin on the face of the land. It was therefore with no disappointment or dissatisfaction that my enquiries and observation did not present to me any incorrigible vices in the noblesse of France, or any abuse which could not be removed by a reform very short of abolition. Your noblesse did not deserve punishment; but to degrade is to punish.

IT WAS WITH THE SAME SATISFACTION I found that the result of my enquiry concerning your clergy was not dissimilar. It is no soothing news to my ears, that great bodies of men are incurably corrupt. It is not with much credulity I listen to any, when they speak evil of those whom they are going to plunder. I rather suspect that vices are feigned or exaggerated, when profit is looked for in their punishment. An enemy is a bad witness: a robber is a worse. Vices and abuses there were undoubtedly in that order, and must be. It was an old establishment, and not frequently revised. [165] But I saw no crimes in the individuals that merited confiscation of their substance, nor those cruel insults and degradations, and that unnatural persecution which has been substituted in the place of meliorating regulation.

If there had been any just cause for this new religious persecution, the atheistic libellers, who act as trumpeters to animate the populace to plunder, do not love any body so much as not to dwell with complacence on the vices of the existing clergy. This they have not done. They find themselves obliged to rake into the histories of former ages (which they have ransacked with a malignant and profligate industry) for every instance of oppression and persecution which has been made by that body or in its favour, in order to justify, upon very iniquitous, because very illogical principles of retaliation, their own persecutions, and their own cruelties. After destroying all other genealogies and family distinctions, they invent a sort of pedigree of crimes. It is not very just to chastise men for the offences of their natural ancestors; but to take the fiction of ancestry in a corporate succession, as a ground for punishing men who have no relation to guilty acts, except in names and general descriptions, is a sort of refinement in injustice belonging to the philosophy of this enlightened age. The assembly punishes men, many, if not most, of whom abhor the violent conduct of ecclesiastics in former times as much as their present persecutors can do, and who would be as loud and as strong in the expression of that sense, if they were not well aware of the purposes for which all this declamation is employed.

Corporate bodies are immortal for the good of the members, but not for their punishment. Nations themselves are such corporations. As well might we in England think of waging inexpiable war upon all Frenchmen for the evils which they have brought upon us in the several periods of our mutual hostilities. You might, on your part, think yourselves [166] justified in falling upon all Englishmen on account of the unparalleled calamities brought upon the people of France by the unjust invasions of our Henries and our Edwards. Indeed we should be mutually justified in this exterminatory war upon each other, full as much as you are in the unprovoked persecution of your present countrymen, on account of the conduct of men of the same name in other times.

We do not draw the moral lessons we might from history. On the contrary, without care it may be used to vitiate our minds and to destroy our happiness. In history a great volume is unrolled for our instruction, drawing the materials of future wisdom from the past errors and infirmities of mankind. It may, in the perversion, serve for a magazine, furnishing offensive and defensive weapons for parties in church and state, and supply the means of keeping alive, or reviving dissensions and animosities, and adding fuel to civil fury. History consists, for the greater part, of the miseries brought upon the world by pride, ambition, avarice, revenge, lust, sedition, hypocrisy, ungoverned zeal, and all the train of disorderly appetites, which shake the public with the same

—— troublous storms that toss
The private state, and render life unsweet.

These vices are the *causes* of those storms. Religion, morals, laws, prerogatives, privileges, liberties, rights of men, are the *pretexts*. The pretexts are always found in some specious appearance of a real good. You would not secure men from tyranny and sedition, by rooting out of the mind the principles to which these fraudulent pretexts apply? If you did, you would root out every thing that is valuable in the human breast. As these are the pretexts, so the ordinary actors and instruments in great public evils are kings, priests, magistrates, senates, parliaments, national assemblies, judges, and captains. You would not cure the [167] evil by resolving, that there should be no more monarchs, nor ministers of state, nor of the gospel; no interpreters of law; no general officers; no public councils. You might change the names. The things in some shape must remain. A certain *quantum* of power must always exist in the community, in some hands, and under some appellation. Wise men will apply their remedies to vices, not to names; to the causes of evil which are permanent, not to the occasional organs by which they act, and the transitory modes in which they appear. Otherwise you will be wise historically, a fool in practice. Seldom have two ages the same fashion in their pretexts and the same modes of mischief. Wickedness is a little more inventive. Whilst you are discussing fashion, the fashion is gone by. The very same vice assumes a new body. The spirit transmigrates; and, far from losing its principle of life by the change of its appearance, it is renovated in its new organs with the fresh vigour of a juvenile activity. It walks abroad; it continues its ravages, whilst you are gibbeting the carcass, or demolishing the tomb. You are terrifying yourself with ghosts and apparitions, whilst your house is the haunt of robbers. It is thus with all those, who, attending only to the shell and husk of history, think they are waging war with intolerance, pride, and cruelty, whilst, under colour of abhorring the ill principles of antiquated parties, they are authorizing and feeding the same odious vices in different factions, and perhaps in worse.

YOUR CITIZENS OF PARIS formerly had lent themselves as the ready instruments to slaughter the followers of Calvin, at the infamous massacre of St. Bartholomew. What should we say to those who could think of retaliating on the Parisians of this day the abominations and horrors of that time? They are indeed brought to abhor *that* massacre. Ferocious as [168] they are, it is not difficult to make them dislike it; because the politicians and fashionable teachers have no interest in giving their passions exactly the same direction. Still however they find it their interest to keep the same savage dispositions alive. It was but the other day that they caused this very massacre to be acted on the stage for the diversion of the descendants of those who committed it. In this tragic farce they produced the Cardinal of Lorraine in his robes of function, ordering general slaughter. Was this spectacle intended to make the Parisians abhor persecution, and loath the effusion of blood? No, it was to teach them to persecute their own pastors; it was to excite them, by raising a disgust and horror of their clergy, to an alacrity in hunting down to destruction an order, which, if it ought to exist at all, ought to exist not only in safety, but in reverence. It was to stimulate their cannibal appetites (which one would think had been gorged sufficiently) by variety and seasoning; and to quicken them to an alertness in new murders and massacres, if it should suit the purpose of the Guises of the day. An assembly, in which sat a multitude of priests and prelates, was obliged to suffer this indignity at its door. The author was not sent to the gallies, nor the players to the house of correction. Not long after this exhibition, those players came forward to the assembly to claim the rites of that very religion which they had dared to expose, and to shew their prostituted faces in the senate, whilst the archbishop of Paris, whose function was known to his people only by his prayers and benedictions, and his wealth only by his alms, is forced to abandon his house, and to fly from his flock, as from ravenous wolves, because, truly, in the sixteenth century, the Cardinal of Lorraine was a rebel and a murderer.[f]

[f. *This is on a supposition of the truth of this story, but he was not in France at the time. One name serves as well as another.*]

[169] Such is the effect of the perversion of history, by those, who, for the same nefarious purposes, have perverted every other part of learning. But those who will stand upon that elevation of reason, which places centuries under our eye, and brings things to the true point of comparison, which obscures little names, and effaces the colours of little parties, and to which nothing can ascend but the spirit and moral quality of human actions, will say to the teachers of the Palais Royal, "The Cardinal of Lorraine was the murderer of the sixteenth century, you have the glory of being the murderers in the eighteenth; and this is the only difference between you." But history, in the nineteenth century, better understood, and better employed, will, I trust, teach a civilized posterity to abhor the misdeeds of both these barbarous ages. It will teach future priests and magistrates not to retaliate upon the speculative and inactive atheists of future times, the enormities committed by the present practical zealots and furious fanatics of that wretched error, which, in its quiescent state, is more than punished, whenever it is embraced. It will teach posterity not to make war upon either religion or philosophy, for the abuse which the hypocrites of both have made of the two most valuable blessings conferred upon us by the bounty of the universal Patron, who in all things eminently favours and protects the race of man.

If your clergy, or any clergy, should shew themselves vicious beyond the fair bounds allowed to human infirmity, and to those professional faults which can hardly be separated from professional virtues, though their vices never can countenance the exercise of oppression, I do admit, that they would naturally have the effect of abating very much of our indignation against the tyrants who exceed measure and justice in their punishment. I can allow in clergymen, through all their divisions, some tenaciousness of their own [170] opinion; some overflowings of zeal for its propagation; some predilection to their own state and office; some attachment to the interest of their own corps; some preference to those who listen with docility to their doctrines, beyond those who scorn and deride them. I allow all this, because I am a man who have to deal with men, and who would not, through a violence of toleration, run into the greatest of all intolerance. I must bear with infirmities until they fester into crimes.

Undoubtedly, the natural progress of the passions, from frailty to vice, ought to be prevented by a watchful eye and a firm hand. But is it true that the body of your clergy had past those limits of a just allowance? From the general style of your late publications of all sorts, one would be led to believe that your clergy in France were a sort of monsters; an horrible composition of superstition, ignorance, sloth, fraud, avarice, and tyranny. But is this true? Is it true, that the lapse of time, the cessation of conflicting interests, the woeful experience of the evils resulting from party rage, have had no sort of influence gradually to meliorate their minds? Is it true, that they were daily renewing invasions on the civil power, troubling the domestic quiet of their country, and rendering the operations of its government feeble and precarious? Is it true, that the clergy of our times have pressed down the laity with an iron hand, and were in all places lighting up the fires of a savage persecution? Did they by every fraud endeavour to encrease their estates? Did they use to exceed the due demands on estates that were their own? Or, rigidly screwing up right into wrong, did they convert a legal claim into a vexatious extortion? When not possessed of power, were they filled with the vices of those who envy it? Were they enflamed with a violent litigious spirit of controversy? Goaded on with the ambition of intellectual sovereignty, were they ready to [171] fly in the face of all magistracy, to fire churches, to massacre the priests of other descriptions, to pull down altars, and to make their way over the ruins of subverted governments to an empire of doctrine, sometimes flattering, sometimes forcing the consciences of men from the jurisdiction of public institutions into a submission to their personal authority, beginning with a claim of liberty and ending with an abuse of power?

These, or some of these, were the vices objected, and not wholly without foundation, to several of the churchmen of former times, who belonged to the two great parties which then divided and distracted Europe.

If there was in France, as in other countries there visibly is, a great abatement, rather than any increase of these vices, instead of loading the present clergy with the crimes of other men, and the odious character of other times, in common equity they ought to be praised, encouraged, and supported, in their departure from a spirit which disgraced their predecessors, and for having assumed a temper of mind and manners more suitable to their sacred function.

WHEN MY OCCASIONS took me into France, towards the close of the late reign, the clergy, under all their forms, engaged a considerable part of my curiosity. So far from finding (except from one set of men, not then very numerous, though very active) the complaints and discontents against that body, which some publications had given me reason to expect, I perceived little or no public or private uneasiness on their account. On further examination, I found the clergy in general, persons of moderate minds and decorous manners; I include the seculars, and the regulars of both sexes. I had not the good fortune to know a great many of the parochial clergy; but in general I received a perfectly good [172] account of their morals, and of their attention to their duties. With some of the higher clergy I had a personal acquaintance; and of the rest in that class, very good means of information. They were, almost all of them, persons of noble birth. They resembled others of their own rank; and where there was any difference, it was in their favour. They were more fully educated than the military noblesse; so as by no means to disgrace their profession by ignorance, or by want of fitness for the exercise of their authority. They seemed to me, beyond the clerical character, liberal and open; with the hearts of gentlemen, and men of honour; neither insolent nor servile in their manners and conduct. They seemed to me rather a superior class; a set of men, amongst whom you would not be surprised to find a *Fénelon*. I saw among the clergy in Paris (many of the description are not to be met with any where) men of great learning and candour; and I had reason to believe, that this description was not confined to Paris. What I found in other places, I know was accidental; and therefore to be presumed a fair sample. I spent a few days in a provincial town, where, in the absence of the bishop, I passed my evenings with three clergymen, his vicars-general, persons who would have done honour to any church. They were all well informed; two of them of deep, general, and extensive erudition, antient and modern, oriental and western; particularly in their own profession. They had a more extensive knowledge of our English divines than I expected; and they entered into the genius of those writers with a critical accuracy. One of these gentlemen is since dead, the Abbé *Morangis*. I pay this tribute, without reluctance, to the memory of that noble, reverend, learned, and excellent person; and I should do the same, with equal cheerfulness, to the merits of the others, who I believe are still living, if I did not fear to hurt those whom I am unable to serve.

[173] Some of these ecclesiastics of rank, are, by all titles, persons deserving of general respect. They are deserving of gratitude from me, and from many English. If this letter should ever come into their hands, I hope they will believe there are those of our nation who feel for their unmerited fall, and for the cruel confiscation of their fortunes, with no common sensibility. What I say of them is a testimony, as far as one feeble voice can go, which I owe to truth. Whenever the question of this unnatural persecution is concerned, I will pay it. No one shall prevent me from being just and

grateful. The time is fitted for the duty; and it is particularly becoming to shew our justice and gratitude, when those who have deserved well of us and of mankind are labouring under popular obloquy and the persecutions of oppressive power.

You had before your revolution about an hundred and twenty bishops. A few of them were men of eminent sanctity, and charity without limit. When we talk of the heroic, of course we talk of rare, virtue. I believe the instances of eminent depravity may be as rare amongst them as those of transcendent goodness. Examples of avarice and of licentiousness may be picked out, I do not question it, by those who delight in the investigation which leads to such discoveries. A man, as old as I am, will not be astonished that several in every description, do not lead that perfect life of self-denial, with regard to wealth or to pleasure, which is wished for by all, by some expected, but by none exacted with more rigour, than by those who are the most attentive to their own interests, or the most indulgent to their own passions. When I was in France, I am certain that the number of vicious prelates was not great. Certain individuals among them not distinguishable for the regularity of their lives, made some amends for their want of the severe [174] virtues, in their possession of the liberal; and were endowed with qualities which made them useful in the church and state. I am told, that with few exceptions, Louis the Sixteenth had been more attentive to character, in his promotions to that rank, than his immediate predecessor; and I believe, as some spirit of reform has prevailed through the whole reign, that it may be true. But the present ruling power has shewn a disposition only to plunder the church. It has punished *all* prelates; which is to favour the vicious, at least in point of reputation. It has made a degrading pensionary establishment, to which no man of liberal ideas or liberal condition will destine his children. It must settle into the lowest classes of the people. As with you the inferior clergy are not numerous enough for their duties; as these duties are, beyond measure, minute and toilsome; as you have left no middle classes of clergy at their ease, in future nothing of science or erudition can exist in the Gallican church. To complete the project, without the least attention to the rights of patrons, the assembly has provided in future an elective clergy; an arrangement which will drive out of the clerical profession all men of sobriety; all who can pretend to independence in their function or their conduct; and which will throw the whole direction of the public mind into the hands of a set of licentious, bold, crafty, factious, flattering wretches, of such condition and such habits of life as will make their contemptible pensions, in comparison of which the stipend of an exciseman is lucrative and honourable, an object of low and illiberal intrigue. Those officers, whom they still call bishops, are to be elected to a provision comparatively mean, through the same arts, (that is, electioneering arts) by men of all religious tenets that are known or can be invented. The new lawgivers have not ascertained any thing whatsoever concerning their qualifications, relative either to doctrine or to morals; no [175] more than they have done with regard to the subordinate clergy; nor does it appear but that both the higher and the lower may, at their discretion, practice or preach any mode of religion or irreligion that they please. I do not yet see what the jurisdiction of bishops over their subordinates is to be; or whether they are to have any jurisdiction at all.

In short, Sir, it seems to me, that this new ecclesiastical establishment is intended only to be temporary, and preparatory to the utter abolition, under any of its forms, of the Christian religion, whenever the minds of men are prepared for this last stroke against it, by the accomplishment of the plan for bringing its ministers into universal contempt. They who will not believe, that the philosophical fanatics who guide in these matters, have long entertained such a design, are utterly ignorant of their character and proceedings. These enthusiasts do not scruple to avow their opinion, that a state can subsist without any religion better than with one; and that they are able to supply the place of any good which may be in it, by a project of their own—namely, by a sort of education they have imagined, founded in a knowledge of the physical wants of men; progressively carried to an enlightened self-interest, which, when well understood, they tell us will identify with an interest more enlarged and public. The scheme of this education has been long known. Of late they distinguish it (as they have got an entire new nomenclature of technical terms) by the name of a *Civic Education.*

I hope their partizans in England, (to whom I rather attribute very inconsiderate conduct than the ultimate object in this detestable design) will succeed neither in the pillage of the ecclesiastics, nor in the introduction of a principle of popular election to our bishoprics and parochial cures. This, in the present condition of the world, would be the last corruption of the church; the utter ruin of the [176] clerical character; the most dangerous shock that the state ever received through a misunderstood arrangement of religion. I know well enough that the bishoprics and cures, under kingly and seignoral patronage, as now they are in England, and as they have been lately in France, are sometimes acquired by unworthy methods; but the other mode of ecclesiastical canvas subjects them infinitely more surely and more generally to all the evil arts of low ambition, which, operating on and through greater numbers, will produce mischief in proportion.

THOSE OF YOU WHO HAVE ROBBED the clergy, think that they shall easily reconcile their conduct to all protestant nations; because the clergy, whom they have thus plundered, degraded, and given over to mockery and scorn, are of the Roman Catholic, that is, of *their own* pretended persuasion. I have no doubt that some miserable bigots will be found here as well as elsewhere, who hate sects and parties different from their own, more than they love the substance of religion; and who are more angry with those who differ from them in their particular plans and systems, than displeased with those who attack the foundation of our common hope. These men will write and speak on the subject in the manner that is to be expected from their temper and character. Burnet says, that when he was in France, in the year 1683, "the method which carried over the men of the finest parts to popery was this— they brought themselves to doubt of the whole Christian religion. When that was once done, it seemed a more indifferent thing of what side or form they continued outwardly." If this was then the ecclesiastic policy of France, it is what they have since but too much reason to repent of. They preferred atheism to a form of religion not agreeable to their ideas. They succeeded in destroying that form; and atheism has succeeded in [177] destroying them. I can readily give credit to Burnet's story; because I have observed too much of a similar spirit (for a little of it is "much too much") amongst ourselves. The humour, however, is not general.

The teachers who reformed our religion in England bore no sort of resemblance to your present reforming doctors in Paris. Perhaps they were (like those whom they opposed) rather more than could be wished under the influence of a party spirit; but they were most sincere believers; men of the most fervent and exalted piety; ready to die, as some of them did die, like true heroes in defence of their particular ideas of Christianity; as they would with equal fortitude, and more chearfully, for that stock of general truth, for the branches of which they contended with their blood. These men would have disavowed with horror those wretches who claimed a fellowship with them upon no other titles than those of their having pillaged the persons with whom they maintained controversies, and their having despised the common religion, for the purity of which they exerted themselves with a zeal, which unequivocally bespoke their highest reverence for the substance of that system which they wished to reform. Many of their descendants have retained the same zeal; but, (as less engaged in conflict) with more moderation. They do not forget that justice and mercy are substantial parts of religion. Impious men do not recommend themselves to their communion by iniquity and cruelty towards any description of their fellow creatures.

We hear these new teachers continually boasting of their spirit of toleration. That those persons should tolerate all opinions, who think none to be of estimation, is a matter of small merit. Equal neglect is not impartial kindness. The species of benevolence, which arises from contempt, is no true charity. There are in England abundance of men who tolerate in the true spirit of toleration. They think the [178] dogmas of religion, though in different degrees, are all of moment; and that amongst them there is, as amongst all things of value, a just ground of preference. They favour, therefore, and they tolerate. They tolerate, not because they despise opinions, but because they respect justice. They would reverently and affectionately protect all religions, because they love and venerate the great principle upon which all agree, and the great object to which they are all directed. They begin more and more plainly to discern, that we have all a common cause, as against a common enemy. They will not be so misled by the spirit of faction, as not to distinguish what is done in favour of their subdivision, from those acts of hostility, which, through some particular description, are aimed at the whole corps, in which they themselves, under another denomination, are included. It is impossible for me to say what may be the character of every description of men amongst us. But I speak for the greater part; and for them, I must tell you, that sacrilege is no part of their doctrine of good works; that, so far from calling you into their fellowship on such title, if your professors are admitted to their communion, they must carefully conceal their doctrine of the lawfulness of the proscription of innocent men; and that they must make restitution of all stolen goods whatsoever. Till then they are none of ours.

You may suppose that we do not approve your confiscation of the revenues of bishops, and deans, and chapters, and parochial clergy possessing independent estates arising from land, because we have the same sort of establishment in England. That objection, you will say, cannot hold as to the confiscation of the goods of monks and nuns, and the abolition of their order. It is true, that this particular part of your general confiscation does not affect England, as a precedent in point: but the reason applies; and it goes a [179] great way. The long parliament confiscated the lands of deans and chapters in England on the same ideas upon which your assembly set to sale the lands of the monastic orders. But it is in the principle of injustice that the danger lies, and not in the description of persons on whom it is first exercised. I see, in a country very near us, a course of policy pursued, which sets justice, the common concern of mankind, at defiance. With the national assembly of France, possession is nothing; law and usage are nothing. I see the national assembly openly reprobate the doctrine of prescription, which* one of the greatest of their own lawyers tells us, with great truth, is a part of the law of nature. He tells us, that the positive ascertainment of its limits, and its security from invasion, were among the causes for which civil society itself has been instituted. If prescription be once shaken, no species of property is secure, when it once becomes an object large enough to tempt the cupidity of indigent power. I see a practice perfectly correspondent to their contempt of this great fundamental part of natural law. I see the confiscators begin with bishops, and chapters, and monasteries; but I do not see them end there. I

* Domat.

see the princes of the blood, who, by the oldest usages of that kingdom, held large landed estates, (hardly with the compliment of a debate) deprived of their possessions, and in lieu of their stable independent property, reduced to the hope of some precarious, charitable pension, at the pleasure of an assembly, which of course will pay little regard to the rights of pensioners at pleasure, when it despises those of legal proprietors. Flushed with the insolence of their first inglorious victories, and pressed by the distresses caused by their lust of unhallowed lucre, disappointed but not discouraged, they have at length ventured completely to subvert all property of all descriptions throughout the extent of a great [180] kingdom. They have compelled all men, in all transactions of commerce, in the disposal of lands, in civil dealing, and through the whole communion of life, to accept as perfect payment and good and lawful tender, the symbols of their speculations on a projected sale of their plunder. What vestiges of liberty or property have they left? The tenant-right of a cabbage-garden, a year's interest in a hovel, the goodwill of an ale-house, or a baker's shop, the very shadow of a constructive property, are more ceremoniously treated in our parliament than with you the oldest and most valuable landed possessions, in the hands of the most respectable personages, or than the whole body of the monied and commercial interest of your country. We entertain an high opinion of the legislative authority; but we have never dreamt that parliaments had any right whatever to violate property, to overrule prescription, or to force a currency of their own fiction in the place of that which is real, and recognized by the law of nations. But you, who began with refusing to submit to the most moderate restraints, have ended by establishing an unheard of despotism. I find the ground upon which your confiscators go is this; that indeed their proceedings could not be supported in a court of justice; but that the rules of prescription cannot bind a legislative assembly.* So that this legislative assembly of a free nation sits, not for the security, but for the destruction of property, and not of property only, but of every rule and maxim which can give it stability, and of those instruments which can alone give it circulation.

WHEN THE ANABAPTISTS of Münster, in the sixteenth century, had filled Germany with confusion by their system of levelling and their wild opinions concerning property, to [181] what country in Europe did not the progress of their fury furnish just cause of alarm? Of all things, wisdom is the most terrified with epidemical fanaticism, because of all enemies it is that against which she is the least able to furnish any kind of resource. We cannot be ignorant of the spirit of atheistical fanaticism, that is inspired by a multitude of writings, dispersed with incredible assiduity and expence, and by sermons delivered in all the streets and places of public resort in Paris. These writings and sermons have filled the populace with a black and savage atrocity of mind, which supersedes in them the common feelings of nature, as well as all sentiments of morality and religion; insomuch that these wretches are induced to bear with a sullen patience the intolerable distresses brought upon them by the violent convulsions and permutations that have been made in property.† The spirit of

---

*Speech of Mr. Camus, published by order of the National Assembly.

†Whether the following description is strictly true I know not; but it is what the publishers would have pass for true, in order to animate others. In a letter from Toul, given in one of their papers, is the following passage concerning the people of that district: "Dans la Révolution actuelle, ils ont résisté à toutes les *séductions du bigotisme, aux persécutions et aux tracasseries* des Ennemis de la Révolution. *Oubliant leurs plus grands intérêts* pour rendre hommage aux vues d'ordre général qui ont déterminé l'Assemblée Nationale, ils voient, *sans se plaindre,* supprimer cette foule d'établissemens ecclésiastiques par lesquels *ils subsistoient;* et même, en perdant leur siège épiscopal, la seule de toutes ces ressources qui pouvoit, ou plutôt *qui devoit, en toute équité,* leur être conservée; con-

proselytism attends this spirit of fanaticism. They have societies to cabal and correspond at home and abroad for the propagation of their tenets. The [182] republic of Berne, one of the happiest, the most prosperous, and the best governed countries upon earth, is one of the great objects, at the destruction of which they aim. I am told they have in some measure succeeded in sowing there the seeds of discontent. They are busy throughout Germany. Spain and Italy have not been untried. England is not left out of the comprehensive scheme of their malignant charity; and in England we find those who stretch out their arms to them, who recommend their examples from more than one pulpit, and who choose, in more than one periodical meeting, publicly to correspond with them, to applaud them, and to hold them up as objects for imitation; who receive from them tokens of confraternity, and standards consecrated amidst their rites and mysteries;* who suggest to them leagues of perpetual amity, at the very time when the power, to which our constitution has exclusively delegated the federative capacity of this kingdom, may find it expedient to make war upon them.

IT IS NOT THE CONFISCATION of our church property from this example in France that I dread, though I think this would be no trifling evil. The great source of my solicitude is, lest it should ever be considered in England as the policy

---

damnés *à la plus effrayante misère,* sans avoir *été ni pu être entendus, ils ne murmurent point,* ils restent fidèles aux principes du plus pur patriotisme; ils sont encore prêts à *verser leur sang* pour le maintien de la Constitution, qui va reduire leur Ville *à la plus déplorable nullité."* These people are not supposed to have endured those sufferings and injustices in a struggle for liberty, for the same account states truly that they had been always free; their patience in beggary and ruin, and their suffering, without remonstrance, the most flagrant and confessed injustice, if strictly true, can be nothing but the effect of this dire fanaticism. A great multitude all over France is in the same condition and the same temper.

*See the proceedings of the confederation at *Nantz.*

of a state, to seek a resource in confiscations of any kind; or that any one description of citizens should be brought to regard any of the others as their proper prey.* Nations are [183] wading deeper and deeper into an ocean of boundless debt. Public debts, which at first were a security to governments, by interesting many in the public tranquillity, are likely in their excess to become the means of their subversion. If governments provide for these debts by heavy impositions, they perish by becoming odious to the people. If they do not provide for them, they will be undone by the efforts of the most dangerous of all parties; I mean an extensive discontented monied interest, injured and not destroyed. The men who compose this interest look for their security, in the first instance, to the fidelity of government; in the second, to its power. If they find the old governments effete, worn out, and with their springs relaxed, so as not to be of sufficient vigour for their purposes, they may seek new ones that shall be possessed of more energy; and this energy will be derived, not from an acquisition of resources, but from a contempt of justice. Revolutions are favourable to confiscation; and it is impossible to know under what obnoxious names the next

---

*"Si plures sunt ii quibus improbe datum est, quam illi quibus injuste ademptum est, idcirco plus etiam valent? Non enim numero haec judicantur, sed pondere. Quam autem habet aequitatem, ut agrum multis annis, aut etiam saeculis ante possessum, qui nullum habuit habeat; qui autem habuit amittat? Ac, propter hoc injuriae genus, Lacedaemonii Lysandrum Ephorum expulerunt: Agin regem (quod nunquam antea apud eos acciderat) necaverunt; exque eo tempore tantae discordiae secutae sunt, ut et tyranni exsisterint, et optimates exterminarentur, et preclarissime constituta respublica dilaberetur. Nec vero solum ipsa cecidit, sed etiam reliquam Graeciam evertit contagionibus malorum, quae a Lacedaemoniis profectae manarunt latius." After speaking of the conduct of the model of true patriots, Aratus of Sicyon, which was in a very different spirit, he says, "Sic par est agere cum civibus; non ut bis jam vidimus, hastam in foro ponere et bona civium voci subjicere praeconis. At ille Graecus (id quod fuit sapientis et praestantis viri) omnibus consulendum esse putavit: eaque est summa ratio et sapientia boni civis, commoda civium non divellere, sed omnes eadem aequitate continere." Cic. Off. l. 2.

confiscations will be authorised. I am sure that the principles predominant in France extend to very many persons and descriptions of persons in all countries who think their innoxious indolence their security. This kind of innocence in proprietors may be argued into inutility; and inutility into an unfitness for their estates. Many parts of Europe are in open disorder. In many others there is a hollow murmuring under ground; a confused movement is felt, that threatens a general earthquake in the political world. Already confederacies and correspondences of the most extraordinary nature are forming, in [184] several countries.* In such a state of things we ought to hold ourselves upon our guard. In all mutations (if mutations must be) the circumstance which will serve most to blunt the edge of their mischief, and to promote what good may be in them, is, that they should find us with our minds tenacious of justice, and tender of property.

But it will be argued, that this confiscation in France ought not to alarm other nations. They say it is not made from wanton rapacity; that it is a great measure of national policy, adopted to remove an extensive, inveterate, superstitious mischief. It is with the greatest difficulty that I am able to separate policy from justice. Justice is itself the great standing policy of civil society; and any eminent departure from it, under any circumstances, lies under the suspicion of being no policy at all.

When men are encouraged to go into a certain mode of life by the existing laws, and protected in that mode as in a lawful occupation—when they have accommodated all their ideas, and all their habits to it—when the law had long made their adherence to its rules a ground of reputation, and their departure from them a ground of disgrace and even of penalty—I am sure it is unjust in legislature, by an arbitrary

---

*See two books intitled, Einige Originalschriften des Illuminatenordens: System und Folgen des Illuminatenordens. München, 1787.

act, to offer a sudden violence to their minds and their feelings; forcibly to degrade them from their state and condition, and to stigmatize with shame and infamy that character and those customs which before had been made the measure of their happiness and honour. If to this be added an expulsion from their habitations, and a confiscation of all their goods, I am not sagacious enough to discover how this despotic sport, made of the feelings, consciences, prejudices, and properties of men, can be discriminated from the rankest tyranny.

[185] If the injustice of the course pursued in France be clear, the policy of the measure, that is, the public benefit to be expected from it, ought to be at least as evident, and at least as important. To a man who acts under the influence of no passion, who has nothing in view in his projects but the public good, a great difference will immediately strike him, between what policy would dictate on the original introduction of such institutions, and on a question of their total abolition, where they have cast their roots wide and deep, and where by long habit things more valuable than themselves are so adapted to them, and in a manner interwoven with them, that the one cannot be destroyed without notably impairing the other. He might be embarrassed, if the case were really such as sophisters represent it in their paltry style of debating. But in this, as in most questions of state, there is a middle. There is something else than the mere alternative of absolute destruction, or unreformed existence. *Spartam nactus es; hanc exorna.* This is, in my opinion, a rule of profound sense, and ought never to depart from the mind of an honest reformer. I cannot conceive how any man can have brought himself to that pitch of presumption, to consider his country as nothing but *carte blanche,* upon which he may scribble whatever he pleases. A man full of warm speculative benevolence may wish his society otherwise constituted than he finds it; but a good patriot, and a true politician, always considers how he shall make the most of the existing materials of his country.

A disposition to preserve, and an ability to improve, taken together, would be my standard of a statesman. Every thing else is vulgar in the conception, perilous in the execution.

There are moments in the fortune of states when particular men are called to make improvements by great mental exertion. In those moments, even when they seem to enjoy the confidence of their prince and country, and to [186] be invested with full authority, they have not always apt instruments. A politician, to do great things, looks for a *power,* what our workmen call a *purchase;* and if he finds that power, in politics as in mechanics he cannot be at a loss to apply it. In the monastic institutions, in my opinion, was found a great *power* for the mechanism of politic benevolence. There were revenues with a public direction; there were men wholly set apart and dedicated to public purposes, without any other than public ties and public principles; men without the possibility of converting the estate of the community into a private fortune; men denied to self-interests, whose avarice is for some community; men to whom personal poverty is honour, and implicit obedience stands in the place of freedom. In vain shall a man look to the possibility of making such things when he wants them. The winds blow as they list. These institutions are the products of enthusiasm; they are the instruments of wisdom. Wisdom cannot create materials; they are the gifts of nature or of chance; her pride is in the use. The perennial existence of bodies corporate and their fortunes, are things particularly suited to a man who has long views; who meditates designs that require time in fashioning; and which propose duration when they are accomplished. He is not deserving to rank high, or even to be mentioned in the order of great statesmen, who, having obtained the command and direction of such a power as existed in the wealth, the discipline, and the habits of such corporations, as those which you have rashly destroyed, cannot find any way of converting it to the great and lasting benefit of his country. On the view of this subject a thousand uses suggest themselves to a contriving mind. To destroy any power, growing wild from the rank productive force of the human mind, is almost tantamount, in the moral world, to the destruction of the apparently active properties of bodies [187] in the material. It would be like the attempt to destroy (if it were in our competence to destroy) the expansive force of fixed air in nitre, or the power of steam, or of electricity, or of magnetism. These energies always existed in nature, and they were always discernible. They seemed, some of them unserviceable, some noxious, some no better than a sport to children; until contemplative ability, combining with practic skill, tamed their wild nature, subdued them to use, and rendered them at once the most powerful and the most tractable agents, in subservience to the great views and designs of men. Did fifty thousand persons, whose mental and whose bodily labour you might direct, and so many hundred thousand a year of a revenue, which was neither lazy nor superstitious, appear too big for your abilities to wield? Had you no way of using the men but by converting monks into pensioners? Had you no way of turning the revenue to account, but through the improvident resource of a spendthrift sale? If you were thus destitute of mental funds, the proceeding is in its natural course. Your politicians do not understand their trade; and therefore they sell their tools.

But the institutions savour of superstition in their very principle; and they nourish it by a permanent and standing influence. This I do not mean to dispute; but this ought not to hinder you from deriving from superstition itself any resources which may thence be furnished for the public advantage. You derive benefits from many dispositions and many passions of the human mind, which are of as doubtful a colour in the moral eye, as superstition itself. It was your business to correct and mitigate every thing which was noxious in this passion, as in all the passions. But is superstition the greatest of all possible vices? In its possible excess I think it becomes a very great evil. It is, however, a moral subject; and of course admits of all degrees and all [188] modifications. Superstition is the religion of feeble minds; and they must be tolerated in an intermixture of it, in some trifling or some enthusiastic shape or other, else you will deprive weak minds of a resource found necessary to the strongest. The body of all true religion consists, to be sure, in obedience to the will of the sovereign of the world; in a confidence in his declarations; and an imitation of his perfections. The rest is our own. It may be prejudicial to the great end; it may be auxiliary. Wise men, who as such are not *admirers,* (not admirers at least of the *Munera Terrae*) are not violently attached to these things, nor do they violently hate them. Wisdom is not the most severe corrector of folly. They are the rival follies, which mutually wage so unrelenting a war; and which make so cruel a use of their advantages, as they can happen to engage the immoderate vulgar on the one side or the other in their quarrels. Prudence would be neuter; but if, in the contention between fond attachment and fierce antipathy concerning things in their nature not made to produce such heats, a prudent man were obliged to make a choice of what errors and excesses of enthusiasm he would condemn or bear, perhaps he would think the superstition which builds, to be more tolerable than that which demolishes; that which adorns a country, than that which deforms it; that which endows, than that which plunders; that which disposes to mistaken beneficence, than that which stimulates to real injustice; that which leads a man to refuse to himself lawful pleasures, than that which snatches from others the scanty subsistence of their self-denial. Such, I think, is very nearly the state of the question between the ancient founders of monkish superstition, and the superstition of the pretended philosophers of the hour.

For the present I postpone all considerations of the supposed public profit of the sale, which however I conceive [189] to be perfectly delusive. I shall here only consider it as a transfer of property. On the policy of that transfer I shall trouble you with a few thoughts.

In every prosperous community something more is produced than goes to the immediate support of the producer. This surplus forms the income of the landed capitalist. It will be spent by a proprietor who does not labour. But this idleness is itself the spring of labour; this repose the spur to industry. The only concern of the state is, that the capital taken in rent from the land, should be returned again to the industry from whence it came; and that its expenditure should be with the least possible detriment to the morals of those who expend it, and to those of the people to whom it is returned.

In all the views of receipt, expenditure, and personal employment, a sober legislator would carefully compare the possessor whom he has recommended to expel, with the stranger who was proposed to fill his place. Before the inconveniences are incurred which *must* attend all violent revolutions in property through extensive confiscation, we ought to have some rational assurance that the purchasers of the confiscated property will be in a considerable degree more laborious, more virtuous, more sober, less disposed to extort an unreasonable proportion of the gains of the labourer, or to consume on themselves a larger share than is fit for the measure of an individual, or that they should be qualified to dispense the surplus in a more steady and equal mode, so as to answer the purposes of a politic expenditure, than the old possessors, call those possessors, bishops, or canons, or commendatory abbots, or monks, or what you please. "The monks are lazy." Be it so. Suppose them no otherwise employed than by singing in the choir. They are as usefully employed as those who neither sing nor say. As usefully even as those who sing upon the stage. They are [190] as usefully employed as if they worked from dawn to dark in the innumerable servile, degrading, unseemly, unmanly, and often most unwholesome and pestiferous occupations, to which by the social oeconomy so many wretches are inevitably doomed. If it were not generally pernicious to disturb the natural course of things, and to impede, in any degree, the great wheel of circulation which is turned by the strangely directed labour of these unhappy people, I should be infinitely more inclined forcibly to rescue them from their miserable industry, than violently to disturb the tranquil repose of monastic quietude. Humanity, and perhaps policy, might better justify me in the one than in the other. It is a subject on which I have often reflected, and never reflected without feeling from it. I am sure that no consideration, except the necessity of submitting to the yoke of luxury, and the despotism of fancy, who in their own imperious way will distribute the surplus product of the soil, can justify the toleration of such trades and employments in a well-regulated state. But for this purpose of distribution, it seems to me, that the idle expences of monks are quite as well directed as the idle expences of us lay-loiterers.

When the advantages of the possession, and of the project, are on a par, there is no motive for a change. But in the present case, perhaps they are not upon a par, and the difference is in favour of the possession. It does not appear to me, that the expences of those whom you are going to expel, do, in fact, take a course so directly and so generally leading to vitiate and degrade and render miserable those through whom they pass, as the expences of those favourites whom you are intruding into their houses. Why should the expenditure of a great landed property, which is a dispersion of the surplus product of the soil, appear intolerable to you or to me, when it takes its course through the accumulation of vast libraries, which are the history of the force and weakness [191] of the human mind; through great collections of antient records, medals, and coins, which attest and explain laws and customs; through paintings and statues, that, by imitating nature, seem to extend the limits of creation; through grand monuments of the dead, which continue the regards and connexions of life beyond the grave; through collections of the specimens of nature, which become a representative assembly of all the classes and families of the world, that by disposition facilitate, and, by exciting curiosity, open the avenues to science? If, by great permanent establishments, all these objects of expence are better secured from the inconstant sport of personal caprice and personal extravagance, are they worse than if the same tastes prevailed in scattered individuals? Does not the sweat of the mason and carpenter, who toil in order to partake the sweat of the peasant, flow as pleasantly and as salubriously, in the construction and repair of the majestic edifices of religion, as in the painted booths and sordid sties of vice and luxury; as honourably and as profitably in repairing those sacred works, which grow hoary with innumerable years, as on the momentary receptacles of transient voluptuousness; in opera-houses, and brothels; and gaming-houses, and club-houses, and obelisks in the Champ de Mars? Is the surplus product of the olive and the vine worse employed in the frugal sustenance of persons, whom the fictions of a pious imagination raise to dignity by construing in the service of God, than in pampering the innumerable multitude of those who are degraded by being made useless domestics subservient to the pride of man? Are the decorations of temples an expenditure less worthy a wise man than ribbons, and laces, and national cockades, and petits maisons, and petit soupers, and all the innumerable fopperies and follies in which opulence sports away the burthen of its superfluity?

[192] We tolerate even these; not from love of them, but for fear of worse. We tolerate them, because property and liberty, to a degree, require that toleration. But why proscribe the other, and surely, in every point of view, the more laudable use of estates? Why, through the violation of all property,

through an outrage upon every principle of liberty, forcibly carry them from the better to the worse?

This comparison between the new individuals and the old corps is made upon a supposition that no reform could be made in the latter. But in a question of reformation, I always consider corporate bodies, whether sole or consisting of many, to be much more susceptible of a public direction by the power of the state, in the use of their property, and in the regulation of modes and habits of life in their members, than private citizens ever can be, or perhaps ought to be; and this seems to me a very material consideration for those who undertake any thing which merits the name of a politic enterprize. So far as to the estates of monasteries.

With regard to the estates possessed by bishops and canons, and commendatory abbots, I cannot find out for what reason some landed estates may not be held otherwise than by inheritance. Can any philosophic spoiler undertake to demonstrate the positive or the comparative evil, of having a certain, and that too a large portion of landed property, passing in succession thro' persons whose title to it is, always in theory, and often in fact, an eminent degree of piety, morals, and learning; a property which, by its destination, in their turn, and on the score of merit, gives to the noblest families renovation and support, to the lowest the means of dignity and elevation; a property, the tenure of which is the performance of some duty, whatever value you may choose to set upon that duty—and the character of whose proprietors demands at least an exterior decorum and gravity of manners; who are to exercise a generous but [193] temperate hospitality; part of whose income they are to consider as a trust for charity; and who, even when they fail in their trust, when they slide from their character, and degenerate into a mere common secular nobleman or gentleman, are in no respect worse than those who may succeed them in their forfeited possessions? Is it better that estates should be held by those who have no duty than by those who have one? By those whose character and destination point to virtues, than by those who have no rule and direction in the expenditure of their estates but their own will and appetite? Nor are these estates held altogether in the character or with the evils supposed inherent in mortmain. They pass from hand to hand with a more rapid circulation than any other. No excess is good; and therefore too great a proportion of landed property may be held officially for life; but it does not seem to me of material injury to any commonwealth, that there should exist some estates that have a chance of being acquired by other means than the previous acquisition of money.

THIS LETTER IS GROWN to a great length, though it is indeed short with regard to the infinite extent of the subject. Various avocations have from time to time called my mind from the subject. I was not sorry to give myself leisure to observe whether, in the proceedings of the national assembly, I might not find reasons to change or to qualify some of my first sentiments. Every thing has confirmed me more strongly in my first opinions. It was my original purpose to take a view of the principles of the national assembly with regard to the great and fundamental establishments; and to compare the whole of what you have substituted in the place of what you have destroyed, with the several members of our British constitution. But this plan is of greater extent than at first I computed, and I find that you have [194] little desire to take the advantage of any examples. At present I must content myself with some remarks upon your establishments; reserving for another time what I proposed to say concerning the spirit of our British monarchy, aristocracy, and democracy, as practically they exist.

I have taken a review of what has been done by the governing power in France. I have certainly spoke of it with freedom. Those whose principle it is to despise the antient permanent sense of mankind, and to set up a scheme of society on new principles, must naturally expect that such of us who think better of the judgment of the human race than of theirs, should consider both them and their devices, as men and schemes upon their trial. They must take it for granted that we attend much to their reason, but not at all to their authority. They have not one of the great influencing prejudices of mankind in their favour. They avow their hostility to opinion. Of course they must expect no support from that influence, which, with every other authority, they have deposed from the seat of its jurisdiction.

I can never consider this assembly as any thing else than a voluntary association of men, who have availed themselves of circumstances, to seize upon the power of the state. They have not the sanction and authority of the character under which they first met. They have assumed another of a very different nature; and have completely altered and inverted all the relations in which they originally stood. They do not hold the authority they exercise under any constitutional law of the state. They have departed from the instructions of the people by whom they were sent; which instructions, as the assembly did not act in virtue of any antient usage or settled law, were the sole source of their authority. The most considerable of their acts have not been done by great majorities; and in this sort of near divisions, which carry [195] only the constructive authority of the whole, strangers will consider reasons as well as resolutions.

If they had set up this new experimental government as a necessary substitute for an expelled tyranny, mankind would anticipate the time of prescription, which, through long usage, mellows into legality governments that were violent in their commencement. All those who have affections which lead them to the conservation of civil order would recognize, even in its cradle, the child as legitimate, which has been produced from those principles of cogent expediency to which all just governments owe their birth, and on which they justify their continuance. But they will be late and reluctant in giving any sort of countenance to the operations of a power, which has derived its birth from no law and no necessity; but which on the contrary has had its origin in those vices and sinister practices by which the social union is often disturbed and sometimes destroyed. This assembly has hardly a year's prescription. We have their own word for it that they have made a revolution. To make a revolution is a measure which, *prima fronte*, requires an apology. To make a revolution is to subvert the antient state of our country; and no common reasons are called for to justify so violent a proceeding. The sense of mankind authorizes us to examine into the mode of acquiring new power, and to criticise on the use that is made of it, with less awe and reverence than that which is usually conceded to a settled and recognized authority.

IN OBTAINING AND SECURING their power, the assembly proceeds upon principles the most opposite from those which appear to direct them in the use of it. An observation on this difference will let us into the true spirit of their conduct. Every thing which they have done, or continue to do, in order to obtain and keep their power, is by the most common [196] arts. They proceed exactly as their ancestors of ambition have done before them. Trace them through all their artifices, frauds, and violences, you can find nothing at all that is new. They follow precedents and examples with the punctilious exactness of a pleader. They never depart an iota from the authentic formulas of tyranny and usurpation. But in all the regulations relative to the public good, the spirit has been the very reverse of this. There they commit the whole to the mercy of untried speculations; they abandon the dearest interests of the public to those loose theories, to which none of them would chuse to trust the slightest of his private concerns. They make this difference, because in their desire of obtaining and securing power they are thoroughly in earnest; there they travel in the beaten road. The public interests, because about them they have no real solicitude, they abandon wholly to chance; I say to chance, because their schemes have nothing in experience to prove their tendency beneficial.

WE MUST ALWAYS SEE with a pity not unmixed with respect, the errors of those who are timid and doubtful of themselves with regard to points wherein the happiness of mankind is concerned. But in these gentlemen there is nothing of the tender parental solicitude which fears to cut up the infant for the sake of an experiment. In the vastness of their promises, and the confidence of their predictions, they far outdo all the boasting of empirics. The arrogance of their pretensions, in a manner provokes, and challenges us to an enquiry into their foundation.

I am convinced that there are men of considerable parts among the popular leaders in the national assembly. Some of them display eloquence in their speeches and their writings. This cannot be without powerful and cultivated talents. But eloquence may exist without a proportionable degree of [197] wisdom. When I speak of ability, I am obliged to distinguish. What they have done towards the support of their system bespeaks no ordinary men. In the system itself, taken as the scheme of a republic constructed for procuring the prosperity and security of the citizen, and for promoting the strength and grandeur of the state, I confess myself unable to find out any thing which displays, in a single instance, the work of a comprehensive and disposing mind, or even the provisions of a vulgar prudence. Their purpose every where seems to have been to evade and slip aside from *difficulty*. This it has been the glory of the great masters in all the arts to confront, and to overcome; and when they had overcome the first difficulty, to turn it into an instrument for new conquests over new difficulties; thus to enable them to extend the empire of their science; and even to push forward beyond the reach of their original thoughts, the land marks of the human understanding itself. Difficulty is a severe instructor, set over us by the supreme ordinance of a parental guardian and legislator, who knows us better than we know ourselves, as he loves us better too. *Pater ipse colendi haud facilem esse viam voluit.* He that wrestles with us strengthens our nerves, and sharpens our skill. Our antagonist is our helper. This amicable conflict with difficulty obliges us to an intimate acquaintance with our object, and compels us to consider it in all its relations. It will not suffer us to be superficial. It is the want of nerves of understanding for such a task; it is the degenerate fondness for tricking short-cuts, and little fallacious facilities, that has in so many parts of the world created governments with arbitrary powers. They have created the late arbitrary monarchy of France. They have created the arbitrary republic of Paris. With them defects in wisdom are to be supplied by the plenitude of force. They get nothing by it. Commencing their labours on a principle of sloth, they have [198] the common fortune of slothful men. The difficulties which they rather had eluded than escaped, meet them again in their course; they multiply and thicken on them; they are involved, through a labyrinth of confused detail, in an industry without limit, and without direction; and, in conclusion, the whole of their work becomes feeble, vitious, and insecure.

It is this inability to wrestle with difficulty which has obliged the arbitrary assembly of France to commence their schemes of reform with abolition and total destruction.* But

---

*A leading member of the assembly, M. Rabaud de St. Etienne, has expressed the principle of all their proceedings as clearly as possible. Nothing can be more simple: "*Tous les établissemens en France couronnent le malheur du peuple: pour le rendre heureux il faut le renouveler; changer ses idées; changer ses loix; changer ses moeurs; . . . . . changer les hommes; changer les choses; changer les mots . . . . . tout détruire; oui, tout détruire; puisque tout est à recréer.*" This gentleman was chosen president in an assembly not sitting at the *Quinze vingt,* or the *Petites*

is it in destroying and pulling down that skill is displayed? Your mob can do this as well at least as your assemblies. The shallowest understanding, the rudest hand, is more than equal to that task. Rage and phrenzy will pull down more in half an hour, than prudence, deliberation, and foresight can build up in an hundred years. The errors and defects of old establishments are visible and palpable. It calls for little ability to point them out; and where absolute power is given, it requires but a word wholly to abolish the vice and the establishment together. The same lazy but restless disposition, which loves sloth and hates quiet, directs these politicians, when they come to work, for supplying the place of what they have destroyed. To make every thing the reverse of what they have seen is quite as easy as to destroy. No difficulties occur in what has never [199] been tried. Criticism is almost baffled in discovering the defects of what has not existed; and eager enthusiasm, and cheating hope, have all the wide field of imagination in which they may expatiate with little or no opposition.

At once to preserve and to reform is quite another thing. When the useful parts of an old establishment are kept, and what is superadded is to be fitted to what is retained, a vigorous mind, steady persevering attention, various powers of comparison and combination, and the resources of an understanding fruitful in expedients are to be exercised; they are to be exercised in a continued conflict with the combined force of opposite vices; with the obstinacy that rejects all improvement, and the levity that is fatigued and disgusted with every thing of which it is in possession. But you may object— "A process of this kind is slow. It is not fit for an assem-

---

Maisons; and composed of persons giving themselves out to be rational beings; but neither his ideas, language, or conduct, differ in the smallest degree from the discourses, opinions, and actions of those within and without the assembly, who direct the operations of the machine now at work in France.

bly, which glories in performing in a few months the work of ages. Such a mode of reforming, possibly might take up many years." Without question it might; and it ought. It is one of the excellencies of a method in which time is amongst the assistants, that its operation is slow, and in some cases almost imperceptible. If circumspection and caution are a part of wisdom, when we work only upon inanimate matter, surely they become a part of duty too, when the subject of our demolition and construction is not brick and timber, but sentient beings, by the sudden alteration of whose state, condition, and habits, multitudes may be rendered miserable. But it seems as if it were the prevalent opinion in Paris, that an unfeeling heart, and an undoubting confidence, are the sole qualifications for a perfect legislator. Far different are my ideas of that high office. The true lawgiver ought to have an heart full of sensibility. He ought to love and respect his kind, and to fear himself. It may be allowed to his temperament to catch his ultimate object with an intuitive [200] glance; but his movements towards it ought to be deliberate. Political arrangement, as it is a work for social ends, is to be only wrought by social means. There mind must conspire with mind. Time is required to produce that union of minds which alone can produce all the good we aim at. Our patience will atchieve more than our force. If I might venture to appeal to what is so much out of fashion in Paris, I mean, to experience, I should tell you, that in my course I have known, and, according to my measure, have co-operated with great men; and I have never yet seen any plan which has not been mended by the observations of those who were much inferior in understanding to the person who took the lead in the business. By a slow but well-sustained progress, the effect of each step is watched; the good or ill success of the first, gives light to us in the second; and so, from light to light, we are conducted with safety through the whole series. We see, that the parts of the system do not clash. The evils latent in the most promising contrivances are provided for as they arise. One advantage is as little as possible sacrificed to another. We compensate, we reconcile, we balance. We are enabled to unite into a consistent whole the various anomalies and contending principles that are found in the minds and affairs of men. From hence arises, not an excellence in simplicity, but one far superior, an excellence in composition. Where the great interests of mankind are concerned through a long succession of generations, that succession ought to be admitted into some share in the councils which are so deeply to affect them. If justice requires this, the work itself requires the aid of more minds than one age can furnish. It is from this view of things that the best legislators have been often satisfied with the establishment of some sure, solid, and ruling principle in government; a power like that which some of the philosophers have called a plastic nature; and [201] having fixed the principle, they have left it afterwards to its own operation.

To proceed in this manner, that is, to proceed with a presiding principle, and a prolific energy, is with me the criterion of profound wisdom. What your politicians think the marks of a bold, hardy genius, are only proofs of a deplorable want of ability. By their violent haste, and their defiance of the process of nature, they are delivered over blindly to every projector and adventurer, to every alchymist and empiric. They despair of turning to account any thing that is common. Diet is nothing in their system of remedy. The worst of it is, that this their despair of curing common distempers by regular methods, arises not only from defect of comprehension, but, I fear, from some malignity of disposition. Your legislators seem to have taken their opinions of all professions, ranks, and offices, from the declamations and buffooneries of satirists; who would themselves be astonished if they were held to the letter of their own descriptions. By listening only to these, your leaders regard all things only on the side of their vices and faults, and view those vices and faults under every colour of exaggeration. It is undoubtedly true, though it may seem paradoxical; but in general, those who are habitually employed in finding and displaying faults, are unqualified for the work of reformation: because their minds are not only unfurnished with patterns of the fair and good, but by habit they come to take no delight in the contemplation of those things. By hating vices too much, they come to love men too little. It is therefore not wonderful, that they should be indisposed and unable to serve them. From hence arises the complexional disposition of some of your guides to pull every thing in pieces. At this malicious game they display the whole of their *quadrimanous* activity. As to the rest, the paradoxes of eloquent writers, brought forth purely as a [202] sport of fancy, to try their talents, to rouze attention, and excite surprize, are taken up by these gentlemen, not in the spirit of the original authors, as means of cultivating their taste and improving their style. These paradoxes become with them serious grounds of action, upon which they proceed in regulating the most important concerns of the state. Cicero ludicrously describes Cato as endeavouring to act in the commonwealth upon the school paradoxes which exercised the wits of the junior students in the stoic philosophy. If this was true of Cato, these gentlemen copy after him in the manner of some persons who lived about his time — *pede nudo Catonem*. Mr. Hume told me, that he had from Rousseau himself the secret of his principles of composition. That acute, though eccentric, observer had perceived, that to strike and interest the public, the marvelous must be produced; that the marvellous of the heathen mythology had long since lost its effect; that giants, magicians, fairies, and heroes of romance which succeeded, had exhausted the portion of credulity which belonged to their age; that now nothing was left to a writer but that species of the marvellous, which might still be produced, and with as great an effect as ever, though in another way; that is, the marvellous in life, in manners, in characters, and in extraordinary situations, giving rise to new and unlooked-for strokes in politics and morals. I believe, that were Rousseau alive, and in one of his lucid intervals, he would be shocked at the practical phrenzy of his scholars, who in their paradoxes are servile imitators; and even in their incredulity discover an implicit faith.

MEN WHO UNDERTAKE considerable things, even in a regular way, ought to give us ground to presume ability. But the physician of the state, who, not satisfied with the cure of distempers, undertakes to regenerate constitutions, [203] ought to shew uncommon powers. Some very unusual appearances of wisdom ought to display themselves on the face of the designs of those who appeal to no practice, and who copy after no model. Has any such been manifested? I shall take a view (it shall for the subject be a very short one) of what the assembly has done, with regard, first, to the constitution of the legislature; in the next place, to that of the executive power; then to that of the judicature; afterwards to the model of the army; and conclude with the system of finance, to see whether we can discover in any part of their schemes the portentous ability, which may justify these bold undertakers in the superiority which they assume over mankind.

IT IS IN THE MODEL of the sovereign and presiding part of this new republic, that we should expect their grand display. Here they were to prove their title to their proud demands. For the plan itself at large, and for the reasons on which it is grounded, I refer to the journals of the assembly of the 29th of September, 1789, and to the subsequent proceedings which have made any alterations in the plan. So far as in a matter somewhat confused I can see light, the system remains substantially as it has been originally framed. My few remarks will be such as regard its spirit, its tendency, and its fitness for framing a popular commonwealth, which they profess theirs to be, suited to the ends for which any commonwealth, and particularly such a commonwealth, is made. At the same time, I mean to consider its consistency with itself, and its own principles.

Old establishments are tried by their effects. If the people are happy, united, wealthy, and powerful, we presume the rest. We conclude that to be good from whence good is derived. In old establishments various correctives have been found for their aberrations from theory. Indeed they are the results of various necessities and expediences. They [204] are not often constructed after any theory; theories are rather drawn from them. In them we often see the end best obtained, where the means seem not perfectly reconcileable to what we may fancy was the original scheme. The means taught by experience may be better suited to political ends than those contrived in the original project. They again re-act upon the primitive constitution, and sometimes improve the design itself from which they seem to have departed. I think all this might be curiously exemplified in the British constitution. At worst, the errors and deviations of every kind in reckoning are found and computed, and the ship proceeds in her course. This is the case of old establishments; but in a new and merely theoretic system, it is expected that every contrivance shall appear, on the face of it, to answer its end; especially where the projectors are no way embarrassed with an endeavour to accommodate the new building to an old one, either in the walls or on the foundations.

The French builders, clearing away as mere rubbish whatever they found, and, like their ornamental gardeners, forming every thing into an exact level, propose to rest the whole local and general legislature on three bases of three different kinds; one geometrical, one arithmetical, and the third financial; the first of which they call the *basis of territory;* the second, the *basis of population;* and the third, the *basis of contribution.* For the accomplishment of the first of these purposes they divide the area of their country into eighty-three pieces, regularly square, of eighteen leagues by eighteen. These large divisions are called *Departments*. These they portion, proceeding by square measurement, into seventeen hundred and twenty districts called *Communes*. These again they subdivide, still proceeding by square measurement, into smaller districts called *Cantons,* making in all 6,400.

[205] At first view this geometrical basis of theirs presents not much to admire or to blame. It calls for no great legislative talents. Nothing more than an accurate land surveyor, with his chain, sight, and theodolite, is requisite for such a plan as this. In the old divisions of the country various accidents at various times, and the ebb and flow of various properties and jurisdictions, settled their bounds. These bounds were not made upon any fixed system undoubtedly. They were subject to some inconveniencies; but they were inconveniencies for which use had found remedies, and habit had supplied accommodation and patience. In this new pavement of square within square, and this organisation and semiorganisation made on the system of Empedocles and Buffon, and not upon any politic principle, it is impossible that innumerable local inconveniencies, to which men are not habituated, must not arise. But these I pass over, because it requires an accurate knowledge of the country, which I do not possess, to specify them.

When these state surveyors came to take a view of their work of measurement, they soon found, that in politics, the most fallacious of all things was geometrical demonstration. They had then recourse to another basis (or rather buttress) to support the building which tottered on that false foundation. It was evident, that the goodness of the soil, the number of the people, their wealth, and the largeness of their contribution, made such infinite variations between square and square as to render mensuration a ridiculous standard of power in the commonwealth, and equality in geometry the

most unequal of all measures in the distribution of men. However, they could not give it up. But dividing their political
and civil representation into three parts, they allotted one of
those parts to the square measurement, without a single fact
or calculation to ascertain whether this territorial proportion
of representation was [206] fairly assigned, and ought upon
any principle really to be a third. Having however given to
geometry this portion (of a third for her dower) out of compliment I suppose to that sublime science, they left the other
two to be scuffled for between the other parts, population
and contribution.

When they came to provide for population, they were
not able to proceed quite so smoothly as they had done
in the field of their geometry. Here their arithmetic came
to bear upon their juridical metaphysics. Had they stuck to
their metaphysic principles, the arithmetical process would
be simple indeed. Men, with them, are strictly equal, and are
entitled to equal rights in their own government. Each head,
on this system, would have its vote, and every man would vote
directly for the person who was to represent him in the legislature. "But soft — by regular degrees, not yet." This metaphysic principle, to which law, custom, usage, policy, reason,
were to yield, is to yield itself to their pleasure. There must
be many degrees, and some stages, before the representative can come in contact with his constituent. Indeed, as we
shall soon see, these two persons are to have no sort of communion with each other. First, the voters in the *Canton*, who
compose what they call *primary assemblies*, are to have a *qualification*. What! a qualification on the indefeasible rights of
men? Yes; but it shall be a very small qualification. Our injustice shall be very little oppressive; only the local valuation of
three days labour paid to the public. Why, this is not much, I
readily admit, for any thing but the utter subversion of your
equalising principle. As a qualification it might as well be let
alone; for it answers no one purpose for which qualifications

are established: and, on your ideas, it excludes from a vote, the man of all others whose natural equality stands the most in need of protection and defence; I mean the man who has nothing else but his natural equality to guard him. [207] You order him to buy the right, which you before told him nature had given to him gratuitously at his birth, and of which no authority on earth could lawfully deprive him. With regard to the person who cannot come up to your market, a tyrannous aristocracy, as against him, is established at the very outset, by you who pretend to be its sworn foe.

The gradation proceeds. These primary assemblies of the *Canton* elect deputies to the *Commune;* one for every two hundred qualified inhabitants. Here is the first medium put between the primary elector and the representative legislator; and here a new turnpike is fixed for taxing the rights of men with a second qualification: for none can be elected into the *Commune* who does not pay the amount of ten days labour. Nor have we yet done. There is still to be another gradation.* These *Communes,* chosen by the *Canton,* choose to the *Department;* and the deputies of the *Department* choose their deputies to the *National Assembly.* Here is a third barrier of a senseless qualification. Every deputy to the national assembly must pay, in direct contribution, to the value of a *mark of silver.* Of all these qualifying barriers we must think alike; that they are impotent to secure independence; strong only to destroy the rights of men.

In all this process, which in its fundamental elements affects to consider only *population* upon a principle of natural

---

*The assembly, in executing the plan of their committee, made some alterations. They have struck out one stage in these gradations; this removes a part of the objection: but the main objection, namely, that in their scheme the first constituent voter has no connection with the representative legislator, remains in all its force. There are other alterations, some possibly for the better, some certainly for the worse; but to the author the merit or demerit of these smaller alterations appear to be of no moment, where the scheme itself is fundamentally vitious and absurd.

right, there is a manifest attention to *property;* which, however just and reasonable on other schemes, is on theirs perfectly unsupportable.

When they come to their third basis, that of *Contribution,* [208] we find that they have more completely lost sight of their rights of men. The last basis rests *entirely* on property. A principle totally different from the equality of men, and utterly irreconcileable to it, is thereby admitted; but no sooner is this principle admitted, than (as usual) it is subverted; and it is not subverted, (as we shall presently see,) to approximate the inequality of riches to the level of nature. The additional share in the third portion of representation, (a portion reserved exclusively for the higher contribution,) is made to regard the *district* only, and not the individuals in it who pay. It is easy to perceive, by the course of their reasonings, how much they were embarrassed by their contradictory ideas of the rights of men and the privileges of riches. The committee of constitution do as good as admit that they are wholly irreconcileable. "The relation, with regard to the contributions, is without doubt *null* (say they) when the question is on the balance of the political rights as between individual and individual; without which *personal equality would be destroyed,* and *an aristocracy of the rich* would be established. But this inconvenience entirely disappears when the proportional relation of the contribution is only considered in the *great masses,* and is solely between province and province; it serves in that case only to form a just reciprocal proportion between the cities, without affecting the personal rights of the citizens."

Here the principle of *contribution,* as taken between man and man, is reprobated as *null,* and destructive to equality; and as pernicious too; because it leads to the establishment of an *aristocracy of the rich.* However, it must not be abandoned. And the way of getting rid of the difficulty is to establish the inequality as between department and department, leaving all the individuals in each department upon an exact par. Observe, that this parity between individuals had been before destroyed when the qualifications [209] within the departments were settled; nor does it seem a matter of great importance whether the equality of men be injured by masses or individually. An individual is not of the same importance in a mass represented by a few, as in a mass represented by many. It would be too much to tell a man jealous of his equality, that the elector has the same franchise who votes for three members as he who votes for ten.

Now take it in the other point of view, and let us suppose their principle of representation according to contribution, that is according to riches, to be well imagined, and to be a necessary basis for their republic. In this their third basis they assume, that riches ought to be respected, and that justice and policy require that they should entitle men, in some mode or other, to a larger share in the administration of public affairs; it is now to be seen, how the assembly provides for the pre-eminence, or even for the security of the rich, by conferring, in virtue of their opulence, that larger measure of power to their district which is denied to them personally. I readily admit (indeed I should lay it down as a fundamental principle) that in a republican government, which has a democratic basis, the rich do require an additional security above what is necessary to them in monarchies. They are subject to envy, and through envy to oppression. On the present scheme, it is impossible to divine what advantage they derive from the aristocratic preference upon which the unequal representation of the masses is founded. The rich cannot feel it, either as a support to dignity, or as security to fortune: for the aristocratic mass is generated from purely democratic principles; and the prevalence given to it in the general representation has no sort of reference to or connexion with the persons, upon account of whose property this superiority of the mass is established. If the contrivers of this scheme meant any

[210] sort of favour to the rich in consequence of their contribution, they ought to have conferred the privilege either on the individual rich, or on some class formed of rich persons (as historians represent Servius Tullius to have done in the early constitution of Rome); because the contest between the rich and the poor is not a struggle between corporation and corporation, but a contest between men and men; a competition not between districts but between descriptions. It would answer its purpose better if the scheme were inverted; that the votes of the masses were rendered equal; and that the votes within each mass were proportioned to property.

Let us suppose one man in a district (it is an easy supposition) to contribute as much as an hundred of his neighbours. Against these he has but one vote. If there were but one representative for the mass, his poor neighbours would outvote him by an hundred to one for that single representative. Bad enough. But amends are to be made him. How? The district, in virtue of his wealth, is to choose, say, ten members instead of one: that is to say, by paying a very large contribution he has the happiness of being outvoted, an hundred to one, by the poor for ten representatives, instead of being outvoted exactly in the same proportion for a single member. In truth, instead of benefitting by this superior quantity of representation, the rich man is subjected to an additional hardship. The encrease of representation within his province sets up nine persons more, and as many more than nine as there may be democratic candidates, to cabal and intrigue, and to flatter the people at his expence and to his oppression. An interest is by this means held out to multitudes of the inferior sort, in obtaining a salary of eighteen livres a day (to them a vast object) besides the pleasure of a residence in Paris and their share in the government of the kingdom. The [211] more the objects of ambition are multiplied and become democratic, just in that proportion the rich are endangered.

Thus it must fare between the poor and the rich in the

province deemed aristocratic, which in its internal relation is the very reverse of that character. In its external relation, that is, its relation to the other provinces, I cannot see how the unequal representation, which is given to masses on account of wealth, becomes the means of preserving the equipoise and the tranquillity of the commonwealth. For if it be one of the objects to secure the weak from being crushed by the strong (as in all society undoubtedly it is) how are the smaller and poorer of these masses to be saved from the tyranny of the more wealthy? Is it by adding to the wealthy further and more systematical means of oppressing them? When we come to a balance of representation between corporate bodies, provincial interests, emulations, and jealousies are full as likely to arise among them as among individuals; and their divisions are likely to produce a much hotter spirit of dissention, and something leading much more nearly to a war.

I see that these aristocratic masses are made upon what is called the principle of direct contribution. Nothing can be a more unequal standard than this. The indirect contribution, that which arises from duties on consumption, is in truth a better standard, and follows and discovers wealth more naturally than this of direct contribution. It is difficult indeed to fix a standard of local preference on account of the one, or of the other, or of both, because some provinces may pay the more of either or of both, on account of causes not intrinsic, but originating from those very districts over whom they have obtained a preference in consequence of their ostensible contribution. If the masses were independent sovereign bodies, who were to provide for a federative treasury by distinct contingents, and that the [212] revenue had not (as it has) many impositions running through the whole, which affect men individually, and not corporately, and which, by their nature, confound all territorial limits, something might be said for the basis of contribution as founded on masses. But of all things, this representation, to be measured by contribution, is the most difficult to settle upon principles of equity in a country, which considers its districts as members of an whole. For a great city, such as Bourdeaux or Paris, appears to pay a vast body of duties, almost out of all assignable proportion to other places, and its mass is considered accordingly. But are these cities the true contributors in that proportion? No. The consumers of the commodities imported into Bourdeaux, who are scattered through all France, pay the import duties of Bourdeaux. The produce of the vintage in Guienne and Languedoc gives to that city the means of its contribution growing out of an export commerce. The landholders who spend their estates in Paris, and are thereby the creators of that city, contribute for Paris from the provinces out of which their revenue arise. Very nearly the same arguments will apply to the representative share given on account of *direct* contribution: because the direct contribution must be assessed on wealth real or presumed; and that local wealth will itself arise from causes not local, and which therefore in equity ought not to produce a local preference.

It is very remarkable, that in this fundamental regulation, which settles the representation of the mass upon the direct contribution, they have not yet settled how that direct contribution shall be laid, and how apportioned. Perhaps there is some latent policy towards the continuance of the present assembly in this strange procedure. However, until they do this, they can have no certain constitution. It must depend at last upon the system of taxation, and must vary [213] with every variation in that system. As they have contrived matters, their taxation does not so much depend on their constitution, as their constitution on their taxation. This must introduce great confusion among the masses; as the variable qualification for votes within the district must, if ever real contested elections take place, cause infinite internal controversies.

To compare together the three bases, not on their political reason, but on the ideas on which the assembly works, and to try its consistency with itself, we cannot avoid observing, that the principle which the committee call the basis of *population*, does not begin to operate from the same point with the two other principles called the bases of *territory* and of *contribution*, which are both of an aristocratic nature. The consequence is, that where all three begin to operate together, there is the most absurd inequality produced by the operation of the former on the two latter principles. Every canton contains four square leagues, and is estimated to contain, on the average, 4,000 inhabitants, or 680 voters in the *primary assemblies,* which vary in numbers with the population of the canton, and send *one deputy* to the *commune* for every 200 voters. *Nine cantons* make a *commune.*

Now let us take a *canton* containing a *sea-port town of trade,* or *a great manufacturing town.* Let us suppose the population of this canton to be 12,700 inhabitants, or 2,193 voters, forming *three primary assemblies,* and sending *ten deputies* to the *commune.*

Oppose to this *one* canton *two* others of the remaining eight in the same commune. These we may suppose to have their fair population of 4,000 inhabitants, and 680 voters each, or 8,000 inhabitants and 1,360 voters, both together. These will form only *two primary assemblies,* and send only *six* deputies to the *commune.*

[214] When the assembly of the *commune* comes to vote on the *basis of territory,* which principle is first admitted to operate in that assembly, the *single canton* which has *half* the territory of the *other two,* will have *ten* voices to *six* in the election of *three deputies* to the assembly of the department, chosen on the express ground of a representation of territory.

This inequality, striking as it is, will be yet highly aggravated, if we suppose, as we fairly may, the *several* other cantons of the *commune* to fall proportionably short of the average population, as much as the *principal canton* exceeds it. Now, as to *the basis of contribution,* which also is a principle admitted first to operate in the assembly of the *commune*. Let us again take *one* canton, such as is stated above. If the whole of the direct contributions paid by a great trading or manufacturing town be divided equally among the inhabitants, each individual will be found to pay much more than an individual living in the country according to the same average. The whole paid by the inhabitants of the former will be more than the whole paid by the inhabitants of the latter—we may fairly assume one third more. Then the 12,700 inhabitants, or 2,193 voters of the canton will pay as much as 19,050 inhabitants, or 3,289 voters of the *other cantons*, which are nearly the estimated proportion of inhabitants and voters of *five* other cantons. Now the 2,193 voters will, as I before said, send only *ten* deputies to the assembly; the 3,289 voters will send *sixteen*. Thus, for an *equal* share in the contribution of the whole *commune*, there will be a difference of *sixteen* voices to *ten* in voting for deputies to be chosen on the principle of representing the general contribution of the whole *commune*.

By the same mode of computation we shall find 15,875 inhabitants, or 2,741 voters of the *other* cantons, who pay *one-sixth* LESS to the contribution of the whole *commune*, will [215] have *three* voices MORE than the 12,700 inhabitants, or 2,193 voters of the *one* canton.

Such is the fantastical and unjust inequality between mass and mass, in this curious repartition of the rights of representation arising out of *territory* and *contribution*. The qualifications which these confer are in truth negative qualifications, that give a right in an inverse proportion to the possession of them.

In this whole contrivance of the three bases, consider it in any light you please, I do not see a variety of objects, reconciled in one consistent whole, but several contradictory principles reluctantly and irreconcileably brought and held together by your philosophers, like wild beasts shut up in a cage, to claw and bite each other to their mutual destruction.

I am afraid I have gone too far into their way of considering the formation of a constitution. They have much, but bad, metaphysics; much, but bad, geometry; much, but false, proportionate arithmetic; but if it were all as exact as metaphysics, geometry, and arithmetic ought to be, and if their schemes were perfectly consistent in all their parts, it would make only a more fair and sightly vision. It is remarkable, that in a great arrangement of mankind, not one reference whatsoever is to be found to any thing moral or any thing politic; nothing that relates to the concerns, the actions, the passions, the interests of men. *Hominem non sapiunt.*

You see I only consider this constitution as electoral, and leading by steps to the National Assembly. I do not enter into the internal government of the Departments, and their genealogy through the Communes and Cantons. These local governments are, in the original plan, to be as nearly as possible composed in the same manner and on the same principles with the elective assemblies. They are each of them bodies perfectly compact and rounded in themselves.

You cannot but perceive in this scheme, that it has a [216] direct and immediate tendency to sever France into a variety of republics, and to render them totally independent of each other, without any direct constitutional means of coherence, connection, or subordination, except what may be derived from their acquiescence in the determinations of the general congress of the ambassadors from each independent republic. Such in reality is the National Assembly, and such governments I admit do exist in the world, though in forms infinitely more suitable to the local and habitual circumstances of their people. But such associations, rather than bodies politic, have generally been the effect of necessity, not choice; and I believe the present French power is the very first body of citizens, who, having obtained full authority to do with their country what they pleased, have chosen to dissever it in this barbarous manner.

It is impossible not to observe, that in the spirit of this geometrical distribution, and arithmetical arrangement, these pretended citizens treat France exactly like a country of conquest. Acting as conquerors, they have imitated the policy of the harshest of that harsh race. The policy of such barbarous victors, who contemn a subdued people, and insult their feelings, has ever been, as much as in them lay, to destroy all vestiges of the antient country, in religion, in polity, in laws, and in manners; to confound all territorial limits; to produce a general poverty; to put up their properties to auction; to crush their princes, nobles, and pontiffs; to lay low every thing which had lifted its head above the level, or which could serve to combine or rally, in their distresses, the disbanded people, under the standard of old opinion. They have made France free in the manner in which those sincere friends to the rights of mankind, the Romans, freed Greece, Macedon, and other nations. They destroyed the bonds of their union, under colour of providing for the independence of each of their cities.

[217] When the members who compose these new bodies of cantons, communes, and departments, arrangements purposely produced through the medium of confusion, begin to act, they will find themselves, in a great measure, strangers to one another. The electors and elected throughout, especially in the rural *cantons,* will be frequently without any civil habitudes or connections, or any of that natural discipline which is the soul of a true republic. Magistrates and collectors of revenue are now no longer acquainted with their districts, bishops with their dioceses, or curates with their parishes. These new colonies of the rights of men bear a strong resemblance to that sort of military colonies which Tacitus has observed upon in the declining policy of Rome. In better and wiser days (whatever course they took with foreign nations) they were careful to make the elements of a methodical subordination and settlement to be coeval; and even to lay the

foundations of civil discipline in the military.* But, when all the good arts had fallen into ruin, they proceeded, as your assembly does, upon the equality of men, and with as little judgment, and as little care for those things which make a republic tolerable or durable. But in this, as well as almost every instance, your new commonwealth is born, and bred, and fed, in those corruptions which mark degenerated and worn out republics. Your child comes into the world with the symptoms of death; the *facies Hippocratica* forms the character of its physiognomy, and the prognostic of its fate.

The legislators who framed the antient republics knew [218] that their business was too arduous to be accomplished with no better apparatus than the metaphysics of an undergraduate, and the mathematics and arithmetic of an exciseman. They had to do with men, and they were obliged to study human nature. They had to do with citizens, and they were obliged to study the effects of those habits which are communicated by the circumstances of civil life. They were sensible that the operation of this second nature on the first produced a new combination; and thence arose many diversities amongst men, according to their birth, their education, their professions, the periods of their lives, their residence in towns or in the country, their several ways of acquiring and of fixing property, and according to the quality of the property itself, all which rendered them as it were so many different species of animals. From hence they thought themselves obliged to dispose their citizens into such classes, and

*Non, ut olim, universae legiones deducebantur cum tribunis, et centurionibus, et sui cujusque ordinis militibus, ut consensu et caritate rempublicam afficerent; sed ignoti inter se, diversis manipulis, sine rectore, sine affectibus mutuis, quasi ex alio genere mortalium, repente in unum collecti, numerus magis quam colonia. Tac. Annal, l. 14. sect. 27. All this will be still more applicable to the unconnected, rotary, biennial national assemblies, in this absurd and senseless constitution.

to place them in such situations in the state as their peculiar habits might qualify them to fill, and to allot to them such appropriated privileges as might secure to them what their specific occasions required, and which might furnish to each description such force as might protect it in the conflict caused by the diversity of interests, that must exist, and must contend in all complex society: for the legislator would have been ashamed, that the coarse husbandman should well know how to assort and to use his sheep, horses, and oxen, and should have enough of common sense not to abstract and equalize them all into animals, without providing for each kind an appropriate food, care, and employment; whilst he, the oeconomist, disposer, and shepherd of his own kindred, subliming himself into an airy metaphysician, was resolved to know nothing of his flocks, but as men in general. It is for this reason that Montesquieu observed very justly, that in their classification of the citizens, the great legislators of antiquity made [219] the greatest display of their powers, and even soared above themselves. It is here that your modern legislators have gone deep into the negative series, and sunk even below their own nothing. As the first sort of legislators attended to the different kinds of citizens, and combined them into one commonwealth, the others, the metaphysical and alchemistical legislators, have taken the direct contrary course. They have attempted to confound all sorts of citizens, as well as they could, into one homogeneous mass; and then they divided this their amalgama into a number of incoherent republics. They reduce men to loose counters merely for the sake of simple telling, and not to figures whose power is to arise from their place in the table. The elements of their own metaphysics might have taught them better lessons. The troll of their categorical table might have informed them that there was something else in the intellectual world besides *substance* and *quantity*. They might learn from the catechism of metaphysics that there were eight heads more,* in every complex deliberation, which they have never thought of, though these, of all the ten, are the subject on which the skill of man can operate any thing at all.

So far from this able disposition of some of the old republican legislators, which follows with a solicitous accuracy, the moral conditions and propensities of men, they have levelled and crushed together all the orders which they found, even under the coarse unartificial arrangement of the monarchy, in which mode of government the classing of the citizens is not of so much importance as in a republic. It is true, however, that every such classification, if properly ordered, is good in all forms of government; and composes a strong barrier against the excesses of despotism, as well as it is the necessary means of giving effect and permanence [220] to a republic. For want of something of this kind, if the present project of a republic should fail, all securities to a moderated freedom fail along with it; all the indirect restraints which mitigate despotism are removed; insomuch that if monarchy should ever again obtain an entire ascendency in France, under this or under any other dynasty, it will probably be, if not voluntarily tempered at setting out, by the wise and virtuous counsels of the prince, the most completely arbitrary power that has ever appeared on earth. This is to play a most desperate game.

The confusion, which attends on all such proceedings, they even declare to be one of their objects, and they hope to secure their constitution by a terror of a return of those evils which attended their making it. "By this," say they, "its destruction will become difficult to authority, which cannot break it up without the entire disorganization of the whole state." They presume, that if this authority should ever come to the same degree of power that they have acquired, it would

---

*Qualitas, Relatio, Actio, Passio, Ubi, Quando, Situs, Habitus.

make a more moderate and chastised use of it, and would piously tremble entirely to disorganise the state in the savage manner that they have done. They expect, from the virtues of returning despotism, the security which is to be enjoyed by the offspring of their popular vices.

I wish, Sir, that you and my readers would give an attentive perusal to the work of M. de Calonne, on this subject. It is indeed not only an eloquent but an able and instructive performance. I confine myself to what he says relative to the constitution of the new state, and to the condition of the revenue. As to the disputes of this minister with his rivals, I do not wish to pronounce upon them. As little do I mean to hazard any opinion concerning his ways and means, financial or political, for taking his country out of its present disgraceful and deplorable situation of servitude, anarchy, bankruptcy, and beggary. [221] I cannot speculate quite so sanguinely as he does: but he is a Frenchman, and has a closer duty relative to those objects, and better means of judging of them, than I can have. I wish that the formal avowal which he refers to, made by one of the principal leaders in the assembly, concerning the tendency of their scheme to bring France not only from a monarchy to a republic, but from a republic to a mere confederacy, may be very particularly attended to. It adds new force to my observations; and indeed M. de Calonne's work supplies my deficiencies by many new and striking arguments on most of the subjects of this Letter.*

It is this resolution, to break their country into separate republics, which has driven them into the greatest number of their difficulties and contradictions. If it were not for this, all the questions of exact equality, and these balances, never to be settled, of individual rights, population, and contribution, would be wholly useless. The representation, though derived from parts, would be a duty which equally regarded

* See L'Etat de la France, p. 363.

the whole. Each deputy to the assembly would be the representative of France, and of all its descriptions, of the many
and of the few, of the rich and of the poor, of the great districts and of the small. All these districts would themselves
be subordinate to some standing authority, existing independently of them; an authority in which their representation,
and every thing that belongs to it, originated, and to which it
was pointed. This standing, unalterable, fundamental government would make, and it is the only thing which could make,
that territory truly and properly an whole. With us, when we
elect popular representatives, we send them to a council, in
which each man individually is a subject, and submitted to
a government complete in all its ordinary functions. With
you the elective assembly is the sovereign, and the sole sovereign: all the members are [222] therefore integral parts of
this sole sovereignty. But with us it is totally different. With us
the representative, separated from the other parts, can have
no action and no existence. The government is the point of
reference of the several members and districts of our representation. This is the center of our unity. This government of
reference is a trustee for the *whole*, and not for the parts. So
is the other branch of our public council, I mean the house
of lords. With us the king and the lords are several and joint
securities for the equality of each district, each province,
each city. When did you hear in Great Britain of any province suffering from the inequality of its representation; what
district from having no representation at all? Not only our
monarchy and our peerage secure the equality on which our
unity depends, but it is the spirit of the house of commons
itself. The very inequality of representation, which is so foolishly complained of, is perhaps the very thing which prevents
us from thinking or acting as members for districts. Cornwall elects as many members as all Scotland. But is Cornwall
better taken care of than Scotland? Few trouble their heads
about any of your bases, out of some giddy clubs. Most of

those, who wish for any change, upon any plausible grounds, desire it on different ideas.

Your new constitution is the very reverse of ours in its principle; and I am astonished how any persons could dream of holding out any thing done in it as an example for Great Britain. With you there is little, or rather no, connection between the last representative and the first constituent. The member who goes to the national assembly is not chosen by the people, nor accountable to them. There are three elections before he is chosen: two sets of magistracy intervene between him and the primary assembly, so as to render him, as I have said, an ambassador of a state, and [223] not the representative of the people within a state. By this the whole spirit of the election is changed; nor can any corrective your constitution-mongers have devised render him any thing else than what he is. The very attempt to do it would inevitably introduce a confusion, if possible, more horrid than the present. There is no way to make a connection between the original constituent and the representative, but by the circuitous means which may lead the candidate to apply in the first instance to the primary electors, in order that by their authoritative instructions (and something more perhaps) these primary electors may force the two succeeding bodies of electors to make a choice agreeable to their wishes. But this would plainly subvert the whole scheme. It would be to plunge them back into that tumult and confusion of popular election, which, by their interposed gradation elections, they mean to avoid, and at length to risque the whole fortune of the state with those who have the least knowledge of it, and the least interest in it. This is a perpetual dilemma, into which they are thrown by the vicious, weak, and contradictory principles they have chosen. Unless the people break up and level this gradation, it is plain that they do not at all substantially elect to the assembly; indeed they elect as little in appearance as reality.

What is it we all seek for in an election? To answer its real purposes, you must first possess the means of knowing the fitness of your man; and then you must retain some hold upon him by personal obligation or dependence. For what end are these primary electors complimented, or rather mocked, with a choice? They can never know any thing of the qualities of him that is to serve them, nor has he any obligation whatsoever to them. Of all the powers unfit to be delegated by those who have any real means of judging, that most peculiarly unfit is what relates to a *personal* choice. [224] In case of abuse, that body of primary electors never can call the representative to an account for his conduct. He is too far removed from them in the chain of representation. If he acts improperly at the end of his two years' lease, it does not concern him for two years more. By the new French constitution, the best and the wisest representatives go equally with the worst into this *Limbus Patrum.* Their bottoms are supposed foul, and they must go into dock to be refitted. Every man who has served in an assembly is ineligible for two years after. Just as the magistrates begin to learn their trade, like chimney-sweepers, they are disqualified for exercising it. Superficial, new, petulant acquisition, and interrupted, dronish, broken, ill recollection, is to be the destined character of all your future governors. Your constitution has too much of jealousy to have much of sense in it. You consider the breach of trust in the representative so principally, that you do not at all regard the question of his fitness to execute it.

This purgatory interval is not unfavourable to a faithless representative, who may be as good a canvasser as he was a bad governor. In this time he may cabal himself into a superiority over the wisest and most virtuous. As, in the end, all the members of this elective constitution are equally fugitive, and exist only for the election, they may be no longer the same persons who had chosen him, to whom he is to be responsible when he solicits for a renewal of his trust. To call all the secondary electors of the *Commune* to account, is ridiculous, impracticable, and unjust; they may themselves have been deceived in their choice, as the third set of electors, those of the *Department,* may be in theirs. In your elections responsibility cannot exist.

Finding no sort of principle of coherence with each other in the nature and constitution of the several new republics of France, I considered what cement the legislators had [225] provided for them from any extraneous materials. Their confederations, their *spectacles,* their civic feasts, and their enthusiasm, I take no notice of; They are nothing but mere tricks; but tracing their policy through their actions, I think I can distinguish the arrangements by which they propose to hold these republics together. The first, is the *confiscation,* with the compulsory paper currency annexed to it; the second, is the supreme power of the city of Paris; the third, is the general army of the state. Of this last I shall reserve what I have to say, until I come to consider the army as an head by itself.

As to the operation of the first (the confiscation and paper currency) merely as a cement, I cannot deny that these, the one depending on the other, may for some time compose some sort of cement, if their madness and folly in the management, and in the tempering of the parts together, does not produce a repulsion in the very outset. But allowing to the scheme some coherence and some duration, it appears to me, that if, after a while, the confiscation should not be found sufficient to support the paper coinage (as I am morally certain it will not) then, instead of cementing, it will add infinitely to the dissociation, distraction, and confusion of these confederate republics, both with relation to each other, and to the several parts within themselves. But if the confiscation should so far succeed as to sink the paper currency, the cement is gone with the circulation. In the mean time its binding force will be very uncertain, and it will straiten or relax with every variation in the credit of the paper.

One thing only is certain in this scheme, which is an effect seemingly collateral, but direct, I have no doubt, in the minds of those who conduct this business, that is, its effect in producing an *Oligarchy* in every one of the republics. A paper circulation, not founded on any real [226] money deposited or engaged for, amounting already to four-and-forty millions of English money, and this currency by force substituted in the place of the coin of the kingdom, becoming thereby the substance of its revenue, as well as the medium of all its commercial and civil intercourse, must put the whole of what power, authority, and influence is left, in any form whatsoever it may assume, into the hands of the managers and conductors of this circulation.

In England we feel the influence of the bank; though it is only the center of a voluntary dealing. He knows little indeed of the influence of money upon mankind, who does not see the force of the management of a monied concern which is so much more extensive, and in its nature so much more depending on the managers than any of ours. But this is not merely a money concern. There is another member in the system inseparably connected with this money management. It consists in the means of drawing out at discretion portions of the confiscated lands for sale; and carrying on a process of continual transmutation of paper into land, and land into paper. When we follow this process in its effects, we may conceive something of the intensity of the force with which this system must operate. By this means the spirit of money-jobbing and speculation goes into the mass of land itself, and incorporates with it. By this kind of operation, that species of property becomes (as it were) volatilized; it assumes an unnatural and monstrous activity, and thereby throws into the hands of the several managers, principal and subordinate, Parisian and provincial, all the representative of money, and perhaps a full tenth part of all the land in France, which has now acquired the worst and most pernicious part of the evil of a paper circulation, the greatest possible uncertainty in its value. They have reversed the Latonian kindness to the landed property of Delos. They have sent theirs to be blown [227] about, like the light fragments of a wreck, *oras et littora circum*.

The new dealers being all habitually adventurers, and without any fixed habits or local predilections, will purchase to job out again, as the market of paper, or of money, or of land shall present an advantage. For though an holy bishop thinks that agriculture will derive great advantages from the "*enlightened*" usurers who are to purchase the church confiscations, I, who am not a good, but an old farmer, with great humility beg leave to tell his late lordship, that usury is not a tutor of agriculture; and if the word "enlightened" be understood according to the new dictionary, as it always is in your new schools, I cannot conceive how a man's not believing in God can teach him to cultivate the earth with the least of any additional skill or encouragement. "Diis immortalibus sero," said an old Roman, when he held one handle of the plough, whilst Death held the other. Though you were to join in the commission all the directors of the two academies to the directors of the *Caisse d' Escompte,* one old experienced peasant is worth them all. I have got more information, upon a curious and interesting branch of husbandry, in one short conversation with a Carthusian monk, than I have derived from all the Bank directors that I have ever conversed with. However, there is no cause for apprehension from the meddling of money-dealers with rural oeconomy. These gentlemen are too wise in their generation. At first, perhaps, their tender and susceptible imaginations may be captivated with the innocent and unprofitable delights of a pastoral life; but in a little time they will find that agriculture is a trade much more laborious, and much less lucrative than that which they had left. After making its panegyric, they will turn their backs on it like their great precursor and prototype. They may, like him, begin by singing, *"Beatus ille"* — but what will be the end?

[228] *Haec ubi locutus faenerator Alphius,*
Jam jam futurus rusticus
Omnem redegit idibus pecuniam,
Quaerit calendis ponere.

They will cultivate the *Caisse d' Église,* under the sacred auspices of this prelate, with much more profit than its vineyards or its corn-fields. They will employ their talents according to their habits and their interests. They will not follow the plough whilst they can direct treasuries, and govern provinces.

Your legislators, in every thing new, are the very first who have founded a commonwealth upon gaming, and infused this spirit into it as its vital breath. The great object in these politics is to metamorphose France from a great kingdom into one great play-table; to turn its inhabitants into a nation of gamesters; to make speculations as extensive as life; to mix it with all its concerns; and to divert the whole of the hopes and fears of the people from their useful channels, into the impulses, passions, and superstitions of those who live on chances. They loudly proclaim their opinion, that this their present system of a republic cannot possibly exist without this kind of gaming fund; and that the very thread of its life is spun out of the staple of these speculations. The old gaming in funds was mischievous enough undoubtedly; but it was so only to individuals. Even when it had its greatest extent, in the Mississippi and South Sea, it affected but few, comparatively; where it extends further, as in lotteries, the spirit has but a single object. But where the law, which in most circumstances forbids, and in none countenances gaming, is itself debauched, so as to reverse its nature and policy, and expressly to force the subject to this destructive table, by bringing the spirit and symbols of gaming into the minutest matters, and engaging every body in it, and in every thing, a more dreadful epidemic distemper of that kind is spread than [229] yet has appeared in the world. With you a man can neither earn nor buy his dinner, without a speculation. What he receives in the morning will not have the same value at night. What he is compelled to take as pay for an old debt, will not be received as the same when he comes to pay a debt contracted by himself; nor will it be the same when by prompt payment he would avoid contracting any debt at all. Industry must wither away. Oeconomy must be driven from your country. Careful provision will have no existence. Who will labour without knowing the amount of his pay? Who will study to encrease what none can estimate? who will accumulate, when he does not know the value of what he saves? If you abstract it from its uses in gaming, to accumulate your paper wealth, would be not the providence of a man, but the distempered instinct of a jackdaw.

The truly melancholy part of the policy of systematically making a nation of gamesters is this; that tho' all are forced to play, few can understand the game; and fewer still are in a condition to avail themselves of the knowledge. The many must be the dupes of the few who conduct the machine of these speculations. What effect it must have on the country-people is visible. The townsman can calculate from day to day: not so the inhabitant of the country. When the peasant first brings his corn to market, the magistrate in the town obliges him to take the assignat at par; when he goes to the shop with this money, he finds it seven per cent. the worse for crossing the way. This market he will not readily resort to again. The townspeople will be inflamed! they will force the country-people to bring their corn. Resistance will begin, and the murders of Paris and St. Dennis may be renewed through all France.

What signifies the empty compliment paid to the country

by giving it perhaps more than its share in the theory of your representation? Where have you placed the real [230] power over monied and landed circulation? Where have you placed the means of raising and falling the value of every man's freehold? Those whose operations can take from, or add ten per cent. to, the possessions of every man in France, must be the masters of every man in France. The whole of the power obtained by this revolution will settle in the towns among the burghers, and the monied directors who lead them. The landed gentlemen, the yeoman, and the peasant have, none of them, habits, or inclinations, or experience, which can lead them to any share in this the sole source of power and influence now left in France. The very nature of a country life, the very nature of landed property, in all the occupations, and all the pleasures they afford, render combination and arrangement (the sole way of procuring and exerting influence) in a manner impossible amongst country-people. Combine them by all the art you can, and all the industry, they are always dissolving into individuality. Any thing in the nature of incorporation is almost impracticable amongst them. Hope, fear, alarm, jealousy, the ephemerous tale that does its business and dies in a day, all these things, which are the reins and spurs by which leaders check or urge the minds of followers, are not easily employed, or hardly at all, amongst scattered people. They assemble, they arm, they act with the utmost difficulty, and at the greatest charge. Their efforts, if ever they can be commenced, cannot be sustained. They cannot proceed systematically. If the country gentlemen attempt an influence through the mere income of their property, what is it to that of those who have ten times their income to sell, and who can ruin their property by bringing their plunder to meet it at market? If the landed man wishes to mortgage, he falls the value of his land, and raises the value of assignats. He augments the power of his enemy by the very means he must take to contend with him. [231] The country gentleman therefore, the officer by sea and land, the man of liberal views and habits, attached to no profession, will be as completely excluded from the government of his country as if he were legislatively proscribed. It is obvious, that in the towns, all the things which conspire against the country gentleman, combine in favour of the money manager and director. In towns combination is natural. The habits of burghers, their occupations, their diversion, their business, their idleness, continually bring them into mutual contact. Their virtues and their vices are sociable; they are always in garrison; and they come embodied and half disciplined into the hands of those who mean to form them for civil, or for military action.

All these considerations leave no doubt on my mind, that if this monster of a constitution can continue, France will be wholly governed by the agitators in corporations, by societies in the towns formed of directors of assignats, and trustees for the sale of church lands, attornies, agents, money-jobbers, speculators, and adventurers, composing an ignoble oligarchy founded on the destruction of the crown, the church, the nobility, and the people. Here end all the deceitful dreams and visions of the equality and rights of men. In the "*Serbonian bog*" of this base oligarchy they are all absorbed, sunk, and lost for ever.

Though human eyes cannot trace them, one would be tempted to think some great offences in France must cry to heaven, which has thought fit to punish it with a subjection to a vile and inglorious domination, in which no comfort or compensation is to be found in any, even of those false splendours, which, playing about other tyrannies, prevent mankind from feeling themselves dishonoured even whilst they are oppressed. I must confess I am touched with a sorrow, mixed with some indignation, at the conduct of a few men, once of great rank, and still of great character, [232] who, deluded with specious names, have engaged in a business too deep for the line of their understanding to fathom;

who have lent their fair reputation, and the authority of their high-sounding names, to the designs of men with whom they could not be acquainted; and have thereby made their very virtues operate to the ruin of their country.

So far as to the first cementing principle.

The second material of cement for their new republic is the superiority of the city of Paris; and this I admit is strongly connected with the other cementing principle of paper circulation and confiscation. It is in this part of the project we must look for the cause of the destruction of all the old bounds of provinces and jurisdictions, ecclesiastical and secular, and the dissolution of all antient combinations of things, as well as the formation of so many small unconnected republics. The power of the city of Paris is evidently one great spring of all their politics. It is through the power of Paris, now become the center and focus of jobbing, that the leaders of this faction direct, or rather command the whole legislative and the whole executive government. Every thing therefore must be done which can confirm the authority of that city over the other republics. Paris is compact; she has an enormous strength, wholly disproportioned to the force of any of the square republics; and this strength is collected and condensed within a narrow compass. Paris has a natural and easy connexion of its parts, which will not be affected by any scheme of a geometrical constitution, nor does it much signify whether its proportion of representation be more or less, since it has the whole draft of fishes in its drag-net. The other divisions of the kingdom being hackled and torn to pieces, and separated from all their habitual means, and even principles of union, cannot, for some time at least, confederate against her. Nothing was to be left in all the subordinate [233] members, but weakness, disconnection, and confusion. To confirm this part of the plan, the assembly has lately come to a resolution, that no two of their republics shall have the same commander in chief.

To a person who takes a view of the whole, the strength of Paris thus formed, will appear a system of general weakness. It is boasted, that the geometrical policy has been adopted, that all local ideas should be sunk, and that the people should no longer be Gascons, Picards, Bretons, Normans, but Frenchmen, with one country, one heart, and one assembly. But instead of being all Frenchmen, the greater likelihood is, that the inhabitants of that region will shortly have no country. No man ever was attached by a sense of pride, partiality, or real affection, to a description of square measurement. He never will glory in belonging to the Checquer, N°. 71, or to any other badge-ticket. We begin our public affections in our families. No cold relation is a zealous citizen. We pass on to our neighbourhoods, and our habitual provincial connections. These are inns and resting-places. Such divisions of our country as have been formed by habit, and not by a sudden jerk of authority, were so many little images of the great country in which the heart found something which it could fill. The love to the whole is not extinguished by this subordinate partiality. Perhaps it is a sort of elemental training to those higher and more large regards, by which alone men come to be affected, as with their own concern, in the prosperity of a kingdom so extensive as that of France. In that general territory itself, as in the old name of provinces, the citizens are interested from old prejudices and unreasoned habits, and not on account of the geometric properties of its figure. The power and preeminence of Paris does certainly press down and hold these republics together, as long as it lasts. But, for the reasons I have already given you, I think it cannot last very long.

[234] Passing from the civil creating, and the civil cementing principles of this constitution, to the national assembly, which is to appear and act as sovereign, we see a body in its constitution with every possible power, and no possible external controul. We see a body without fundamen-

tal laws, without established maxims, without respected rules of proceeding, which nothing can keep firm to any system whatsoever. Their idea of their powers is always taken at the utmost stretch of legislative competency, and their examples for common cases, from the exceptions of the most urgent necessity. The future is to be in most respects like the present assembly; but, by the mode of the new elections and the tendency of the new circulations, it will be purged of the small degree of internal controul existing in a minority chosen originally from various interests, and preserving something of their spirit. If possible, the next assembly must be worse than the present. The present, by destroying and altering every thing, will leave to their successors apparently nothing popular to do. They will be roused by emulation and example to enterprises the boldest and the most absurd. To suppose such an assembly sitting in perfect quietude is ridiculous.

Your all-sufficient legislators, in their hurry to do every thing at once, have forgot one thing that seems essential, and which, I believe, never has been before, in the theory or the practice, omitted by any projector of a republic. They have forgot to constitute a *Senate,* or something of that nature and character. Never, before this time, was heard of a body politic composed of one legislative and active assembly, and its executive officers, without such a council; without something to which foreign states might connect themselves; something to which, in the ordinary detail of government, the people could look up; something which might give a bias and steadiness and preserve something [235] like consistency in the proceedings of state. Such a body kings generally have as a council. A monarchy may exist without it; but it seems to be in the very essence of a republican government. It holds a sort of middle place between the supreme power exercised by the people, or immediately delegated from them, and the mere executive. Of this there are no traces in your constitution; and in providing nothing of this kind, your Solons and

Numas have, as much as in any thing else, discovered a sovereign incapacity.

LET US NOW TURN OUR EYES to what they have done towards the formation of an executive power. For this they have chosen a degraded king. This their first executive officer is to be a machine, without any sort of deliberative discretion in any one act of his function. At best he is but a channel to convey to the national assembly such matter as may import that body to know. If he had been made the exclusive channel, the power would not have been without its importance; though infinitely perilous to those who would choose to exercise it. But public intelligence and statement of facts may pass to the assembly, with equal authenticity, through any other conveyance. As to the means, therefore, of giving a direction to measures by the statement of an authorized reporter, this office of intelligence is as nothing.

To consider the French scheme of an executive officer in its two natural divisions of civil and political — In the first it must be observed, that, according to the new constitution, the higher parts of judicature, in either of its lines, are not in the king. The king of France is not the fountain of justice. The judges, neither the original nor the appellate, are of his nomination. He neither proposes the candidates, nor has a negative on the choice. He is not even the public prosecutor. He serves only as a notary to authenticate [236] the choice made of the judges in the several districts. By his officers he is to execute their sentence. When we look into the true nature of his authority, he appears to be nothing more than a chief of bumbailiffs, serjeants at mace, catchpoles, jailers, and hangmen. It is impossible to place any thing called royalty in a more degrading point of view. A thousand times better it had been for the dignity of this unhappy prince, that he had nothing at all to do with the administration of justice, deprived as he is of all that is venerable, and all that is consolatory in that function, without power of originating any process; without a power of suspension, mitigation, or pardon. Every thing in justice that is vile and odious is thrown upon him. It was not for nothing that the assembly has been at such pains to remove the stigma from certain offices, when they were resolved to place the person who lately had been their king in a situation but one degree above the executioner, and in an office nearly of the same quality. It is not in nature, that situated as the king of the French now is, he can respect himself, or can be respected by others.

View this new executive officer on the side of his political capacity, as he acts under the orders of the national assembly. To execute laws is a royal office; to execute orders is not to be a king. However, a political executive magistracy, though merely such, is a great trust. It is a trust indeed that has much depending upon its faithful and diligent performance, both in the person presiding in it and in all his subordinates. Means of performing this duty ought to be given by regulation; and dispositions towards it ought to be infused by the circumstances attendant on the trust. It ought to be environed with dignity, authority, and consideration, and it ought to lead to glory. The office of execution is an office of exertion. It is not from impotence we are to expect the tasks of power. What sort of person [237] is a king to command executory service, who has no means whatsoever to reward it? Not in a permanent office; not in a grant of land; no, not in a pension of fifty pounds a year; not in the vainest and most trivial title. In France the king is no more the fountain of honour than he is the fountain of justice. All rewards, all distinctions are in other hands. Those who serve the king can be actuated by no natural motive but fear; by a fear of every thing except their master. His functions of internal coercion are as odious, as those which he exercises in the department of justice. If relief is to be given to any municipality, the assembly gives it. If troops are to be sent to reduce them to obedience to the assembly, the king is to execute the order; and upon every occasion he is to be spattered over with the blood of his people. He has no negative; yet his name and authority is used to enforce every harsh decree. Nay, he must concur in the butchery of those who shall attempt to free him from his imprisonment, or shew the slightest attachment to his person or to his antient authority.

Executive magistracy ought to be constituted in such a manner, that those who compose it should be disposed to love and to venerate those whom they are bound to obey. A purposed neglect, or, what is worse, a literal but perverse and malignant obedience, must be the ruin of the wisest counsels. In vain will the law attempt to anticipate or to follow such studied neglects and fraudulent attentions. To make men act zealously is not in the competence of law. Kings, even such as are truly kings, may and ought to bear the freedom of subjects that are obnoxious to them. They may too, without derogating from themselves, bear even the authority of such persons if it promotes their service. Louis the XIIIth mortally hated the cardinal de Richlieu; but his support of that minister against his rivals was the source of all the glory of his reign, and the solid foundation of his [238] throne itself. Louis the XIVth, when come to the throne, did not love the cardinal Mazarin; but for his interests he preserved him in power. When old, he detested Louvois; but for years, whilst he faithfully served his greatness, he endured his person. When George the IId took Mr. Pitt, who certainly was not agreeable to him, into his councils, he did nothing which could humble a wise sovereign. But these ministers, who were chosen by affairs, not by affections, acted in the name of, and in trust for, kings; and not as their avowed, constitutional, and ostensible masters. I think it impossible that any king, when he has recovered his first terrors, can cordially infuse vivacity and vigour into measures which he knows to be dictated by those who he must be persuaded are in the highest degree ill affected to his person. Will any ministers, who serve such a king (or whatever he may be called) with but a decent appearance of respect, cordially obey the orders of those whom but the other day in his name they had committed to the Bastile? will they obey the orders of those whom, whilst they were exercising despotic justice upon them, they conceived they were treating with lenity; and for whom, in a prison, they thought they had provided an asylum? If you expect such obedience, amongst your other innovations and regenerations, you ought to make a revolution in nature, and provide a new constitution for the human mind. Otherwise, your supreme government cannot harmonize with its executory system. There are cases in which we cannot take up with names and abstractions. You may call half a dozen leading individuals, whom we have reason to fear and hate, the nation. It makes no other difference, than to make us fear and hate them the more. If it had been thought justifiable and expedient to make such a revolution by such means, and through such persons, as you have made yours, it would have been more wise to have completed the [239] business of the fifth and sixth of October. The new executive officer would then owe his situation to those who are his creators as well as his masters; and he might be bound in interest, in the society of crime, and (if in crimes there could be virtues) in gratitude, to serve those who had promoted him to a place of great lucre and great sensual indulgence; and of something more: For more he must have received from those who certainly would not have limited an aggrandized creature, as they have done a submitting antagonist.

A king circumstanced as the present, if he is totally stupified by his misfortunes, so as to think it not the necessity, but the premium and privilege of life, to eat and sleep, without any regard to glory, never can be fit for the office. If he feels as men commonly feel, he must be sensible, that an office so circumstanced is one in which he can obtain no fame or reputation. He has no generous interest that can excite him to action. At best, his conduct will be passive and defensive. To inferior people such an office might be matter of honour. But to be raised to it, and to descend to it, are different things, and suggest different sentiments. Does he *really* name the ministers? They will have a sympathy with him. Are they forced upon him? The whole business between them and the nominal king will be mutual counteraction. In all other countries, the office of ministers of state is of the highest dignity. In France it is full of peril and incapable of glory. Rivals however they will have in their nothingness, whilst shallow ambition exists in the world, or the desire of a miserable salary is an incentive to short-sighted avarice. Those competitors of the ministers are enabled by your constitution to attack them in their vital parts, whilst they have not the means of repelling their charges in any other than the degrading character of culprits. The ministers of state in France are the only persons in that country who are incapable [240] of a share in the national councils. What ministers! What councils! What a nation! But they are responsible. It is a poor service that is to be had from responsibility. The elevation of mind, to be derived from fear, will never make a nation glorious. Responsibility prevents crimes. It makes all attempts against the laws dangerous. But for a principle of active and zealous service, none but idiots could think of it. Is the conduct of a war to be trusted to a man who may abhor its principle; who, in every step he may take to render it successful, confirms the power of those by whom he is oppressed? Will foreign states seriously treat with him who has no prerogative of peace or war; no, not so much as in a single vote by himself or his ministers, or by any one whom he can possibly influence? A state of contempt is not a state for a prince: better get rid of him at once.

I know it will be said, that these humours in the court and executive government will continue only through this generation; and that the king has been brought to declare the dauphin shall be educated in a conformity to his situation. If he is made to conform to his situation, he will have no education at all. His training must be worse even than that of an arbitrary monarch. If he reads—whether he reads or not, some good or evil genius will tell him his ancestors were kings. Thenceforward his object must be to assert himself, and to avenge his parents. This you will say is not his duty. That may be; but it is Nature; and whilst you pique Nature against you, you do unwisely to trust to Duty. In this futile scheme of polity, the state nurses in its bosom, for the present, a source of weakness, perplexity, counteraction, inefficiency, and decay; and it prepares the means of its final ruin. In short, I see nothing in the executive force (I cannot call it authority) that has even an appearance of vigour, or that has the smallest degree of just [241] correspondence or symmetry, or amicable relation, with the supreme power, either as it now exists, or as it is planned for the future government.

You have settled, by an oeconomy as perverted as the policy, two* establishments of government; one real, one fictitious. Both maintained at a vast expence; but the fictitious at, I think, the greatest. Such a machine as the latter is not worth the grease of its wheels. The expence is exorbitant; and neither the shew nor the use deserve the tenth part of the charge. Oh! but I don't do justice to the talents of the legislators. I don't allow, as I ought to do, for necessity. Their scheme of executive force was not their choice. This pageant must be kept. The people would not consent to part with it. Right; I understand you. You do, in spite of your grand theories, to which you would have heaven and earth to bend, you do know how to conform yourselves to the nature and circumstances of things. But when you were obliged to conform thus far to circumstances, you ought to have carried your

* In reality three, to reckon the provincial republican establishments.

submission farther, and to have made what you were obliged to take, a proper instrument, and useful to its end. That was in your power. For instance, among many others, it was in your power to leave to your king the right of peace and war. What! to leave to the executive magistrate the most dangerous of all prerogatives? I know none more dangerous; nor any one more necessary to be so trusted. I do not say that this prerogative ought to be trusted to your king, unless he enjoyed other auxiliary trusts along with it, which he does not now hold. But, if he did possess them, hazardous as they are undoubtedly, advantages would arise from such a constitution, more than compensating the risque. There is no other way of keeping the several potentates of Europe from intriguing distinctly and personally with the members [242] of your assembly, from intermeddling in all your concerns, and fomenting, in the heart of your country, the most pernicious of all factions; factions in the interest and under the direction of foreign powers. From that worst of evils, thank God, we are still free. Your skill, if you had any, would be well employed to find out indirect correctives and controls upon this perilous trust. If you did not like those which in England we have chosen, your leaders might have exerted their abilities in contriving better. If it were necessary to exemplify the consequences of such an executive government as yours, in the management of great affairs, I should refer you to the late reports of M. de Montmorin to the national assembly, and all the other proceedings relative to the differences between Great Britain and Spain. It would be treating your understanding with disrespect to point them out to you.

I hear that the persons who are called ministers have signified an intention of resigning their places. I am rather astonished that they have not resigned long since. For the universe I would not have stood in the situation in which they have been for this last twelvemonth. They wished well, I take it for granted, to the Revolution. Let this fact be as it may, they could not, placed as they were upon an eminence, though an eminence of humiliation, but be the first to see collectively, and to feel each in his own department, the evils which have been produced by that revolution. In every step which they took, or forbore to take, they must have felt the degraded situation of their country, and their utter incapacity of serving it. They are in a species of subordinate servitude, in which no men before them were ever seen. Without confidence from their sovereign, on whom they were forced, or from the assembly who forced them upon him, all the noble functions of their office are executed by committees of the assembly, without any regard whatsoever [243] to their personal, or their official authority. They are to execute, without power; they are to be responsible, without discretion; they are to deliberate, without choice. In their puzzled situation, under two sovereigns, over neither of whom they have any influence, they must act in such a manner as (in effect, whatever they may intend) sometimes to betray the one, sometimes the other, and always to betray themselves. Such has been their situation; such must be the situation of those who succeed them. I have much respect, and many good wishes, for Mr. Necker. I am obliged to him for attentions. I thought when his enemies had driven him from Versailles, that his exile was a subject of most serious congratulation—*sed multae urbes et publica vota vicerunt.* He is now sitting on the ruins of the finances, and of the monarchy of France.

A great deal more might be observed on the strange constitution of the executory part of the new government; but fatigue must give bounds to the discussion of subjects, which in themselves have hardly any limits.

AS LITTLE GENIUS AND TALENT am I able to perceive in the plan of judicature formed by the national assembly. According to their invariable course, the framers of your constitution have begun with the utter abolition of the parliaments.

These venerable bodies, like the rest of the old government, stood in need of reform, even though there should be no change made in the monarchy. They required several more alterations to adapt them to the system of a free constitution. But they had particulars in their constitution, and those not a few, which deserved approbation from the wise. They possessed one fundamental excellence; they were independent. The most doubtful circumstance attendant on their office, that of its being vendible, contributed however to this independency of character. They held for life. Indeed [244] they may be said to have held by inheritance. Appointed by the monarch, they were considered as nearly out of his power. The most determined exertions of that authority against them only shewed their radical independence. They composed permanent bodies politic, constituted to resist arbitrary innovation; and from that corporate constitution, and from most of their forms, they were well calculated to afford both certainty and stability to the laws. They had been a safe asylum to secure these laws in all the revolutions of humour and opinion. They had saved that sacred deposit of the country during the reigns of arbitrary princes, and the struggles of arbitrary factions. They kept alive the memory and record of the constitution. They were the great security to private property; which might be said (when personal liberty had no existence) to be, in fact, as well guarded in France as in any other country. Whatever is supreme in a state, ought to have, as much as possible, its judicial authority so constituted as not only to depend upon it, but in some sort to balance it. It ought to give a security to its justice against its power. It ought to make its judicature, as it were, something exterior to the state.

These parliaments had furnished, not the best certainly but some considerable corrective to the excesses and vices of the monarchy. Such an independent judicature was ten times more necessary when a democracy became the absolute power of the country. In that constitution, elective, temporary, local judges, such as you have contrived, exercising their dependent functions in a narrow society, must be the worst of all tribunals. In them it will be vain to look for any appearance of justice towards strangers, towards the obnoxious rich, towards the minority of routed parties, towards all those who in the election have supported unsuccessful candidates. It will be impossible to keep the new tribunals clear of the worst spirit of faction. All [245] contrivances by ballot, we know experimentally, to be vain and childish to prevent a discovery of inclinations. Where they may the best answer the purposes of concealment, they answer to produce suspicion, and this is a still more mischievous cause of partiality.

If the parliaments had been preserved, instead of being dissolved at so ruinous a charge to the nation, they might have served in this new commonwealth, perhaps not precisely the same (I do not mean an exact parallel) but near the same purposes as the court and senate of Areopagus did in Athens; that is, as one of the balances and correctives to the evils of a light and unjust democracy. Every one knows, that this tribunal was the great stay of that state; every one knows with what care it was upheld, and with what a religious awe it was consecrated. The parliaments were not wholly free from faction, I admit; but this evil was exterior and accidental, and not so much the vice of their constitution itself, as it must be in your new contrivance of sexennial elective judicatories. Several English commend the abolition of the old tribunals, as supposing that they determined every thing by bribery and corruption. But they have stood the test of monarchic and republican scrutiny. The court was well disposed to prove corruption on those bodies when they were dissolved in 1771. Those who have again dissolved them would have done the same if they could; but both inquisitions having failed, I conclude, that gross pecuniary corruption must have been rather rare amongst them.

It would have been prudent, along with the parliaments,

to preserve their antient power of registering, and of remonstrating at least, upon all the decrees of the national assembly, as they did upon those which passed in the time of the monarchy. It would be a means of squaring the occasional decrees of a democracy to some principles of general jurisprudence. The vice of the antient democracies, and one [246] cause of their ruin, was, that they ruled, as you do, by occasional decrees, *psephismata*. This practice soon broke in upon the tenour and consistency of the laws; it abated the respect of the people towards them; and totally destroyed them in the end.

Your vesting the power of remonstrance, which, in the time of the monarchy, existed in the parliament of Paris, in your principal executive officer, whom, in spite of common sense, you persevere in calling king, is the height of absurdity. You ought never to suffer remonstrance from him who is to execute. This is to understand neither council nor execution; neither authority nor obedience. The person whom you call king, ought not to have this power, or he ought to have more.

Your present arrangement is strictly judicial. Instead of imitating your monarchy, and seating your judges on a bench of independence, your object is to reduce them to the most blind obedience. As you have changed all things, you have invented new principles of order. You first appoint judges, who, I suppose, are to determine according to law, and then you let them know, that, at some time or other, you intend to give them some law by which they are to determine. Any studies which they have made (if any they have made) are to be useless to them. But to supply these studies, they are to be sworn to obey all the rules, orders, and instructions, which from time to time they are to receive from the national assembly. These if they submit to, they leave no ground of law to the subject. They become complete, and most dangerous instruments in the hands of the governing power, which, in the midst of a cause, or on the prospect of it, may wholly change the rule of decision. If these orders of the National

Assembly come to be contrary to the will of the people who locally choose those judges, such confusion must happen as is terrible to think of. For [247] the judges owe their place to the local authority; and the commands they are sworn to obey come from those who have no share in their appointment. In the mean time they have the example of the court of *Chatelet* to encourage and guide them in the exercise of their functions. That court is to try criminals sent to it by the National Assembly, or brought before it by other courses of delation. They sit under a guard, to save their own lives. They know not by what law they judge, nor under what authority they act, nor by what tenure they hold. It is thought that they are sometimes obliged to condemn at peril of their lives. This is not perhaps certain, nor can it be ascertained; but when they acquit, we know, they have seen the persons whom they discharge, with perfect impunity to the actors, hanged at the door of their court.

The assembly indeed promises that they will form a body of law, which shall be short, simple, clear, and so forth. That is, by their short laws, they will leave much to the discretion of the judge; whilst they have exploded the authority of all the learning which could make judicial discretion, (a thing perilous at best) deserving the appellation of a *sound* discretion.

It is curious to observe, that the administrative bodies are carefully exempted from the jurisdiction of these new tribunals. That is, those persons are exempted from the power of the laws, who ought to be the most entirely submitted to them. Those who execute public pecuniary trusts, ought of all men to be the most strictly held to their duty. One would have thought, that it must have been among your earliest cares, if you did not mean that those administrative bodies should be real sovereign independent states, to form an awful tribunal, like your late parliaments, or like our king's-bench, where all corporate officers might obtain protection in the legal exercise of their functions, and would [248] find coercion if they trespassed against their legal duty. But the cause of the exemption is plain. These administrative bodies are the great instruments of the present leaders in their progress through democracy to oligarchy. They must therefore be put above the law. It will be said, that the legal tribunals which you have made are unfit to coerce them. They are undoubtedly. They are unfit for any rational purpose. It will be said too, that the administrative bodies will be accountable to the general assembly. This, I fear, is talking without much consideration of the nature of that assembly, or of these corporations. However, to be subject to the pleasure of that assembly, is not to be subject to law, either for protection or for constraint.

This establishment of judges as yet wants something to its completion. It is to be crowned by a new tribunal. This is to be a grand state judicature; and it is to judge of crimes committed against the nation, that is, against the power of the assembly. It seems as if they had something in their view of the nature of the high court of justice erected in England during the time of the great usurpation. As they have not yet finished this part of the scheme, it is impossible to form a direct judgment upon it. However, if great care is not taken to form it in a spirit very different from that which has guided them in their proceedings relative to state offences, this tribunal, subservient to their inquisition, *the committee of research,* will extinguish the last sparks of liberty in France, and settle the most dreadful and arbitrary tyranny ever known in any nation. If they wish to give to this tribunal any appearance of liberty and justice, they must not evoke from, or send to it, the causes relative to their own members, at their pleasure. They must also remove the seat of that tribunal out of the republic of Paris.*

[249] HAS MORE WISDOM been displayed in the constitution of your army than what is discoverable in your plan of

---

*For further elucidations upon the subject of all these judicatures, and of the committee of research, see M. de Calonne's work.

judicature? The able arrangement of this part is the more difficult, and requires the greater skill and attention, not only as a great concern in itself, but as it is the third cementing principle in the new body of republics, which you call the French nation. Truly it is not easy to divine what that army may become at last. You have voted a very large one, and on good appointments, at least fully equal to your apparent means of payment. But what is the principle of its discipline? or whom is it to obey? You have got the wolf by the ears, and I wish you joy of the happy position in which you have chosen to place yourselves, and in which you are well circumstanced for a free deliberation, relatively to that army, or to any thing else.

The minister and secretary of state for the war department, is M. de la Tour du Pin. This gentleman, like his colleagues in administration, is a most zealous assertor of the revolution, and a sanguine admirer of the new constitution, which originated in that event. His statement of facts, relative to the military of France, is important, not only from his official and personal authority, but because it displays very clearly the actual condition of the army in France, and because it throws light on the principles upon which the assembly proceeds in the administration of this critical object. It may enable us to form some judgment how far it may be expedient in this country to imitate the martial policy of France.

M. de la Tour du Pin, on the 4th of last June, comes to give an account of the state of his department, as it exists under the auspices of the national assembly. No man knows it so well; no man can express it better. Addressing himself to the National Assembly, he says, "His Majesty has *this day* sent me to apprize you of the multiplied disorders [250] of which *every day* he receives the most distressing intelligence. The army (le corps militaire) threatens to fall into the most turbulent anarchy. Entire regiments have dared to violate at once the respect due to the laws, to the King, to the order established by your decrees, and to the oaths which they have taken with the most awful solemnity. Compelled by my duty to give you information of these excesses, my heart bleeds when I consider who they are that have committed them. Those, against whom it is not in my power to withhold the most grievous complaints, are a part of that very soldiery which to this day have been so full of honour and loyalty, and with whom, for fifty years, I have lived the comrade and the friend.

"What incomprehensible spirit of delirium and delusion has all at once led them astray? Whilst you are indefatigable in establishing uniformity in the empire, and moulding the whole into one coherent and consistent body; whilst the French are taught by you, at once the respect which the laws owe to the rights of man, and that which the citizens owe to the laws, the administration of the army presents nothing but disturbance and confusion. I see in more than one corps the bonds of discipline relaxed or broken; the most unheard-of pretensions avowed directly and without any disguise; the ordinances without force; the chiefs without authority; the military chest and the colours carried off; the authority of the King himself [*risum teneatis*] proudly defied; the officers despised, degraded, threatened, driven away, and some of them prisoners in the midst of their corps, dragging on a precarious life in the bosom of disgust and humiliation. To fill up the measure of all these horrors, the commandants of places have had their throats cut, under the eyes, and almost in the arms, of their own soldiers.

"These evils are great; but they are not the worst consequences [251] which may be produced by such military insurrections. Sooner or later they may menace the nation itself. *The nature of things requires,* that the army should never act but as *an instrument.* The moment that, erecting itself into a deliberative body, it shall act according to its own resolutions, the *government, be it what it may, will immediately degenerate into a military democracy;* a species of political monster, which has always ended by devouring those who have produced it.

"After all this, who must not be alarmed at the irregular consultations, and turbulent committees, formed in some regiments by the common soldiers and non-commissioned officers, without the knowledge, or even in contempt of the authority of their superiors; although the presence and concurrence of those superiors could give no authority to such monstrous democratic assemblies [comices]."

It is not necessary to add much to this finished picture: finished as far as its canvas admits; but, as I apprehend, not taking in the whole of the nature and complexity of the disorders of this military democracy, which, the minister at war truly and wisely observes, wherever it exists, must be the true constitution of the state, by whatever formal appellation it may pass. For, though he informs the assembly, that the more considerable part of the army have not cast off their obedience, but are still attached to their duty, yet those travellers who have seen the corps whose conduct is the best, rather observe in them the absence of mutiny than the existence of discipline.

I cannot help pausing here for a moment, to reflect upon the expressions of surprise which this Minister has let fall, relative to the excesses he relates. To him the departure of the troops from their antient principles of loyalty and honour seems quite inconceivable. Surely those to whom he addresses himself know the causes of it but too well. [252] They know the doctrines which they have preached, the decrees which they have passed, the practices which they have countenanced. The soldiers remember the 6th of October. They recollect the French guards. They have not forgot the taking of the King's castles in Paris, and at Marseilles. That the governors in both places, were murdered with impunity, is a fact that has not passed out of their minds. They do not abandon the principles, laid down so ostentatiously and laboriously, of the equality of men. They cannot shut their eyes to the degradation of the whole noblesse of France; and the suppression of the very idea of a gentleman. The total abolition of titles and distinctions is not lost upon them. But Mr. du Pin is astonished at their disloyalty, when the doctors of the assembly have taught them at the same time the respect due to laws. It is easy to judge which of the two sorts of lessons men with arms in their hands are likely to learn. As to the authority of the King, we may collect from the minister himself (if any argument on that head were not quite superfluous) that it is not of more consideration with these troops, than it is with every body else. "The King," says he, "has over and over again repeated his orders to put a stop to these excesses: but, in so terrible a crisis, *your* [the assembly's] concurrence is become indispensably necessary to prevent the evils which menace the state. *You* unite to the force of the legislative power, *that of opinion* still more important." To be sure the army can have no opinion of the power or authority of the king. Perhaps the soldier has by this time learned, that the assembly itself does not enjoy a much greater degree of liberty than that royal figure.

It is now to be seen what has been proposed in this exigency, one of the greatest that can happen in a state. The Minister requests the assembly to array itself in all its terrors, and to call forth all its majesty. He desires that the [253] grave and severe principles announced by them may give vigour to the King's proclamation. After this we should have looked for courts civil and martial; breaking of some corps, decimating others, and all the terrible means which necessity has employed in such cases to arrest the progress of the most terrible of all evils; particularly, one might expect, that a serious inquiry would be made into the murder of commandants in the view of their soldiers. Not one word of all this, or of any thing like it. After they had been told that the soldiery trampled upon the decrees of the assembly promulgated by the King, the assembly pass new decrees; and they authorise the King to make new proclamations. After the Secretary at War had stated that the regiments had paid no regard to oaths *prêtés avec la plus imposante solemnité*—they propose—what? More oaths. They renew decrees and proclamations as they experience their insufficiency, and they multiply oaths in proportion as they weaken, in the minds of men, the sanctions of religion. I hope that handy abridgments of the excellent sermons of Voltaire, d'Alembert, Diderot, and Helvetius, on the Immortality of the Soul, on a particular superintending Providence, and on a Future State of Rewards and Punishments, are sent down to the soldiers along with their civic oaths. Of this I have no doubt; as I understand, that a certain description of reading makes no inconsiderable part of their military exercises, and that they are full as well supplied with the ammunition of pamphlets as of cartridges.

To prevent the mischiefs arising from conspiracies, irregular consultations, seditious committees, and monstrous democratic assemblies ["comitia," "comices"] of the soldiers, and all the disorders arising from idleness, luxury, dissipation, and insubordination, I believe the most astonishing means have been used, that ever occurred to men, even in all the inventions of this prolific age. It is no less than [254] this: The King has promulgated in circular letters to all the regiments his direct authority and encouragement, that the several corps should join themselves with the clubs and confederations in the several municipalities, and mix with them in their feasts and civic entertainments! This jolly discipline, it seems, is to soften the ferocity of their minds; to reconcile them to their bottle companions of other descriptions; and to merge particular conspiracies in more general associations.*

---

*Comme sa Majesté y a reconnu, non une systême d'associations particulières, mais une réunion de volontés de tous les François pour la liberté et la prosperité communes, ainsi pour le maintien de l'ordre publique; il a pensé qu'il convenoit que chaque régiment prit part a ces fêtes civiques pour multiplier les rapports, et reserrer les liens d'union entre les citoyens et les

---

That this remedy would be pleasing to the soldiers, as they are described by Mr. de la Tour du Pin, I can readily believe: and that, however mutinous otherwise, they will dutifully submit themselves to *these* royal proclamations. But I should question whether all this civic swearing, clubbing, and feasting, would dispose them more than at present they are disposed, to an obedience to their officers; or teach them better to submit to the austere rules of military discipline. It will make them admirable citizens after the French mode, but not quite so good soldiers after any mode. A doubt might well arise, whether the conversations at these good tables, would fit them a great deal the better for the character of *mere instruments*, which this veteran officer and statesman justly observes, the nature of things always requires an army to be.

Concerning the likelihood of this improvement in discipline, by the free conversation of the soldiers with the municipal festive societies, which is thus officially encouraged by royal authority and sanction, we may judge by the state of the municipalities themselves, furnished to us by the war [255] minister in this very speech. He conceives good hopes of the success of his endeavours towards restoring order *for the present* from the good disposition of certain regiments; but he finds something cloudy with regard to the future. As to preventing the return of confusion "for this, the administration (says he) cannot be answerable to you, as long as they see the municipalities arrogate to themselves an authority over the troops, which your institutions have reserved wholly to the monarch. You have fixed the limits of the military authority and the municipal authority. You have bounded the action, which you have permitted to the latter over the former, to the right of requisition; but never did the letter

---

troupes.—Lest I should not be credited, I insert the words, authorising the troops to feast with the popular confederacies.

or the spirit of your decrees authorise the commons in these municipalities to break the officers, to try them, to give orders to the soldiers, to drive them from the posts committed to their guard, to stop them in their marches ordered by the King, or, in a word, to enslave the troops to the caprice of each of the cities or even market towns through which they are to pass."

Such is the character and disposition of the municipal society which is to reclaim the soldiery, to bring them back to the true principles of military subordination, and to render them machines in the hands of the supreme power of the country! Such are the distempers of the French troops! Such is their cure! As the army is, so is the navy. The municipalities supersede the orders of the assembly, and the seamen in their turn supersede the orders of the municipalities. From my heart I pity the condition of a respectable servant of the public, like this war minister, obliged in his old age to pledge the assembly in their civic cups, and to enter with a hoary head into all the fantastick vagaries of these juvenile politicians. Such schemes are not like propositions coming from a man of fifty years wear and tear amongst mankind. They seem rather such as ought to be [256] expected from those grand compounders in politics, who shorten the road to their degrees in the state; and have a certain inward fanatical assurance and illumination upon all subjects; upon the credit of which one of their doctors has thought fit, with great applause, and greater success, to caution the assembly not to attend to old men, or to any persons who valued themselves upon their experience. I suppose all the ministers of state must qualify, and take this test; wholly abjuring the errors and heresies of experience and observation. Every man has his own relish. But I think, if I could not attain to the wisdom, I would at least preserve something of the stiff and peremptory dignity of age. These gentlemen deal in regeneration; but at any price I should hardly yield my rigid fibres to be regenerated by them; nor begin, in my grand climacteric, to squall in their new accents, or to stammer, in my second cradle, the elemental sounds of their barbarous metaphysics.* *Si isti mihi largiantur ut repuerascam, et in eorum cunis vagiam, valde recusem!*

The imbecility of any part of the puerile and pedantic system, which they call a constitution, cannot be laid open without discovering the utter insufficiency and mischief of every other part with which it comes in contact, or that bears any the remotest relation to it. You cannot propose a remedy for the incompetence of the crown, without displaying the debility of the assembly. You cannot deliberate on the confusion of the army of the state, without disclosing the worse disorders of the armed municipalities. The military lays open the civil, and the civil betrays the military anarchy. I wish every body carefully to peruse the eloquent speech (such it is) of Mons. de la Tour du Pin. He attributes the salvation of the municipalities to the good behaviour [257] of some of the troops. These troops are to preserve the well-disposed part of those municipalities, which is confessed to be the weakest, from the pillage of the worst disposed, which is the strongest. But the municipalities affect a sovereignty, and will command those troops which are necessary for their protection. Indeed, they must command them, or court them. The municipalities, by the necessity of their situation, and by the republican powers they have obtained, must, with relation to the military, be the masters, or the servants, or the confederates, or each successively; or they must make a jumble of all together, according to circumstances. What government is there to coerce the army but the municipality, or the municipality but the army? To preserve concord where authority is extinguished, at the hazard of all consequences, the assembly attempts to cure the distempers by the distempers themselves; and they hope to preserve themselves from a purely

---

*This war minister has since quitted the school and resigned his office.

military democracy, by giving it a debauched interest in the municipal.

If the soldiers once come to mix for any time in the municipal clubs, cabals, and confederacies, an elective attraction will draw them to the lowest and most desperate part. With them will be their habits, affections, and sympathies. The military conspiracies, which are to be remedied by civic confederacies; the rebellious municipalities, which are to be rendered obedient by furnishing them with the means of seducing the very armies of the state that are to keep them in order; all these chimeras of a monstrous and portentous policy, must aggravate the confusions from which they have arisen. There must be blood. The want of common judgment manifested in the construction of all their descriptions of forces, and in all their kinds of civil and judicial authorities, will make it flow. Disorders may be quieted in one time and in one part. They will break out in others; [258] because the evil is radical and intrinsic. All these schemes of mixing mutinous soldiers with seditious citizens, must weaken still more and more the military connection of soldiers with their officers, as well as add military and mutinous audacity to turbulent artificers and peasants. To secure a real army, the officer should be first and last in the eye of the soldier; first and last in his attention, observance, and esteem. Officers it seems there are to be, whose chief qualification must be temper and patience. They are to manage their troops by electioneering arts. They must bear themselves as candidates not as commanders. But as by such means power may be occasionally in their hands, the authority by which they are to be nominated becomes of high importance.

What you may do finally, does not appear; nor is it of much moment, whilst the strange and contradictory relation between your army and all the parts of your republic, as well as the puzzled relation of those parts to each other and to the whole, remain as they are. You seem to have given the provisional nomination of the officers, in the first instance, to the king, with a reserve of approbation by the National Assembly. Men who have an interest to pursue are extremely sagacious in discovering the true seat of power. They must soon perceive that those who can negative indefinitely, in reality appoint. The officers must therefore look to their intrigues in that assembly, as the sole certain road to promotion. Still, however, by your new constitution they must begin their solicitation at court. This double negotiation for military rank seems to me a contrivance as well adapted, as if it were studied for no other end, to promote faction in the assembly itself, relative to this vast military patronage; and then to poison the corps of officers with factions of a nature still more dangerous to the safety of government, upon any bottom on which it can be placed, [259] and destructive in the end to the efficiency of the army itself. Those officers, who lose the promotions intended for them by the crown, must become of a faction opposite to that of the assembly which has rejected their claims, and must nourish discontents in the heart of the army against the ruling powers. Those officers, on the other hand, who, by carrying their point through an interest in the assembly, feel themselves to be at best only second in the good-will of the crown, though first in that of the assembly, must slight an authority which would not advance, and could not retard their promotion. If to avoid these evils you will have no other rule for command or promotion than seniority, you will have an army of formality; at the same time it will become more independent, and more of a military republic. Not they but the king is the machine. A king is not to be deposed by halves. If he is not every thing in the command of an army, he is nothing. What is the effect of a power placed nominally at the head of the army, who to that army is no object of gratitude, or of fear? Such a cypher is not fit for the administration of an object of all things the most delicate, the supreme command of military men. They must be constrained (and their inclinations lead them to what their necessities require) by a real, vigorous, effective, decided, personal authority. The authority of the assembly itself suffers by passing through such a debilitating channel as they have chosen. The army will not long look to an assembly acting through the organ of false shew, and palpable imposition. They will not seriously yield obedience to a prisoner. They will either despise a pageant, or they will pity a captive king. This relation of your army to the crown will, if I am not greatly mistaken, become a serious dilemma in your politics.

It is besides to be considered, whether an assembly like yours, even supposing that it was in possession of another [260] sort of organ through which its orders were to pass, is fit for promoting the obedience and discipline of an army. It is known, that armies have hitherto yielded a very precarious and uncertain obedience to any senate, or popular authority; and they will least of all yield it to an assembly which is to have only a continuance of two years. The officers must totally lose the characteristic disposition of military men, if they see with perfect submission and due admiration, the dominion of pleaders; especially when they find, that they have a new court to pay to an endless succession of those pleaders, whose military policy, and the genius of whose command (if they should have any) must be as uncertain as their duration is transient. In the weakness of one kind of authority, and in the fluctuation of all, the officers of an army will remain for some time mutinous and full of faction, until some popular general, who understands the art of conciliating the soldiery, and who possesses the true spirit of command shall draw the eyes of all men upon himself. Armies will obey him on his personal account. There is no other way of securing military obedience in this state of things. But the moment in which that event shall happen, the person who really commands the army is your master; the master (that is little) of your king, the master of your assembly, the master of your whole republic.

How came the assembly by their present power over the army? Chiefly, to be sure, by debauching the soldiers from their officers. They have begun by a most terrible operation. They have touched the central point, about which the particles that compose armies are at repose. They have destroyed the principle of obedience in the great essential critical link between the officer and the soldier, just where the chain of military subordination commences, and on which the whole of that system depends. The soldier is told, he is a citizen, and has the rights of man and citizen. The right of [261] a man, he is told, is to be his own governor, and to be ruled only by those to whom he delegates that self-government. It is very natural he should think, that he ought most of all to have his choice where he is to yield the greatest degree of obedience. He will therefore, in all probability, systematically do, what he does at present occasionally; that is, he will exercise at least a negative in the choice of his officers. At present the officers are known at best to be only permissive, and on their good behaviour. In fact, there have been many instances in which they have been cashiered by their corps. Here is a second negative on the choice of the king; a negative as effectual at least as the other of the assembly. The soldiers know already that it has been a question, not ill received in the national assembly, whether they ought not to have the direct choice of their officers, or some proportion of them? When such matters are in deliberation, it is no extravagant supposition that they will incline to the opinion most favourable to their pretensions. They will not bear to be deemed the army of an imprisoned king, whilst another army in the same country, with whom too they are to feast and confederate, is to be considered as the free army of a free constitution. They will cast their eyes on the other and more permanent army; I mean the municipal. That corps, they well know, does actually elect its own officers. They may not be able to discern the grounds of distinction on which they are not to elect a Marquis de la

Fayette (or what is his new name) of their own? If this election of a commander in chief be a part of the rights of men, why not of theirs? They see elective justices of peace, elective judges, elective curates, elective bishops, elective municipalities, and elective commanders of the Parisian army. Why should they alone be excluded? Are the brave troops of France the only men in that nation who are not the fit judges of military merit, and of the qualifications necessary for a commander [262] in chief? Are they paid by the state, and do they therefore lose the rights of men? They are a part of that nation themselves, and contribute to that pay. And is not the king, is not the national assembly, and are not all who elect the national assembly, likewise paid? Instead of seeing all these forfeit their rights by their receiving a salary, they perceive that in all these cases a salary is given for the exercise of those rights. All your resolutions, all your proceedings, all your debates, all the works of your doctors in religion and politics, have industriously been put into their hands; and you expect that they will apply to their own case just as much of your doctrines and examples as suits your pleasure!

Every thing depends upon the army in such a government as yours; for you have industriously destroyed all the opinions, and prejudices, and, as far as in you lay, all the instincts which support government. Therefore the moment any difference arises between your national assembly and any part of the nation, you must have recourse to force. Nothing else is left to you; or rather you have left nothing else to yourselves. You see by the report of your war minister, that the distribution of the army is in a great measure made with a view of internal coercion.* You must rule by an army; and you have infused into that army by which you rule, as well as into the whole body of the nation, principles which after a time must disable you in the use you resolve to make of

---

*Courier François, 30 July, 1790. Assemblée Nationale, Numéro 210.

it. The king is to call out troops to act against his people, when the world has been told, and the assertion is still ringing in our ears, that troops ought not to fire on citizens. The colonies assert to themselves an independent constitution and a free trade. They must be constrained by troops. In what chapter of your code of the rights of men are they able to read, that it is a part of the rights of men to [263] have their commerce monopolized and restrained for the benefit of others? As the colonists rise on you, the negroes rise on them. Troops again—Massacre, torture, hanging! These are your rights of men! These are the fruits of metaphysic declarations wantonly made, and shamefully retracted! It was but the other day that the farmers of land in one of your provinces refused to pay some sorts of rents to the lord of the soil. In consequence of this, you decree that the country people shall pay all rents and dues, except those which as grievances you have abolished; and if they refuse, then you order the king to march troops against them. You lay down metaphysic propositions which infer universal consequences, and then you attempt to limit logic by despotism. The leaders of the present system tell them of their rights, as men, to take fortresses, to murder guards, to seize on kings without the least appearance of authority even from the assembly, whilst, as the sovereign legislative body, that assembly was sitting in the name of the nation; and yet these leaders presume to order out the troops, which have acted in these very disorders, to coerce those who shall judge on the principles, and follow the examples, which have been guarantied by their own approbation!

The leaders teach the people to abhor and reject all feodality as the barbarism of tyranny, and they tell them afterwards how much of that barbarous tyranny they are to bear with patience. As they are prodigal of light with regard to grievances, so the people find them sparing in the extreme with regard to redress. They know that not only certain quit-rents and personal duties, which you have permitted them to redeem (but have furnished no money for the redemption) are as nothing to those burthens for which you have made no provision at all. They know, that almost the whole system of landed property in its origin is feudal; that it is the distribution of the possessions of the [264] original proprietors, made by a barbarous conqueror to his barbarous instruments; and that the most grievous effects of conquest are the land rents of every kind, as without question they are.

The peasants, in all probability, are the descendants of these antient proprietors, Romans or Gauls. But if they fail, in any degree, in the titles which they make on the principles of antiquaries and lawyers, they retreat into the citadel of the rights of men. There they find that men are equal; and the earth, the kind and equal mother of all, ought not to be monopolized to foster the pride and luxury of any men, who by nature are no better than themselves, and who, if they do not labour for their bread, are worse. They find, that by the laws of nature the occupant and subduer of the soil is the true proprietor; that there is no prescription against nature; and that the agreements (where any there are) which have been made with their landlords, during the time of slavery, are only the effect of duresse and force; and that when the people re-entered into the rights of men, those agreements were made as void as every thing else which had been settled under the prevalence of the old feudal and aristocratic tyranny. They will tell you that they see no difference between an idler with a hat and a national cockade, and an idler in a cowl or in a rochet. If you ground the title to rents on succession and prescription, they tell you, from the speech of Mr. Camus, published by the national assembly for their information, that things ill begun cannot avail themselves of prescription; that the title of these lords was vicious in its origin; and that force is at least as bad as fraud. As to the title by succession, they will tell you, that the succession of those who have cultivated the soil is the true pedigree of property, and not rotten parchments and silly substitutions; that the lords have enjoyed the usurpation too long; and that if they allow to [265] these lay monks any charitable pension, they ought to be thankful to the bounty of the true proprietor, who is so generous towards a false claimant to his goods.

When the peasants give you back that coin of sophistic reason, on which you have set your image and superscription, you cry it down as base money, and tell them you will pay for the future with French guards, and dragoons, and hussars. You hold up, to chastise them, the second-hand authority of a king, who is only the instrument of destroying, without any power of protecting either the people or his own person. Through him, it seems, you will make yourselves obeyed. They answer, You have taught us that there are no gentlemen; and which of your principles teach us to bow to kings whom we have not elected? We know, without your teaching, that lands were given for the support of feudal dignities, feudal titles, and feudal offices. When you took down the cause as a grievance, why should the more grievous effect remain? As there are now no hereditary honours, and no distinguished families, why are we taxed to maintain what *you* tell us ought to exist? You have sent down our old aristocratic landlords in no other character, and with no other title, but that of ex-actors under your authority. Have you endeavoured to make these your rent-gatherers respectable to us? No. You have sent them to us with their arms reversed, their shields broken, their impresses defaced; and so displumed, degraded, and metamorphosed, such unfeathered two-legged things, that we no longer know them. They are strangers to us. They do not even go by the names of our antient lords. Physically they may be the same men; though we are not quite sure of that, on your new philosophic doctrines of personal identity. In all other respects they are totally changed. We do not see why we have not as good a right to refuse them their rents, as you have to abrogate all their honours, titles, and distinctions. [266] This we have never commissioned you to do; and it is one instance, among many indeed, of your assumption of undelegated power. We see the burghers of Paris, through their clubs, their mobs, and their national guards, directing you at their pleasure, and giving that as law to you, which, under your authority, is transmitted as law to us. Through you, these burghers dispose of the lives and fortunes of us all. Why should not you attend as much to the desires of the laborious husbandman with regard to our rent, by which we are affected in the most serious manner, as you do to the demands of these insolent burghers, relative to distinctions and titles of honour, by which neither they nor we are affected at all? But we find you pay more regard to their fancies than to our necessities. Is it among the rights of man to pay tribute to his equals? Before this measure of yours, we might have thought we were not perfectly equal. We might have entertained some old, habitual, unmeaning prepossession in favour of those landlords; but we cannot conceive with what other view than that of destroying all respect to them, you could have made the law that degrades them. You have forbidden us to treat them with any of the old formalities of respect, and now you send troops to sabre and to bayonet us into a submission to fear and force, which you did not suffer us to yield to the mild authority of opinion.

The ground of some of these arguments is horrid and ridiculous to all rational ears; but to the politicians of metaphysics who have opened schools for sophistry, and made establishments for anarchy, it is solid and conclusive. It is obvious, that on a mere consideration of the right, the leaders in the assembly would not in the least have scrupled to abrogate the rents along with the titles and family ensigns. It would be only to follow up the principle of their reasonings, and to complete the analogy of their conduct. But [267] they had newly possessed themselves of a great body of landed property by confiscation. They had this commodity at market; and the market would have been wholly destroyed, if they were to permit the husbandmen to riot in the speculations with which they so freely intoxicated themselves. The only security which property enjoys in any one of its descriptions, is from the interests of their rapacity with regard to some other. They have left nothing but their own arbitrary pleasure to determine what property is to be protected and what subverted.

Neither have they left any principle by which any of their municipalities can be bound to obedience; or even conscientiously obliged not to separate from the whole, to become independent, or to connect itself with some other state. The people of Lyons, it seems, have refused lately to pay taxes. Why should they not? What lawful authority is there left to exact them? The king imposed some of them. The old states, methodised by orders, settled the more antient. They may say to the assembly, Who are you, that are not our kings, nor the states we have elected, nor sit on the principles on which we have elected you? And who are we, that when we see the gabelles, which you have ordered to be paid, wholly shaken off, when we see the act of disobedience afterwards ratified by yourselves—who are we, that we are not to judge what taxes we ought or ought not to pay, and who are not to avail ourselves of the same powers, the validity of which you have approved in others? To this the answer is, We will send troops. The last reason of kings is always the first with your assembly. This military aid may serve for a time, whilst the impression of the increase of pay remains, and the vanity of being umpires in all disputes is flattered. But this weapon will snap short, unfaithful to the hand that employs it. The assembly keep a school where, systematically, and with unremitting [268] perseverance, they teach principles, and form regulations, destructive to all spirit of subordination, civil and military—and then they expect that they shall hold in obedience an anarchic people by an anarchic army!

The municipal army, which, according to their new policy, is to balance this national army, if considered in itself only, is of a constitution much more simple, and in every respect less exceptionable. It is a mere democratic body, unconnected with the crown or the kingdom; armed, and trained, and officered at the pleasure of the districts to which the corps severally belong; and the personal service of the individuals who compose it, or the fine in lieu of personal service, are directed by the same authority.* Nothing is more uniform. If, however, considered in any relation to the crown, to the national assembly, to the public tribunals, or to the other army, or considered in a view to any coherence or connection between its parts, it seems a monster, and can hardly fail to terminate its perplexed movements in some great national calamity. It is a worse preservative of a general constitution, than the systasis of Crete, or the confederation of Poland, or any other ill-devised corrective which has yet been imagined, in the necessities produced by an ill-constructed system of government.

HAVING CONCLUDED my few remarks on the constitution of the supreme power, the executive, the judicature, the military, and on the reciprocal relation of all these establishments, I shall say something of the ability shewed by your legislators with regard to the revenue.

[269] In their proceedings relative to this object, if possible, still fewer traces appear of political judgment or finan-

---

*I see by M. Necker's account, that the national guards of Paris have received, over and above the money levied within their own city, about 145,000*l.* sterling out of the public treasure. Whether this be an actual payment for the nine months of their existence, or an estimate of their yearly charge, I do not clearly perceive. It is of no great importance, as certainly they may take whatever they please.

cial resource. When the states met, it seemed to be the great object to improve the system of revenue, to enlarge its connection, to cleanse it of oppression and vexation, and to establish it on the most solid footing. Great were the expectations entertained on that head throughout Europe. It was by this grand arrangement that France was to stand or fall; and this became, (in my opinion, very properly,) the test by which the skill and patriotism of those who ruled in that assembly would be tried. The revenue of the state is the state. In effect all depends upon it, whether for support or for reformation. The dignity of every occupation wholly depends upon the quantity and the kind of virtue that may be exerted in it. As all great qualities of the mind which operate in public, and are not merely suffering and passive, require force for their display, I had almost said for their unequivocal existence, the revenue, which is the spring of all power, becomes in its administration the sphere of every active virtue. Public virtue, being of a nature magnificent and splendid, instituted for great things, and conversant about great concerns, requires abundant scope and room, and cannot spread and grow under confinement, and in circumstances straitened, narrow, and sordid. Through the revenue alone the body politic can act in its true genius and character, and therefore it will display just as much of its collective virtue, and as much of that virtue which may characterise those who move it, and are, as it were, its life and guiding principle, as it is possessed of a just revenue. For from hence, not only magnanimity, and liberality, and beneficence, and fortitude, and providence, and the tutelary protection of all good arts, derive their food, and the growth of their organs, but continence, and self-denial, and labour, and vigilance, and frugality, and whatever else there is in [270] which the mind shews itself above the appetite, are no where more in their proper element than in the provision and distribution of the public wealth. It is therefore not without reason that the science of speculative and practical finance, which must take to its aid so many auxiliary branches of knowledge, stands high in the estimation not only of the ordinary sort, but of the wisest and best men; and as this science has grown with the progress of its object, the prosperity and improvement of nations has generally encreased with the encrease of their revenues; and they will both continue to grow and flourish, as long as the balance between what is left to strengthen the efforts of individuals, and what is collected for the common efforts of the state, bear to each other a due reciprocal proportion, and are kept in a close correspondence and communication. And perhaps it may be owing to the greatness of revenues, and to the urgency of state necessities, that old abuses in the constitution of finances are discovered, and their true nature and rational theory comes to be more perfectly understood; insomuch that a smaller revenue might have been more distressing in one period than a far greater is found to be in another; the proportionate wealth even remaining the same. In this state of things, the French assembly found something in their revenues to preserve, to secure, and wisely to administer, as well as to abrogate and alter. Though their proud assumption might justify the severest tests, yet in trying their abilities on their financial proceedings, I would only consider what is the plain obvious duty of a common finance minister, and try them upon that, and not upon models of ideal perfection.

The objects of a financier are, then, to secure an ample revenue; to impose it with judgment and equality; to employ it oeconomically; and when necessity obliges him to make use of credit, to secure its foundations in that instance, [271] and for ever, by the clearness and candour of his proceedings, the exactness of his calculations, and the solidity of his funds. On these heads we may take a short and distinct view of the merits and abilities of those in the national assembly, who have taken to themselves the management of this arduous concern. Far from any encrease of revenue in their hands, I find, by a report of M. Vernier, from the committee of finances, of the second of August last, that the amount of the national revenue, as compared with its produce before the revolution, was diminished by the sum of two hundred millions, or *eight millions sterling* of the annual income — considerably more than one third of the whole!

If this be the result of great ability, never surely was ability displayed in a more distinguished manner, or with so powerful an effect. No common folly, no vulgar incapacity, no ordinary official negligence, even no official crime, no corruption, no peculation, hardly any direct hostility which we have seen in the modern world, could in so short a time have made so complete an overthrow of the finances, and with them, of the strength, of a great kingdom. *Cedo quî vestram rempublicam tantam amisistis tam cito?*

The sophisters and declaimers, as soon as the assembly met, began with decrying the antient constitution of the revenue in many of its most essential branches, such as the public monopoly of salt. They charged it, as truly as unwisely, with being ill-contrived, oppressive, and partial. This representation they were not satisfied to make use of in speeches preliminary to some plan of reform; they declared it in a solemn resolution or public sentence, as it were judicially, passed upon it; and this they dispersed throughout the nation. At the time they passed the decree, with the same gravity they ordered this same absurd, oppressive, and partial tax to be paid, until they could find a revenue to replace it. The consequence was inevitable. [272] The provinces which had been always exempted from this salt monopoly, some of whom were charged with other contributions, perhaps equivalent, were totally disinclined to bear any part of the burthen, which by an equal distribution was to redeem the others. As to the assembly, occupied as it was with the declaration and violation of the rights of men, and with their arrangements for general confusion, it had neither leisure nor capacity to contrive, nor authority to enforce any plan of any kind relative to the replacing the tax or equalizing it, or compensating the provinces, or for conducting their minds to any scheme of accommodation with the other districts which were to be relieved.

The people of the salt provinces, impatient under taxes damned by the authority which had directed their payment, very soon found their patience exhausted. They thought themselves as skilful in demolishing as the assembly could be. They relieved themselves by throwing off the whole burthen. Animated by this example, each district, or part of a district, judging of its own grievance by its own feeling, and of its remedy by its own opinion, did as it pleased with other taxes.

We are next to see how they have conducted themselves in contriving equal impositions, proportioned to the means of the citizens, and the least likely to lean heavy on the active capital employed in the generation of that private wealth, from whence the public fortune must be derived. By suffering the several districts, and several of the individuals in each district, to judge of what part of the old revenue they might withhold, instead of better principles of equality, a new inequality was introduced of the most oppressive kind. Payments were regulated by dispositions. The parts of the kingdom which were the most submissive, the most orderly, or the most affectionate to the commonwealth, bore the whole burthen of the state. Nothing turns [273] out to be so oppressive and unjust as a feeble government. To fill up all the deficiencies in the old impositions, and the new deficiencies of every kind which were to be expected, what remained to a state without authority? The national assembly called for a voluntary benevolence; for a fourth part of the income of all the citizens, to be estimated on the honour of those who were to pay. They obtained something more than could be rationally calculated, but what was far indeed from answerable to their real necessities, and much less to their fond expectations. Rational people could have hoped for little from this their tax in the disguise of a benevolence; a tax, weak, ineffective, and unequal; a tax by which luxury, avarice, and selfishness were screened, and the load thrown upon productive capital, upon integrity, generosity, and public spirit—a tax of regulation upon virtue. At length the mask is thrown off, and they are now trying means (with little success) of exacting their benevolence by force.

This benevolence, the ricketty offspring of weakness, was to be supported by another resource, the twin brother of the same prolific imbecility. The patriotic donations were to make good the failure of the patriotic contribution. John Doe was to become security for Richard Roe. By this scheme they took things of much price from the giver, comparatively of small value to the receiver; they ruined several trades; they pillaged the crown of its ornaments, the churches of their plate, and the people of their personal decorations. The invention of these juvenile pretenders to liberty, was in reality nothing more than a servile imitation of one of the poorest resources of doting despotism. They took an old huge full-bottomed perriwig out of the wardrobe of the antiquated frippery of Louis XIV., to cover the premature baldness of the national assembly. They produced this old-fashioned formal folly, though it had been so abundantly [274] exposed in the Memoirs of the Duke de St. Simon, if to reasonable men it had wanted any arguments to display its mischief and insufficiency. A device of the same kind was tried in my memory by Louis XV., but it answered at no time. However, the necessities of ruinous wars were some excuse for desperate projects. The deliberations of calamity are rarely wise. But here was a season for disposition and providence. It was in a time of profound peace, then enjoyed for five years, and promising a much longer continuance, that they had recourse to this desperate trifling. They were sure to lose more reputation by sporting, in their serious situation, with these toys and playthings of finance, which have filled half their journals, than could possibly be compensated by the poor temporary supply which they afforded. It seemed as if those who adopted such projects were wholly ignorant of their circumstances, or wholly unequal to their necessities. Whatever virtue may be in these devices, it is obvious that neither the patriotic gifts, nor the patriotic contribution, can ever be resorted to again. The resources of public folly are soon exhausted. The whole indeed of their scheme of revenue is to make, by any artifice, an appearance of a full reservoir for the hour, whilst at the same time they cut off the springs and living fountains of perennial supply. The account not long since furnished by Mr. Necker was meant, without question, to be favourable. He gives a flattering view of the means of getting through the year; but he expresses, as it is natural he should, some apprehension for that which was to succeed. On this last prognostic, instead of entering into the grounds of this apprehension, in order by a proper foresight, to prevent the prognosticated evil, Mr. Necker receives a sort of friendly reprimand from the president of the assembly.

As to their other schemes of taxation, it is impossible to say any thing of them with certainty; because they have [275] not yet had their operation; but nobody is so sanguine as to imagine they will fill up any perceptible part of the wide gaping breach which their incapacity has made in their revenues. At present the state of their treasury sinks every day more and more in cash, and swells more and more in fictitious representation. When so little within or without is now found but paper, the representative not of opulence but of want, the creature not of credit but of power, they imagine that our flourishing state in England is owing to that bank-paper, and not the bank-paper to the flourishing condition of our commerce, to the solidity of our credit, and to the total exclusion of all idea of power from any part of the transaction. They forget that, in England, not one shilling of paper-money of any description is received but of choice; that the whole has had its origin in cash actually deposited; and that it is convertible, at pleasure, in an instant, and without the smallest loss, into cash again. Our paper is of value in commerce, because in law it is of none. It is powerful on Change, because in Westminster-hall it is impotent. In payment of a debt of twenty shillings, a creditor may refuse all the paper of the bank of England. Nor is there amongst us a single public security, of any quality or nature whatsoever, that is enforced by authority. In fact it might be easily shewn, that our paper wealth, instead of lessening the real coin, has a tendency to encrease it; instead of being a substitute for money, it only facilitates its entry, its exit, and its circulation; that it is the symbol of prosperity, and not the badge of distress. Never was a scarcity of cash, and an exuberance of paper, a subject of complaint in this nation.

Well! But a lessening of prodigal expences, and the oeconomy which has been introduced by the virtuous and sapient assembly, makes amends for the losses sustained in the receipt of revenue. In this at least they have fulfilled [276] the duty of a financier. Have those, who say so, looked at the expences of the national assembly itself? of the municipalities? of the city of Paris? of the increased pay of the two armies? of the new police? of the new judicatures? Have they even carefully compared the present pension-list with the former? These politicians have been cruel, not oeconomical. Comparing the expences of the former prodigal government, and its relation to the then revenues, with the expences of this new system as opposed to the state of its new treasury, I believe the present will be found beyond all comparison more chargeable.*

---

*The reader will observe, that I have but lightly touched (my plan demanded nothing more) on the condition of the French finances, as connected with the demands upon them. If I had intended to do otherwise, the materials in my hands for such a task are not altogether perfect. On this subject I

It remains only to consider the proofs of financial ability furnished by the present French managers when they are to raise supplies on credit. Here I am a little at a stand; for credit, properly speaking, they have none. The credit of the antient government was not indeed the best: but they could always, on some terms, command money, not only at home, but from most of the countries of Europe where a surplus capital was accumulated; and the credit of that government was improving daily. The establishment of a system of liberty would of course be supposed to give it new strength; and so it would actually have done, if a [277] system of liberty had been established. What offers has their government of pretended liberty had from Holland, from Hamburgh, from Switzerland, from Genoa, from England, for a dealing in their paper? Why should these nations of commerce and oeconomy enter into any pecuniary dealings with a people who attempt to reverse the very nature of things; amongst whom they see the debtor prescribing, at the point of the bayonet, the medium of his solvency to the creditor; discharging one of his engagements with another; turning his very penury into his resource; and paying his interest with his rags?

Their fanatical confidence in the omnipotence of church plunder, has induced these philosophers to overlook all care of the public estate, just as the dream of the philosopher's stone induces dupes, under the more plausible delusion of

refer the reader to M. de Calonne's work; and the tremendous display that he has made of the havock and devastation in the public estate, and in all the affairs of France, caused by the presumptuous good intentions of ignorance and incapacity. Such effects, those causes will always produce. Looking over that account with a pretty strict eye, and, with perhaps too much rigour, deducting every thing which may be placed to the account of a financier out of place, who might be supposed by his enemies desirous of making the most of his cause, I believe it will be found, that a more salutary lesson of caution against the daring spirit of innovators than what has been supplied at the expence of France, never was at any time furnished to mankind.

the hermetic art, to neglect all rational means of improving their fortunes. With these philosophic financiers, this universal medicine made of church mummy is to cure all the evils of the state. These gentlemen perhaps do not believe a great deal in the miracles of piety; but it cannot be questioned that they have an undoubting faith in the prodigies of sacrilege. Is there a debt which pressed them? Issue *assignats*. Are compensations to be made, or a maintenance decreed to those whom they have robbed of their freehold in their office, or expelled from their profession? *Assignats*. Is a fleet to be fitted out? *Assignats*. If sixteen millions sterling of these *assignats*, forced on the people, leave the wants of the state as urgent as ever—issue, says one, thirty millions sterling of *assignats*—says another, issue fourscore millions more of *assignats*. The only difference among their financial factions is on the greater or the lesser quantity of *assignats* to be imposed on the publick sufferance. They are all professors of *assignats*. Even those, whose natural good sense and knowledge [278] of commerce, not obliterated by philosophy, furnish decisive arguments against this delusion, conclude their arguments, by proposing the emission of *assignats*. I suppose they must talk of *assignats*, as no other language would be understood. All experience of their inefficacy does not in the least discourage them. Are the old *assignats* depreciated at market? What is the remedy? Issue new *assignats*. *Mais si maladia, opiniatria, non vult se garire, quid illi facere? Assignare; postea assignare; ensuita assignare.* The word is a trifle altered. The Latin of your present doctors may be better than that of your old comedy; their wisdom, and the variety of their resources, are the same. They have not more notes in their song than the cuckow; though, far from the softness of that harbinger of summer and plenty, their voice is as harsh and as ominous as that of the raven.

Who but the most desperate adventurers in philosophy and finance could at all have thought of destroying the settled revenue of the state, the sole security for the public credit, in the hope of rebuilding it with the materials of confiscated property? If, however, an excessive zeal for the state should have led a pious and venerable prelate, by anticipation a father of the church,* to pillage his own order, and, for the good of the church and people, to take upon himself the place of grand financier of confiscation, and comptroller-general of sacrilege, he and his coadjutors were, in my opinion, bound to shew, by their subsequent conduct, that they knew something of the office they assumed. When they had resolved to appropriate to the *Fisc* a certain portion of the landed property of their conquered country, it was their business to render their bank a real fund of credit, as far as such a bank was capable of becoming so.

[279] To establish a current circulating credit upon any Land-bank, under any circumstances whatsoever, has hitherto proved difficult at the very least. The attempt has commonly ended in bankruptcy. But when the assembly were led, through a contempt of moral, to a defiance of oeconomical principles, it might at least have been expected that nothing would be omitted on their part to lessen this difficulty, to prevent any aggravation of this bankruptcy. It might be expected that to render your Land-bank tolerable, every means would be adopted that could display openness and candour in the statement of the security; every thing which could aid the recovery of the demand. To take things in their most favourable point of view, your condition was that of a man of a large landed estate, which he wished to dispose of for the discharge of a debt, and the supply of certain services. Not being able instantly to sell, you wished to mortgage. What would a man of fair intentions, and a commonly clear understanding, do in such circumstances? Ought he not first to ascertain the gross value of the estate; the charges of its man-

---

*La Bruyère of Bossuet.

agement and disposition; the encumbrances, perpetual and temporary, of all kinds, that affect it; then, striking a net surplus, to calculate the just value of the security? When that surplus, the only security to the creditor, had been clearly ascertained, and properly vested in the hands of trustees; then he would indicate the parcels to be sold, and the time, and conditions of sale; after this, he would admit the public creditor, if he chose it, to subscribe his stock into this new fund; or he might receive proposals for an *assignat* from those who would advance money to purchase this species of security.

This would be to proceed like men of business, methodically and rationally; and on the only principles of public and private credit that have an existence. The dealer would [280] then know exactly what he purchased; and the only doubt which could hang upon his mind would be, the dread of the resumption of the spoil, which one day might be made (perhaps with an addition of punishment) from the sacrilegious gripe of those execrable wretches who could become purchasers at the auction of their innocent fellow-citizens.

An open and exact statement of the clear value of the property, and of the time, the circumstances, and the place of sale, were all necessary, to efface as much as possible the stigma that has hitherto been branded on every kind of Landbank. It became necessary on another principle, that is, on account of a pledge of faith previously given on that subject, that their future fidelity in a slippery concern might be established by their adherence to their first engagement. When they had finally determined on a state resource from church booty, they came, on the 14th of April 1790, to a solemn resolution on the subject; and pledged themselves to their country, "that in the statement of the public charges for each year there should be brought to account a sum sufficient for defraying the expences of the R. C. A. religion, the support of the ministers at the altars, the relief of the poor, the pensions to the ecclesiastics, secular as well as regular, of the one and of the other sex, *in order that the estates and goods which are at the disposal of the nation may be disengaged of all charges, and employed by the representatives, or the legislative body, to the great and most pressing exigencies of the state.*" They further engaged, on the same day, that the sum necessary for the year 1791 should be forthwith determined.

In this resolution they admit it their duty to show distinctly the expence of the above objects, which, by other resolutions, they had before engaged should be first in the order of provision. They admit that they ought to shew [281] the estate clear and disengaged of all charges, and that they should shew it immediately. Have they done this immediately, or at any time? Have they ever furnished a rent-roll of the immoveable estates, or given in an inventory of the moveable effects which they confiscate to their *assignats*? In what manner they can fulfil their engagements of holding out to public service "an estate disengaged of all charges," without authenticating the value of the estate, or the *quantum* of the charges, I leave it to their English admirers to explain. Instantly upon this assurance, and previously to any one step towards making it good, they issue, on the credit of so handsome a declaration, sixteen millions sterling of their paper. This was manly. Who, after this masterly stroke, can doubt of their abilities in finance? But then, before any other emission of these financial *indulgences*, they took care at least to make good their original promise! If such estimate, either of the value of the estate or the amount of the incumbrances, has been made, it has escaped me. I never heard of it.

At length they have spoken out, and they have made a full discovery of their abominable fraud, in holding out the church lands as a security for any debts or any service whatsoever. They rob only to enable them to cheat; but in a very short time they defeat the ends both of the robbery and the fraud, by making out accounts for other purposes, which blow up their whole apparatus of force and of deception. I am obliged to M. de Calonne for his reference to the document which proves this extraordinary fact: it had, by some means, escaped me. Indeed it was not necessary to make out my assertion as to the breach of faith on the declaration of the 14th of April 1790. By a report of their Committee it now appears, that the charge of keeping up the reduced ecclesiastical establishments, and other expences attendant on religion, and maintaining the [282] religious of both sexes, retained or pensioned, and the other concomitant expences of the same nature, which they have brought upon themselves by this convulsion in property, exceeds the income of the estates acquired by it in the enormous sum of two millions sterling annually; besides a debt of seven millions and upwards. These are the calculating powers of imposture! This is the finance of philosophy! This is the result of all the delusions held out to engage a miserable people in rebellion, murder, and sacrilege, and to make them prompt and zealous instruments in the ruin of their country! Never did a state, in any case, enrich itself by the confiscations of the citizens. This new experiment has succeeded like all the rest. Every honest mind, every true lover of liberty and humanity must rejoice to find that injustice is not always good policy, nor rapine the high road to riches. I subjoin with pleasure, in a note, the able and spirited observations of M. de Calonne on this subject.*

* "Ce n'est point à l'assemblée entière que je m'adresse ici; je ne parle qu'à ceux qui l'égarent, en lui cachant sous des gazes séduisantes le but où ils l'entraînent. C'est à eux que je dis: Votre objet, vous n'en disconviendrez pas, c'est d'ôter tout espoir au clergé, & de consommer sa ruine; c'est-là, en ne vous soupçonnant d'aucune combinaison de cupidité, d'aucun regard sur le jeu des effets publics, c'est-là ce qu'on doit croire que vous avez en vue dans la terrible opération que vous proposez; c'est ce qui doit en être le fruit. Mais le peuple que vous y intéressez, quel avantage peut-il y trouver? En vous servant sans cesse de lui, que faites vous pour lui? Rien, absolument rien; &, au contraire, vous faites ce qui ne conduit qu'à l'accabler de nouvelles charges. Vous avez rejeté, à son préjudice, une offre de 400 millions, dont l'acceptation pouvoit devenir un moyen de soulagement en sa faveur; & à cette ressource, aussi profitable que légitime, vous avez substitué une injustice ruineuse, qui, de

---

[283] In order to persuade the world of the bottom-less resource of ecclesiastical confiscation, the assembly have proceeded to other confiscations of estates in offices, which could not be done with any common colour without being compensated out of this grand confiscation of landed property. They have thrown upon this fund, which was to shew a surplus, disengaged of all charges, a new charge; namely, the compensation to the whole body of the disbanded judicature; and of all suppressed offices and estates; a charge which I cannot ascertain, but which unquestionably amounts to many French millions. Another of the new charges, is an annuity of four hundred and eighty thousand pounds sterling, to be paid (if they choose to keep faith) by daily payments, for the interest of the first assignats. Have they ever given themselves the trouble to state fairly the expence of the management of the church lands in the hands of the municipalities, to whose care, skill, and diligence, and that of their legion of unknown under-agents, they have chosen to commit the charge of the forfeited estates, and the consequence of which had been so ably pointed out by the bishop of Nancy?

But it is unnecessary to dwell on these obvious heads of in-cumbrance. Have they made out any clear state of the grand incumbrance of all, I mean the whole of the general and municipal establishments of all sorts, and compared it with the regular income by revenue? Every deficiency in these be-comes a charge on the confiscated estate, before the creditor can plant his cabbages on an acre of church property. There

---

votre propre aveu, charge le trésor public, & par conséquent le peuple, d'un surcroît de dépense annuelle de 50 millions au moins, & d'un remboursement de 150 millions.

"Malheureux peuple! voilà ce que vous vaut en dernier résultat l'expro-priation de l'Eglise, & la dureté des décrets taxateurs du traitement des min-istres d'une religion bienfaisante; & désormais ils seront à votre charge: leurs charités soulageoient les pauvres; & vous allez être imposés pour subvenir à leur entretien!"—*De l'État de la France,* p. 81. See also p. 92, and the follow-ing pages.

is no other prop than this confiscation to keep the whole state from tumbling to the ground. In this situation they have purposely covered all that they ought industriously to have cleared, with a thick fog; and then, blindfold themselves, like bulls that shut their eyes when they push, they drive, by the point of the bayonets, their slaves, [284] blindfolded indeed no worse than their lords, to take their fictions for currencies, and to swallow down paper pills by thirty-four millions sterling at a dose. Then they proudly lay in their claim to a future credit, on failure of all their past engagements, and at a time when (if in such a matter any thing can be clear) it is clear that the surplus estates will never answer even the first of their mortgages, I mean that of the four hundred million (or sixteen millions sterling) of *assignats*. In all this procedure I can discern neither the solid sense of plain-dealing, nor the subtle dexterity of ingenious fraud. The objections within the assembly to pulling up the flood-gates for this inundation of fraud, are unanswered; but they are thoroughly refuted by an hundred thousand financiers in the street. These are the numbers by which the metaphysic arithmeticians compute. These are the grand calculations on which a philosophical public credit is founded in France. They cannot raise supplies; but they can raise mobs. Let them rejoice in the applauses of the club at Dundee, for their wisdom and patriotism in having thus applied the plunder of the citizens to the service of the state. I hear of no address upon this subject from the directors of the Bank of England; though their approbation would be of a little more weight in the scale of credit than that of the club at Dundee. But, to do justice to the club, I believe the gentlemen who compose it to be wiser than they appear; that they will be less liberal of their money than of their addresses; and that they would not give a dog's-ear of their most rumpled and ragged Scotch paper for twenty of your fairest *assignats*.

Early in this year the assembly issued paper to the amount

of sixteen millions sterling. What must have been the state
into which the assembly has brought your affairs, that the relief afforded by so vast a supply has been hardly perceptible?
This paper also felt an almost immediate [285] depreciation
of five per cent., which in little time came to about seven.
The effect of these *assignats* on the receipt of the revenue is
remarkable. Mr. Necker found that the collectors of the revenue, who received in coin, paid the treasury in *assignats*. The
collectors made seven per cent. by thus receiving in money,
and accounting in depreciated paper. It was not very difficult to foresee that this must be inevitable. It was, however,
not the less embarrassing. Mr. Necker was obliged (I believe,
for a considerable part, in the market of London) to buy
gold and silver for the mint, which amounted to about twelve
thousand pounds above the value of the commodity gained.
That minister was of opinion, that whatever their secret nu-
tritive virtue might be, the state could not live upon *assignats*
alone; that some real silver was necessary, particularly for the
satisfaction of those, who having iron in their hands, were
not likely to distinguish themselves for patience, when they
should perceive that whilst an encrease of pay was held out
to them in real money, it was again to be fraudulently drawn
back by depreciated paper. The minister, in this very natural
distress, applied to the assembly, that they should order the
collectors to pay in specie what in specie they had received.
It could not escape him, that if the treasury paid three per
cent. for the use of a currency, which should be returned
seven per cent. worse than the minister issued it, such a dealing could not very greatly tend to enrich the publick. The
assembly took no notice of his recommendation. They were
in this dilemma; if they continued to receive the assignats,
each must become an alien to their treasury: if the treasury
should refuse those paper *amulets,* or should discountenance
them in any degree, they must destroy the credit of their sole
resource. They seem then to have made their option; and

to have given some sort of credit to their paper by taking it themselves; at the same time in their speeches [286] they made a sort of swaggering declaration, something, I rather think, above legislative competence; that is, that there is no difference in value between metallic money and their assignats. This was a good stout proof article of faith, pronounced under an anathema, by the venerable fathers of this philosophic synod. *Credat* who will—certainly not *Judaeus Apella.*

A noble indignation rises in the minds of your popular leaders, on hearing the magic lanthorn in their shew of finance compared to the fraudulent exhibitions of Mr. Law. They cannot bear to hear the sands of his Mississippi compared with the rock of the church, on which they build their system. Pray let them suppress this glorious spirit, until they shew to the world what piece of solid ground there is for their *assignats,* which they have not pre-occupied by other charges. They do injustice to that great, mother fraud, to compare it with their degenerate imitation. It is not true, that Law built solely on a speculation concerning the Mississippi. He added the East India trade; he added the African trade; he added the farms of all the farmed revenue of France. All these together unquestionably could not support the structure which the public enthusiasm, not he, chose to build upon these bases. But these were, however, in comparison, generous delusions. They supposed, and they aimed at, an increase of the commerce of France. They opened to it the whole range of the two hemispheres. They did not think of feeding France from its own substance. A grand imagination found in this flight of commerce something to captivate. It was wherewithal to dazzle the eye of an eagle. It was not made to entice the smell of a mole, nuzzling and burying himself in his mother earth, as yours is. Men were not then quite shrunk from their natural dimensions by a degrading and sordid philosophy, and fitted for low and vulgar deceptions. Above all remember, [287] that in imposing on the imagination, the then managers of the system made a compliment to the freedom of men. In their fraud there was no mixture of force. This was reserved to our time, to quench the little glimmerings of reason which might break in upon the solid darkness of this enlightened age.

On recollection, I have said nothing of a scheme of finance which may be urged in favour of the abilities of these gentlemen, and which has been introduced with great pomp, though not yet finally adopted in the national assembly. It comes with something solid in aid of the credit of the paper circulation; and much has been said of its utility and its elegance. I mean the project for coining into money the bells of the suppressed churches. This is their alchymy. There are some follies which baffle argument; which go beyond ridicule; and which excite no feeling in us but disgust; and therefore I say no more upon it.

It is as little worth remarking any farther upon all their drawing and re-drawing, on their circulation for putting off the evil day, on the play between the treasury and the *Caisse d' Escompte,* and on all these old exploded contrivances of mercantile fraud, now exalted into policy of state. The revenue will not be trifled with. The prattling about the rights of men will not be accepted in payment for a biscuit or a pound of gunpowder. Here then the metaphysicians descend from their airy speculations, and faithfully follow examples. What examples? the examples of bankrupts. But, defeated, baffled, disgraced, when their breath, their strength, their inventions, their fancies desert them, their confidence still maintains its ground. In the manifest failure of their abilities they take credit for their benevolence. When the revenue disappears in their hands, they have the presumption, in some of their late proceedings, to value *themselves* on the relief given to the people. They did not [288] relieve the people. If they entertained such intentions, why did they order the obnoxious taxes to be paid? The people relieved themselves in spite of the assembly.

But waiving all discussion on the parties who may claim the merit of this fallacious relief, has there been, in effect, any relief to the people, in any form? Mr. Bailly, one of the grand agents of paper circulation, lets you into the nature of this relief. His speech to the National Assembly contained an high and laboured panegyric on the inhabitants of Paris for the constancy and unbroken resolution with which they have borne their distress and misery. A fine picture of public felicity! What! great courage and unconquerable firmness of mind to endure benefits, and sustain redress? One would think from the speech of this learned Lord Mayor, that the Parisians, for this twelvemonth past, had been suffering the straits of some dreadful blockade; that Henry the Fourth had been stopping up the avenues to their supply, and Sully thundering with his ordnance at the gates of Paris; when in reality they are besieged by no other enemies than their own madness and folly, their own credulity and perverseness. But Mr. Bailly will sooner thaw the eternal ice of his atlantic regions, than restore the central heat to Paris, whilst it remains "smitten with the cold, dry, petrifick mace" of a false and unfeeling philosophy. Some time after this speech, that is, on the thirteenth of last August, the same magistrate, giving an account of his government at the bar of the same assembly, expresses himself as follows: "In the month of July 1789," (the period of everlasting commemoration) "the finances of the city of Paris were *yet* in good order; the expenditure was counterbalanced by the receipt, and she had at that time a million (forty thousand pounds sterling) in bank. The expences which she has been constrained to incur *subsequent to the revolution,* amount to 2,500,000 livres. [289] From these expences, and the great falling off in the product of the *free gifts,* not only a momentary but a *total* want of money has taken place." This is the Paris upon whose nourishment, in the course of the last year, such immense sums, drawn from the vitals of all France, have been expended! As long as Paris stands in the place of antient Rome, so long she will be maintained by the subject provinces. It is an evil inevitably attendant on the dominion of sovereign democratic republics. As it happened in Rome, it may survive that republican domination which gave rise to it. In that case despotism itself must submit to the vices of popularity. Rome, under her emperors, united the evils of both systems; and this unnatural combination was one great cause of her ruin.

To tell the people that they are relieved by the dilapidation of their public estate, is a cruel and insolent imposition. Statesmen, before they valued themselves on the relief given to the people by the destruction of their revenue, ought first to have carefully attended to the solution of this problem: Whether it be more advantageous to the people to pay considerably, and to gain in proportion; or to gain little or nothing, and to be disburthened of all contribution? My mind is made up to decide in favour of the first proposition. Experience is with me, and, I believe, the best opinions also. To keep a balance between the power of acquisition on the part of the subject, and the demands he is to answer on the part of the state, is a fundamental part of the skill of a true politician. The means of acquisition are prior in time and in arrangement. Good order is the foundation of all good things. To be enabled to acquire, the people, without being servile, must be tractable and obedient. The magistrate must have his reverence, the laws their authority. The body of the people must not find the principles of natural subordination, by art rooted out of their minds. [290] They must respect that property of which they cannot partake. They must labour to obtain what by labour can be obtained; and when they find, as they commonly do, the success disproportioned to the endeavour, they must be taught their consolation in the final proportions of eternal justice. Of this consolation, whoever deprives them, deadens their industry, and strikes at the root of all acquisition as of all conservation. He that does this is the cruel oppressor, the merciless enemy of the poor and wretched; at the same time that by his wicked speculations he exposes the fruits of successful industry, and the accumulations of fortune, to the plunder of the negligent, the disappointed, and the unprosperous.

Too many of the financiers by profession are apt to see nothing in revenue, but banks, and circulations, and annuities on lives, and tontines, and perpetual rents, and all the small wares of the shop. In a settled order of the state, these things are not to be slighted, nor is the skill in them to be held of trivial estimation. They are good, but then only good, when they assume the effects of that settled order, and are built upon it. But when men think that these beggarly contrivances may supply a resource for the evils which result from breaking up the foundations of public order, and from causing or suffering the principles of property to be subverted, they will, in the ruin of their country, leave a melancholy and lasting monument of the effect of preposterous politics, and presumptuous, short-sighted, narrow-minded wisdom.

THE EFFECTS OF THE INCAPACITY shewn by the popular leaders in all the great members of the commonwealth are to be covered with the "all-atoning name" of liberty. In some people I see great liberty indeed; in many, if not in the most, an oppressive, degrading servitude. But what is [291] liberty without wisdom, and without virtue? It is the greatest of all possible evils; for it is folly, vice, and madness, without tuition or restraint. Those who know what virtuous liberty is, cannot bear to see it disgraced by incapable heads, on account of their having high-sounding words in their mouths. Grand, swelling sentiments of liberty, I am sure I do not despise. They warm the heart; they enlarge and liberalise our minds; they animate our courage in a time of conflict. Old as I am, I read the fine raptures of Lucan and Corneille with pleasure. Neither do I wholly condemn the little arts and devices of popularity. They facilitate the carrying of many points of moment; they keep the people together; they refresh the mind in its exertions; and they diffuse occasional gaiety over the severe brow of moral freedom. Every politician ought to sacrifice to the graces; and to join compliance with reason. But in such an undertaking as that in France, all these subsidary sentiments and artifices are of little avail. To make a government requires no great prudence. Settle the seat of power; teach obedience; and the work is done. To give freedom is still more easy. It is not necessary to guide; it only requires to let go the rein. But to form a *free government;* that is, to temper together these opposite elements of liberty and restraint in one consistent work, requires much thought; deep reflection; a sagacious, powerful, and combining mind. This I do not find in those who take the lead in the national assembly. Perhaps they are not so miserably deficient as they appear. I rather believe it. It would put them below the common level of human understanding. But when the leaders choose to make themselves bidders at an auction of popularity, their talents, in the construction of the state, will be of no service. They will become flatterers instead of legislators; the instruments, not the guides of the people. If any of them should happen to propose a scheme of [292] liberty, soberly limited, and defined with proper qualifications, he will be immediately outbid by his competitors, who will produce something more splendidly popular. Suspicions will be raised of his fidelity to his cause. Moderation will be stigmatized as the virtue of cowards, and compromise as the prudence of traitors; until, in hopes of preserving the credit which may enable him to temper and moderate on some occasions, the popular leader is obliged to become active in propagating doctrines, and establishing powers, that will afterwards defeat any sober purpose at which he ultimately might have aimed.

But am I so unreasonable as to see nothing at all that deserves commendation in the indefatigable labours of this assembly? I do not deny that among an infinite number of acts of violence and folly, some good may have been done. They who destroy every thing certainly will remove some grievance. They who make every thing new, have a chance that they may establish something beneficial. To give them credit for what they have done in virtue of the authority they have usurped, or which can excuse them in the crimes by which that authority has been acquired, it must appear, that the same things could not have been accomplished without producing such a revolution. Most assuredly they might; because almost every one of the regulations made by them, which is not very equivocal, was either in the cession of the king, voluntarily made at the meeting of the states, or in the concurrent instructions to the orders. Some usages have been abolished on just grounds; but they were such that if they had stood as they were to all eternity, they would little detract from the happiness and prosperity of any state. The improvements of the national assembly are superficial; their errors, fundamental.

Whatever they are, I wish my countrymen rather to recommend to our neighbours the example of the British constitution, [293] than to take models from them for the improvement of our own. In the former they have got an invaluable treasure. They are not, I think, without some causes of apprehension and complaint; but these they do not owe to their constitution, but to their own conduct. I think our happy situation owing to our constitution; but owing to the whole of it, and not to any part singly; owing in a great measure to what we have left standing in our several reviews and reformations, as well as to what we have altered or superadded. Our people will find employment enough for a truly patriotic, free, and independent spirit, in guarding what they possess, from violation. I would not exclude alteration neither; but even when I changed, it should be to preserve. I should be led to my remedy by a great grievance. In what I did, I should follow the example of our ancestors. I would make the reparation as nearly as possible in the style of the building. A politic caution, a guarded circumspection, a moral rather than a complexional timidity, were among the ruling principles of our forefathers in their most decided conduct. Not being illuminated with the light of which the gentlemen of France tell us they have got so abundant a share, they acted under a strong impression of the ignorance and fallibility of mankind. He that had made them thus fallible, rewarded them for having in their conduct attended to their nature. Let us imitate their caution, if we wish to deserve their fortune, or to retain their bequests. Let us add, if we please; but let us preserve what they have left; and, standing on the firm ground of the British constitution, let us be satisfied to admire rather than attempt to follow in their desperate flights the aëronauts of France.

I have told you candidly my sentiments. I think they are not likely to alter yours. I do not know that they ought. You are young; you cannot guide, but must follow the fortune of your country. But hereafter they may be of [294] some use to you, in some future form which your commonwealth may take. In the present it can hardly remain; but before its final settlement it may be obliged to pass, as one of our poets says, "through great varieties of untried being," and in all its transmigrations to be purified by fire and blood.

I have little to recommend my opinions, but long observation and much impartiality. They come from one who has been no tool of power, no flatterer of greatness; and who in his last acts does not wish to belye the tenour of his life. They come from one, almost the whole of whose public exertion has been a struggle for the liberty of others; from one in whose breast no anger durable or vehement has ever been kindled, but by what he considered as tyranny; and who snatches from his share in the endeavours which are used by good men to discredit opulent oppression, the hours he has employed on your affairs; and who in so doing persuades himself he has not departed from his usual office.

They come from one who desires honours, distinctions, and emoluments, but little, and who expects them not at all; who has no contempt for fame, and no fear of obloquy; who shuns contention, though he will hazard an opinion: from one who wishes to preserve consistency; but who would preserve consistency by varying his means to secure the unity of his end; and, when the equipoise of the vessel in which he sails may be endangered by overloading it upon one side, is desirous of carrying the small weight of his reasons to that which may preserve its equipoise.

FINIS

NOTES

PAGE 85. *The Revolution in France.* The term "Revolution," from its application to the events of 1688, had acquired in England a sense exclusively favourable. "Revolution principles" meant the principles of English constitutional liberty. The Tories who supported the Hanoverian succession, while opposing the rest of the policy of the Whigs, called themselves "Revolution Tories." Hence the name "Revolution Society" meant much the same as "Constitutional Society." This use of the term *in bonam partem,* which was still in vogue, though in its decline, at the time of the French Revolution, from that time disappears from the English language. Burke was at first unwilling to apply the term to a series of events which in his opinion amounted to the total subversion of the framework of a national society, and was based on what he called "spurious Revolution principles," p. 103, l. 26: but custom soon sanctioned its use in England. In France it had been in common use for forty years, and had passed from a favourable sense to one almost legendary and heroic. Thus, on the use of it made by Barbier in 1751, M. Aubertin writes; "Voilà donc ce mot de 'révolution' qui abonde sous la plume des contemporains, et pour un temps illimité prend possession de notre histoire. Désormais, l'idée sinistre d'une catastrophe nécessaire, d'une péripétie tragique, obsède les imaginations françaises; la vie politique de notre pays sort des conditions d'un développement normal pour entrer dans les brusques mouvements et dans l'horreur mystérieuse d'un drame." L'Esprit Public au XVIIIe Siècle, p. 282. On the use of the word shortly before the event, see Mercier, New Picture of Paris, ch. 3: "Every book that bore the title of *Revolution* was bought up and carried away . . . . We were always hearing the words, 'Give me the Roman Revolutions—the Revolutions of Sweden—of Italy'; and booksellers, in order to sell their old books, printed false titles, and took the purchase on the credit merely of the label."

IBID. *Eleventh Edition,* 1791. Within a few months after its first publication, the work had reached this, its permanent form. Burke made some alterations in the text as it appears in the first edition, which will be noticed so far as they are material. A few short annotations, which appear in editions subsequent to the one adopted as the text,

Notes

are printed with it (see note to [296] p. 173, l. 33): but it does not appear that Burke, even if he penned these, intended them for the press. This Eleventh Edition appeared in the second year of publication. The circulation of the work in Burke's lifetime was estimated at 30,000 copies, which Lord Stanhope thinks an exaggeration; but as at the death of James Dodsley in 1797 it appeared that he had sold no less than 18,000, if we take into account the French and German translations, Irish and American Reprints, &c., it cannot be a great one. There is a curious abridged and cheap edition, published by "S. J." in 1793, in 12mo., for popular circulation, as an antidote to the writings of the Jacobins. The editor professes to have "pruned some little exuberances of genius and effusions of fancy into which the lively imagination of the excellent writer had sometimes betrayed him."

IBID. *Argument.* Burke says (p. 95, l. 24) that he writes with very little attention to formal method. This distribution of the work into sections is only approximative, and intended to assist the reader in marking the salient points, and thus more readily seizing the drift of the work. The brief headings given in this "Argument" only indicate the thread of the thought, by no means include all that hangs upon it. Those who desire a minute analysis can consult the translations of Gentz and Dupont: but such an analysis tends to impair the effect of the work, which is essentially discursive and informal.

P. 87, L. 24. *a very young gentleman at Paris.* M. Dupont, who afterwards translated the work into French. He became acquainted with Burke in London, and visited him at Beaconsfield.

L. 27. *an answer was written,* &c. See Burke's Corr. vol. iii. p. 102. This letter will be found valuable as a means of acquiring a first and general idea of Burke's views. It bears evidence of great pains taken in the composition. Sir Philip Francis, whose taste was so much offended by the "Reflections," thought this letter "in point of writing, much less exceptionable."

P. 88, L. 1. *upon prudential considerations*—i. e. for fear of the letter being opened, and the receiver endangered by the opinions contained in it. Cp. p. 88, l. 26.

L. 4. *assigned in a short letter*—which was then sent in its stead. They appear to have been afterwards incorporated in the letter itself (Corr. vol. iii. pp. 103, 104).

L. 8. *early in the last spring.* The "Substance of Mr. Burke's Speech in the Debate on the Army Estimates, Feb. 9, 1790," published very soon after, in which his views on French events were freely stated, was followed by Lord Stanhope's Letter in answer to it, dated Feb. 24, in which he says, "From the title of another pamphlet, which an advertisement in the papers has announced is speedily to be expected from you, it is conjectured that the Revolution Society in London was in your contemplation when you made that Speech," p. 20. Lord Stanhope was chairman of that society. The advertisement was in the London Chronicle for Feb. 16, 1790, and runs as follows: "In the Press, and will speedily be published, Reflections on certain [297] Proceedings of the Revolution Society of the 4th of November, 1789, concerning the Affairs of France. In a Letter from Mr. Edmund Burke to a gentleman in Paris. Printed for J. Dodsley in Pall Mall." Burke lent to Sir Philip Francis on Feb. 18, 1790, proof sheets which embraced more than one third of the entire work as it now stands (Corr. vol. iii. p. 128), and perhaps included the first two-thirds, which are here represented as the First Part (pp. 88–269). Much excitement was produced by this advertisement. "The mere idea of Mr. Burke's intention soon to write, gives life to the world of letters." Public Advertiser, Feb. 18.

P. 88, L. 29. *neither for nor from any description of men.* Thus far the publication bears a different character to those of the Constitutional and Revolution Societies. Burke, however, claims throughout the first part of the work to be expressing the opinions of all true Englishmen (p. 179).

P. 89, L. 3. *spirit of rational liberty,* &c. Cp. the Letter to Depont, Corr. vol. iii. p. 105: "You hope that I think the French deserving liberty. I certainly do. I certainly think that all men who desire it, deserve it. It is not the reward of our merit, or the acquisition of our industry. It is our inheritance. It is the birthright of our species. We cannot forfeit our right to it, but by what forfeits our title to the privileges of our kind—I mean, the abuse, or oblivion of our rational faculties, and a ferocious indocility which makes us prompt to wrong and violence, destroys our social nature, and transforms us into something little better than the description of wild beasts."

L. 4. *a permanent body,* &c. See the same Letter, pp. 107–113.

L. 13. *more clubs than one.* The allusion is especially to the Whig club "Brooks's," of which Burke became a member in 1783.

L. 33. *the Constitutional Society—seven or eight years' standing.* Really somewhat more, having been founded by Major Cartwright in the spring of 1780, "after whole months of strenuous exertion." It numbered among its members the Dukes of Norfolk and Richmond, the

Earls of Derby, Effingham, and Selkirk, together with many other persons of rank and members of Parliament.

P. 90, L. 2. *circulation of many books*, &c. An apologist for the Society says that portions of the works of the old Whig authors, such as Sidney, Locke, Trenchard, Lord Somers, &c., were distributed gratis by the Society. But the chief object of the Society was to circulate the writings of Cartwright, Capel Lofft, Jebb, Northcote, Sharp, and other pamphleteers of the day. It is to these that Burke alludes l. 15, in deprecating "the greater part of the publications circulated by that Society."

L. 5. *booksellers* = publishers.

L. 7. charitably *read*—The word is repeated, by the figure called *traductio*, in a contemptuous way. Burke hints that the books were not worth reading, and were in fact not read.

L. 10. *much talk of the lights*, &c. Cp. the French Correspondent of the St. James's Chronicle, Dec. 15, 1789: "It is you, O ye noble inhabitants of [298] the British Isles, who have set the example to my country —it is our commerce with you—it is the perusal of your free writings, which have impressed on our minds an idea of the dignity of man," &c.

L. 12. *meliorated.* Burke always uses this (the correct form) instead of the modern "ameliorate."

P. 91, L. 3. *a club of Dissenters.* Dr. Kippis and Dr. Rees were distinguished members. The Society was established by dissenters, but for some years then past it had numbered among its adherents many members of the Church of England. Lord Surrey, and the Dukes of Norfolk, Leeds, Richmond, and Manchester, sometimes attended their meetings, together with many members of the House of Commons.

L. 3. *of what denomination*, &c. In the time of Burke the lines which separated dissenting denominations from each other and from the Church were less sharply defined than now. The Unitarians were recognised by other denominations, and allowed to preach in their meeting-houses. Dr. Price was nominally an "Independent," though his doctrines were Unitarian.

L. 16. *new members may have entered.* It is stated by Lord Stanhope in his Life of Pitt, that this society had then been lately "new-modelled," with a view to co-operating with the French revolutionists. In this way it came to be a "Society for Revolutions," as Burke calls it at p. 110, l. 4.

P. 92, L. 24. *who they are—personal abilities*, &c. We trace here

Burke's inflexible practice of connecting measures and opinions with the *persons* who support them. Cp. the Letter to Depont, p. 115: "Never wholly separate in your mind the merits of any political question from the men who are concerned in it."

P. 93, L. 8. *nakedness and solitude of metaphysical abstraction.* Perhaps an echo of Butler:

> He took her (viz. matter) *naked,* all *alone,*
> Before one rag of form was on.
> > Hudibras, Part i. Canto i. l. 561.

L. 9. *circumstances,* &c. One of the so-called truisms often insisted on by Aristotle.

L. 14. *government, as well as liberty.* Cp. note to vol. i. p. 70, l. 22. By "government," Burke means here, as often elsewhere, a state or habit of political regulation. Burke ends as well as begins the book with the distinction between true and false liberty. See p. 361.

L. 15. *ten years ago.* After the fall of Turgot, when the French government was at its worst.

L. 26. *the scene of the criminals.* See Don Quixote, Part i. ch. 22. This masterpiece seems to have been a favourite with Burke. "Blessings on his soul, that first invented sleep, said Don Sancho Panza the wise! All those blessings, and ten thousand times more, on him who found out abstraction, personification, and impersonals." Fourth Letter on Regicide Peace.

L. 27. *the metaphysic knight.* Burke uses with but little discrimination the forms metaphysic, metaphysical; ecclesiastic, ecclesiastical; theatric, [299] theatrical; politic, political; practic, practical. By the term "metaphysic," he alludes to the Knights freeing the criminals on the ground of the abstract right to liberty, without regard to circumstances.

L. 29. *spirit of liberty* . . . . *wild gas,* &c. Crabbe is frequently indebted for a hint to Burke, his early patron;

> I for that freedom make, said he, my prayer,
> That suits with all, like atmospheric air;
>
> . . . .
> The lighter gas, that taken in the frame
> The spirit heats, and sets the blood on flame, —
> Such is the freedom which when men approve,
> They know not what a dangerous thing they love.
> > Crabbe, Tales of the Hall.

NOTES

L. 31. *the fixed air.* Then the scientific term for carbonic acid gas. The gas was discovered by Van Helmont. This name was given to it by Dr. Black, in 1755, on account of its property, discovered by him, of readily losing its elasticity, and fixing itself in many bodies, particularly those of a calcareous kind.

L. 32. *the first effervescence.* Cp. infra p. 263, l. 7. "Fixed air" is contained in great quantity in fermented liquors, to which it gives their briskness.

P. 94, L. 2. *Flattery corrupts both the receiver and the giver.* The idea is adapted from Shakespeare:

. . . . It is twice blessed:
It blesseth him that gives, and him that takes.
Merch. of Ven., Act iv. sc. 1.

IBID. *Flattery; adulation.* Intended to express a difference between this vice as a private and as a public practice.

L. 5. *how it had been combined with government,* &c. The Second Part (p. 269 to end) is here anticipated.

L. 9. *Solidity* = stability.

L. 13. *do what they please.* "Mais la liberté politique ne consiste point à faire ce que l'on veut . . . . La liberté ne peut consister qu'à pouvoir faire ce que l'on doit vouloir." De l'Esprit des Lois, Liv. xi. ch. 3.

L. 17. *liberty . . . is power.* "On a confondu le pouvoir du peuple avec la liberté du peuple." Id. ch. 2. In France, says M. Mignet candidly, the love of liberty is equivalent to the love of power.

L. 22. *those who appear the most stirring,* &c. It was believed that the Duke of Orleans was the prime mover, although he did not take the most active part in the scene.

L. 28. *on my coming to town*—for the winter season of 1789–90.

IBID. *an account of these proceedings.* "A Discourse on the Love of our Country, delivered on Nov. 4, 1789, at the Meeting House in the Old Jewry to the Society for commemorating the Revolution in Great Britain. With an Appendix containing the Report of the Committee of the Society; an [300] account of the population of France; and the Declaration of Right by the National Assembly of France. Third Edition, with additions to the Appendix, containing communications from France occasioned by the Congratulatory Address of the Revolution Society to the National Assembly of France, with the Answers to them. By Richard Price, D.D., LL.D., F.R.S.," &c. The Letter of the Duke of Rochefoucauld is an informal one addressed to Dr. Price, and dated Dec. 2, 1789. That of the Archbishop of Aix (as President of the National Assembly) formally addressed to Lord Stanhope, as Chairman of the Society, and dated Dec. 5, 1789, was accompanied by an official extract from the Procès Verbal of the Assembly, dated Nov. 25, 1789. The appendix also contains Resolutions of thanks sent to the Society from Dijon and Lille, together with the Answers transmitted to them by the Society.

P. 95, L. 8. *prudence of an higher order.* Burke always recognizes a good and bad form of moral habits and feelings, without much reference to their names and common acceptations. Hence such striking expressions as "false, reptile prudence," "fortitude of rational fear," &c., abound in his writings.

L. 10. *feeble enough—infancy still more feeble.* Burke was too much disposed to refer the Revolution to the spirit of contemporary Jacobinism as a prime cause. Such a spirit may help, but it can never originate, much less carry into effect, similar convulsions, which always have powerful *material* causes. There was much Jacobinism in England; more than we can now understand. One fifth of the active political forces of this country were classed by Burke as Jacobin; but there was no such irresistible series of material causes as, in the face of material resistance, produced the explosion of 1789.

L. 12. *heap mountains on mountains.* Cp. Waller, On the Head of a Stag:

Heav'n with these Engines had been scal'd,
When mountains heap'd on mountains fail'd.

The allusion is to the Titans. See Virg. Georg. i. 281.

L. 13. *our neighbour's house on fire,* &c.

Nam tua res agitur, paries quum proximus ardet.

Hor. Ep. Lib. i. xviii. 84.

See the idea developed in Burke's justification of interference in the affairs of France, grounded on the "law of civil vicinity," in the First Letter on a Regicide Peace—"Vicini vicinorum facta praesumuntur scire—this principle, which, like the rest, is as true of nations as of individual men, has bestowed on the grand vicinage of Europe a right to know, and a right to prevent, any capital innovation which may amount to the erection of a dangerous nuisance." The politicians of France had denied such a right, on the abstract principle that to every nation belongs the unmolested regulation of its domestic affairs.

L. 22. *freedom of epistolary intercourse; little attention to formal method.* "The arrangement of his work is as singular as the matter. Availing himself of all the privileges of epistolary effusion, in their utmost latitude and [301] laxity, he interrupts, dismisses, and resumes arguments at pleasure. His subject is as extensive as political science—his allusions and excursions reach almost every region of human knowledge. It must be confessed, that in this miscellaneous and desultory warfare, the superiority of a man of genius over common men is infinite. He can cover the most ignominious retreat by a brilliant allusion. He can parade his arguments with masterly generalship, where they are strong. He can escape from an untenable position into a splendid declamation. He can sap the most impregnable conviction by pathos, and put to flight a host of syllogisms with a sneer. Absolved from the laws of vulgar method, he can advance a groupe of magnificent horrors to make a breach in our hearts, through which the most undisciplined rabble of arguments may enter in triumph." Vindiciae Gallicae, Preface.

L. 28. *perhaps of more than Europe.* The designs of Bonaparte, and actual events in Egypt, Syria, India, and the West Indies, justify this forecast. The Revolution forced on the independence of Spanish and Portuguese America.

L. 32. *by means the most absurd,* &c. Balzac (the earlier), "Aristippe": "Les grands événements ne sont pas toujours produits par de grandes causes. Les ressorts sont cachés, et les machines paraissent; et quand on vient à découvrir ces ressorts, on s'étonne de les voir et si faibles et si petits. On a honte de l'opinion qu'on en avait eue." Cp. in the beginning of the First Letter on a Regicide Peace; "It is often impossible, in these political enquiries, to find any proportion between the apparent force of any moral causes we may assign, and their known operation . . . . A common soldier, a child, a girl at the door of an inn, have changed the face of fortune, and almost of nature." In that place, as here, he is considering the fact that "in that its acmé of human prosperity and greatness, in the high and palmy state of the monarchy of France, it fell to the ground without a struggle." So Dr. Johnson: "Politicians have long observed, that the greatest events may be often traced back to slender causes. Petty competition, or casual friendship, the prudence of a slave, or the garrulity of a woman, have hindered or promoted the most important schemes, and hastened or retarded the revolutions of Empire." The Rambler, No. 141.

P. 96, L. 12. *Machiavelian.* The old adjective, from the French form "Machiavel," then in use in England. The *ch* is pronounced soft. We now say "Machiavelli" and "Machiavellian," pronouncing the *ch* hard.

L. 15. *Dr. Richard Price . . . minister of eminence.* Now an old man and in failing health. He was a political economist of some repute, cp. p. 228, l. 31. His writings procured him the friendship of Lord Rockingham's Whig rival, Lord Shelburne, who wished him to become his private secretary, on his accession to office in 1782. By Burke and his party Lord Shelburne was bitterly detested. Shelburne's party, minus their leader, were now in power under Pitt: and hence there might be presumed by foreigners some connexion between Price and the English government. Political disappointment thus contributes to the virulence with which Burke attacks [302] him. Price was true to his early education, having been the son of a dissenting minister, and he was the friend of Franklin, Turgot, and Howard. Mrs. Chapone's character of Simplicius (Miscellanies, Essay I.) is intended for him, and Dr. Doran, in his "Last Journal of Horace Walpole," has mentioned many facts highly creditable to his personal character and ability.

L. 21. *ingredient in the cauldron.* Alluding to Macbeth, Act iv. sc. 1.

P. 97, L. 2. *oracle—philippizes.* The celebrated expression of Demosthenes. Aesch. in Ctes. p. 72.

L. 8. The Reverend *Hugh Peters.* Applied derisively. "Reverend" as a title dates from some time after Peters.

L. 15. *your league in France.* The Holy League of the Catholics. Burke may have had in mind Grey's note on Hudibras, Part i. Canto ii. l. 651.

L. 19. *politics and the pulpit,* &c. The common cry of professional politicians. Silence with regard to public matters neither can nor ought to be kept in the pulpits of a free nation in stirring times. "I abhorred making the pulpit a scene for the venting of passion, or the serving of interests." Burnet, Own Times, Ann. 1684. The practice was by no means confined to the Revolutionists. On the 30th of January, 1790, the Bishop of Chester had preached before the House of Peers a political diatribe full of violent invective against the French nation and the National Assembly. The House voted him thanks, and ordered the sermon to be printed. As to the introduction of politics in the pulpit, Fox agrees with Burke: "Dr. Price, in his sermon on the anniversary of

NOTES

the English Revolution, delivered many noble sentiments, worthy of an enlightened philosopher . . . . But, though I approve of his general principles, I consider his arguments as unfit for the pulpit. The clergy, in their sermons, ought no more to handle political affairs, than this House ought to discuss subjects of morality and religion." Speech on the Test Act, 1790.

L. 28. *Inexperienced in all its affairs, on which they pronounce with so much confidence.* "Try experiments, as sound philosophers have done, and on them raise a legislative system!" This is a specimen of the wisdom of the Rev. Robert Robinson, another of these political divines; once famous as a Baptist minister at Cambridge.

P. 98, L. 3. *The hint given to a noble and reverend lay-divine.* The Duke of Grafton, whom Junius and Burke had united in attacking twenty years before. He had lately written a pamphlet on the subject of the Liturgy and Subscription, entitled "Hints &c., submitted to the serious attention of the Clergy, Nobility, and Gentry, newly assembled." Price calls it "a pamphlet ascribed to a great name, and which would dignify any name." It is chiefly remarkable as having called forth Bishop Horsley's Apology for the Liturgy and Clergy of the Church of England. Mathias alludes to "the *pious* Grafton," and his hostility to the Church, in his "Pursuits of Literature," Dialogue iv. l. 191, where he adds a note, "See the Duke's *Hints*—rather broad." Again at l. 299:

> With Symonds, and with Grafton's Duke would vie,
> A Dilettante in Divinity.

[303] Dr. John Symonds was Professor of Modern History at Cambridge. While sneering at "the lower orders of people," for "sinking into an enthusiasm in religion lately revived" (alluding to the Methodists), Price opposed the reform of the Liturgy and Articles, and urged those who were dissatisfied "to set up a separate worship for themselves."

P. 98, L. 4. *lay-divine.* The Duke held Unitarian opinions. Besides some writings of his own, he had done service to religious enquiry by printing for popular circulation the celebrated recension of the New Testament by Griesbach.

IBID. *high in office in one of our Universities.* Cp. Junius, Letter xv. The Duke was Chancellor of the University of Cambridge. Gray's Ode on his installation is well known. The text hints at the impropriety of such an office being held by a frequenter of the Unitarian meeting-house of Dr. Disney in Essex Street.

REFLECTIONS ON THE REVOLUTION IN FRANCE

L. 5. *to other lay-divines of rank.* The allusion is to the friend and patron of Price and Priestly, the Marquis of Lansdowne (Earl of Shelburne), who also held Unitarian opinions.

L. 7. *Seekers.* The Seekers were a Puritan sect who professed no determinate form of religion. Sir Harry Vane was at their head.

L. 8. *old staple*—as in Shakespeare, = material, especially used of woollen tissues. "Spun into the primitive staple of their frame," Fourth Letter on Regicide Peace. Cp. infra p. 302, l. 26.

L. 10. *to improve upon non-conformity.* Cp. note vol. i. p. 240, l. 1.

L. 22. *calculating divine.* Alluding to Price's labours as a political arithmetician.

L. 23. *great preachers.* Ps. xlviii. v. 11. The repetition of *great* is ironical, alluding to the rank of these *lay-divines.*

L. 26. *hortus siccus.* A collection of dried plants.

P. 99, L. 1. *baron bold.* Milton, L'Allegro, l. 119.

L. 3. *this town.* The work was written in Burke's house in Gerrard Street, Soho.

IBID. *uniform round of its vapid dissipations.* Alluding to the London season, which at this date began late in the autumn, and terminated late in the spring. Cp. Johnson's homily on the Close of the Season, Rambler No. 124 (May 25, 1751).

L. 5. *Mess-Johns* = Parsons, in the *familiar* sense. "Mess" is an archaic corruption of Magister. The term is of Scottish origin. Cp. Fergusson (the precursor of Burns), Hollow-fair;

See there is Bill-Jock and auld Hawkie,
And yonder's Mess-John and auld Nick.

L. 18. *Utinam nugis,* &c. Juv. Sat. iv. 150.

L. 22. *is almost the only lawful king,* &c. From the insolent form of words in which Price says he would have congratulated the king on his recovery, "in a style very different from that of most of the addresses." (p. 25), alluded to infra, p. 116.

[304] **L. 27.** *meridian* fervour = blaze.

IBID. *twelfth century.* Burke alludes to the pontificate of Innocent III, 1198–1216. Cp. the Abridgment of Eng. Hist. Book iii. chap. 8. "At length the sentence of excommunication was fulminated against the king (John). In the same year the same sentence was pronounced

NOTES

upon the Emperor Otho; and this daring pope was not afraid at once to drive to extremities the two greatest princes in Europe . . . . Having first released the English subjects from their oath of allegiance, by an unheard-of presumption he formally deposed John from his throne and dignity; he invited the king of France to take possession of the forfeited crown," &c.

P. 100, L. 23. *gradually habituated to it.* Cp. infra p. 157, l. 2.

L. 26. *condo et compono,* &c. Hor. Epist. I. 1. 12.

P. 101, L. 17. *at a remote period, elective.* "Reges ex nobilitate . . . sumunt," Tacitus, Germ. c. 7. Bolingbroke, N. Bacon, &c., make much of the fact as applied to the Saxon kings, and to Stephen and John after the Conquest.

L. 23. *and whilst the legal conditions,* &c. Cp. infra p. 108, l. 16.

L. 29. *electoral college.* The collective style of the nine Electors to the Empire. "College" (collegium) is used in its technical sense in Roman law.

P. 102, L. 20. *lives and fortunes.* A very ancient formula, the original words of which survive in the German "Mit Gut und Blut." So the 8th section of the Bill of Rights: "That they will stand to, maintain, and defend their said Majesties . . . . with their lives and estates, against all persons whatsoever," &c. This will explain the reference in the next sentence. The expression recalls the once common "life and property addresses" from public bodies to the crown.

L. 26. *Revolution of* 1688. It must be confessed that the argument which Burke here begins, and sustains with much force and ingenuity through twenty pages, is a complete failure. Mr. Hallam has refuted it at almost every point. It must be remembered that Burke is writing not as a judge, or a philosophical historian, but as an advocate. He conceived that the constitution would be endangered by the tenets of the Society, if they came into general credit, and made up his mind to lend the whole weight of his authority and his skill as a debater to support the opposite views (cp. the concluding paragraph of the work).

L. 29. *confounding all the three together.* Burke, using the expression of Sir Joseph Jekyl, says, that the Revolution of 1688 "was, in truth and in substance, a revolution not made, but prevented." In the Revolution of "forty years before," which good sense and good faith on the part of one man might have prevented, the *letter* of our liberties was insisted on quite as strictly as by the Old Whigs, or by Burke.

REFLECTIONS ON THE REVOLUTION IN FRANCE

P. 103, L. 11. *Declaration of Right.* Commonly called the Bill of Rights. It is printed in the Appendix to Professor Stubbs's Select Charters, p. 505.

[305] **L. 12.** *cornerstone.* Cp. vol. i. p. 179, l. 22.

L. 19. *A few years after this period.* 12 & 13 Will. III. cap. 2. By this Act the Crown was settled, after the death of William III and Anne without issue, upon the Princess Sophia, youngest daughter of Elizabeth Queen of Bohemia (daughter of James I.), and the heirs of her body, being protestants. Burke does not mention the Act 6 Anne, cap. 7, which asserts the right of the legislature to regulate the descent of the Crown, and makes it treasonable to maintain the contrary.

P. 104, L. 5. *gypsey predictions*—i. e. ignorant, random utterances. Burke called the republican nomenclature of the months "gipsey jargon."

L. 6. *the wisdom of the nation*—i. e. the collected opinion of wise politicians.

L. 7. *case of necessity—rule of law.* Cp. in the Fragment of Speech on the Acts of Uniformity; "When tyranny is extreme, and abuses of government intolerable, men resort to the rights of nature to shake it off. When they have done so, the very same principle of necessity of human affairs, to establish some other authority, which shall preserve the order of this new institution, must be obeyed, until they grow intolerable; and you shall not be suffered to plead original liberty against such an institution. See Holland, Switzerland."

L. 10. *a small and temporary deviation—regular hereditary succession.* This is hardly worthy of Burke. Hallam most truly says: "Our new line of sovereigns scarcely ventured to hear of their hereditary right. . . . This was the greatest change that affected our monarchy by the fall of the House of Stuart. The laws were not so materially altered as the spirit and sentiments of the people. Hence those who look only at the former have been prone to underrate the magnitude of this revolution. The fundamental maxims of the constitution, both as they regard the king and the subject, may seem nearly the same; but the disposition with which they were received and interpreted was entirely different." The truth of this last statement is undeniable.

L. 14. *Privilegium non transit in exemplum.* A maxim of the Civil law. "Privilegium" is used in the technical sense of an enactment that has for its object particular persons, as distinguished from a public mea-

Notes

sure. "C'est un grand mal," says Pascal, "de suivre l'exception au lieu de la règle. Il faut être sévère et contraire à l'exception."

L. 17. *its not being done at that time*, &c. "The Commons," says Hallam, "did not deny that the case was one of election, though they refused to allow that the monarchy was thus rendered perpetually elective."

L. 24. *on that of his wife.* By which, as Bentinck said, the prince would have become "his wife's gentleman-usher."

Ibid. *eldest born of the issue . . . . acknowledged as undoubtedly his.* The allusion is to the reported spuriousness of the prince born in 1688. Until that unfortunate event, which precipitated the Revolution, the Princess was heir presumptive to the crown. In acquiescing in the Revolution, the [306] Tories were obliged to presume the truth of this utterly groundless report. The devolution of the crown on the Princess was so far admitted by the Lords in the convention, that they omitted the important clause which pronounced the throne vacant, on its desertion by James.

L. 29. *choice . . . act of necessity.* If this were really said in seriousness, it is a sophism which could scarcely mystify an intelligent schoolboy. Two very different things are indicated by the term "choice."

P. 105, L. 15. *to reign over us*, &c. The best comment on this is, that it required a distinct Act of Parliament (2 W. and M. ch. 6) to enable the queen to exercise the regal power during the king's absence from England.

P. 106, L. 10. *repeating as from a rubric.* A process which always commanded Burke's respect, in matters of the constitution. Cp. vol. i. p. 267, l. 26, &c.

L. 31. *limitation of the crown.* In the technical sense, alluding to the succession being made conditional on the profession of Protestantism (see § 9 of the Declaration).

P. 107, L. 3. *for themselves and for all their posterity for ever.* It is impossible to defend Burke in this literal reading of the Declaration, in which he follows the genuine Tory Swift (Examiner, No. 16). This paper of Swift's will illustrate the difference between real Toryism and the Whig-Toryism of Bolingbroke. The words "for ever," copied from the Act of 1st Elizabeth, are mere surplusage, as in the expression "heirs for ever," in relation to private property. The right of Parliament to regulate the succession to the crown was too well established to make it worth while to have recourse to this verbal quibble. "The Parliament," says Sir Thomas Smith (Secretary of State temp. Elizabeth), "*giveth form of succession to the Crown*. To be short, all that ever the people of Rome might do either *in centuriatis comitiis* or *tribunitiis*, the same may be done by the Parliament of England." Commonwealth of England, p. 77, Ed. 1633. Priestley remarked that Burke had rendered himself, by denying this competency in Parliament, liable to the charge of high treason under an act framed by his own idol, Lord Somers: and Lord Stanhope declared his intention of impeaching him for it. The right of binding posterity was denied, on general grounds, by Locke, Treatise Concerning Government, Book ii. ch. viii. 116, to whom Swift alludes in the Examiner: "Lawyers may explain this, or call them words of form, as they please; and reasoners may argue that such an obligation is against the nature of government: but a plain reader, &c."

L. 4. The question as to a power of a people to bind their posterity is argued and settled according to Burke's opinion in a well-known passage in Absalom and Achitophel.

L. 6. *better Whig than Lord Somers,* &c. Note, vol. i. p. 148, l. 34. See Burke's panegyric upon the "Old Whigs"; "They were not *umbratiles doctores,* men who had studied a free constitution only in its anatomy, and upon dead systems. They knew it alive, and in action." Burke really [307] presumes too much on the ignorance of his readers. The mere title-page of Lord Somers's "Judgement of Whole Kingdoms and Nations," which affirms "the Rights of the People and Parliament of Britain to resist and deprive their Kings for evil government," is a sufficient answer to this tirade. Throughout these pages Burke exhibits the heat and the preoccupation of the advocate, not the judicial calm of the critic.

L. 12. *aided* with *the powers.* Burke generally uses *with* to express the instrument. We now say "*by* the powers." Cp. p. 115, l. 10, &c.

L. 18. *difficult . . . to give limits to the mere abstract competence of the supreme power.* The distinction between abstract and moral competence had an important place in Burke's reasoning on the American question. *Perimus licitis.* Cp. vol. i. p. 254, and see note.

L. 27. *house of lords — not morally competent,* &c. "The legislative can have no power to transfer their authority of making laws, and place it in other hands." — "The house of lords is not morally competent to dissolve itself, nor to abdicate, if it would, its portion in the legislature of the kingdom." These passages are quoted, the former from Locke,

NOTES

the latter from Bushel, by Grattan, in his Speech against the Union, Feb. 8, 1810. The argument is merely an idle *non possumus;* and on Grattan's deduction from it, the verdict of succeeding generations has been against it.

L. 34. *constitution—constituent parts.* The old "constitutional" doctrine is here very clearly stated. Had Burke lived a century later, he would have seen that it completely failed when it came to be generally applied. No principle is now better established than the unity and indivisibility of national sovereignty.

P. 108, L. 10. *not changing the substance—describing the persons—same force—equal authority.* Burke does not add force to his subtleties by this parody of the Athanasian Creed. Yet he cautions his readers, a few lines further, against getting "entangled in the mazes of metaphysic sophistry"!

L. 14. *communi sponsione reipublicae.* The Editor does not call to mind the phrase as a quotation. It was possibly invented by Burke, to express his meaning with the more weight.

L. 19. *mazes of metaphysic sophistry.* See note to vol. i. p. 215, l. 11. The outcry against "metaphysic sophistry" was no invention of Burke's. It is a favourite topic with Bolingbroke and other politicians who opposed the philosophical Whiggism of the School of Locke.

L. 23. *extreme emergency.* Mr. Hallam says most truly that this view, which "imagines some extreme cases of intolerable tyranny, some, as it were, lunacy of despotism, as the only plea and palliation of resistance," is merely a "pretended modification of the slavish principles of absolute obedience."

P. 109, L. 10. *states.* i. e. the Lords and Commons; the English Parliament in its original form being an imitation of the States-General of France. Our Liturgy until lately spoke of "the Three Estates of the Realm of [308] England assembled in Parliament." Cp. Milton, of the Assembly in Pandemonium;

> The bold design
> Pleas'd highly those infernal States, and joy
> Sparkl'd in all their eyes.

> Par. Lost, ii. 386.

L. 11. *organic moleculae of a disbanded people.* The idea is fully explained in the First Letter on Regicide Peace; "The body politic of France existed in the majesty of its throne, in the dignity of its nobility, in the honour of its gentry, in the sanctity of its clergy, in the reverence of its magistracy, in the weight and consideration due to its landed property in the several bailliages, in the respect due to its moveable substance represented by the corporations of the kingdom. All these particular *moleculae* united form the great mass of what is truly the body politic in all countries."

L. 25. *Some time after the conquest,* &c. "Five kings out of the seven that followed William the Conqueror were usurpers, according at least to modern notions" (Hallam). The facts seem to be as follows. Even in private succession, the descent of an inheritance as between the brother and the son of the owner was settled by no certain rule of law in the time of Glanvil. The system of Tanistry, which prevailed in Ireland down to the time of James I., and under which the land descended to the "eldest and most worthy" of the same blood, who was commonly ascertained by election, was thus partially in force. No better mode, says Mr. Hallam, could have been devised for securing a perpetual supply of civil quarrels. The principle of inheritance *per stirpem* which sound policy gradually established in private possessions, was extended by the lawyers about the middle of the 13th century to the Crown. Edward I. was proclaimed immediately upon his father's death, though absent in Sicily. Something however of the old principle may be traced in this proclamation, issued in his name by the guardians of the realm, where he asserts the Crown of England "to have devolved upon him by hereditary succession and the will of his nobles." These last words were omitted in the proclamation of Edward II.; since whose time the Crown has been absolutely hereditary. The question was thus settled at the period when the English constitution, according to Professor Stubbs, took its definite and permanent form. For illustrations of the question from ancient history see Grotius de Jure Bell. et Pac., Lib. ii. ch. 7, § 24.

L. 27. *the heir* per capita—*the heir* per stirpes. The distinction is produced by taking two different points of view; the one regarding the crown as the right of the reigning *family,* the other as the right of the reigning *person.* In the first case, when the reigning member of the family died, the whole of the members of the *family* (capita) re-entered into the family rights, and the crown fell to the "eldest and most worthy." In the second case, the crown descended to the legal heir or representative of the reigning person (*per stirpem*). By the heir *per capita,* Burke means the "eldest and most worthy" of the same blood. Elsewhere, following the [309] modern jurists, he calls the right of such an heir, "the right of consanguinity," that of the lineal heir, "the right of representation," from his standing in the place of, and thus *representing*, the former possessor (Abridgment of Eng. Hist., Book iii. ch. 8). Burke acutely traced the old principle of Tanistry in some of the details of the feudal law. "For what is very singular, and I take it otherwise unaccountable, a collateral warranty bound without any descending assets, where the lineal did not, unless something descended; and this subsisted invariably in the law until this century" (Id., Book ii. ch. 7). Collateral warranties were deprived of this effect by 4 Ann, ch. 16, § 21.

L. 30. *the inheritable principle survived,* &c. Burke says of the kings before the Conquest, "Very frequent examples occur where the son of a deceased king, if under age, was entirely passed over, and his uncle or some remoter relation raised to the Crown; but there is not a single instance where the election has carried it out of the blood" (Abr. Eng. Hist., Bk. ii. ch. 7).

L. 32. *multosque per annos,* &c. Virg. Georg. iv. 208. The quotation had been used as a motto to No. 72 of the Spectator, and in the Dedication to Bolingbroke's Dissertation on Parties.

P. 110, L. 6. *take the deviation . . . for the principle.* It was not in Burke's plan here to argue against the elective principle; but in the Annual Register for 1763, on the occasion of the then impending elections of a King of Poland and a King of the Romans, he says; "Those two elective sovereignties not only occasion many mischiefs to those who live under them, but have frequently involved a great part of Europe in blood and confusion. Indeed, these existing examples prove, beyond all speculation, the infinite superiority, in every respect, of hereditary monarchy; since it is evident, that the method of election constantly produces all those intestine divisions, to which, by its nature, it appears so liable, and also fails in that which is one of its principal objects, and which might be expected from it, the securing government for many successions in the hands of persons of extraordinary merit and uncommon capacity. We find by experience, that those kingdoms, where the throne is an inheritance, have had, in their series of succession, full as many able princes to govern them, as either Poland or Germany, which are elective."

L. 14. *dragged the bodies of our antient sovereigns out of the quiet of their tombs.* The allusion is to the outrages committed by the Roundhead troopers in Winchester Cathedral. There may also be an allusion to the plundering of the Abbey of Faversham, at the dissolution of monasteries, when the remains of King Stephen were disinterred and thrown into the Swale, for the sake of the leaden coffin. Cp. in the Draft of Letter to Markham (1770); "My passions are not to be roused, either on the side of partiality, or on that of hatred, by those who lie in their cold lead, quiet and innoxious, in the chapel of Henry, or the churches of Windsor Castle or La Trappe — *quorum Flaminia tegitur cinis atque Latina.*"

[310] **L. 15.** *attaint and disable backwards.* In the manner of the Chinese law of attainder, by which its effect extends to a man's ancestors though not to his descendants.

L. 26. *Statute* de tallagio non concedendo—(Anno 1297). Not originally a statute, though referred to as such in the preamble to the Petition of Right, and decided by the judges in 1637 to be a Statute. See Stubbs' Select Charters, p. 487. Cp. vol. i. p. 237, l. 33.

L. 27. *Petition of Right.* See Stubbs' Select Charters, p. 505.

P. 111, L. 5. *The law,* &c. Burke, as we might expect, turns to the Act of Settlement without saying a word of the cause which led to its being passed, namely, the failure of issue, not of Queen Mary, but of William himself. The final limitation of the Bill of Rights was to William's own heirs: so that if after Mary's death he had married some one else, and had a son, the crown would have passed completely out of the English royal family.

L. 27. *Stock and root of inheritance—temporary administratrix of a power.* This shifts the argument to a different position. The doctrines of the Revolution Society obviously referred to the latter ground of choice. But Burke would scarcely have maintained that the merit of William as an administrator did not weigh with the English nation, when they associated him with Mary on the throne.

L. 32. *is daughter,* &c. Others however, nearer in blood, but of the Catholic faith, were passed over: especially those of the Palatine family, whose ancestors having been strong assertors of the Protestant religion, it was thought likely that some of them might return to it.

P. 112, L. 34. *A few years ago,* &c. Burke commands more attention when he confesses his reason for all this deliberate mystification. No sophistry was ever too gross for the public ear; but the occasion which turned Burke for the time into a Tory casuist must have appeared to him critical indeed.

Notes

P. 113, L. 14. *export to you in illicit bottoms.* The allusion is to the Act of Navigation. See vol. i. p. 179, and note. "Bottom" (Dutch *Bodem*) is the old technical term for a ship. It is still used in such mercantile phrases as "foreign bottoms," and survives in the term "bottomry," applied to the advance of money on the security of the ship for the purposes of the voyage.

L. 27. *pledge of the stability and perpetuity,* &c. The following passage is proper to be quoted here, as being a complete expression of the idea in the text, and at the same time the one which was selected by De Quincey as the most characteristic passage in the works of Burke, from the literary point of view. It is also a necessary illustration to the argument at p. 141, ll. 23–35.

> Such are *their* ideas; such *their* religion; and such *their* law. But as to *our* country, and *our* race, as long as the well-compacted structure of our church and state, the sanctuary, the holy of holies of that ancient law, defended by reverence, defended by power, a fortress at once and a temple, shall stand inviolate on the brow of the British Sion—as long as the British monarchy, not more limited than fenced by the orders of the state, shall, like [311] the proud Keep of Windsor, rising in the majesty of proportion, and girt with the double belt of its kindred and coeval towers—as long as this awful structure shall oversee and guard the subjected land*—so long the mounds and dykes of the low, fat Bedford Level will have nothing to fear from all the pickaxes of all the levellers of France. As long as our sovereign lord the king, and his faithful subjects, the lords and commons of this realm—the triple cord, which no man can break; the solemn, sworn, constitutional frank-pledge of this nation; the firm guarantees of each others' being, and each others' rights; the joint and several securities,† each in its place and order, for every kind and every quality of property and of dignity; as long as these endure, so long the Duke of Bedford is safe; and we are all safe together—the high, from the blights of envy and the spoliations of rapacity; the low, from the iron hand of oppression and the insolent spurn of contempt. Amen! and so be it! and so it *will* be —

*The allusion is obviously to the striking view of Windsor Castle and the valley of the Thames, from the uplands of Buckinghamshire, in which stood Burke's country-house, where this Letter was written. There is a similar allusion to the imposing effect of an ancient castle in the Fourth Letter on a Regicide Peace.

†Cp. p. 296, l. 23.

REFLECTIONS ON THE REVOLUTION IN FRANCE

Dum domus Aeneae Capitoli immobile saxum
Accolet; imperiumque pater Romanus habebit.
Letter to a Noble Lord, p. 53.

P. 114, L. 1. *It is common for them to dispute,* &c. But cp. Hallam, Const. Hist. chap. xiv. "Since the extinction of the House of Stuart's pretensions, and other events of the last half century, we have seen those exploded doctrines of indefeasible hereditary right revived under another name, and some have been willing to misrepresent the transactions of the Revolution and the Act of Settlement as if they did not absolutely amount to a deposition of the reigning sovereign, and an election of a new dynasty by the representatives of the nation in parliament." Mr. Hallam wished to be understood as explicitly affirming (in contradiction of Burke) what had been already stated by Paley (see Princ. of Moral and Political Philos. p. 411), that the great advantage of the Revolution was what many regarded as its reproach, and more as its misfortune—that it broke the line of succession. After stating precisely the votes, and pointing out the impossibility of reconciling them with such a construction as Burke's, he goes on to say—"It was only by recurring to a kind of paramount, and what I may call hyperconstitutional law, a mixture of force and regard to the national good, which is the best sanction of what is done in revolutions, that the vote of the Commons could be defended. They proceeded not by the stated rules of the English government, but by the general rights of mankind. They looked not so much to Magna Charta as to the original compact of society; and rejected Coke and Hale for Hooker and Grotius." Hallam in effect subscribes to the criticism contained in the 3rd, 4th, and 5th Letters of Dr. Priestley on this question. Cp. Grotius, Lib. ii. c. 7, § 27.

[312] **L. 2.** *exploded fanatics of slavery.* The allusion is to Heylin, Filmer, &c. Priestley, who is followed by Hallam (cp. note to p. 108, l. 23), charges Burke with advancing principles equivalent in effect to those of passive obedience and non-resistance (Preface to Letters).

L. 7. *new fanatics,* &c. Rousseau attacked Grotius quite as unreasonably as Filmer had done. We may exclaim too often with Burke, "One would think that such a thing as a medium had never been heard of in the moral world!"

L. 11. *more of a divine sanction,* &c. It would be superfluous to show the inaccuracy of such a notion.

P. 115, L. 17. *broken the original contract—more than misconduct.* That is, a higher degree of misconduct than Dr. Price meant to be understood by his use of the word. The argument really amounts to no more than a criticism of Dr. Price's English.

L. 35. *popular representative* = the House of Commons. Cp. vol. i. p. 118, l. 17.

L. 36. *the next great constitutional act*—the Act of Settlement, 12 and 13 W. III, cap. 2. "It was determined," says Mr. Hallam, "to accompany this settlement with additional securities for the subject's liberty. The Bill of Rights was reckoned hasty and defective: some matters of great importance had been omitted, and in the twelve years which had since elapsed, new abuses had called for new remedies." One of these abuses was the number of placemen and pensioners in the House (cp. note to vol. i. p. 138, l. 27).

P. 116, L. 3. *no pardon—pleadable to an impeachment.* This question arose upon the plea of pardon put in bar of prosecution by the Earl of Danby in 1679, and resisted with what Mr. Hallam considers culpable violence, by two successive Houses of Commons. It remained undecided until the Act of Settlement. The expressions in the enacting clause of this Act, says Mr. Hallam, "seem tacitly to concede the Crown's right of granting a pardon *after* sentence; which, though perhaps it could not be well distinguished in point of law from a pardon pleadable in bar, stands on a very different footing with respect to constitutional policy."

L. 7. *practical claim of impeachment.* Always strongly insisted upon by Burke as an important guarantee of constitutional liberty. Cp. vol. i. p. 120, l. 33, and note.

L. 17. *more properly the servant,* &c. The idea that a governing functionary is a servant, and that national sovereignty is inalienable, was strongly insisted on by Rousseau in the "Contrat Social" (Liv. ii. ch. 1. 2). It is an advance on the Whig doctrine, maintained by Burke, that government consists in a compact between the king and people, as equal contracting parties, which neither is at liberty to break so long as its original conditions are fulfilled. Cp. Selden's Table-Talk, head "Contracts." "If our fathers have lost their liberty, why may not we labour to regain it?" Ans. "We must look to the contract; if that be rightly made, we must stand to it: if once we grant we may recede from contracts, upon any inconveniency that [313] may afterwards happen, we shall have no bargain kept." The doctrine of Dr. Price had been advocated at least two centuries before by Althusius (see Bayle),

REFLECTIONS ON THE REVOLUTION IN FRANCE

who held "omnes reges nihil aliud esse quam magistratus," "quod summa reipublicae cujusvis jure sit penes solum populum," &c. "Error pestilens," is the comment of Conringius, "et turbando orbi aptus"!

L. 22. *Haec commemoratio,* &c. Ter. And., Act i. sc. 1. l. 17. The steward Sosia, no longer a slave, in these words resents his master's reminding him of the change in his condition. Burke's repartees to Dr. Price, which fill up the rest of the page, are in his most effective parliamentary style.

P. 117, L. 7. *Kings, in one sense,* &c. Cp. vol. i. p. 118, l. 10.

L. 18. *speak only the primitive language of the law.* Cp. vol. i. p. 268, l. 11.

L. 24. *the Justicia of Arragon.* See Hallam's account of Arragon. His functions did not differ in essence from those of the Chief Justice of England, as divided among the judges of the King's Bench, but practically they were much more extensive and important. The office is to be traced to the year 1118, but it was not till the Cortes of 1348 that it was endowed with an authority which "proved eventually a more adequate barrier against oppression than any other country could boast." From that time he held his post for life. It was penal for any one to obtain letters from the king impeding the execution of the justiza's process. See Hallam's account of the successful resistance of the justiza Juan de Cerda to John I.: "an instance of judicial firmness and integrity, to which, in the fourteenth century, no country perhaps in Europe could offer a parallel." Middle Ages, chap. iv.

P. 118, L. 3. *Let these gentlemen,* &c. Selden gives as the original meaning of the maxim that the king can do no wrong, that "no process can be granted against him" (at Common Law).

L. 6. *positive statute law which affirms that he is not.* Burke clearly alludes to a provision in the Act for attainting the Regicides, 12 Car. II. cap. 30, which runs thus: "And be it hereby declared, that by the undoubted and fundamental laws of this kingdom, neither the Peers of this realm, nor the Commons, nor both together in Parliament or out of Parliament, nor the People collectively or representatively, nor any other Persons whatsoever, ever had, have, hath, or ought to have, any coercive power over the persons of the Kings of this realm." We can hardly wonder that Burke did not think fit to indicate precisely this "positive statute law."

L. 11. *Laws are commanded,* &c. The "inter arma leges silent" of Cicero.

NOTES

L. 15. *Justa bella quibus necessaria.* Burke, as usual, quotes from memory. "Justa piaque sunt arma, quibus necessaria; et necessaria, quibus nulla nisi in armis spes salutis." Livy, Lib. ix. cap. 1. The passage is alluded to by Sidney, and also in the famous pamphlet "Killing no Murder"; "His (Cromwell's) indeed have been pious arms," &c., p. 8.

L. 24. *faint, obscure,* &c. Cp. notes, vol. i. p. 105, l. 13, and p. 225, l. 30.

[314] **P. 119, L. 2.** *a revolution will be the very last resource,* &c. "I confess that events in France have corrected several opinions which I previously held. . . . I can hardly frame to myself the condition of a people, in which I would not rather desire that they should continue, than to fly to arms, and to seek redress through the unknown miseries of a revolution." Fox, Speech on the Suspension of the Habeas Corpus Act, 1794.

L. 4. *The third head,* &c. On this Burke does not expend so much useless force. Feeling that after all he had something better to do than to split hairs with Dr. Price, he soon pushes on to the proper business of the book. He avoids actually *denying* the rights of men, but alleges that Englishmen have not had occasion to insist on them.

P. 120, L. 1. *They endeavour to prove,* &c. Similarly the Americans had based their claims to liberty on law and precedent.

L. 18. *rights of men — rights of Englishmen.* "Our ancestors, for the most part, took their stand, not on a general theory, but on the particular constitution of the realm. They asserted the rights, not of men, but of Englishmen." Macaulay, Essay on Mackintosh's History of the Revolution. Burke however himself alludes to the "common rights of men," in distinction from the "disputed rights and privileges of freedom," in the Letter to the Sheriffs of Bristol. And every Englishman familiar with the literature of his own time must have known that Burke exaggerated. The "rights of men" were a common Whig topic. Bp. Warburton, for instance, says in one of his Sermons that to call an English king "the Lord's Anointed" is "a violation of the rights of men."

L. 20. *other profoundly learned men.* The allusion is to Coke and Glanvil. Cp. vol. i. p. 238, l. 7.

L. 22. *general theories.* Hooker and Grotius are alluded to. See also Book I. of Selden "De Jure Naturae et Gentium secundum disciplinam Hebraeorum."

P. 121, L. 14. *you will observe,* &c. Burke here terminates his quotations from the archives of the English constitution, and passes on

REFLECTIONS ON THE REVOLUTION IN FRANCE

to his "Reflections" on the French Revolution. He effects the transition in three paragraphs, in which he contrives to rise, at once, and without an effort, to the full "height of his great argument." These three paragraphs, evidently composed with great pains, sum up the conclusions of the previous pages as to matter, and as to style are so regulated as to prepare for the gravity and force which characterize the next section of the work.

L. 15. *uniform policy.* Cp. note to vol. i. p. 180, l. 17.

L. 16. *entailed inheritance.* "Major hereditas venit unicuique nostrum a jure et legibus, quam a parentibus," is the well-known motto from Cicero, prefixed to Coke upon Littleton.

L. 17. *derived to us from our forefathers, to be transmitted to our posterity.* The spirited lines of Cato (Act III.) were familiar to Burke:

Remember, O my friends! the laws, the rights,
The generous plan of pow'r deliver'd down
[315] From age to age, by your renown'd forefathers
(So dearly bought, the price of so much blood),
O let it never perish in your hands,
But piously transmit it to your children.

L. 21. *unity, diversity.* Cp. vol. i. p. 255, l. 11.

L. 22. *an house of commons* and a *people.* Observe the claim here insinuated, suggested by Burke's Whiggish theory of Parliament. It is now understood that the rights of the House of Commons are not distinguishable from, and are immediately resolvable into those of the people.

L. 26. *following nature, which is wisdom without reflection,* &c. Cp. infra p. 174, l. 32, p. 181, l. 27, &c. So in the Third Letter on Regicide Peace; "Never was there a jar or discord between genuine sentiment and sound policy. Never, no, never, did Nature say one thing, and Wisdom say another." A literal translation of Juvenal, Sat. xiv. l. 321;

Nunquam aliud Natura, aliud Sapientia dixit.

The formula is borrowed from the Stoic philosophy, so popular in Rome. Burke often had in mind the description of his favourite author, Lucan;

Hi mores, haec duri immota Catonis
Secta fuit; servare modum, finemque tenere,
Naturamque sequi, patriaeque impendere vitam;
Non sibi, sed toti genitum se credere mundo.

Phars. II. 380, &c.

NOTES

The use Burke makes of the idea is, however, a relic of his study of the Essayists. See the Spectator, No. 404. It occurs more than once in Chesterfield's Essays in the "World." The doctrine is well put by Beccaria; "It is not only in the fine arts that the imitation of nature is the fundamental principle; it is the same in sound policy, which is no other than the art of uniting and directing to the same end the natural and immutable sentiments of mankind."

L. 28. *A spirit of innovation.* Burke does not mean a spirit of *Reform.* "It cannot, at this time, be too often repeated—line upon line; precept upon precept; until it comes into the currency of a proverb— *to innovate is not to reform.*" Letter to a Noble Lord.

IBID. *the result of a selfish temper,* &c. This might well be illustrated by the attempted innovations on the constitution in the early part of the reign (see vol. i., passim), and by the history of the Stuarts. "Charles II.," says Clarendon, "had in his nature so little reverence and esteem for antiquity, and did in truth so much contemn old orders, forms, and institutions, that the objection of novelty rather advanced than obstructed any proposition."

L. 29. *People will not look forward,* &c. "Vous vivez tout entiers dans le moment présent; vous y êtes consignés par une passion dominante: et tout ce qui ne se rapporte pas à ce moment vous parait antique et suranné. Enfin, vous êtes tellement en votre personne et de coeur et d'esprit, que, croyant former à vous seuls un point historique, les ressemblances éternelles entre le [316] temps et les hommes échappent à votre attention, et l'autorité de l'expérience vous semble une fiction, ou une vaine garantie destinée uniquement au crédit des vieillards." Madame De Stael, Corinne, liv. xii.

P. 122, L. 3. *family settlement—mortmain.* By which landed property is secured inalienably (subject to important legal restrictions) in families and corporations (in the legal sense) respectively.

L. 4. *grasped as in a kind of mortmain* (mortua manus, mainmorte). There is an allusion to the fanciful explanation of the term, "that it is called mortmaine by resemblance to the holding of a man's hand that is ready to die, for what he then holdeth he letteth not go till he be dead" (Co. Litt. 2 b). The tenure was really so called because it yielded no service to the superior lord.

L. 10. *Our political system,* &c. Compare with these weighty conclusions the opinion of Bacon; "Those things which have long gone together are, as it were, confederate within themselves. . . . It were good, therefore, if men, in their innovations, would follow the example of time itself, which indeed innovateth greatly, but quietly, and by degrees scarcely to be perceived." Essay on Innovations. Cp. Hooker, Eccl. Pol., Book i. ch. 10, par. 9, last clause.

L. 15. *great mysterious incorporation.* Cp. vol. i. p. 288, l. 12.

L. 20. *never wholly new,* &c. Cp. Introd. to vol. i. p. 29, l. 20, &c. Cp. also the theory of the true Social Contract, p. 192 infra.

L. 30. . . . . . *our sepulchres and our altars.* The germ of the argument is to be found in the 14th of South's Posthumous Sermons: "And herein does the admirable wisdom of God appear, in modelling the great economy of the world, so uniting public and private advantages, that those affections and dispositions of mind, that are most conducible to the safety of government and society, are also most advantageous to man in his personal capacity." The argument is amplified in Dr. Chalmers' Bridgewater Treatise.

P. 123, L. 9. *a noble freedom.* The epithet is not used in the moral sense, but indicates an *aristocratic* character. The image, however, is not intended to degrade but to elevate the character of popular liberty.

L. 15. *their age.* But see note to vol. i. p. 138, l. 13, and Arist. Pol., Lib. ii. c. 5.

L. 27. *possessed in some parts,* &c. Burke carries on the idea of the last paragraph, likening the mass of the nation to a nobleman succeeding to his paternal estate.

L. 31. *very nearly as good as could be wished.* Was it so? This question was much debated before the meeting of the States-General. The Revolutionists wished for a constitution, to which the privileged classes replied that France already had a very good constitution, to which nothing was wanting but a restoration to its pristine vigour. This paradox is supported by Burke. A statesman so far removed from suspicion of prejudice as J. J. Mounier, is quite of another opinion. Burke likened the States-General [317] to the English Parliament. Cp. p. 109, l. 9, p. 115, l. 24. Nothing, however, could be farther from the constitution of the latter, composed, in the Commons, of proprietors elected by proprietors, and in the Lords, of a descendible personal magistracy: and never was a nation governed, even temporarily, by a more absurd constitution than that of the revived States-General. "Supposons, contre toute vraisemblance, que les ordres séparés eussent agi de consent, et que la paix n'eut point été troublée par leurs prétentions respectives, ils auroient sanctionné cette monstrueuse composition d'états-généraux. Ils auroient décidé, qu'on réuniroit périodiquement tous les François âgés de plus de vingt cinq ans, pour délibérer séparément, les uns comme nobles, les autres comme plébéiens, sur tous les intérêts de l'état, non seulement dans chaque ville, mais encore jusques dans le dernier village, pour rédiger par écrit leurs demandes et leurs projets, et les confier à des députés, soumis dans l'assemblée des réprésentans aux ordres de ceux qui les auroient choisis. Ainsi l'on auroit établi une aristocratie violente et une démocratie tumultueuse, dont la lutte inévitable n'eut pas tardé de produire l'anarchie et un bouleversement général." Mounier, De l'influence attribuée aux philosophes, &c., p. 90. Sir P. Francis, in a letter to Burke, pointed out the error Burke here makes.

L. 32. *States,* i. e. States-General.

P. 124, L. 8. *subject of compromise.* Cp. vol. i. p. 278, l. 29.

L. 9. *temperaments.* Cp. note to vol. i. p. 124, l. 17.

L. 33. *low-born servile wretches.* Notice the variation from an earlier opinion in vol. i. p. 107, l. 16. The passage of Rousseau quoted in the note to that place may be here appropriately refuted by stating, in the words of Burke, the steady policy of the French monarchy, which had subsisted, and even been strengthened, by the generation or support of republics. The Swiss republics grew under the guardianship of the French monarchy. The Dutch republics were hatched and cherished under the same incubation. A republican constitution was afterwards, under the influence of France, established in the Empire, against the pretensions of its chief; and while the republican protestants were crushed at home (cp. note to p. 97, l. 19, ante) the French monarchs obtained their final establishment in Germany as a law of the Empire, by the treaty of Westphalia. See the Second Letter on Regicide Peace (1796).

P. 125, L. 2. *Maroon slaves.* Maroon (borrowed from the French West Indies, *Marron*) means a runaway slave.

L. 3. *house of bondage.* Exodus, xx. 2.

L. 20. *looked to your neighbours in this land.* But how impossible it was, very properly insists De Tocqueville, to do as England had done, and gradually to change the spirit of the ancient institutions by practice! By no human device can a year be made to do the work of centuries. The Frenchman felt himself every hour injured in his fortune, his comfort, or his pride, by some old law, some political usage, or some remnant of old power, and saw within his reach no remedy applicable to the particular [318] ill—for him the only alternatives were, to suffer everything, or to destroy everything.

L. 34. *to* overlay *it* = to stifle or smother.

P. 126, L. 8. *never can remove.* Cp. post, pp. 360, 361.

L. 11. *not more happy.* Cp. post, p. 198.

L. 12. *a smooth and easy career.* This is putting far too fair a face on the possibilities of the crisis. Any power capable of effectually controlling the antagonistic interests might have directed such a career; but where was such a power to be found?

L. 25. *All other nations,* &c. Cp. Burnet, History of his own Time, vol. i., on this characteristic in the Bohemian revolution.

L. 27. *some rites . . . of religion—severer manners.* The allusion seems to be especially to the English Commonwealth.

P. 127, L. 3. disgraced *the tone of lenient council,* &c. i. e. thrown into disfavour. Cp. infra, p. 172, l. 12 sqq.

L. 5. *its most potent topics* = the best arguments in its favour.

L. 28. *medicine of the state.* Cp. p. 155, l. 9.

IBID. *They have seen,* &c. Notice the strength of the antitheses. The whole section is a fine example of Burke's most powerful style.

P. 128, L. 6. *national bankruptcy the consequence.* Contentio. See note to vol. i. p. 167, l. 2.

L. 11. *species* = descriptions of money (Fr. espèces), i. e. gold and silver.

L. 13. *hid themselves in the earth from whence they came.* The germ of this dignified figure is from the Parable of the Talents. There is a passage in Swift's Drapier's Letters, writes Arthur Young, which accounts fully for gold and silver so absolutely disappearing in France; I change only *Wood's pence* for *assignats.* "For my own part, I am already resolved what to do; I have a pretty good shop of stuffs and silks, and instead of taking *assignats,* I intend to truck with my neighbours, the butcher and baker, and brewer, and the rest, goods for goods; and the little gold and silver I have, I will keep by me like my heart's blood, till better times; till I am just ready to starve, and then I will buy *assignats.*" Example of France a Warning to Britain, 3rd Edition, p. 127. The louis d'or (20 livres) was at one time worth 1800 livres in assignats! Much gold and silver was at first hoarded in concealment, but during the year 1791 the treasure of France began to be imported into England.

NOTES

The price of 3 per cent. Consols, which during the previous five years had averaged £75, at midsummer in that year stood at £88.

L. 20. *fresh ruins of France.* The rest of Europe was at this time under the extraordinary delusion that France was really ruined; in Burke's words, "not politically existing." This persuasion partly accounts for the terror and astonishment which soon succeeded it.

L. 28. *the last stake reserved,* &c. Cp. ante, p. 119, l. 2, and post, p. 176, l. 12. Burke means that insurrection and bloodshed are the extreme medicine of the state, and only to be used in the last resort, when everything [319] else has failed. A similar expression is put by Fielding into the mouth of Jonathan Wild; "Never to do more mischief than was necessary, for that mischief was too precious a thing to be wasted." Cp. Lucan, Book vii.; "Ne quâ parte sui pereat scelus."

L. 31. *their pioneers*—the philosophers and economists.

P. 129, L. 1. *their shoe buckles.* Alluding to the "patriotic donations" of silver plate. See p. 345.

L. 14. *of ten thousand times greater consequence,* &c. "They (the Jacobins) are always considering the formal distributions of power in a constitution; the moral basis they consider as nothing. Very different is my opinion; I consider the moral basis as everything; the formal arrangements, further than as they promote the moral principles of government, and the keeping desperately wicked persons as the subjects of laws, and not the makers of them, to be of little importance. What signifies the cutting and shuffling of cards, while the pack still remains the same?" Fourth Letter on Regicide Peace.

L. 29. *lay their ordaining hands—promise of revelation.* The allusion is to the practice of the Church (see Acts ch. viii).

P. 130, L. 2. *talents—practical experience in the state.* "Nous n'avons jamais manqué de philosophes et d'orateurs," says De Sacy, in his critique on Rathery's Histoire des États-Généraux; "nous n'avons eu faute que d'hommes d'état."

L. 7. *those who will lead,* &c. This canon was the result of Burke's observation of the English Parliament. Cp. vol. i. note to p. 208, l. 28. For the parallels in Greek and Roman life, see Plato, Rep., Book vi. p. 493, and Cicero, Rep., Book ii.

P. 131, L. 2. *six hundred persons.* The double representation of the Tiers État, advocated by Sieyès and D'Entragues, had already been admitted in the provincial assemblies. It was now adopted by Necker with the view of overbalancing the influence of the privileged orders, and overcoming their selfish and impolitic resistance to taxation, and their general determination to thwart the royal policy.

L. 11. *soon resolved into that body.* The states met on the 5th of May; and the Third Estate on the 17th of June, upon the motion of Sieyès, constituted itself the National Assembly. "The memorable decree of the 17th of June," says M. Mignet, "contained the germ of the 4th of August."

L. 14. *a very great proportion,* &c. The intervention of the lawyer in so many of the acts of civil life, and the complexity of the different bodies of common law (coûtumes), 300 in number, which prevailed in different parts of the country,* always greatly swelled the numbers of the profession. [320] "Sous le regne du Roy François premier de ce nom, un Villanovanus fit un Commentaire sur Ptolomée, dedans lequel il disoit, qu'en ceste France il y avoit plus de gens de robbe longue, qu'en toute l'Allemagne, l'Italie, et l'Espagne; et croy certes qu'il disoit vray." Pasquier, Les Recherches de la France, Liv. ix. c. 38. Montaigne, about the same time, remarks (Ess., Liv. i. ch. 22) that the lawyers might be considered as a Fourth Estate. As it was the lawyers who were best acquainted with the wrongs of the people, and alone possessed the knowledge requisite for putting them forward, they were very appropriate representatives of the people. Burke has in mind, of course, the state of things in England, in which the landed gentry, dealing honourably with the people and enjoying their sympathy and confidence, always furnished the majority of their representatives. But how could he have supposed that the French people would or could return the landowners as their representatives?

L. 15. *a majority of the members who attended.* This cannot be correct. 652 members took their seats: and they were classed as follows:

2	Priests.
12	Gentlemen.
12	Mayors or Consuls of Towns.
162	Magistrates of different tribunals.
272	Advocates.

* "Nous avons en France plus de loix que tout le reste du monde ensemble et plus qu'il n'en fauldroit à regler touts les mondes d'Epicurus. *Ut olim flagitiis, sic nunc legibus laboramus.*" Montaigne, Ess., Liv. iii. ch. 13.

NOTES

16 Physicians.
176 Merchants, monied men, and farmers.
___
652
===

L. 16. *practitioners in the law.* Cp. note to vol. i. p. 241, l. 10. The remarks of Dr. Ramsay in his History of the American Revolution, on the share of the lawyers in the revolt, are quoted very appositely in Priestley's second Letter to Burke, in answer to these remarks. See also vol. i. p. 249, ll. 8–11.

L. 17. *not of distinguished magistrates.* The magistrates of the supreme courts and bailliages belonged to the order of the Nobility, and were represented in its representation to the number of 28; and even if they had been eligible, the electors of the Third Estate would hardly have entrusted them with their interests. But 162 magistrates of other tribunals were among the representatives of the Third Estate. "La députation des communes," says Mounier, "était à-peu-pres aussi bien composée qu'elle pouvoit l'être, et il est difficile qu'elle le soit mieux, tant qu'on séparera la représentation des plébéiens de celle des gentilshommes." Recherches sur les causes, &c. Vol. i. p. 257.

L. 21. *inferior . . . members of the profession.* On the complaints against practising lawyers in parliament, and their exclusion in the 46th of Edward III, see Hallam, ch. viii. part 3. Cp. the Parliamentum Indoctorum, or lack-learning Parliament, of Henry IV. In Bacon's Draught for a Proclamation [321] for a Parliament, he admonishes the electors "Thirdly and lastly, that they be truly sensible not to disvalue or disparage the house . . . . with lawyers of mean account and estimation." See generally on this subject, the debate in the Commons, November, 1649, in Whitelock's Memoirs.

L. 23. *distinguished exceptions.* There were one or two advocates of profound learning and in large practice, like Camus. There were others, like Mounier and Malouet, distinguished for the wisdom and moderation of their political views.

L. 28. *saw distinctly—all that was to follow.* Compare with the paragraphs which follow, the Thoughts on French Affairs, under the head "Effect of the Rota." Paine denies that these were the views of Burke at the time, and says that it was impossible to make him believe that there would be a revolution in France: his opinion being that the French had neither spirit to undertake it, nor fortitude to support it. This had been the opinion of the best informed statesmen since the failure of Turgot. Cp. note to p. 271, l. 9.

P. 132, L. 18. *daring, subtle, active,* &c. Cp. vol. i. p. 242, l. 3.

L. 25. *inevitable.* See p. 131, l. 28.

P. 133, L. 6. *Supereminent authority,* &c. — *Contentio.* Cp. note to vol. i. p. 167, l. 2.

L. 7. *country clowns — traders.* The 176 (note to p. 131, l. 15).

L. 9. *traders — never known anything beyond their counting-house.* The Memoirs of the *bourgeois* Hardy, Barbier, and Marais afford valuable illustrations of the views of affairs taken by peaceable men of useful and uniform lives, and evidence that their ideas were not bounded by their counting-house. There is no reason to think that they were exceptions in their class.

L. 16. *pretty considerable.* This expression has ceased to be classical in England, but survives in America. There were only 16 physicians in the Assembly.

L. 17. *this faculty had not,* &c. The French *Ana* are full of gibes upon the medical profession. Burke possibly had in mind the constant ridicule of the faculty of medicine by his favourite French author, Molière. Cp. infra, p. 349, l. 25.

L. 32. *natural landed interest.* But how unreasonable to expect it! The natural landed interest was surely sufficiently represented in the nobility.

L. 35. *sure operation of adequate causes,* &c. Burke thought that the House of Commons was and ought to be something very much more than what was implied in the vulgar idea of a "popular representation"; that it contained within itself a much more subtle and artificial combination of parts and powers, than was generally supposed; and that it would task the leisure of a contemplative man to exhibit thoroughly the working of its mechanism. See Letter to a Member of the National Assembly.

P. 134, L. 4. politic *distinction* = political. See note to p. 93, l. 27, ante.

[322] **L. 18.** *it cannot escape observation.* See the character of Mr. Grenville, vol. i. p. 185, and notes.

L. 26. *After all,* &c. The defects of the preceding observations do

Notes

not impair the justice of the censure contained in the concluding paragraph, which was amply established by events. Burke's glance was often too rapid to be quite exact, but it was unerring in its augury of the essential bearing of a movement.

L. 32. *dissolve* us. Burke writes as if speaking in the House.

P. 135, L. 1. *breakers of law in India,* &c. See the Speech on the Nabob of Arcot's Debts, in which Paul Benfield, who made (including himself) no fewer than eight members of Parliament, and others, are treated in a rhetorical strain of indignant irony which has no parallel in profane literature.

L. 16. *fools rush in,* &c. Pope, Essay on Criticism, l. 625.

L. 27. *mere country* curates. (Curés.) Not in the modern sense of an *assistant,* but in the old and proper one of a *beneficed* clergyman or his *substitute* (vicaire). Bailey's dictionary has: Curate, a parson or vicar of a parish. The order of the clergy was represented by 48 archbishops and bishops, 35 abbots or canons, and 208 curates or parish priests. The income of a beneficed *curé* averaged £28 per annum: that of a *vicaire,* about half that sum.

L. 31. *hopeless poverty.* The Revolution, says Arthur Young, was an undoubted benefit to the lower clergy, who comprised five-sixths of the whole. They were not too numerously represented, if the representation were to mean anything at all.

P. 136, L. 6. *those by whom,* &c. i. e. the lawyers.

L. 26. *turbulent, discontented men of quality.* These remarks, applying to the Duke of Orleans, Mirabeau, Talleyrand, the two Lameths, Duport, d'Aiguillon, de Noailles, &c., were indirectly aimed at contemporary English nobles of the class of the Duke of Bedford, Lord Lansdowne, Lord Stanhope, and Lord Lauderdale, who whilst inflated with exaggerated Whig sentiments of liberty, had long disavowed the Whig principle of acting in connexion, and effectually ruined the political power of the party to which they professed to belong. Cp. vol. i. pp. 150 sqq.

L. 31. *to be attached,* &c. Cp. Pope, Essay on Man, iv. 361 sqq.

L. 32. *the first principle of public affections.* See p. 107, l. 9 sqq. The argument may be traced in Cic. De Officiis, Lib. i. c. 17. Since Burke's time, it has become a trite commonplace. Dr. Blair wrote a whole sermon upon it. So Robert Hall; "The order of nature is ever from particulars to generals. As in the operations of intellect we proceed from the contemplation of individuals to the formation of general abstractions, so in the developement of the passions in like manner we advance from private to public affections; from the love of parents, brothers, and sisters, to those more expanded regards which embrace the immense society of human kind." Sermon on Modern Infidelity. On the other hand, the private [323] affections are attacked, with the same metaphysical weapons, but with a very different object, by Jonathan Edwards and Godwin.

L. 33. *first link*, &c. Cp. note to vol. i. p. 148, l. 1.

P. 137, L. 7. *the then Earl of Holland.* "This (reprieving Lord Goring, and not Lord Holland) may be a caution to us against the affectation of popularity, when you see the issue of it in this noble gentleman, who was as full of generosity and courtship to all sorts of persons, and readiness to help the oppressed, and to stand for the rights of the people, as any person of his quality in this nation. Yet this person was by the representatives of the people given up to execution for treason; and another lord, who never made profession of being a friend to liberty, either civil or spiritual, and exceeded the Earl as much in his crimes as he came short of him in his popularity, the life of this lord was spared by the people." (Whitelock, March 8, 1649.) The bounties prodigally bestowed on him were a reward for his carrying out as chief-justice in eyre the illegal claims made by Charles I., in virtue of the forestal rights (cp. vol. i. p. 77, l. 7). He became one of the leaders of the Parliament party, but deserted them, and paid the penalty with his life. Hallam charges him with ingratitude to both king and queen.

L. 24. *when men of rank,* &c. The allusion is again to those noblemen who patronised the Revolution Society.

P. 138, L. 2. *if the terror, the ornament of their age.* Burke perhaps had in mind the well-known epitaph of Richelieu (cp. l. 25), by Des Bois, in which he is described as "Tam saeculi sui tormentum quam ornamentum."

> Born to subdue insulting tyrants' rage,
> The ornament and terror of the age.
> > (Halifax, Lines on William III.)

L. 7. *great bad men.* So Pope, Essay on Man, iv. 284;

> Cromwell, damn'd to everlasting fame.

Burke perhaps had in mind Milton, Par. Lost, ii. 5;

NOTES

Satan exalted sat, by merit rais'd
To that bad eminence.

L. 8. *a favourite poet.* Waller; "Panegyric to my Lord Protector." After the Restoration, Waller made a panegyric upon Charles; and when the king satirically remarked that that on Cromwell was the better one, replied, with witty servility, that poets succeeded better in dealing with fiction than with truth. Waller was of kin to the Protector through his mother, a sister of John Hampden. Burke was familiar with the domestic history of the Wallers from the circumstance that his estate was in the same parish as theirs (Beaconsfield).

L. 19. *destroying angel.* Cp. vol. i. p. 214, l. 23.

IBID. *smote the country—communicated to it the force and energy,* &c. Similarly Junius, Feb. 6, 1771; "With all his crimes, he (Cromwell) had the spirit of an Englishman. The conduct of such a man must always be an exception to vulgar rules. He had abilities sufficient to reconcile contradictions, and to make a great nation at the same time unhappy and formidable." [324] In the Letter to a Member of the National Assembly the policy of Cromwell is illustrated by his rejecting meaner men of his own party, and choosing Hale as his chief-justice.

L. 29. *how very soon France,* &c. France has always been distinguished for the most elastic internal powers. Burke in after times quoted in illustration of this the lines,

Per damna, per caedes, ab ipso
Ducit opes animumque ferro.

L. 33. *not slain the* mind *in their country.* Mackintosh retorts this dignified figure on the ministers whom Burke after the Revolution conceived it to be his duty to support.

P. 139, L. 6. *palsy.* Fr. *paralysie,* now generally disused, in favour of the original term *paralysis.*

L. 16. *levellers.* A term applied to the English Jacobins of the period of the Commonwealth.

L. 17. load *the edifice* = overload. So Oldham, 1st Satire on Jesuits;

Vassals to every ass that loads a throne.

L. 25. oratorial *flourish.* The spelling is correct.

L. 29. *occupation of an hair-dresser,* &c. Cp. Arist. Pol., Lib. iii. c. 5.

P. 140, L. 4. *of* that *sophistical,* &c. Cp. note to vol. i. p. 193, l. 6.

L. 15. *woe to the country,* &c. Burke's support of the Test Act has been adduced to show how little practical meaning there was in this tirade. The question, however, here, is one of political, not religious disability. The term "religious" (l. 17) appears only to allude to the established church.

P. 141, L. 3. *sortition or rotation.* Harrington, the English constitution-monger, made the latter an essential principle in his scheme. Milton, however, wished "that this wheel, or partial wheel in state, if it be possible, might be avoided, as having too much affinity with the wheel of fortune." It will hardly be credited that a practical member of Parliament and shrewd thinker like Soame Jenyns, approved the principle of sortition, and deliberately proposed to have an annual ministry chosen by lot from 30 selected members of the House of Peers, and 100 of the House of Commons! See his "Scheme for the Coalition of Parties," 1782. Well might Burke call that "one of the most critical periods in our annals" (Letter to a Noble Lord). Had the then proposed parliamentary reforms taken place, Burke thought that "not France, but England, would have had the honour of leading up the death-dance of Democratic Revolution. Other projects, exactly coincident in time with those, struck at the very existence of the kingdom under any constitution" (ib.).

L. 7. *road to eminence and power from obscure condition . . . not to be made too easy.* There is here possibly an allusion to the preceding generation, and the career of men like Lord Melcombe. The road was always easy enough in England, and by this time in most other countries. Struensee had governed Denmark. Writers had busied themselves in vain to discover the [325] grandfather of l'Hôpital. On the day when the States-General met in France, three out of eight ministers who composed the cabinet (Necker, Vergennes, and Sartine) were not of noble birth.

L. 13. *Virtue . . . never tried but by some difficulty*—περὶ τὸ χαλεπώτερον ἀεὶ καὶ τέχνη γίνεται καὶ ἀρετή. Arist. Eth., Lib. ii. c. 3. Cp. p. 272, l. 29 sqq.

L. 15. *its ability as well as its property.* "Jacobinism," wrote Burke several years afterwards, when the whole civilised world was in affright at the word, without understanding very well what it meant, "is the revolt of the enterprising talents of a country against its property."

L. 23. *the great masses which excite envy,* &c. Cp. the Letter to a Noble Lord, in which the vast property of the Duke of Bedford is used to illustrate this doctrine. The extract given in a previous note (to p. 113, l. 27) contains the substance of its argument.

P. 142, L. 1. *the power of perpetuating our property in our families,* &c. Burke alludes to the practice of family settlements.

L. 5. *grafts benevolence,* &c. Because it encourages a man to other objects than a selfish lavishment of his fortune on his private wishes. The expression is slightly altered from the 1st Edition.

L. 12. *sole judge of all property,* &c. See the motion relative to the Speech from the Throne, 14th June, 1784, in which this fact is used in justification of the disapproval, expressed by the Commons, of the corruption and intimidation employed by the ministers and peers. The judicial power of the Lords is historically traced by Hallam, ch. xiii.

L. 26. *constitution of a kingdom—a problem in arithmetic.* Notwithstanding the sarcasm, which became very popular, the principle has now been recognised not only in England, but in most constitutional governments.

> That British liberty's an empty name
> Till each fair burgh, numerically free,
> Shall choose its members by the Rule of Three.
> Canning, New Morality.

Rousseau's theory, however, referred not to the rule of three, but to the rule of the *square root!* See "Contrat Social," Liv. iii. ch. 1.

L. 28. *lamp-post.* (Lanterne), alluding to the summary executions by the mob (see infra, p. 166), which began, during the riots which preceded the 14th of July, with punishing thieves by dragging them to the Grève, and hanging them by the ropes which were used to fasten the lanterns. De Launay, De Losme, Solbay, and Flesselles, were soon afterwards "lynched" in the same way.

P. 143, L. 12. *completed its work . . . accomplished its ruin.* Cp. a similar expression, vol. i. p. 207, l. 11.

L. 27. *dismembered their country.* Cp. infra, p. 192, l. 27.

P. 145, L. 1. *ever-waking vigilance.* Cp. note to vol. i. p. 76, l. 30. The allusion is of course to the "fair Hesperian tree," which

> Laden with blooming gold, had need the guard
> Of dragon-watch and uninchanted eye.—Comus, l. 393.

[326] **L. 13.** milky *good-nature* = childish. So "milky gentleness," Shakspeare, King Lear, Act i. scene 4. Cp. vol. i. p. 100, l. 10, "milkiness

of infants." The expression seems to be adopted from the Spectator (No. 177), speaking of constitutional good-nature, "which Mr. Dryden somewhere calls a milkiness of blood."

L. 14. *heroic fortitude towards the sufferers.* Cp. note to vol. i. p. 149, l. 27. This idea, often repeated by Burke, is derived from the "Thoughts on Various Subjects," by Pope and Swift: "I never knew any man in my life, who could not bear another's misfortunes perfectly like a Christian."

L. 19. *Is our monarchy,* &c. By the next page it will be seen that Dr. Price had marked as the fundamental grievance of the English people the inadequacy of popular representation. Could Burke really wish to be understood as declaring that a reform of Parliament in England would lead to the changes here set out? If so, what is the meaning of the high praise he proceeds to bestow on the English people for their steadiness of temperament? It is, however, superfluous to point out all the logical excesses of a heated advocate.

L. 22. *done away.* Strictly correct. So to do out, do up, do off, do on (dout, dup, doff, don), &c. The modern phrase, to "do away *with,*" has arisen from confusion with the interjectional expression, "Away with." Spenser;

To do away vain doubt, and needless dread.

L. 23. *house of lords to be voted useless.* Alluding to the Resolution of the Commons, Feb. 6, 1649, "That the House of Peers in Parliament is useless and dangerous, and ought to be abolished." On that day the Lords met, and adjourned "till ten o'clock to-morrow." That morrow, says Mr. Hallam, was the 25th of April, 1660.

L. 29. *land-tax — malt-tax — naval strength.* The land-tax and malt-duty were the only imposts included in the estimate of "ways and means" for raising the "supplies," which provided for the navy, ordnance, army, and miscellaneous services. Taken together, these imposts did rather more than pay for the navy, which then cost about two-and-half millions annually.

P. 146, L. 3. *in the increase.* i. e. in the form of an increase.

L. 16. *dull sluggish race—mediocrity of freedom.* Cp. Letter to Elliott; "My praises of the British government, loaded with all its incumbrances; clogged with its peers and its beef; its parsons and its pudding; its commons and its beer; and its dull slavish liberty of going about just as one pleases," &c.

NOTES

L. 19. *began by affecting to admire,* &c. There was not much in this. The excellence of the British constitution consisted not in its formal, but in its moral basis; in the unity, the cordial recognition, and the substantial justice, which subsisted between class and class, and this was beyond the reach of French politicians. Formally regarded, not only the French leaders, but some English philosophers, not without a certain justice, always "looked upon it with a sovereign contempt." It is this moral basis which [327] Burke, following his master Aristotle, is always insisting on as the essence of political life and stability.

L. 21. *the friends of your National Assembly,* &c. The theory of the English constitution was first systematically attacked by Bentham, in his Fragment on Government, 1775.

L. 24. *has discovered,* &c. It is notorious that England at this time was not free in the sense in which it has now been free for forty years.

L. 31. *representation is partial—possesses liberty only partially.* For several years such phrases had been so dinned into the ears of the English nation, as to become a byword for the wits. Of the abstract principle that all men are born free, Soame Jenyns says, "This is so far from being true, that the first infringement of their liberty is being born at all; which is imposed upon them without their consent, given either by themselves or their representatives." Disquisition on Government and Civil Liberty.

P. 147, L. 15. *treat the humbler part of the community with the greatest contempt.* Nowhere are more flagrant examples of this to be found than in Milton. When he finds or imagines the mass of the people to be with him, he treats them with the greatest respect; when there is a reaction, or a chance of it, they become "the blockish vulgar"—"the people, exorbitant and excessive in all their notions"—"the mad multitude"—"a miserable, credulous, deluded thing called the vulgar" (Eikonoklastes)—"a multitude, ready to fall back, or rather to creep back, to their once abjured and detested thraldom of kingship"— "the inconsiderate multitude" (Mode of Establishing a Free Commonwealth)—"the simple laity" (Tenure of Kings). The mild Spenser calls the people "the rascal many." So the chorus in Samson;

> Nor do I name of men the common rout,
> That wand'ring loose about,
> Grow up and perish, like the summer flie,
> Heads without name no more remembered.

"Tout peuple," wrote Marat, "est naturellement moutonnier" (Journal de Marat, Mars 5, 1793). On the contempt of the demagogues of the ancient world for their audience, cp. Arbuthnot's (Swift's?) paper "Concerning the Altercation or Scolding of the Ancients."

L. 22. *under which we have long prospered.* See Bentham's Book of Fallacies, or Sydney Smith's review of it, for a consideration of this trite argument.

L. 23. *perfectly adequate,* &c. "If there is a doubt, whether the House of Commons represents perfectly the whole commons of Great Britain (I think there is none) there can be no question but that the Lords and Commons together represent the sense of the whole people to the crown, and to the world." Third Letter on a Regicide Peace.

P. 148, L. 19. *that house is no representative of the people at all, even in semblance or in form.* Directly at variance with all constitutional history, Selden maintains that the Lords "sit for the commonwealth." In the "Present [328] Discontents" (vol. i. p. 118, l. 11), Burke maintains Selden's view (see Introd. to vol. i. p. 20). It would be idle to maintain that Burke's views had suffered no change: but the change was certainly not produced by the French Revolution. It dated from the claim set up by the Whig rivals of Burke's party, when in office, and speaking through the Throne, to convey the sense of the people to the House of Commons, in a manner implying distrust and reproach; and this claim was supported by the doctrine that the Lords represented the people, as well as the Commons. Burke singled out specially for refutation on this occasion the following passage from Lord Shelburne's Speech of April 8, 1778; "I will never submit to the doctrines I have heard this day from the woolsack, that the other House [House of Commons] are the only representatives and guardians of the people's rights; I boldly maintain the contrary—I say this House [House of Lords] *is equally the representatives of the people.*" It was not that the exigencies of party warfare induced Burke to relinquish his position; it was that the doctrine was now inspired with an entirely different meaning. Its assertion in the Present Discontents, and its denial fourteen years after, were made with the same intention, that of preventing liberty from being wounded through its forms (see Motion relative to the Speech from the Throne, 1784). It would be more correct to keep to the Whig form of words and say that the Crown and Lords are *trustees* for the people.

L. 25. *built . . . upon a basis not more solid,* &c. Cp. vol. i. p. 213, l. 28, p. 270, l. 31.

L. 31. *Something they must destroy,* &c. Burke altered the commencement of this paragraph, which stands thus in the 1st Edition; "Some of them are so heated with their particular religious theories, that they

Notes

give more than hints that the fall of the civil powers, with all the dreadful consequences of that fall, provided they might be of service to their theories, could not be unacceptable to them," &c. This was done to make clearer the serious charge here brought against Priestley, which was the beginning of the persecution which finally drove him from the country.

P. 149, L. 4. *appear quite certain.* Convinced, however, only by the harmless enthusiasm which thinks it necessary to attach a specific meaning to the visions of the seer in the Apocalypse. It was not until 1794 that Dr. Priestley offered this apology for it.

L. 6. *a man . . . of great authority.* Dr. Priestley. The offensive passage is that which concludes his formidable "History of the Corruptions of Christianity," and finishes the considerations addressed to the advocates for the civil establishment of religion, and especially to Bishop Hurd. It is as follows; "It is nothing but the *alliance* of the kingdom of Christ with the kingdoms of this world (an alliance which our Lord Himself expressly disclaimed) that supports the grossest corruptions of Christianity; and perhaps we must wait for the fall of the civil powers before this most unnatural alliance be broken. Calamitous, no doubt, will that time be. But what convulsion in the political world ought to be a subject of lamentation, if it [329] be attended with so desirable an event? May the kingdom of God, and of Christ, (that which I conceive to be intended in the Lord's Prayer,) truly and fully come, though all the kingdoms in the world be removed in order to make way for it!" The publication of this in 1782, at or very near one of the most critical periods of our domestic history, when a religious enthusiasm which had already reduced much of the metropolis to ashes, threatened to ally itself with an equally formidable political element (cp. note to p. 141, l. 3), justifies much of the obloquy that followed when Burke called attention to it.

L. 7. *alliance between church and state.* The well-known doctrine of Bishop Warburton, alluded to post, p. 188, l. 7 sqq.

L. 8. *fall of the* civil powers. The meaning of this was not to be mistaken. Immediately before, Priestley has been asking why Lutheranism and Anglicanism had been established, while the Anabaptists of Münster, and the Socinians, had been persecuted? "I know of no reason why, but that the opinions of Luther and Cranmer had the sanction of the *civil powers,* which those of Socinus and others of the same age, and who were equally well qualified to judge for themselves, had not."

REFLECTIONS ON THE REVOLUTION IN FRANCE

L. 10. *Calamitous no doubt,* &c. Dr. Priestley on the 28th of Feb., 1794, the day appointed for a general fast, preached at the Gravel-pit Meeting in Hackney a sermon, entitled "The Present State of Europe compared with Ancient Prophecies," in which he repeats and justifies the offensive paragraph, and warns his congregation of the "danger to the civil powers of Europe, in consequence of their connexion with antichristian ecclesiastical systems." He also apologised for it in a letter dated Northumberland, Nov. 10, 1802, addressed to the editor of the Monthly Magazine, by saying that it was not intended for England, but for Europe generally, "especially those European States which had been parts of the Roman Empire, but were then in communion with the Church of Rome. . . . Besides that the interpretation of prophecy ought to be free to all, it is the opinion, I believe, of every commentator that these states are doomed to destruction." In an Appendix to the Fast Sermon, he prints a long extract from Hartley's "Observations on Man" (1749), in which the fall of the civil and ecclesiastical powers was predicted with similar coolness. "It would be great rashness," says Hartley in his conclusion, "to fix a time for the breaking of the storm that hangs over our heads, as it is blindness and infatuation not to see it, nor to be aware that it may break; and yet this infatuation has always attended all falling states."

L. 19. possessed *by these notions.* In the sense of diabolical possession. "An obstinate man," says Butler, "does not hold opinions, but they hold him; for when once he is possessed with an error, 'tis like the devil, not to be cast out but with great difficulty."

L. 22. *solid test of long experience.* Cp. note to p. 147, l. 22, ante.

L. 25. *wrought under-ground a mine . . . the "rights of men."* Locke and Sidney were the founders of the school of the "Rights of Men," and first [330] made the Rights of the Englishman, in theory, ancillary to the general pretensions to liberty on behalf of the *man.* The argument of Sidney is first, that all men have by nature certain rights, second, that Englishmen have ever enjoyed those rights. But how was it possible for Frenchmen to assert a similar claim? The "rights of man" were literally the only basis in reasoning on which their claims could have been founded. In England, on the other hand, the particular liberties of the subject were so well established, that Sidney himself rests the great body of his arguments on the rights of the Englishman. He is liable, as much as Burke, to the very charge which Rousseau brings against Grotius; "Sa plus constante manière de raisonner est d'établir toujours le droit par le fait."

NOTES

P. 150, L. 8. *Illa se jactet in aula,* &c. Virg. Aen. i. 140.

L. 10. *Levanter* = a tempestuous East wind.

L. 11. *break up the fountains of the great deep.* Cp. note to vol. i. p. 186, l. 10.

L. 15. *the* real *rights of men.* The profound and just remarks which follow are a fine example of that "dower of spanning wisdom" in which Burke was so rich, and expressed with an unusual strength and simplicity of construction.

L. 22. *as between their fellows*—i. e. as between themselves and their fellows.

L. 24. *means of making their industry fruitful*—i. e. to the occupation of the soil, without prejudice to the rights of the owner. Cp. vol. i. p. 247, l. 26.

L. 25. *acquisitions of their parents.* Without prejudice, of course, to the right of the parent to dispose of it himself. Cp. ante, p. 142, l. 1.

L. 27. *instruction in life, consolation in death*—alluding to the Church establishment.

L. 31. *In this partnership,* &c. This happy illustration is an afterthought, and is wanting in the First Edition.

P. 151, L. 3. *deny to be amongst the direct original rights,* &c. Equality of power might even be denied to be among the physical *possibilities* of civil society.

L. 7. *offspring of convention.* Burke here admits the fundamental doctrines relating to the Social Contract, and proceeds to show how they change their significance in practice.

L. 14. *one of the first motives to civil society,* &c. The process is traced with his usual clearness by Hooker, Ecc. Pol., Book i. § 10. Burke seems to have in mind Hooker's disciple Locke, Treat. of Government, Book ii. ch. 7, § 90; "For the end of civil society being to avoid and remedy those inconveniences of the state of nature, which necessarily follow from every man's being a judge in his own case," &c.

L. 16. *judge in his own cause.* Cp. vol. i. p. 252, l. 8, and the "Letter to the Sheriffs of Bristol," in which the argument from this principle is expanded and applied to the relations of states between themselves. "When any community is subordinately connected with another, the great danger of [331] the connexion is the extreme pride and self-complacency of the superior which in all matters of controversy will probably decide in its own favour," &c.

L. 22. *rights of an uncivil and a civil state together.* Cp. Lucretius, v. 1147;

> Acrius ex ira quod enim se quisque parabat
> Ulcisci, quam nunc concessum est legibus aequis,
> Hanc ob rem est homines pertaesum vi colere aevum.

Other illustrations from the classics are given in Grotius, Lib. ii. c. 20.

L. 25. *secure some liberty, makes a surrender in trust of the whole of it.* "Il me semble que l'homme, sortant de l'état naturel, pour arriver à l'état social, perd son indépendance pour acquérir plus de sûreté. L'homme quitte ses compagnons des bois qui ne le gênent pas, mais qui peuvent le dévorer, pour venir trouver une société qui ne le dévorera pas, mais qui doit le gêner. Il stipule ses intérêts du mieux qu'il peut, et, lorsqu'il entre dans une bonne constitution, il céde le moins de son indépendance, et obtient le plus de sûreté qu'il est possible." Rivarol, Journal Politique. Liberty is a compromise between independence and security. This "surrender in trust" resembles the surrender, in the contract of insurance, of a portion of your property, for the security of the whole.

L. 27. *not made in virtue of natural rights.* Cp. note to vol. i. p. 100, l. 23.

P. 152, L. 4. *even in the mass and body,* &c. "With all respect for popular assemblies be it spoken," says Swift, "it is hard to recollect one folly, infirmity, or vice, to which a single man is subjected, and from which a body of commons, either collective or represented, can be wholly exempt." Contests and Discussions in Athens and Rome, ch. iv.

L. 7. *power out of themselves.* Compare this with the trivial sophism of Sieyès, "Il ne faut pas placer le régulateur hors de la machine." Burke truly says elsewhere; "An ignorant man, who is not fool enough to meddle with his clock, is however sufficiently confident to think he can safely take to pieces, and put together at his pleasure, a moral machine of another guise, importance, and complexity, composed of far other wheels, and springs, and balances, and counteracting and co-operating powers. Men little think how immorally they act in meddling with what they do not understand." Rivarol says, in the same view, "Rien ne ressemble moins à une balance que la machine du gouvernement; rien ne ressemble moins à un équilibre que la marche des corps politiques," &c. Oeuvres, vol. iv. p. 265.

L. 10. *restraints on men—among their rights.* Cp. ante, p. 93, l. 21.

L. 21. *most delicate and complicated skill.* Cp. note to p. 152, l. 7.

L. 26. *recruits* = fresh supplies of nourishment.

L. 27. *What is the use,* &c. Observe the close similarity to Aristotle.

P. 153, L. 1. *real effects of moral causes.* "Moral" is used as commonly by Burke, for the contrary of "physical."

[332] **L. 14.** *More experience than any person can gain in his whole life.* The democratical theory appears to be that political judgment comes to a man with puberty. The truth is, that like practical wisdom in private matters, it comes to none who have not laboriously worked for it, and therefore to most people not at all.

L. 16. *pulling down an edifice.* "To construct," wrote Burke six years before, "is a matter of skill; to demolish, force and fury are sufficient." Similar expressions are used by Soame Jenyns.

L. 19. approved *utility* = proved.

L. 21. *like rays of light.* An admirable illustration. Cp. Bacon's observation that the human understanding is not a "dry light," but imbued with the colours of the will and passions.

L. 34. *ignorant of their trade.* Cp. infra, p. 263, l. 23.

P. 154, L. 12. *in proportion as they are metaphysically true,* &c. Burke takes up a cant paradox of the day. Soame Jenyns; "It is a certain though a strange truth, that in politics all principles which are speculatively right, are practically wrong; the reason of which is, that they proceed on a supposition that men act rationally; which being by no means true, all that is built on so false a foundation, on experiment falls to the ground." Reflections on Several Subjects. "Metaphysics" was commonly applied as a term of reproach by English writers after the promulgation of the philosophy of Locke, and especially so used by the Essayists.

L. 16. *balances, compromises.* Cp. vol. i. p. 278, l. 29.

L. 21. *denominations.* In the arithmetical sense = numbers.

L. 22. *right—power.* Cp. note to p. 107, l. 18, ante.

L. 27. *first of all virtues, prudence* = φρόνησις. Cp. Arist. Eth., Lib. vi. c. 8, &c. In a previous work Burke calls prudence "the God of this lower world," perhaps in allusion to Juv. Sat. x. 365.

L. 29. *Liceat perire poetis,* &c. Hor. de Arte Poet. 465, 466.

REFLECTIONS ON THE REVOLUTION IN FRANCE

IBID. *one of them.* Empedocles. The allusion is of course to him in his philosophical rather than his poetical character.

L. 34. *or divine.* The allusion is to Dr. Price, as may be seen from the opening of the next paragraph. Burke means that at the end of an honourable career, Price was playing the fool, like the philosopher in the legend. Cp. Butler, Fragments;

> Empedocles, to be esteem'd a God,
> Leapt into Aetna, with his sandals shod,
> That b'ing blown out, discover'd what an ass
> The great philosopher and juggler was,
> That to his own new deity sacrific'd,
> And was himself the victim and the priest.

So Milton, Par. Lost, iii. 469;

> Others came single; he who to be deem'd
> A god, leap'd fondly into *Aetna* flames,
> Empedocles.

[333] **P. 155, L. 12.** *cantharides.* The Spanish or blistering fly, sometimes taken internally as a stimulant.

L. 14. *relaxes the spring.* Burke often employs this image, which was very fashionable in the times when the most usual illustration of a government was some piece of inanimate mechanism.

L. 18. *cum perimit saevos,* &c. Juv. vii. 151.

L. 22. *almost all the* high-bred *republicans*—i. e. *extreme.* Cp. vol. i. p. 76, l. 11, &c., and note. The Bedford Whigs, the Grenville Whigs (excepting their head, Lord Temple), and finally the party of Lord Chatham, had yielded in succession to the attraction of the Court party. This high-bred republicanism, extending even to equality of rank and property, seems to have been much in vogue in the reign of Anne, when it was often advanced in Parliament, fortified by the abstract reasoning to which Burke was so hostile. Its currency was commonly laid to the account of the writings of Locke; but it is easy to trace it to much earlier and more general causes. A democratical tone was frequently assumed by Whig politicians in the succeeding reigns, in order to conciliate popular favour.

L. 26. *those of us,* &c. The Rockingham party.

L. 28. *Hypocrisy,* &c. Cp. vol. i. p. 151, l. 2, and note.

L. 34. *civil and legal resistance.* Cp. with this paragraph, the passage in the "Letter to the Sheriffs of Bristol" in which the Party system is defended against the attacks of "those who pretend to be strong as-sertors of liberty." "This moral levelling is a servile principle. It leads to practical passive obedience far better than all the doctrines which the pliant accommodation of theology to power has ever produced. It cuts up by the roots, not only all idea of forcible resistance, but even of civil opposition."

P. 156, L. 4. *think lightly of all public principle.* See the description of the process of *Ratting* at the end of the "Observations on a late State of the Nation" (1769).

P. 157, L. 13. *well-placed sympathies.* Cp. note to vol. i. p. 153, l. 2.

L. 23. *still unanimating repose of public prosperity.* "Still" is an adverb = ever. Cp. ante, note to p. 146, l. 16.

L. 27. *Pisgah of his pulpit.* Deut. xxxiv. 1.

L. 26. *Peters had not the fruits,* &c. He was tried at the Restoration, and executed with other regicides at Charing Cross.

P. 158, L. 28. *Another of these reverend gentlemen.* Who this was does not appear. Mr. Rutt, the laborious editor and annotator of Dr. Priestley, notices the quotation, but gives no information. The writer alluded to may perhaps be the person quoted in the foot-note at p. 181.

P. 159, L. 34. *unmanly.* A characteristic epithet with Burke.

P. 160, L. 2. *well-born* = generous, liberal, Gr. εὐφυής.

L. 5. *procession of American savages.* A reminiscence of Burke's read-ing in the preparation of one of his early works, the "Account of Euro-pean Settlements in America." See that work, part ii. ch. 4.

IBID. *entering into Onondaga.* An Indian village in the western part of what [334] is now the State of New York, which was the central station of the French Jesuit missionaries, in whose accounts these scenes are described. See "Relation de ce qui est passé, &c., au pays de la Nouvelle France és années 1655 et 1656," by J. de Quens, and Bancroft, Hist. U.S. vol. iii. p. 143 sqq.

L. 8. *women as ferocious as themselves.* "The women, forgetting the human as well as the female nature, and transformed into something worse than furies, act their parts, and even out-do the men in this scene of horror." Sett. in America, vol. i. p. 198. It is unnecessary to illustrate this by the incidents of the Revolution.

L. 21. *their situation.* That of absolute dependence on the will of an organisation of mobs.

L. 25. *foreign republic.* The city of Paris.

L. 26. *whose constitution,* &c. The municipal government of Paris, which had passed out of the hands of the 300 electors, was at this time shared between 60 departments. Each department was a caricature of a Greek democratic state, was considered by its inhabitants as a sovereign power, and passed resolutions, which had the force of laws within its limits. This division into 60 departments was first introduced to facilitate the election to the States-General; but the easy means which it afforded of summoning the people of each district upon short notice, and of communicating a show of regularity and unanimity to their proceedings, made it too useful a system to be discarded. Much of that appearance of order and government which characterises the first year of the Revolution is due rather to this device, than to that self-restraint which made "anarchy tolerable" in Massachusetts. (See vol. i. pp. 244–45.)

L. 26. *emanated neither from the charter of their king,* &c. Having arisen out of temporary and mechanical arrangements. Necker, however, had by a grave error in policy recognised the 300 electors as a legal body. Their functions properly extended only to the choosing of representatives in the States-General; and they were entrusted with power by the people on the 13th of July merely because they were the only body in whom the public could immediately confide.

L. 28. *an army not raised either by the authority,* &c. The National Guards, formed in haste after the dismission of Necker on the 11th of July. "Thirty thousand citizens, totally unaccustomed to arms, were soon seen armed at all points, and in a few hours training assumed some appearance of order and discipline. The French Guards now shewed the benefits of their late education and improvements; they came in a body to tender their services to the people."

L. 31. *There they sit,* &c. The first edition represented *all* the moderate members as having been driven away. "There they sit, after a gang of assassins had driven away all the men of moderate minds and moderating authority among them, and left them as a sort of dregs and refuse, under the apparent lead of those in whom they do not so much as pretend to [335] have any confidence. There they sit, in mockery of legislation, repeating in resolutions the words of those whom they detest and despise. Captives themselves, they compel a captive king,"

&c. M. de Menonville, one of the moderate party, wrote to Burke on the 17th of November, to point out the inaccuracy of this, and some other statements; and Burke in the next edition corrected it. "Some of the errors you point out to me in my printed letter are really such. One only I find to be material. It is corrected in the edition I take the liberty of sending to you." Letter to a Member of the National Assembly, Jan. 19, 1791. In this letter he made them ample amends by a glowing panegyric. "Sir, I do look on you as true martyrs; I regard you as soldiers who act far more in the spirit of our Commander-in-Chief, and the Captain of our salvation, than those who have left you; though I must first bolt myself very thoroughly, and know that I can do better, before I can answer *them*." He proceeds while commending Abbé Maury, Cazalès, &c., who remained at their post, to apologise for those who, like Mounier and Lally-Tollendal, had abandoned it.

P. 161, L. 4. *decided before they are debated.* The clubs governed in the departments of Paris, and through them, in the National Assembly.

L. 9. *all conditions, tongues and nations.* Aristocrats and clergymen joined and even took the lead in these assemblies. Germans, Italians, Englishmen, Swiss, and Spaniards were found among them. The greater part of the Central Committee at the Évêché were not Frenchmen.

L. 14. *Academies . . . set up in all the places of public resort.* The allusion is to the *Conciliabules*. "The Parisians," says Mercier, "have wished to imitate the English, who meet in taverns, and discuss the most important affairs of the state; but that did not take, because every one wished to preside at these meetings."

L. 24. *Embracing in their arms,* &c. Burke refers to the circumstances attending the condemnation, for a bank-note forgery, of the brothers Agasse, which occurred in the middle of January, 1790. Dr. Guillotin had some time previously proposed to the Assembly to inflict the punishment of death in a painless manner, and to relieve the relations of the criminal from the feudal taint of felony. The Abbé Pépin, on this occasion, procured the enactment of the last of these changes; and while the criminals lay under sentence of hanging, their brother and cousin, with the view of marking this triumph of liberty, were promoted to be lieutenants in the Grenadier Company of the Battalion of National Guards for the district of St. Honoré, on which occasion, in defiance of public decency and natural feeling, they were publicly feasted and complimented. See Mr. Croker's Essay on the Guillotine in the Quarterly Review for December, 1843.

L. 34. Explode *them* = hoot off, reject, Lat. explodo. Cp. "exploding hiss," Par. Lost, x. 546.

P. 162, L. 3. *gallery . . . house.* Alluding to the English House of Commons.

L. 5. *Nec color imperii,* &c. Lucan, Phars. ix. 207 (*erat* for *erit*). From [336] the gloomy presages put into the mouth of Cato, on the death of Pompey; from which are also taken the lines quoted in vol. i. p. 206.

L. 6. *power given them . . . to subvert and to destroy.* The allusion seems to be to the expression so common in the Apocalypse (see ch. xiii. 7, &c.).

L. 8. *none to construct.* See the Second Part of the work, in which their efforts to construct are criticised.

L. 13. *institute* = institution.

LL. 22, 24. *"Un beau jour." "That the vessel of the state,"* &c. Bailly and Mirabeau, infra, p. 167, note.

L. 29. *slaughter of innocent gentlemen in their houses.* Foulon and Berthier, who were, however, murdered by the *lanterne* at the Grève, "with every circumstance of refined insult and cruelty which could have been exhibited by a tribe of cannibals."

L. 30. *the blood spilled was not the most pure.* The remark of Barnave, when Lally-Tollendal was describing this horrid scene, and Mirabeau told him "it was a time to think rather than to feel."

P. 163, L. 6. *felicitation on the present New Year.* Alluding to the address presented to the king and queen on the 3rd of January by a deputation of 60 members of the Assembly. "They (the Assembly) look forward to the happy day, when appearing in a body before a prince, the friend of the people, they shall present to him a collection of laws calculated for his happiness, and the happiness of all the French; when their respectful affection shall entreat a beloved king to forget the disorders of a tempestuous epoch," &c.

L. 18. *frippery.* In the proper sense of old clothing furbished up for second sale. Cp. the French words, friper, fripier, friperie.

IBID. *still in the old cut.* "Those French fashions, which of late years have brought their principles, both with regard to religion and government, a little in question." Lord Chesterfield, The World, No. 146 (1755).

L. 27. *ordinary* = chaplain.

NOTES

L. 34. *leze nation.* The new name given by the Assembly to the offence of treason against the nation, which was put under the cognisance of the Chatelet. It is imitated from the name lèse majesté (laesa majestas, treason).

P. 164, L. 6. *balm of hurt minds.* Macbeth, Act ii. sc. 2.

L. 22. *the centinel at her door.* M. de Miomandre. "After bravely resisting for a few minutes, finding himself entirely overpowered, he opened the queen's door, and called out with a loud voice, *Save the queen, her life is aimed at! I stand alone against two thousand tigers!* He soon after sunk down covered with wounds, and was left for dead."

L. 25. *cut down.* He recovered, however, from his wounds.

L. 27. *pierced . . . the bed.* This has been denied. It is impossible to say whether it is true.

P. 165, L. 5. *Two had been selected, &c.* M. de Huttes and M. Varicourt, two of the guards.

[337] **L. 21.** *one of the old palaces.* The Tuileries, where the King was whilst Burke was writing.

P. 166, L. 16. *fifth monarchy.* Cp. note to p. 149, l. 6, ante. The fifth monarchy was the dream of a large sect of enthusiasts in the Puritan times.

L. 18. *in the midst of this joy.* An allusion to Lucretius, iv. 1129;

.... medio de fonte leporum
Surgit amari aliquid, quod in ipsis floribus angat.

L. 24. *a groupe of regicide . . . What hardy pencil, &c.* Burke only too clearly foresaw what was to happen. In his next piece on French affairs, the "Letter to a Member of the National Assembly," he repeats his belief that they would assassinate the king as soon as he was no longer necessary to their design. He thought, however, that the queen would be the first victim. Cp. infra, p. 169, l. 17. In the Second Letter on a Regicide Peace, he defends his anticipation on this point. "It was accident, and the momentary depression of that part of the faction, that gave to the husband the happy priority in death."

P. 169, L. 13. *offspring of a sovereign, &c.* Maria Theresa.

L. 15. *Roman matron.* Burke had in mind some story such as that of Lucretia.

IBID. *that in the last extremity, &c.* Alluding to the queen's carrying poison about with her.

Reflections on the Revolution in France

L. 18. *It is now,* &c. Burke to Sir P. Francis, Feb. 20, 1790; "I tell you again, that the recollection of the manner in which I saw the Queen of France, in the year 1774, and the contrast between that brilliancy, splendour, and beauty, with the prostrate homage of a nation to her — and the abominable scene of 1789, which I was describing, *did* draw tears from me, and wetted my paper. These tears came again into my eyes, almost as often as I looked at the description; they may again. You do not believe this fact, nor that these are my real feelings: but that the whole is affected, or, as you express it, downright foppery."

L. 21. *just above the horizon.* Cp. a similar image in vol. i. p. 208, l. 1.

L. 27. *titles of veneration,* i. e. that of queen.

L. 28. *sharp antidote.* Cp. second note to p. 169, l. 15.

L. 34. *the age of chivalry is gone.* This famous theatrical passage has been perhaps too roughly handled by the critics. The lament for chivalry is as old as the birth of what we regard as modern ideas. See the famous stanzas of Ariosto on the loyalty and frankness of the old knightly days.

IBID. *Sophisters* = sophists.

P. 170, L. 2. *generous loyalty.* Some readers of M. Taine may have been startled by his comment on the term *loyalty*—"MOT INTRADUI-SIBLE, qui désigne le sentiment de subordination, quand il est noble" (Les Écrivains Anglais Contemporains, p. 318). So completely has the idea been effaced from the French mind! The word "loyauté" has a different meaning.

L. 3. *proud submission.* The "modestie superbe" of the courtier is mentioned by Montesquieu, Liv. iv. ch. 2.

[338] **L. 5.** *the spirit of an exalted freedom.* This conclusion pervades the writings of Bolingbroke upon mediaeval English history, especially the reign of Edward III. It coincides also with the well-known conclusion of Gibbon, that the spirit of freedom breathes throughout the feudal institutions. So in Second Letter on Regicide Peace: "In all these old countries, the state has been made to the people, and not the people conformed to the state. . . . This comprehensive scheme virtually produced a degree of personal liberty in forms the most adverse to it. That liberty was formed, under monarchies stiled absolute, in a degree unknown to the ancient commonwealths."

L. 6. *nurse of manly sentiment and heroic enterprise, is gone.* "Ces vertus mâles qui nous seraient le plus nécessaires et que nous n'avons presque plus—un véritable esprit d'indépendance, le goût des grandes choses, la foi en nous-mêmes et dans une cause." De Tocqueville, Preface to Ancien Régime, p. ix.

L. 8. *that chastity of honour.* Bowles, Verses to Burke;

No, Burke! thy heart, by juster feelings led,
Mourns for the spirit of high Honour fled;
Mourns that Philosophy, abstract and cold,
With'ring should smite life's fancy-flowered mould;
And many a smiling sympathy depart,
That graced the sternness of the manly heart.

IBID. *felt a stain like a wound*—A reminiscence of South. "And if the conscience has not wholly lost its native tenderness, it will not only dread the infection of a wound, but also the aspersion of a blot." Sermon lxiv (Deliverance from Temptation the Privilege of the Righteous).

L. 10. *ennobled whatever it touched.* An allusion to the well-known expression in Johnson's Epitaph on Goldsmith, usually, but incorrectly, quoted as "Nihil tetigit quod non ornavit."

L. 11. *lost half its evil,* &c. One of Burke's old phrases, borrowed from the essayists. In Sett. in America, vol. i. p. 200, he says that civilisation, if it has "abated the force of some of the natural virtues," by the luxury which attends it, has "taken out likewise the sting of our natural vices, and softened the ferocity of the human race without enervating their courage." Cp. p. 240, l. 14. So Fourth Letter on Regicide Peace; "The reformed and perfected virtues, the polished mitigated vices, of a great capital." Cp. generally with this famous passage the following from the Fourth Letter on a Regicide Peace; "Morals, as they were— decorum, the great outguard of the sex, and the proud sentiment of honour, which makes virtue more respectable where it is, and conceals human frailty where virtue may not be, will be banished from this land of propriety, modesty, and reserve." The passage is cleverly plagiarised by Macaulay, Ess. on Hallam; "We look in vain for those qualities which lend a charm to the errors of high and ardent natures, for the generosity, the tenderness, the chivalrous delicacy, which ennoble appetites into passions, and impart to vice itself a portion of the majesty of virtue."

[339] **L. 17.** *It is this which has given its character to modern Europe.* "Chivalry, uniting with the genius of our policy, has probably suggested those peculiarities in the law of nations by which modern states

---

are distinguished from the ancient." Dr. Fergusson's Essay on the History of Civil Society (1767), p. 311.

L. 32. *obedience liberal.* Vol. i. p. 288, l. 27.

L. 33. *bland assimilation* = digestion. Two of Milton's phrases are here blended. Par. Lost, v. 4, 5, 412.

P. 171, L. 2. *decent drapery of life,* &c. The notion is Johnson's. "Life," he would say, "is barren enough surely, with all her trappings: let us therefore be cautious how we strip her." Mrs. Piozzi's Anecdotes. It is curious to trace here the influence which Johnson, with his zeal for subordination, his hatred to innovation, and his reverence for the feudal times, exercised upon Burke in his early years.

L. 3. *superadded ideas,* &c. Bowles, in his Verses to Burke, says of chivalry—

> Her milder influence shall she still impart,
> To decorate, but not disguise, the heart:
> To nurse the tender sympathies that play
> In the short sunshine of life's early way;
> For female worth and meekness to inspire
> Homage and love, and temper rude desire.

L. 5. *which the heart owns, and the understanding ratifies.* There seems here to be a reminiscence of Bishop Horsley's Sermon on the Poor (Sermon xxxv), May 18, 1786; "For although I should not readily admit that the proof of moral obligation cannot in any instance be complete unless the connection be made out between the action which the heart naturally approves, and that which a right understanding of the interests of mankind would recommend, (on the contrary—to judge practically of right and wrong, we should feel rather than philosophise; and we should act from sentiment rather than from policy) yet we surely acquiesce with the most cheerfulness in our duty, when we perceive how the useful and the fair are united in the same action."

L. 21. *cold hearts and muddy understandings.* A good parallel to Burke's observations on the philosophers is to be found in the fourth Book of the Dunciad, which shadows forth the ruin of society by men furnished with

A brain of feathers and a heart of lead.

Pope and Burke agree in making moral and intellectual decay proceed together under the delusion of improvement.

L. 23. *laws to be supported only by their own terrors . . . nothing is left*

Notes

which engages the affections. On this subject see the wise doctrines of Bishop Horsley, Sermon xii.

L. 27. *visto.* See note to vol. i. p. 178, l. 27.

IBID. *nothing but the gallows.* A curious coincidence with an old Italian poet:

[340] Vanno al giardino . . . . .
Risiede in mezzo il paretaio de Nemi
D'un pergolato, il quale a ogni corrente
Sostien, con quattro braccia di cavezza
Penzoloni, che sono una bellezza.
　　　　　　　Lippi, Malmantile Racquistato, cant. vi. st. 50.

"Paretaio de Nemi" is slang for gallows or gibbet.

L. 29. *mechanic* = mechanical, in malam partem.

P. 172, L. 3. *Non satis est,* &c. Hor. de Arte Poet. 99. A "Spectator" motto (No. 321). Cp. p. 311, l. 8 sqq.

L. 7. *But power,* &c. If in the concluding sentence we read "rulers" for "kings," we have a forcible statement of an ordinary historical process, which was about to be repeated in France.

L. 13. *by freeing kings from fear,* &c. The idea is borrowed from Hume; "But history and experience having since convinced us that this practice (tyrannicide) increases the jealousy and cruelty of princes, a Timoleon and a Brutus, though treated with indulgence on account of the prejudice of their times, are now considered as very improper models for imitation." Dissertation on the Passions. It may be remarked that Burke follows the fashion of his age, in treating "kings" as a political species. Selden, more profound in his distinctions, says, "Kings are all individual, this or that king: there is no species of kings."

L. 19. *Kings will be tyrants,* &c. This paragraph is quoted by Dr. Whately, in his *Rhetoric,* as a fine example of Method. Cp. note to vol. i. p. 123, l. 30.

L. 26. *prosperous state . . . owing to the spirit of our old manners.* Cp. the reflections of Cicero at the beginning of the Fifth Book of the Republic, which commences with the line of Ennius,

Moribus antiquis res stat Romana virisque.

L. 34. *Nothing is more certain,* &c. The addition made to this conclusion by Hallam, though not insisted on by Burke in the present passage, is quite consonant with his general views; "There are, if I may say so, three powerful spirits, which have from time to time moved over the face of the waters, and given a predominant impulse to the moral sentiments and energies of mankind. These are the spirits of LIBERTY, of RELIGION, and of HONOUR. It was the principal business of chivalry to cherish the last of these three." Middle Ages, chap. ix. part ii.

P. 173, L. 1. *this European world of ours.* The First Letter on a Regicide Peace contains a remarkable description of the unity of law, education, and manners in the Europe of the Middle Ages. "No citizen of Europe could be altogether an exile in any part of it. There was nothing more than a pleasing variety to recreate and instruct the mind, to enrich the imagination, and to meliorate the heart. When a man travelled or resided for health, pleasure, business, or necessity, from his own country, he never felt himself quite abroad."

[341] **L. 15.** *trodden down under the hoofs of a swinish multitude.* The idea is derived from St. Matthew vii. 6. The much resented expression "swinish multitude" afterwards became a toast with the English Jacobins.

L. 33. This note, together with those printed at pp. 209, 211, 212, 213, 245, seems to have been added by a subsequent editor from a copy of the work used by the author in his last years.

P. 174, L. 12. *whether you took them from us.* Such a view is inconsistent with a comparative knowledge of the facts of English and continental history. Burke perhaps alludes to the legendary chivalry of the Court of Arthur, of which Brittany had its share.

L. 13. *to you—we trace them best.* Mr. Hallam calls France "the fountain of chivalry."

L. 14. *gentis incunabula nostrae.* (cunabula.) Virg. Aen. iii. 105. The writer perhaps had in mind the expression of Cicero, "Montes patrios, incunabula nostra." Ep. Att. ii. 15.

L. 15. *when your fountain is choaked up,* &c. This presage has not been verified. England and Germany are likely to transmit to future generations much that is worth preserving of the spirit of chivalry.

L. 24. *a revolution in sentiments,* &c. "Il y a une révolution générale qui change le goût des esprits, aussi bien que les fortunes du monde." Rochefoucault, Maximes. Burke went so far as to say that the present one amounted to a "revolution in the constitution of the human mind." The fact is that the sentimental basis on which the estimation of political institutions rested was passing away. The true way of regarding the question is in the light of the change in English public opinion between 1815–1830.

L. 27. *forced to apologize,* &c. Notice the keenness and strength of the expression.

L. 31. *For this plain reason.* The phrase is from Pope's Essay on Man.

IBID. *because it is natural,* cp. p. 181, l. 27.

P. 175, L. 7. *Our minds are purified,* &c. From the well-known definition of Tragedy in the Poetics of Aristotle, ch. vi. 2. The work on the Sublime and Beautiful shows traces of the study of the Poetics. Cp. also Rhet., Lib. ii. ch. 8; Pol., Lib. viii. 7. 3.

L. 16. *Garrick . . . Siddons.* Burke was an enthusiastic lover of the stage. The former famous actor was among his most cherished friends. Fourth Letter on Regicide Peace; "My ever dear friend, Garrick, who was the most acute observer of nature I ever knew."

L. 28. *as they once did in the antient stage.* The allusion, as clearly appears by the context, is to the "hypothetical proposition" put by Euripides into the mouth of Eteocles (Phoen. 524);

εἴπερ γὰρ ἀδικεῖν χρή, τυραννίδος πέρι
κάλλιστον ἀδικεῖν, τἄλλα δ' εὐσεβεῖν χρεών.

Cicero (De Off. iii. 21) says that Caesar often repeated these lines. But [342] Burke's memory fails him when he says that the Athenian audience "rejected" them. Those which they thus condemned were the more harmless ones which occurred in a speech of Bellerophon;

εἰ δ' ἡ Κύπρις τοιοῦτον ὀφθαλμοῖς ὁρᾷ,
οὐ θαῦμ', ἔρωτας μυρίους αὐτὴν τρέφειν.

See Seneca, Epist. 115, Dindorf, Fr. Eur. No. 288, and Schlegel's Dramatic Literature, Lect. viii.

P. 176, L. 19. *fear more dreadful than revenge.* A striking prophecy of the horrors of the Reign of Terror.

L. 34. *to remit his prerogatives, and to call his people to a share of freedom.* If we regard the transactions between the king and the parliament of Paris, this is a clear misrepresentation. Such remissions of prerogative had been wrested from the king by the parliament. That body charged the king with having formed a fixed system for the overthrow of the established constitution, which had been in train ever since 1771. Burke, however, alludes to the institution of the provincial assemblies, and the work done by the Assembly of Notables (the

REFLECTIONS ON THE REVOLUTION IN FRANCE

abolition of the *corvée,* and of the restrictions on internal traffic, especially that in corn). The Notables also had before them a project for abolishing the *gabelles.*

P. 177, L. 5. *provide force . . . the remnants of his authority.* Alluding to the arrest of magistrates.

L. 14. *look up with a sort of complacent awe,* &c. The allusion is evidently to Frederick the Great.

L. 15. know *to keep firm,* &c. = know how. The expression is French. "Il est affreux," says Mounier, "penser qu'avec une âme moins bienfaisante, un autre prince eût peut-être trouvé les moyens de maintenir son pouvoir." Rech. sur les causes, &c., p. 25.

L. 20. *listed* = enlisted.

L. 31. *with truth been said to be consolatory to the human mind.* The allusion is to the fine chorus in Samson Agonistes;

"O how comely it is, and how reviving
To the spirits of just men long oppress'd,
When God into the hands of their deliverer
Puts invincible might," &c.

P. 178, L. 1. *Louis the Eleventh.* The founder of the absolute system completed by Louis XIV. His character abundantly indicates the genuine tyrant. See Commines, and the "Scandalous Chronicle."

IBID. *Charles the Ninth.* Who authorised and took a personal part in the massacre of St. Bartholomew, 1572.

L. 2. *murder of Patkul.* The Livonian patriot, surrendered to him under a treaty by Augustus of Poland, and judicially murdered in 1707. See Voltaire's History of Charles XII.

L. 3. *murder of Monaldeschi.* An Italian gentleman who had been a favourite of the queen, but in revenge for neglect had composed a book in which her intrigues were unveiled. She had him dragged into her presence, [343] and then and there assassinated, Oct. 10, 1657. Leibnitz, to his disgrace, was among the apologists for this crime, which took place at Fontainebleau.

L. 6. *King of the French.* So the king was styled after the 4th of August. The title of King of France was thought to savour of feudal usurpation.

L. 29. *flower-de-luce on their shoulder.* The notorious Lamotte, whose scandalous book appeared in London in 1788. She had been branded with the fleur-de-lis and the word *voleuse* on both shoulders.

L. 30. *Lord George Gordon fast in Newgate.* This mischievous maniac had been convicted June 6, 1787, amongst other things for a libel on the queen of France: but before the time fixed for coming up to receive sentence, he made off to the continent. He soon returned, and in August took up his residence in one of the dirtiest streets in Birmingham, when he became a proselyte to the religion, and assumed the dress and manners of the Jews. He was arrested there on the 7th of December on a warrant for contempt of court, and committed to Newgate, where his freaks were for some time a topic of public amusement, as may be seen from the contemporary newspapers.

L. 31. *public proselyte.* He had assumed the name and style of the Right Hon. Israel Bar Abraham George Gordon. He nourished a long beard, and refused to admit to his presence any Jew who appeared without one. See a ridiculous letter on the subject in the Public Advertiser, Oct. 16, 1789.

L. 33. *raised a mob,* &c. This is a mild description of the terrible No-Popery riots. On the evening of Tuesday, June 6, 1780, six-and-thirty fires were to be seen blazing in different parts of London. "During the whole night men, women and children were running up and down with such goods and effects as they wished most to preserve. The tremendous roar of the authors of these horrible scenes was heard at one instant, and at the next, the dreadful reports of soldiers' musquets, firing in platoons, and from different quarters; in short, every thing served to impress the mind with ideas of universal anarchy and approaching desolation." Ann. Register.

P. 179, L. 12. *Dr. Price has shewn us,* &c. In his Treatise on Reversionary Payments, and other economical works.

L. 34. *near forty years.* Burke arrived in London early in 1750.

P. 180, L. 9. *attempt to hide their total want of consequence,* &c. Burke no doubt had in mind a passage in Hurd's Sermons on Prophecy, Serm. xii; "A few fashionable men make a noise in the world: and this clamour, being echoed on all sides from the shallow circles of their admirers, misleads the unwary into an opinion that the irreligious spirit is universal and uncontrollable." So Canning, Speech at Liverpool, March 18, 1820; "A certain number of ambulatory tribunes of the people, self-elected to that high function, assumed the name and authority of whatever plan they thought proper to select for a place of meeting; their rostrum was pitched, sometimes here, sometimes there, according to the fancy of the mob, or the patience of the magistrates: but the proposition and the proposer were in all places [344] nearly alike; and when, by a sort of political ventriloquism, the same voice had been made to issue from half a dozen different corners of the country, it was impudently assumed to be a 'concord of sweet sounds,' composing the united voice of the people of England!"

L. 14. *grasshoppers . . . make the field ring with their* importunate *chink.* From Burke's favourite author, Virgil;

> Ubi quarta sitim coeli collegerit hora,
> Et cantu *querulae* rumpent arbusta cicadae.

Georg. iii. 327.

See also Ecl. ii. 13, Culex 151, &c. "Importunate" is a favourite epithet of Burke's. Cp. vol. i. p. 204, l. 2. The illustration is a relic of Boccalini's story of the foolish traveller who dismounted to kill the grasshoppers which disturbed his meditations as he journeyed. See The Craftsman, No. 73 (1727).

L. 15. *thousands of great cattle . . . chew the cud and are silent.* One of those quaint and strong images, so frequent in the later writings of Burke, which seem to the modern critic ridiculous or farfetched. On such points Burke perhaps has a claim to be judged by no other standard than himself.

L. 26. *I deprecate such hostility.* Rhetorical *occultatio* (cp. vol. i. note to p. 172, l. 17). From p. 258, l. 16, we see that Burke had already begun to contemplate that crusade which he heralded in the Letters on Regicide Peace.

L. 28. *formerly have had a king of France,* &c. John the Good, taken prisoner at the battle of Poitiers, Sept. 19, 1356.

L. 29. *you have read,* &c. In the Chronicle of Froissart.

L. 30. *victor in the field.* Edward the Black Prince. In the last century, when the main object of English policy was to triumph over France, the Black Prince was naturally exalted into a hero of the first rank. Cp. Warton, Ode xviii;

> The prince in sable steel that sternly frown'd,
> And Gallia's captive king, and Cressy's wreath renown'd.

L. 32. *not materially changed.* The persistence or continuity of the English national character which Burke here hints at would be no uninteresting matter of study. It is perhaps this, as much as anything,

NOTES

which makes the monuments of our literature, in a degree far higher than those of any other, living and speaking realities. To no Englishman can Chaucer and Shakspere, Addison and Fielding, ever become a dead letter.

P. 181, L. 1. *generosity and dignity of thinking,* &c. Bolingbroke speaks in this strain of the reign of Edward III, which was then considered the acme of Old English national life. Cp. Johnson, "London";

> Illustrious Edward! from the realms of day,
> The land of heroes and of saints survey.

More accurate history ranks this particular period less highly. Professor Stubbs considers it to be characterised by a "splendid formal hollowness . . . the life, the genius, the spirit of all, fainting and wearing out under the incubus of [345] false chivalry, cruel extravagance, and the lust of war" (Select Charters, p. 418). A modern author has said of the specious attractions of the Middle Ages, that they resemble the brilliant colouring of some old pictures— *il ne leur reste plus que le vernis.* Touch them, and their splendour turns to dust. Chivalry was but the perishable flower of national life: the fruit of substantial civilisation succeeded it.

It is so rarely that we can detect any real variation of opinion in Burke, even between his earliest and his latest works, that it is worth while to note that in the beginning of the Account of European Settlements in America he declares the manners of Europe before the Renaissance to have been "wholly barbarous." "A wild romantic courage in the Northern and Western parts of Europe, and a wicked policy in the Italian states, was the character of that age. If we look into the manners of the courts, there appear but very faint marks of cultivation and politeness. The interview between our Edward IV and his brother of France, wherein they were both caged up like wild beasts, shews dispositions very remote from a true sense of honour, or any just ideas of politeness and humanity."

L. 3. *Subtilized . . . into savages.* A similar expression occurs in Goguet's character of the Spartans, inserted by Burke in the Annual Register for 1760. In the volume for 1761, he alludes to this as "the character of a famous nation, improved, if we may say so, by one styled a Philosopher, into brutes." The Philosopher is Lycurgus, the idol of Rousseau. "The project," writes Mercier, "was to form an entire new race of men; and we have been transformed into savages." New Picture of Paris, ch. 3. So Matthias, Pursuits of Literature, iv. 11;

But chief, Equality's vain priest, Rousseau,
A sage in sorrow nursed and gaunt with woe —
. . . .
What time his work the citizen began,
And gave to France the social savage, Man.

L. 4. *Rousseau . . . Voltaire . . . Helvetius.* The spirit of free-thinking, which gives so distinct a character to the last century, was by no means the produce of that century. It had been militant for at least two centuries, before in the middle of that century it became triumphant. It came from Italy with the Renaissance. Lanoue, in his *Discours* (1585), calculates the atheists of France at a million. Père Mersenne, in 1636, reckons 50,000 in Paris alone; "Quae (Lutetia) si luto plurimum, multo tamen magis atheismo foetet." See more on this subject in M. Aubertin's Introduction, and cp. especially Burton's section on "Religious Melancholy in defect."

L. 7. *no discoveries to be made in morality.* So in the Letter to M. de Menonville, Burke insists that to effect a real reform, every vestige must be effaced of "that philosophy which pretends to have made discoveries in the *terra australis* of morality." This letter contains Burke's final judgment on Rousseau.

L. 9. *understood long before we were born.* Cp. ante, p. 120, l. 21.

[346] **L. 12.** *silent tomb . . . pert loquacity.* So the Anthology;

Πολλὰ λαλεῖς, ἄνθρωπε, χαμαὶ δὲ τίθῃ μετὰ μικρόν,
   Σίγα, καὶ μελέτα ζῶν ἔτι τὸν θάνατον.

L. 20. *blurred* = blotted, scribbled over.

L. 22. *real hearts of flesh,* &c. Ezekiel xi. 19.

P. 182, L. 17. *many of our men of speculation.* Alluding to the school of English essayists, with Addison at its head; and especially to Dr. Johnson. See especially the "World," Nos. 112–114. Lord Chesterfield's Essays in the World, which appeared in Burke's younger days, evidently attracted his attention. The following extracts are from No. 112, which commences with the quotation of one of Bolingbroke's showy and shallow generalisations on the subject of prejudice, and is interesting from its bearing on the present text. "It is certain that there has not been a time when the prerogative of human reason was more freely asserted, nor errors and prejudices more ably attacked and exposed by the best writers, than now. But may not the principle of enquiry and detection be carried too far, or at least made too general? And should not a prudent discrimination of cases be attended to? A

NOTES

prejudice is by no means (though generally thought so) an error; on the contrary, it may be a most unquestioned truth, though it be still a prejudice in those who, without any examination, take it upon trust and entertain it by habit. There are even some prejudices, founded upon error, which ought to be connived at, or perhaps encouraged; their effects being more beneficial to society than their detection can possibly be. . . . The bulk of mankind have neither leisure nor knowledge sufficient to reason right; why then should they be taught to reason at all? Will not honest instinct prompt, and wholesome prejudices guide them, much better than half reasoning? . . . Honest, useful, home-spun prejudices . . . in themselves undoubted and demonstrable truths, and ought therefore to be cherished even in their coarsest dress."

L. 29. *habit . . . series of unconnected acts.* The distinction is an important part of the moral system of Aristotle, Eth., Lib. ii. iii.

P. 183, L. 8. *at inexpiable war with all establishments.* Cp. infra, p. 187, l. 1. See the beginning of the famous article in the Encyclopédie on *Foundations,* written by Turgot. There are indications in subsequent works that Burke had read it. The author, not content with exposing the abuses and weak points of old establishments, avowedly endeavours "to excite an aversion to new foundations."

IBID. *inexpiable war.* A curious expression of Livy, which seems to have stuck in Burke's memory. "Ex quibus pro certo habeat, Patres, adversus quos tenderet, bello inexpiabili se persecuturos." Lib. iv. c. 35. It is repeated at p. 243, l. 3, and in the Letter to Mr. Baron Smith.

L. 13. *singular species of compact.* Bishop Horsley, after tracing the theory of an original compact of government to the Crito of Plato, says; "It is remarkable that this fictitious compact, which in modern times hath been made the basis of the unqualified doctrine of resistance, should have [347] been set up by Plato in the person of Socrates as the foundation of the opposite doctrine of the passive obedience of the individual." Serm. xliv. Jan. 30, 1793.

P. 184, L. 7. *refused to change their law,* &c. Alluded to by Bolingbroke in his Remarks on the History of England. See Blackstone, vol. iv. ch. 8, and especially Milman, History of Latin Christianity, Book xiii. ch. 6; "Parliament with one indignant voice declared the surrender of the realm by John null and void, as without the consent of Parliament, and contrary to the king's coronation oath (40 Edw. III). . . . Parliament was as resolute against the other abuse (the possession of rich benefices by foreigners). The first Statute of Provisors had been passed in the reign of Edward I (35 Edw. I). Twice already in the reign of Edward III (in 1351 and 1353) was this law re-enacted, with penalties rising above one another in severity. It was [now, 1373] declared that the Court of Rome could present to no bishopric or benefice in England." "In the year 1390 (15 Rich. II) the Commons extorted the renewal of the Statute of Provisors in the strongest terms."

L. 16. *we must provide as Englishmen.* Cp. ante, note to p. 95, l. 13. Burke considered the rest of Europe as "linked by a contignation" with the political edifice of France.

L. 24. *a cabal calling itself philosophic.* The term "philosophic" then implied, as it perhaps still does in France, unbelief in Christianity. Coleridge's character of the philosophy brought into vogue by Voltaire, D'Alembert, Diderot, &c., is given here, not because it is altogether just, but because it illustrates the views of Burke, by which it was undoubtedly inspired;

> Prurient, bustling, and revolutionary, this French wisdom has never more than grazed the surface of knowledge. As political economy, in its zeal for the increase of food, it habitually overlooked the qualities and even the sensations of those that were to feed on it. As ethical philosophy, it recognised no duties which it could not reduce into debtor and creditor accounts on the ledgers of self-love, where no coin was sterling which could not be rendered into agreeable sensations. And even in its height of self-complacency as chemical art, greatly am I deceived if it has not from the very beginning mistaken the products of destruction, *cadavera rerum,* for the elements of composition: and most assuredly it has dearly purchased a few brilliant inventions at the loss of all communion with life and the spirit of nature. As the process, such the result!—a heartless frivolity alternating with a sentimentality as heartless—an ignorant contempt of antiquity—a neglect of moral self-discipline—a deadening of the religious sense, even in the less reflecting forms of natural piety—a scornful reprobation of all consolations and secret refreshings from above *
> —and as the *caput mortuum* [348] of human nature evaporated, a French nature of rapacity, levity, ferocity, and presumption. The Statesman's Manual, Appendix C.

L. 34. *Collins and Toland,* &c. All that is worth knowing of these

---

* Coleridge borrows these beautiful expressions from the Chorus in "Samson Agonistes."

writers may be read in Mr. Pattison's Essay on the "Tendencies of Religious Thought in England, 1688–1750." The representative man of the sect was Tindal. Cp. Pope, Imit. of Horace, i. 6;

> But art thou one whom new opinions sway,
> One who believes as Tindal leads the way?
> Who virtue and a church alike disowns,
> Thinks that but words, and this but brick and stones?

P. 185, L. 2. *Who now reads Bolingbroke?* Cp. infra, p. 226, l. 11. It has been remarked that Burke is ungenerous to his literary master. Some, however, consider his obligations to Bolingbroke slighter than has been generally supposed, and look upon Addison as his literary parent. Cp. note to p. 182, l. 17, sup. The "Sublime and Beautiful" certainly bears the marks of much study of Addison, both as to style and as to matter. Burke repeats his opinion of Bolingbroke in the First Letter on a Regicide Peace; "When I was very young, a general fashion told me I was to admire some of the writings against that minister (Sir R. Walpole). A little more maturity taught me as much to despise them."

L. 5. *few successors.* The allusion is to Hume.

Ibid. *family vault of "all the Capulets."* Romeo and Juliet, Act iv. sc. 1:

> Thou shalt be borne to that same ancient vault,
> Where all the kindred of the Capulets lie.

L. 9. *never acted in corps.* With Burke, a sure sign of being worthless and abnormal excrescences of civil society. Vide "Present Discontents." This observation on the atheistical freethinkers is made by Bolingbroke himself! Burke has in mind the chorus in Samson;

> If any be (atheists) they walk obscure;
> For of such doctrine never was there school,
> But the heart of the fool,
> And no man therein doctor but himself.

L. 20. *native plainness and directness of understanding.* The English are remarkable for a rooted dislike to all chicanery and sophistication. Good miscellaneous illustrations of English character are the author of "Hudibras," as reflected in his writings, the Sir Roger de Coverly of Addison, the principal characters of Fielding, Boswell's portraiture of Dr. Johnson, and the "Christopher North" of Blackwood's Magazine (Professor John Wilson).

L. 22. *those who have successively obtained authority among us.* Burke evidently alludes to Sir Robert Walpole, Lord Chatham, and Lord

Rockingham, denying, by implication, the same merit to those who had been in power since Rockingham's death.

L. 28. *no rust of superstition,* &c. So Bacon, Essay of Atheism; "I had [349] rather believe all the Fables in the *Legend,* and the *Talmud,* and the *Alcoran,* than that this universal frame is without a mind."

P. 186, L. 7. *temple . . . unhallowed fire.* Alluding to the sacred fire on the altar of Vesta at Rome: possibly also to Numbers, ch. xvi.

L. 15. *Greek—Armenian—Roman—Protestant.* Burke speaks elsewhere of the "four grand divisions of Christianity," evidently intending the same as here. (Letter to W. Smith, Esq.) He was of opinion that the "three religions, prevalent more or less in various parts of these islands, ought all, in subordination to the legal establishments, as they stand in the several countries to be countenanced, protected, and cherished; and that in Ireland particularly the Roman Catholic religion should be upheld in high respect and veneration . . . and not tolerated as an inevitable evil." The character of Burke by Shackleton, who, it should be remembered, was a Quaker, contains the following remarkable passage; "He believes the Papists wrong, he doubts if the Protestants are altogether right. He has not been favoured to find that church which would lead him to the indubitable certainty of true religion, undefiled with the mixture of human inventions." We trace here the line of thought which was adopted by Coleridge, and carried into practice by Irving. Cp. the Doctrine of Toleration, infra, pp. 253, 254.

P. 187, L. 16. *in antient Rome.* The allusion is to the constitution of the Decemvirate; the state visited was Athens, in the time of Pericles. Niebuhr discredited the story, but afterwards retracted his opinion.

L. 20. *our church establishment.* No student of history will allow this to be a fair statement of contemporary public opinion. It is totally opposed to the views of the Warburtonian school, which included the most thoughtful and practical churchmen of the time.

LL. 28, 30. *august fabric . . . sacred temple.* The "templum in modum arcis" of Tacitus, speaking of the temple of Jerusalem, which is alluded to in the passage quoted in note to p. 113, l. 27.

P. 188, L. 31. *act in trust.* Cp. note to vol. i. p. 118, l. 10.

P. 189, L. 10. *Janissaries.* Cp. note to vol. i. p. 96, l. 1.

L. 24. *the most shameless thing,* &c. Cp. Dryden's Satire on the Dutch. See the arguments of the Athenians to the Melians, Thucydides, Book v. ch. 85.

Notes

L. 27. *the people at large never ought,* &c. Cp. vol. i. p. 74, p. 251, &c. "Quicquid multis peccatur inultum est," Lucan, Phars. v. 260. The quotation had been employed by Burke in his appeal for mercy on behalf of the convicted rioters of 1780. He often appeals to the general doctrine.

P. 190, L. 4. *false shew of liberty*—"Falsa species libertatis," from the passage in Tacitus (Hist. i. 1) quoted in vol. i. p. 125, l. 23.

L. 19. *will and reason the same.* The doctrine that reason and will are identical in the Divine mind is a conclusion of the Schoolmen often used by the English theologians.

L. 25. *confer that power on those only,* &c. Cp. p. 129, l. 23 sqq.

P. 191, L. 5. *Life-renters.* Tenants for life, i. e. those who are entitled to receive the rents for life.

[350] L. 9. *cut off the entail.* The usual expression for formally depriving persons on whom settlements have been made, of the benefit of such settlements. By an entail, strictly speaking, property is settled on persons and the heirs of their bodies: but cutting off the entail also defeats all the supplementary contingent interests.

IBID. *commit waste.* The technical term for permanent injury done on a landed estate, as by pulling down houses, cutting timber, &c.

L. 18. *link with the other.* Cp. ante, p. 121.

L. 20. *science of jurisprudence.* In the First Letter on a Regicide Peace, Burke says that Lord Camden shared his views on this point. "No man, in a public or private concern, can divine by what rule or principle her judgments are to be directed; nor is there to be found a professor in any university, or a practitioner in any court, who will hazard an opinion of what is or is not law in France, in any case whatever." He goes on to remark on that disavowal of all principles of public law which outlawed the French Republic in Europe.

L. 22. *collected reason of ages.* A similar vindication of law from the wit of a pert sciolist is attributed to Dr. Johnson. See that of Blackstone, vol. iii. ch. 22.

L. 25. *Personal self-sufficiency,* &c. So Daniel;

For self-opinion would be seen more wise
  Than present counsels, customs, orders, laws;
And to the end to have them otherwise
  The Commonwealth into confusion draws,

As if ordain'd to embroil the world with wit,
As well as grossness to dishonour it.
Chorus to Tragedy of Philotas.

P. 192, L. 22. *that no man should approach,* &c.

If ancient fabrics nod and threat to fall,
To patch their flaws, and buttress up the wall,
So far is duty; but here fix the mark:
For all beyond it, is to touch the ark.
Dryden, Abs. and Achit.

L. 29. *hack that aged parent in pieces.* So in Speech on Parliamentary Reform, 1782; "I look with filial reverence on the constitution of my country, and never will cut it in pieces, and put it into the kettle of any magician, in order to boil it, with the puddle of their compounds, into youth and vigour." Alluding to the legend of the daughters of Pelias, King of Thessaly, who "by the counsel of Medea, chopped him in pieces, and set him a boiling with I know not what herbs in a cauldron, but could not revive him again," Hobbes, De Corpore Politico, Part ii. cap. 8. Hobbes, like Burke, uses the story to illustrate "cutting the Commonwealth in pieces, upon pretence or hope of reformation." Cowley employs it in a similar way, in his famous Essay on the Government of Oliver [351] Cromwell. It was an obvious illustration of events in 1789. Cp. infra, note to p. 227, l. 13, and p. 328, l. 34.

P. 193, L. 8. *It is a partnership,* &c. A fine example of Burke's way of taking an abused abstract principle, and correcting it in its application, while he enlarges and intensifies its signification. Burke exposes the fallacies involved in the French use of the term *Société,* which literally means "partnership" as well as "society."

L. 11. *cannot be obtained in many generations.* The germs of this profound argument are to be found in Cicero, but it was never put in shape so ably, nor enforced so powerfully, as in the present passage.

P. 194, L. 14. *"Quod illi principi,"* &c. From the dream of Scipio, Cic. de Rep., Lib. vi. The passage is used as a motto on the title-page of Vattel's Law of Nations, a favourite authority of Burke's.

L. 17. *of the head and heart.* Cp. ante, p. 171, l. 5.

IBID. *great name*—Scipio.

L. 18. *greater name*—Cicero.

L. 27. *cast* = caste, birth.

NOTES

P. 195, L. 6. *oblation of the state itself, as a worthy offering,* &c. Perhaps a reminiscence of a passage in the Communion Service.

L. 9. *dignity of persons.* The allusion is to the various ecclesiastical dignitaries from the Bishop downwards.

P. 197, L. 10. *as ample and as early a share—modern world.* Burke uses the word modern in its strict sense = the world of to-day. The "ample and early share" is not intended to extend beyond the age of Hooker and Bacon. In any more extended sense, except in the names of a few Schoolmen, and very rare cases like Chaucer, it would be difficult to justify the claim.

P. 198, L. 4. *estate of the church . . . private property.* In his Speech on the Petition against the Acts of Uniformity (1772), Burke maintained the contrary. He then held that the church was a voluntary society, favoured by the State, and endowed by it with the tithes as a public tax.

L. 9. *Euripus.* The strait between Boeotia and Euboea. The Mediterranean being in general almost tideless, the periodical rise and fall of the water here and in the Straits of Messina was a standing puzzle to the ancients.

IBID. *funds and actions.* "Actions" Fr. = shares in a joint stock. (German *Actien.*)

L. 16. *mere invention,* &c. Cp. the well-known line, "Si Dieu n'existait pas, il faudrait l'inventer."

L. 25. *preached to the poor.* St. Luke vii. 22, &c.

L. 32. *miserable great* (great = rich, powerful). "Great persons," says South, "unless their understandings are very great too, are of all others the most miserable." So Gray, Ode to Spring;

How vain the ardour of the crowd—
How low, how little are the proud,
    How indigent the great!

[352] **P. 199, L. 13.** *They too are among the unhappy.* Crabbe consoles the poor man by enumerating some of the sorrows of the rich;

Ah! go in peace, good fellow, to thine home,
Nor fancy these escape the general doom;
Gay as they seem, be sure with them are hearts
With sorrow tried, there's sadness in their parts;
If thou could'st see them, when they think alone,
Mirth, music, friends, and these amusements gone;
Could'st thou discover every secret ill

That pains their spirit, or resists their will;
Could'st thou behold forsaken love's distress,
Or envy's pang at glory or success,
Or beauty, conscious of the spoils of time,
Or guilt alarm'd when memory shows the crime;
All that gives sorrow, terror, grief and gloom—
Content would cheer thee trudging to thine home.

Crabbe, "Amusements."

L. 14. *personal pain.* The pleasure of wealth, says South, is so far from reaching the soul, that it scarce pierces the skin. "What would a man give to purchase a release, nay, but a small respite from the extreme pains of the gout or stone? And yet, if he could fee his physician with both the Indies, neither art nor money can redeem, or but reprieve him from his misery. No man feels the pangs and tortures of his present distemper (be it what it will) at all the less for being rich. His riches indeed may have occasioned, but they cannot allay them. No man's fever burns the gentler for his drinking his juleps in a golden cup." See the rest of this, the concluding argument of the fine sermon "On Covetousness."

L. 19. *range without limit.* This reminds us something of Pascal's gloomy observations on the secret instinct which leads man to seek diversion and employment in something outside himself.

L. 33. *The people of England know,* &c. These considerations are repeated from earlier Church politicians. "Where wealth is held in so great admiration as generally in this golden age it is, that without it angelical perfections are not able to deliver from extreme contempt, surely to make bishops poorer than they are, were to make them of less account and estimation than they should be." Hooker, Eccl. Pol., Book vii. ch. xxiv. 19. So also South, Sermon iv. (Ecclesiastical Policy the Best Policy): "The vulgar have not such logical heads, as to be able to abstract such subtile conceptions as to separate the man from the minister, or to consider the same person under a double capacity, and so honour him as a divine, while they despise him as poor. . . . Let the minister be abject and low, his interest inconsiderable, the Word will suffer for his sake. The message will still find reception according to the dignity of the messenger." Swift, Project for the Advancement of Religion; "It so happens that men of pleasure, who never go to church, nor use themselves to read books of devotion, [353] form their ideas of the clergy from a few poor strollers they often observe in the streets, or sneaking out of some person of quality's house, where they are hired by the lady at ten shillings a month. . . . And let some reasoners think what they please, it is certain that men must be brought to esteem and love the clergy before they can be persuaded to be in love with religion. No man values the best medicine, if administered by a physician whose person he hates and despises."

P. 200, L. 5. *If the poverty were voluntary,* &c. Hazlitt, Essay on the Want of Money: "Echard's book on the Contempt of the Clergy is unfounded. It is surely sufficient for any set of individuals, raised above actual want, that their characters are not merely respectable, but sacred. Poverty, when it is voluntary, is never despicable, but takes an heroical aspect."

L. 13. *Those who are to instruct presumptuous ignorance,* &c. "With what a face shall a pitiful underling encounter the solemn looks of an oppressing grandee? With what hope of success shall he adventure to check the vicious extravagances of a ruffling gallant? Will he dare to contradict the opinion, or disallow the practice of that wealthy or this powerful neighbour, by whose alms, it may be, he is relieved, and supported by his favour?" Barrow, Consecration Sermon on Ps. cxxxii. 16. For a remarkable instance of the indebtedness of modern politicians to Burke, compare with this passage Sir R. Peel's Speech at the Glasgow Banquet, 1837.

L. 20. *No! we will have her to exalt her mitred front,* &c. "Christ would have his body, the church, not meagre and contemptible, but replenished and borne up with sufficiency, displayed to the world with the beauties of fulness, and the most ennobling proportions." South, Posthumous Sermons, No. ii.

L. 34. *They can see a bishop of Durham,* &c. The argument is from what he elsewhere calls "the excellent queries of the excellent Berkeley." "If the revenues allotted for the encouragement of religion and learning were made hereditary in the hands of a dozen lay lords, and as many overgrown commoners, whether the public would be much the better for it?" Queries, No. 340. Similarly Swift, Arguments against Enlarging the Power of the Bishops: "I was never able to imagine what inconvenience would accrue to the public by one thousand or two thousand a year being in the hands of a protestant bishop, any more than of a lay person. The former, generally speaking, lives as piously and hospitably as the other, pays his debts as honestly, and spends as much of his revenue amongst his tenants; besides, if they are his immediate tenants, you may distinguish them at first sight, by their habits and horses, or, if you go to their houses, by their comfortable way of living."

P. 201, L. 2. *this Earl, or that Squire.* The argument is wittily amplified by Sydney Smith, in his Second Letter to Archdeacon Singleton: "Take, for instance, the Cathedral of Bristol, the whole estates of which are about equal to keeping a pack of foxhounds. If this had been in the hands of a [354] country gentleman, instead of Precentor, Succentor, Dean, and Canons, and Sexton, you would have had huntsman, whipper-in, dog-feeders, and stoppers of earths; the old squire, full of foolish opinions, and fermented liquids, and a young gentleman of gloves, waistcoats, and pantaloons; and how many generations might it be before the fortuitous concourse of noodles would produce such a man as Professor Lee, one of the Prebendaries of Bristol, and by far the most eminent Oriental scholar in Europe?"

L. 3. *So many dogs and horses are not kept,* &c. The reader might fancy he had Cobbett before him instead of Burke. Burke was a true friend to the poor who lived near his estate. See Prior's Life of Burke, ch. xiv.

L. 8. *It is better to cherish,* &c. The principle had been put forth by Bishop Horsley in his Sermon on the poor not ceasing out of the land (Deut. xv. 11), May 18, 1786. He maintains that the best and most natural mode of relief is by voluntary contributions. "The law should be careful not to do too much."

L. 15. *Too much and too little are treason against property.* This striking aphorism is a type peculiar to Burke. Cp. note to vol. i. p. 186, l. 20.

P. 202, L. 3. *We shall believe those reformers,* &c. "If they abuse the goods of the Church unto pomp and vanity, such faults we do not excuse in them: only we wish it to be considered whether such faults be verily in them, or else but objected against them by such as gape after spoil, and therefore are no competent judges of what is moderate and what is excessive. . . . If the remedy for the disease is good, let it be unpartially applied. *Interest reipublicae ut re suâ quisque bene utatur.* Let all states be put to their moderate pensions, let their livings and lands be taken away from them, whosoever they be, in whom such ample possessions are found to have been matters of grievous abuse; were this just? would noble families think this reasonable?" Hooker, Eccl. Pol., Book vii. xxiv. 24. So Crabbe, "Religious Sects":

> "In pomp," they cry, "is England's Church arrayed,
> Our cool reformers wrought like men afraid —
> We would have pulled her gorgeous temples down,
> And spurned her mitre, and defiled her gown —
> We would have trodden low both bench and stall,
> Nor left a tithe remaining, great or small!"

NOTES

Let us be serious—should such trials come,
Are they themselves prepared for martyrdom?

L. 23. *cup of their abominations.* Revelation of St. John, xvii. 4.

L. 28. *selfish enlargement of mind,* &c. Cp. note to vol. i. p. 151, l. 2.

P. 203, L. 15. *harshly driven—harpies of usury.* The allusion is to Virg. Aen. iii. 212, sqq.

P. 204, L. 6. *academies of the Palais Royal.* The court yard of the Palais Royal, surrounded by restaurants and shops, was and is still a noted place of meeting—the Forum of stump-orators and newsmongers. Mr. [355] Carlyle names it *Satan-at-home.* The Club of Jacobins took their afterwards too famous name from meeting in the hall of a convent of monks of the order of St. James of Compostella.

L. 35. *dungeons and iron cages of their old masters.* The allusion is to the cruelties of Louis XI, thus described by Commines: "Il est vray qu'il avoit fait de rigoureuses prisons, comme cages de fer et autres de bois, couvertes de plaques de fer par le dehors et par le dedans, avec terribles ferrures de quelques huict pieds de large, et de la hauteur d'un homme et un pied de plus. Le premier qui les devisa fut l'évesque de Verdun, qui en la première qui fut faite fut mis incontinent, et y a couché quatorze ans." Mém. Liv. vi. ch. 12.

P. 207, L. 17. *Family settlements.* In French technical language, *substitutions fidei-commissaires,* see p. 337, l. 2 (to be distinguished from the use of these terms in the civil law). Several coutumes, however, including those of Normandy and Brittany, disallowed them. The law on the subject had been fixed by an ordinance in 1741. In the Encyclopédie they are regarded like many other institutions, as useful in their day, but unsuited to the age. The writer of the article approves the English restrictions on settlements, which forbid their operation beyond the life of a person living at the time when they are made, and twenty-one years after. "On dit que le droit coutumier d'Angleterre abhorre les successions à perpetuité; et en conséquence, elles y sont plus limitées que dans aucune autre monarchie de l'Europe." The writer also looks enviously on the protection to leaseholders against entails, which was peculiar to Britain. In France the protection of the leaseholder against heirs and purchasers formerly extended only to nine years from the commencement of the lease, Louis XIV. having fixed this short limit in order to make the tax on alienations more frequently exigible. Among the reforms of Turgot, this period had been increased to twenty-seven years, but the Encyclopedist considers this too short.

REFLECTIONS ON THE REVOLUTION IN FRANCE

L. 18. *the jus retractus = droit de retrait,* or right of recovery, usually known as *prélation.* The French law admitted more than twenty species of this right, the most important of which were the *Retrait Seigneurial* and the *Retrait Lignager.* By the former the lord could at any time compulsorily repurchase alienated lands which had once formed part of his fief. By the latter the heirs of a landowner could similarly repurchase any portion of their ancestors' estates which he had alienated. These rights prevailed not only in the *pays coutumiers,* but in the *pays de droit écrit.* Cp. the Assise of Jerusalem.

L. 19. *mass of landed property held by the crown . . . unalienably.* The private estates of the monarch had formerly been distinguished from the crown estates, and could be alienated: but after the Ordinance of Moulins (Ordonnance du domaine, 1566) the distinction disappeared, and all estates which came in any way to the monarch were united to the crown lands. The policy of non-alienation, however, dates from a time anterior to St. Louis. It was one of the weakest points of the *ancien régime,* and was [356] ably attacked in the Traité de la Finance des Romains, 1740, before the Encyclopedists brought forward their arguments against it, and Turgot formed his wise plan for abolishing it. The crown lands were often alienated, but such alienations were always subject to the *jus retractus.*

L. 21. *vast estates of the ecclesiastic corporations.* Their wealth had been much exaggerated. Some estimated it at one half, others at one third, of the rental of the kingdom. Condorcet, in his Life of Turgot, estimates it at less than a fifth.

P. 208, L. 7. *not noble or newly noble.* "Les gens d'esprit et les gens riches trouvaient donc la noblesse insupportable; et la plupart la trouvaient si insupportable qu'ils finissaient par l'acheter. Mais alors commençait pour eux un nouveau genre de supplice; ils étaient des anoblis, des gens nobles, mais n'étaient pas gentilshommes." Rivarol, Journal Politique.

P. 209, L. 7. *two academies of France.* The famous Académie des Sciences (*The* Academy), and the Académie des Inscriptions, so called because its special office was the devising of inscriptions in honour of the *grand Monarque,* and in celebration of his various civil and military triumphs.

IBID. *vast undertaking of the Encyclopaedia.* Commenced in 1751 by Diderot and D'Alembert. There had been Encyclopaedias ever since the middle of the sixteenth century: but the present work, in which may be traced the first form of "Positivism," purposed to purge the world of knowledge and practice of all that was obsolete or prejudicial. It was republished (1782 sq.) in sections, under the title of Encyclopédie Méthodique. "It was intended to comprise sketches, at once accurate and elementary, of the subjects of human knowledge: and to exhibit the most certain, the most useful and important truths, in the different branches of science. It was besides to contain a discussion of every question that interests the learned or the humane; opinions of the greatest universality or celebrity, with the origin and progress of those opinions, and the arguments, whether just or fallacious, on which they had been supported." Condorcet, Life of Turgot, ch. ii. It might have been added that the work was based on the labours of Ephraim Chambers, and was at first intended to be little more than a translation of his dictionary.

L. 12. *pursued with a degree of zeal,* &c. See Rousseau's Essay on the Sciences.

L. 31. *bigotry of their own.* The tone of the Encyclopédie, however, is far removed from open bigotry. The English Jacobins outdid their models. The London Corresponding Society are said to have resolved that the pernicious belief in a God was to be an exception to their general principle of toleration! (Sir J. Mackintosh, in the British Critic, Aug. 1800). Burke's meaning is well amplified by Dr. Liddon: "Religion does not cease to influence events among those who reject its claims: it excites the strongest passions, not merely in its defenders, but in its enemies. The claim to hold communion with an unseen world irritates, when it does not win and satisfy. Atheism has again and again been a fanaticism: it has been a missionary [357] and a persecutor by turns; it is lashed into passion by the very presence of the sublime passion to which it is opposed." Some Elements of Religion, Lect. i.

P. 210, L. 11. *desultory and faint persecution.* Alluding to the proceedings against the Encyclopedists, commenced when seven volumes had been published, and weakened by being carried on by two parties so opposite as Jesuits and Jansenists. The former had proposed to contribute the theological articles, and were piqued at being repulsed. The Parliament of Paris in the end appointed a commission to supervise the publication. It is remarkable that the article on the Soul, which was marked in the Mémoires as the most offensive of all, was proved to have been written by a licentiate of the Sorbonne, whose orthodoxy was unimpeachable! This persecution caused a closer union between most of the members of the *secte*

Encyclopédique, but it deprived them of the assistance of others, in particular of Turgot.

P. 211, L. 10. *in their satires.* See the smaller works of Voltaire, Diderot, &c.

P. 212, L. 21. *new morality.* The term was adopted by Canning as a title for his well-known satirical poem in the Anti-jacobin.

L. 33. *comptrollers-general.* Burke might have excepted from this sweeping denunciation one who lost the office, in part from the desperate opposition of the bankers whom his predecessors employed— Turgot. When Turgot had to resign, and his prudent and liberal policy was reversed, there was but one way in France. It was rather the *farmers-general* who should have been thus stigmatised.

P. 213, L. 4. *Mr. Laborde.* Jean Joseph (Marquis) de Laborde, a wealthy merchant of Bayonne, employed extensively as a banker and financial contractor by the government of Louis XV, first in the Seven Years' War. He was a Spaniard by birth, his proper name being Dort. He took the name of Laborde from an estate with which the marquisate urged on him by the Duc de Choiseul was connected. He acquired enormous wealth, chiefly, perhaps, as Burke hints, by his public jobs. He retired from affairs on the disgrace of Choiseul. He was condemned during the Reign of Terror for the exportation of bullion, with the supposed intent of depreciating assignats, and guillotined 18th April, 1794.

L. 9. *Duke de Choiseul.* Minister 1758–1770. Alluded to in vol. i. p. 108.

L. 14. *to have been in Paris,* &c. The circumstance is again alluded to, in connection with the partition of Poland, in the Second Letter on a Regicide Peace. See next note.

L. 16. *Duke d'Aiguillon.* The richest *seigneur* in France, after the king, and one of the few members of the *noblesse* who took up the cause of the Revolution in the Assembly. He had been Minister of Foreign Affairs to Louis XV, after the disgrace of Choiseul. He is immortal in history owing to the fact that from his supine and miserable policy, no opposition was offered to the partition of Poland, always an instrument of France, and whose [358] ruin decided action on the part of France, might, it was thought, have prevented. "Si Choiseul avait été encore là," said Louis XV, "ce partage n'aurait pas eu lieu." He distinguished himself in his latter years, during which he was entrusted with the government of Brittany, by hiding himself in a mill, when the English landed at St. Cast, and coming out upon their repulse, "covered, not with glory, but with flour." The "Livre Rouge" says that he twice nearly occasioned a civil war and the ruin of the state, and twice escaped the scaffold.

L. 17. *protecting despotism.* The protecting hand was that of Madame du Barry.

L. 20. *The noble family of Noailles had long been servants,* &c. For two centuries and a half. The Maréchal de Noailles had especially been distinguished in the War of the Austrian Succession, 1742–1748, and afterwards as a minister. His son Louis, duc de Noailles, was notorious as a private agent of Louis XVI. One of his sayings is worth quoting. Louis had said that the farmers-general were the support of the state: "Oui, Sire—comme la corde soutient le pendu." He died shortly after the execution of the King, and his widow, daughter, and granddaughter were afterwards guillotined, July 22, 1794. Burke here alludes particularly to the Vicomte de Noailles, a younger son, who took a prominent part, together with the Duc d'Aiguillon, in the debates of the Assembly, particularly in the proceedings of the 4th of August.

L. 25. *Duke de Rochefoucalt.* François Alexandre Frédéric, duc de Rochefoucauld-Liancourt, often called duc de Liancourt, eminent as a political economist.

L. 29. *make a good use,* &c. See Arthur Young's Travels in France, vol. i. p. 62.

L. 31. *his brother.* See foot-note. Dominique de la Rochefoucauld, the Archbishop, was descended from a poor and unconsidered branch of the family. He was President of the Order of the Clergy in the States-general of 1789.

P. 214, L. 8. *crudelem illam Hastam.* Cicero, alluding to the sales under the confiscations of Sylla: "Nec vero unquam bellorum civilium semen et causa deerit, dum homines perditi hastam illam cruentam et meminerint et sperabunt." De Officiis, ii. 8, 29. So Fourth Philippic, 4, 9: "Quos non illa infinita hasta satiavit."

L. 32. *Harry the Eighth.* "Harry" is simply the ancient and French way of pronouncing "Henry."

P. 215, L. 4. *rob the abbies.* Mr. Hallam is of opinion that the alienation of the abbey lands was on the whole beneficial to the country. His opinion was probably, however, modified by his doctrine that the property of a corporate body stands on a different footing from that of private individuals. Bolingbroke considers it a politic measure.

P. 220, L. 2. *an offer of a contribution.* The Archbishop, on behalf of the clergy, offered an unconditional surrender of the tithes, if they were [359] allowed to keep the church lands. This compromise was discountenanced by Sieyès.

P. 221, L. 20. *Bank of discount.* The Caisse d'Escompte, planned by the masterly statesman Turgot, while Comptroller-general, and carried out by his successor.

P. 222, L. 2. *old independent judicature of the parliaments.* The position of king, parliaments, and people, will be best understood from the words of Mounier: "Dans le plupart des états de l'Europe, les différens pouvoirs se sont livrés des combats à mort, ou ont fait des traités de partage, de sorte que les sujêts savent clairement quels sont ceux qui ont le droit de commander, et dans quels cas ils doivent obéir. La France seule, peut-être, offroit le spectacle extraordinaire de deux autorités alternativement victorieuses ou soumises, concluant des trèves, mais jamais de traités définitifs; et dans le choc de leurs prétentions, dictant au peuple des volontés contraires. Ces deux autorités étoient celle du roi et celle des parlemens ou tribunaux supérieurs." Recherches sur les causes, &c., pp. 10, 11.

P. 223, L. 5. *sort of fine.* Alluding to the practice of granting leases for lives or years at low rents, in consideration of a *fine*, or lump sum paid down at the commencement of the term.

L. 6. *sort of gift.* "Gift" (donum) is used in the technical sense in feudal law. The word *dedi* usually implied services to be rendered by the donee and his heirs to the donor and his heirs. It was of wider comprehension than other terms, and was considered by lawyers "the aptest word of feoffment."

L. 13. *waste.* See second note to p. 191, l. 9.

IBID. *hands habituated to the gripings of usury.* Burke evidently has in mind the *soucars* of India. See Speech on Nabob of Arcot's Debts.

L. 32. *advocates for servitude.* Burke here answers by anticipation the reproaches which the work brought upon him from the English Whigs and Revolutionists.

P. 224, L. 10. *hereditary wealth. . . . dignity.* The House of Lords.

NOTES

L. 13. *permanent organ.* The House of Commons.

L. 22. *pure democracy . . . only tolerable form.* The austere doctrine of Sieyès. It may now be said that the thinking world of Europe has thoroughly unlearnt this speculative dogma, the product of superficial knowledge and superficial reasoning.

L. 29. *direct train. . . . oligarchy.* The presage was fulfilled by the establishment of the Fifth of Fructidor (the Directory).

L. 32. *I reprobate no form of government,* &c. The opinions contained in these lines are developed in the Appeal from the New to the Old Whigs. "He (Mr. Burke) never abused all republics. He has never professed himself a friend or an enemy to republics or to monarchies in the abstract. He thought that the circumstances and habits of every country, which it is always perilous and productive of the greatest calamities to force, are to decide upon the form of its government. There is nothing in his nature, his temper, or [360] his faculties, which should make him an enemy to any republic, modern or ancient. Far from it. He has studied the form and spirit of republics very early in life; he has studied them with great attention; and with a mind undisturbed by affection or prejudice. He is indeed convinced that the science of government would be poorly cultivated without that study. But the result in his mind from that investigation has been, and is, that neither England nor France, without infinite detriment to them, as well in the event as in the experiment, could be brought into a republican form; but that everything republican which can be introduced with safety into either of them, must be built upon a monarchy." The history of political sentiment in both countries amply justifies this view.

L. 35. *very few, and very particularly circumstanced.* The Swiss confederation still survives, and the kingdom of the Netherlands is really a republic, as it was formerly in Burke's time. The republics of Genoa and Venice were also in existence when Burke wrote. The Italian republics established by Bonaparte (the Ligurian, Cisalpine, Roman, Parthenopean, &c.) were of short duration.

P. 225, L. 4. *better acquainted with them.* And their verdict was unanimously against them. A study of Thucydides, Plato, and Aristotle will prove how little homage pure democracy met with from the best minds of the age when it was best understood.

L. 25. *learned friend.* No doubt, Dr. French Laurence.

P. 226, L. 11. *Bolingbroke. . . . presumptuous and superficial writer.* See note ante, p. 185, l. 2. Not only Burke, but Pitt, learnt much from

Bolingbroke. Pitt was recommended by his father to study parts of Bolingbroke's writings, and get them by heart.

L. 13. *one observation.* "Among many reasons which determine me to prefer monarchy to every other form of government, this is a principal one. When monarchy is the essential form, it may be more easily and more usefully tempered with aristocracy, or democracy, or both, than either of them, when they are the essential forms, can be tempered with monarchy. It seems to me, that the introduction of a real permanent monarchical power, or anything more than the pageantry of it, into either of these, must destroy them and extinguish them, as a greater light extinguishes a less. Whereas it may easily be shewn, and the true form of our government will demonstrate, without seeking any other example, that very considerable aristocratical and democratical powers may be grafted on a monarchical stock, without diminishing the lustre, or restraining the power and authority of the prince, enough to alter in any degree the essential form." — Patriot King, p. 98. So Dean Lockier in Spence's Anecdotes: "Whatever is good, either in monarchies or republics, may be enjoyed in limited monarchies. The whole force of the nation is as ready to be turned one way as in [absolute] monarchies; and the liberties of the people may be as well secured as in republics."

L. 21. *the fawning sycophant of yesterday.* Perhaps a hard criticism on [361] some of the savants. More than one article of the Encyclopédie was written in the palace of Versailles.

L. 32. *full of abuses.* Burke omits one most important link in the chain of causes which led to the Revolution. The great system of abuses had been thoroughly penetrated, and a comprehensive, gradual scheme for remedying them had been commenced by Turgot. The principles which guided this great man in the preparation of this scheme have been since tried, affirmed, and developed. They have given the key to the reforms of the present century in our own and other countries. But Turgot was only suffered to remain in office twenty months, and nearly everything which he had time to effect was reversed. The interested classes, the nobility, clergy, parliaments, and farmers-general, were too strong for him. If any body could have done what Burke blames the French for not doing, it was he. What was left, but a general convulsion, proceeding from lower sources, if oppression was to be thrown off at all? Irritated by hesitation, retrogression, and mistrust, the people had lost all faith in their established government: and in dealing with the monarchy, which they wished in some way to preserve, naturally went to extremes in the safeguards which they provided for the concessions they had extorted. Facts seem to strengthen the conclusion of Mackintosh, that under such circumstances the *shock* of a revolution is necessary to the accomplishment of great reforms.

P. 227, L. 9. *All France was of a different opinion,* &c. True; but the *Cahiers* only too clearly indicated what was smouldering beneath. They repeatedly affirm, on the part of the *Tiers État,* the right of Property, and demand for it the protection of the law, as a thing that was in great jeopardy. They prove that every principle of society had been universally made the subject of question, and that very various opinions were entertained as to what ought to be done. They reveal a Harringtonian spirit in every corner of the kingdom. No one who reads them can fail to see in the "Declaration of the Rights of Man" their inevitable sequel.

L. 12. *projects for the reformation,* &c. More than this—they are full of abstract ideas, of the passion for definition, uniformity, and paper government. The Cahiers, in the briefest summary or index of contents, are perfectly bewildering. M. de Tocqueville insists, however, that whoso wishes to understand the Revolution, must study incessantly the whole series of folios.

L. 13. *without the remotest suggestion,* &c. Calonne is nearer the mark; "C'est d'abord une puérilité que d'argumenter du mot *régénérer le royaume,* qui se trouve dans quelques-uns des cahiers, et peut-être aussi dans quelques phrases employées par le Roi; comme si l'on pouvoit en conclure que le Roi et les cahiers, en se servant de cette expression métaphorique, auroient entendu que l'Assemblée devoit culbuter la Monarchie de fond en comble, et créer un gouvernement absolument nouveau. 'Régénérer' est un terme de religion, qui loin de présenter l'idée d'une destruction universelle, n'annonce qu'une salutaire vivification. Le baptême régénère l'homme en effaçant la [362] tâche qui le souilloit, et non en détruisant son existence; mais dans le sens de la révolution, régénérer c'est anéantir. Une telle interprétation rappelle l'histoire de ce Roi de Thessalie que ses filles égorgèrent," &c. (Cp. supra, note to p. 192, l. 29.) People saw that the kingdom needed "regeneration," and when they were about it made up their minds that it should be a thorough one.

L. 15. *been but one voice.* This is hardly justifiable. American independence had certainly raised similar hopes in France. Nor would it have been possible for the impulse to a republic to spring up and ripen in so short a time.

L. 29. *Taehmas Kouli Khan.* The military usurper whose exploits were a romance to the Western world in Burke's youth, and ended in the national prostration of Persia, from which the country has never recovered.

L. 35. *human race itself melts away and perishes under the eye of the observer.* "Men grow up thin," says Bacon, "where the Turcoman's horse sets his foot." Perhaps Burke had in mind the description of the miraculous smiting of the Philistines by Jonathan; "And the watchmen of Saul in Gibeah of Benjamin *looked;* and behold, the multitude *melted away,*" &c. 1 Sam. xiv. 16.

P. 228, L. 12. *state of its population.* The increase of the population, taken in connexion with the inequality of imposts, and the burdens of the poor, ought to have been estimated among the causes of the Revolution.

P. 229, L. 15. *considerable tracts of it are barren.* It was calculated in 1846 that nearly one-seventh of the whole superficies consisted of unproductive expanses of sand, heath, &c., chiefly lying near the seashores of Gascony and Languedoc, and in Champagne and French Flanders.

L. 19. *Generality of Lisle.* A Generality was the district under the official care of an Intendant-general. Lille was populous because it had been part of Flanders, the flourishing condition of which as compared with France was conspicuous in the Middle Ages. In Belgium the density of the population is still more than double that of the average of France; the former having 166, the latter 70 inhabitants to the square kilométre.

P. 230, L. 13. *whole British dominions.* Burke only means the British Isles.

L. 28. *species.* Plural.

P. 231, L. 25. *when I consider the face of the kingdom of France.* This Ciceronian page is well worth studying for its method, and the way in which the expressions which form the vehicle of the reflection are varied. The force of the argument is much enhanced by keeping in mind that this magnificent face of affairs had been mainly produced by the policy of Louis XIV. Thomson's description of the civilization of France clearly afforded Burke some hints:

            . . . . Diffusive shot
O'er fair extents of land, the shining road:

NOTES

The flood-compelling arch: the long canal,
[363] Through mountains piercing, and uniting seas:
The dome resounding sweet with infant joy,
From famine saved, or cruel-handed shame,
And that where valour counts his noble scars.
"Liberty," Part V. 471.

L. 26. *multitude and opulence of her cities.* Then much greater in comparison with Britain. The British Isles now contain twice as many towns having more than 100,000 inhabitants, as France.

L. 27. *useful magnificence of her spacious high roads,* &c. In which respect France was at least half a century in advance of England. The principal "grands chemins" were made by the government in the times of Louis XIV and XV. It was imagined that they might facilitate invasion, an idea which is laughed to scorn in the Encyclopédie. It is certain that they facilitated the Revolution.

L. 28. *opportunity* = opportuneness.

IBID. *her artificial canals,* &c. Canals were constructed in Italy in the eleventh, twelfth, and thirteenth centuries, and had an almost equally early beginning in the Netherlands. The first French canal was that of Briare, joining the Seine and Loire, begun in 1605 and finished in 1642.

L. 29. *opening the conveniences . . . through a solid continent.* Alluding to the canal of Languedoc, the greatest work of the kind on the continent, reaching from Narbonne to Toulouse, and forming a communication between the Atlantic and the Mediterranean. It was begun and finished by Pierre Paul de Riquet, in the reign of Louis XIV, and cost above 1,300,000*l.* sterling. Corneille, says Sir J. Stephen, has celebrated the junction of the two seas in some noble verses, whose only fault is that they say far too much of Louis XIV, and nothing at all of Riquet or of Colbert.

L. 31. *ports and harbours . . . naval apparatus.* Especially the naval stations of Brest, Toulon, and Cherbourg. The navy of France was another creation of Colbert's.

L. 33. *fortifications.* Most of them designed and carried out at a vast expense by S. le Prestre de Vauban, to whom and other French writers, as Blondel, Belidor, &c., modern fortification and military engineering in general owe their origin almost exclusively.

P. 232, L. 1. *impenetrable barrier.* He has in mind especially the "iron frontier" towards the Netherlands.

REFLECTIONS ON THE REVOLUTION IN FRANCE

L. 3. *to what complete perfection,* &c. Especially the vine, hardly known in Gaul until the Roman conquest.

L. 7. *in some particulars not second.* Burke alludes to the English silk manufacture, which was eclipsed by France, in consequence, as was shewn by Mr. Huskisson, of the prohibitive system established in favour of the weavers of Spitalfields.

L. 8. *grand foundations of charity.* The Hôtel-Dieu, École Militaire, Invalides, &c., of Paris; The Dames de la Charité, founded by St. Vincent de Paul, Redemptorists, Lazarists, and the numerous bodies of Hospitallers, &c., &c.

[364] **L. 9.** *state of all the arts.* France in the last century was at the head of all Europe in the arts—painting, architecture, decorative design, and music.

L. 10. *men she has bred,* &c. It would take up too much space to trace this out in its details, and compare France in this respect with the rest of Europe. It would be an easy and interesting task for the student. See Dr. Bridges' "Colbert and Richelieu," where, however, the worth of French intellect is overrated.

L. 27. *Whoever has examined,* &c. But the character of the monarch was against what Burke assumes to be the spirit of the monarchy. "Il commençait toutes les reformes par justice, et n'en achevant aucune par indolence, et par abandon de lui-même, irritant la passion d'innover sans la satisfaire, faisant entrevoir le bien sans l'opérer. Roi populaire dans les rues, il redevenait Roi gentilhomme à Versailles—reformateur auprès de Turgot et de Necker, honteux de ses reformes dans la société brillante et legère de Marie Antoinette; Roi constitutional par goût, Roi absolu par habitude," &c.—De Sacy.

L. 30. *earnest endeavour towards the prosperity,* &c. In spite, however, not in consequence, of the institutions Burke was defending. After the peace of 1763 (See Vol. i. "Present Discontents") a spirit of reformation had sprung up and spread over all parts of Europe, even to Constantinople. Agriculture and trade had been the special objects of this movement in France. "Another no less laudable characteristic (of the present times) is, that spirit of reform and improvement, under the several heads of legislation, of the administration of justice, the mitigation of penal laws, the affording some greater attention to the ease and security of the lower orders of the people, with the cultivation of those acts most generally useful to mankind, and particularly the public encouragement given to agriculture as an art, which is becoming prevalent in every part of Europe." Annual Register, 1786.

NOTES

P. 233, L. 5. *censurable degree of facility.* "If in many respects the force of received opinions has in the present times been too much impaired, and perhaps too wide and indiscriminate a scope given to speculation on the domains of antiquity and practice, it is, however, a just cause of triumph, that prejudice and bigotry were the earliest victims. Happy will it be, if the blows which were aimed at the foundations and the buttresses, shall only shake off the useless incumbrances of the edifice. And this, we are to hope, will be the case." Ibid.

L. 11. *trespassed more by levity and want of judgment,* &c. For instance, the attempt suddenly to relieve the working classes from the disadvantages imposed on them by the system of industrial corporations. Rash and highsounding promises on many other points were issued in the name of the King, which stimulated the opposition of the privileged classes. In the quarrel of 1772 between the King and the Parliament of Toulouse, the latter body accused the government of endangering the people's means of subsistence [365] by its rash measures. The King retorted that public distress was caused by the ambition of the Parliament and the covetousness of the wealthy classes. In this way the idea was thoroughly worked into the people, that all their troubles were caused by the interests of one or other of the powers above them.

L. 20. *dwell perpetually on the donation to favourites,* &c. Burke alludes in the note to the publication of extracts from the famous *Livre Rouge.* Calonne shows that of the 228 millions of livres included in the accounts of this book for sixteen years, under different ministers, 209 millions were accountable for on other scores (foreign subsidies and secret service money, expenses of administration, personal expenses of the King and Queen, payment of the debts of the King's brothers, indemnities, &c.). The pamphlet circulated with so much industry is chiefly made up of scandalous reflections on the persons pensioned, and accounts of their lives and services. We find in it under the account of Mirabeau, 5000 liv. in 1776 for the "MS. of a work composed by him, entitled *Des Lettres de Cachet*"; and 195,000 liv. in 1789, "upon his word of honour [!] to counteract the plans of the National Assembly."

L. 28. *told* = counted. So "tale," p. 234, l. 2.

P. 234, L. 5. *considerable emigrations.* This was before the beginning of the great tide of emigration, which occasioned the decree against leaving the country, in 1791, pronouncing a sentence of civil death, and confiscation of goods, against the emigrant.

L. 7. *Circean liberty.* See Hom. Od. Lib. x. &c.

L. 14. *learned Academicians of Laputa,* &c. The satire of both Butler and Swift was much employed against what was called "virtuosodom," or the cultivation of the minute philosophy and natural science, in the infancy of those pursuits. Swift anticipates with curious foresight the situation of a country under the exclusive dominion of philosophers.

P. 236, L. 11. *those of Germany, at the period,* &c.—i. e. after the death of Frederick II, in 1250. "Every nobleman exercised round his castle a licentious independence; the cities were obliged to seek protection from their walls and confederacies; and from the Rhine and Danube to the Baltic, the names of peace and justice were unknown." —Gibbon.

L. 14. *Orsini and Vitelli.* Perhaps these particular names were put down without sufficient reflection. The Orsini were indeed distinguished in the twelfth century at Rome; but the Vitelli were first known as *condottieri* in the fifteenth, and the Orsini derive their chief celebrity in the same way. The two families were associated in resisting Pope Alexander VI. This was long after the period when robber knights "used to sally from their fortified dens," &c. Burke apparently, like his translator Gentz, thought they were famous in the wars of the Guelphs and Ghibellines.

L. 16. *Mamalukes.* Who constituted a military republic in Egypt and Syria.

IBID. *Nayres on the coast of Malabar.* The Nairs are the military caste who [366] long had the ruling power on this coast, and are still numerous and influential. They are not strictly a noble caste, as Burke implies, but, like some other low castes, have assumed the functions and rights of a noble caste. They were reduced in 1763 by Hyder Ali, by the fall of whose son and successor, Tippoo Sultan, before the English arms, the Malabar coast came to the East India Company.

L. 19. *Equity and Mercy.* Both were personified as coast deities in ancient Rome.

L. 27. *civil war between the vices.* Cp. infra, p. 264, l. 14, p. 274, l. 26, &c.

P. 237, L. 6. *breathe the spirit of liberty as warmly,* &c. Not universally true, though not unjustifiable as a general statement.

L. 16. *principles of a British constitution.* Which was proposed as a model by Maury, Lally-Tollendal, Mounier, &c. The hostility of the victorious party to anything like the English constitution seemed a bond of union between them and the English Jacobins, at whom the present work is mainly levelled.

P. 238, L. 4. *never abandoning for a moment,* &c. M. Depont, to whom the work was addressed, objected to the severity of this part of the character of Henry IV, and Burke in a letter to him on the subject, justifies his view. The "scaffold" (l. 7) alludes to the execution of the Maréchal de Biron. "If he thought that M. de Biron was capable of bringing on such scenes as we have lately beheld, and of producing the same anarchy, confusion, and distress in his kingdom, as preliminary to the establishment of that humiliating as well as vexatious tyranny, we now see on the point of being settled, under the name of a constitution, in France, he did well, very well, to cut him off in the crude and immature infancy of his treasons. He would not have deserved the crown which he wore, and wore with so much glory, if he had scrupled, by all the preventive mercy of rigorous law, to punish those traitors and enemies of their country and of mankind. For, believe me, there is no virtue where there is no wisdom. A great, enlarged, protecting and preserving benevolence has it, not in its incidents and circumstances, but in its very essence, to exterminate vice, and disorder, and oppression from the world." Correspondence, iii. 160. The letter is printed at the end of Dupont's Translation.

L. 9. *merited* = earned. Lat. mereor.

L. 31. *beyond what is common in other countries.* The contrast especially applies to England, where the *noblesse,* as a body, did not exist, the greater part of the nobility being of middle class origin, and really commoners with coronets on their coats of arms.

L. 33. *officious*—i. e. disposed to do kind services. So Dr. Johnson's Epitaph on Levett;

Officious, innocent, sincere,
Of every friendless name the friend.

P. 239, L. 8. *to strike any person.* A form of outrage never very uncommon in this country.

[367] **L. 12.** *attacks upon the property,* &c. To this it may be said that it was well understood that the nobility possessed already so much unjust advantage, that such attacks were out of the question, in the existing state of feeling and intelligence among the lower classes.

L. 19. *When the letting of the land was by rent.* It would even appear that the tenant enjoyed a security in this respect unknown to

English law. "Pareillement de même que la bonne foi ne permet pas au vendeur de vendre au-delà du juste prix, elle ne permet pas aussi au bailleur d'imposer par le bail la charge d'une rente trop forte qui excède le juste prix de l'héritage." Pothier, Traité du Contrat de Bail à Rente, p. 34. In addition, the rent reserved on a lease was commonly made redeemable, by a special clause, at a specified sum, or, in default, at a valuation.

L. 21. *partnership with the farmer.* Known as *métairie,* the farmer being called métayer. The usual form was that the landowner advanced the necessary stock, seed, &c., for carrying on the cultivation, and received as his share one half of the produce. This primitive contract is largely in use in India, Brazil, and other backward agricultural countries.

L. 30. *much of the civil government,* &c. See De Tocqueville, De l'Ancien Régime. The civil government had passed almost entirely out of the hands of the nobility into that of the central power; and the feudal dues and privileges which in former times had been cheerfully yielded to them when they had the responsibility of administration and police, were consequently grudged and resisted.

P. 240, L. 7. *A foolish imitation,* &c. "Anglomanie," which had been increasing in vogue all through the century. See the amusing description of it at the beginning of Mr. Carlyle's Hist. of the French Revolution. Previously the cry was against our following the example of the French,

> Whose manners still our tardy apish nation
> Limps after, in base awkward imitation.
> Shakespeare, Rich. II.

L. 18. *Those of the commons,* &c. Cp. ante, note to p. 208, l. 7.

L. 23. *less than in Germany.* Where the prejudice still subsists in all its force. The first question asked of a stranger in that country is, "Sind Sie von Adel?" The saying there goes that there are three bodies whose strength lies in their corporate cohesion, the Jews, the Jesuits, and the Nobility.

P. 241, L. 6. *The strong struggle,* &c. See Chalmer's Bridgewater Treatise, Chapter on "The Affections which conduce to the well-being of Society."

L. 12. *civil order.* A double meaning perhaps here flashed through Burke's mind—"order" signifying an architectural combination, as well as a state of political regulation.

Notes

L. 13. *Corinthian capital.* The Corinthian is the most graceful and ornamental of the orders of architecture.

IBID. *Omnes boni,* &c. Cic. pro P. Sextio, ix. 21.

[368] **L. 18.** *giving a body to opinion,* &c. Whether the system of such an institution ought not to be revised, in a totally different state of society, is of course, another question. "C'est une terrible chose que la Qualité," says Pascal—"elle donne à un enfant qui vient de naitre une considération que n'obtiendraient pas cinquante ans de travaux et de virtus." Burke says nothing of the tendency, inherent in descended nobility, to sink below the level of its source. Young, Sat. I:

> Men should press forward in fame's glorious chase;
> Nobles look backward, and so lose the race.

L. 31. *It was with the same satisfaction,* &c. Throughout these pages Burke purposely confounds two distinct questions. "Mr. Burke has grounded his eloquent apology purely on their (the clergy) *individual and moral character.* This, however, is totally irrelative to the question; for we are not discussing what place they ought to occupy in society as individuals, but as a body. We are not considering the demerit of citizens whom it is fit to punish, but the spirit of a body which it is politic to dissolve. We are not contending that the Nobility and Clergy were in their private capacity bad citizens, but that they were members of corporations which could not be preserved with security to civil freedom."—Mackintosh.

P. 243, L. 14. *without care it may be used,* &c. History ought not to be written without a strong moral bias. Burke elsewhere censures the cold manner of Tacitus and Machiavelli in narrating crime and oppression. Macaulay is in this respect a good model.

L. 26. *troublous storms,* &c.

> Long were to tell the troublous storms that toss
> The private state, and make the life unsweet.
>   Spenser, Faery Queene, Book ii. c. 7, st. 14.

L. 28. *Religion,* &c., *the pretexts.* "If men would say they took up arms for anything but religion, they might be beaten out of it by reason; out of that they never can, for they will not believe you whatever you say. The very *arcanum* of pretending religion in all wars is, that something may be found out in which all men may have interest. In this the groom has as much interest as the lord. Were it for lands, one has a thousand acres, and the other but one; he would not venture so far, as he that has a thousand. But religion is equal to both. Had all men land alike, by a *lex agraria,* then all men would say they fought for land."—Selden, Table-talk.

P. 244, L. 10. *Wise men will apply,* &c. Cp. vol. i. p. 75 seqq.

P. 246, L. 25. *If your clergy,* &c. One of those passages so common in Burke, which strike by their very temperance, and arrest attention by their mild and tolerant spirit.

L. 32. *through all their divisions.* Not of rank, but of sect and country.

P. 247, L. 6. *I must bear with infirmities,* &c. Notice the epigram, which appears also in Burke's Tracts on the Popery Laws. "The law punishes delinquents, not because they are not good men, but because they are [369] intolerably wicked. It does bear, and must, with the vices and the follies of men, until they actually strike at the root of order."

L. 25. *rigidly screwing up right into wrong.*

In vain thy reason finer webs shall draw,
Entangle justice in her net of law,
And right, too rigid, harden into wrong.
Pope, Essay on Man, iii. 191.

L. 29. *ambition of intellectual sovereignty,* &c. Burke clearly has in mind as a secondary object the Revolutionists at whom the whole work is levelled. Their enthusiasm resembled in a high degree that of the Protestant Reformers. Burke afterwards put this forward more clearly, in showing that the Revolution was one of speculative dogma, and that the war against it was one against that most formidable of opponent forces, an *armed doctrine.*

P. 248, L. 5. *two great parties.* Catholic and Protestant.

L. 15. *When my occasions,* &c. Burke speaks of nearly twenty years before. He refers to the subject in his "Remarks on the Policy of the Allies." It may be said that the prevalence of freethinking did no credit to the clergy, and that the emigrant nobility were equally followers of the philosophers. "The atheism of the new system, as opposed to the piety of the old, is one of the weakest arguments I have yet heard in favour of this political crusade."—Sheridan, Speech on the Address on the War with France, Feb. 12, 1793.

P. 249, L. 12. *provincial town.* Auxerre.

IBID. *the bishop.* M. de Cicé, under whose protection young Burke

NOTES

lived for some time at Auxerre. When the bishop came an impoverished and aged emigrant to England, the Burkes were able to requite his kindness.

L. 13. *three clergymen.* One of whom seems to have been the Abbé Vaullier. Correspondence, vol. i. p. 426.

L. 20. *Abbé Morangis.* Dupont spells the name, in his translation, "*Monrangies.*"

P. 250, L. 5. *an hundred and twenty Bishops.* The exact number of Archbishops and Bishops was 131, of whom forty-eight had seats in the Assembly. The Assembly reduced them to eighty-three (assigning one to each department), which is the number now in existence.

L. 8. *eminent depravity.* Such examples may have been rare, but they were brought prominently into notice, by their existence in the midst of the society of Paris. Clermont, the Abbé of St. Germain des Prés, in the preceding generation, was a notorious instance. He enjoyed 2000 benefices, which he made a practice of selling. He devoted his revenues among other objects to the education of *danseuses.* Talleyrand was an obvious contemporary instance.

L. 32. *pensionary* = stipendiary, the salaries of church officials being made charges on the nation.

[370] **P. 251, L. 4.** *nothing of science or erudition.* Certainly the Gallican church has shown nothing since to compare with the time of Louis XV.

L. 19. *ascertained* = fixed.

L. 29. *intended only to be temporary.* It was but temporary, but it is too much to say that it was intended to be so.

P. 252, L. 7. *enlightened self-interest.* An idea borrowed, like many others, from the English philosophers, but carried out to its consequences by the French, especially by Helvetius.

L. 12. *Civic education.* See the ideas on Public Education at the end of the work of Helvetius "De l'Esprit."

L. 16. *principle of popular election.* Burke evidently has in mind the discussion of the question by Dr. Johnson in his Tract on Lay Patronage: "But it is evident that, as in all other popular elections, there will be a contrariety of judgment, and acrimony of passion; a parish, upon every vacancy, would break into factions, and the contest for the choice of a minister would set neighbours at variance, and bring

REFLECTIONS ON THE REVOLUTION IN FRANCE

discord into families. The minister would be taught all the arts of a candidate, would flatter some, and bribe others . . . and it is hard to say what bitterness of malignity would prevail in a parish where these elections should happen to be frequent, and the enmity of opposition should be rekindled before it had cooled."

P. 253, L. 8. *Burnet says, &c.* History of His Own Times, Book iii.

L. 25. *under the influence of a party spirit, &c.* The allusion is in particular to Cranmer.

L. 29. *as they would with equal fortitude, &c.* This must be taken with some reservation. "Toute opinion est assez forte pour se faire épouser au prix de la vie," says Montaigne. Sectarian heat is often the fiercer the narrower the point of issue.

P. 254, L. 6. *justice and mercy are substantial parts of religion.* Micah vi. 8: "What doth the Lord require of thee, but to do justly, and to love mercy, and to walk humbly with thy God?"

L. 17. *dogmas of religion—all of moment.* Cp. ante, note to p. 186, l. 15. See especially the Tracts on the Popery Laws. Perhaps the judgment of Bacon, acquiesced in by Burke, preferring the extreme of superstition to that of free-thought, may be reconsidered in the light of modern experience. The Rev. R. Cecil, an acute and philosophical divine, thought less of the dangers of Infidelity than of those of Popery. "Popery debases and alloys Christianity; but Infidelity is a furnace, wherein it is purified and refined. The injuries done to it by Popery are repaired by the very attacks of Infidelity." Remains, p. 136.

L. 25. *common cause—common enemy.* That of religion against principled non religionists. Experience, however, shows that the danger has been exaggerated. Notwithstanding the fluctuating prevalence of free-thought in different societies in Europe since the Italian Renaissance, it has nowhere taken root in such a way as to threaten the religion of the nation, from [371] the fact that it cannot adapt itself to the moral needs of the mass of mankind. "Infidelity," says Mr. Cecil, "is a suicide; it dies by its own malignity; it is *known and read of all men.* No man was ever injured essentially by it, who was fortified with a small portion of the genuine spirit of Christianity—its contrition and its docility."

P. 255, L. 18. *I see, in a country very near us, &c.* Cp. note to p. 95, l. 12. Burke here also pretends to the right to censure the unjust domestic policy of a neighbouring nation.

NOTES

L. 23. *one of the greatest of their own lawyers.* I cannot point to any passage in the works of Domat, in which the second thesis, here attributed to him (l. 25), is maintained. Burke was apparently quoting from memory. Often as he makes verbal mistakes, it is rarely that he makes material ones. Here, however, seems to be a material error of memory. The doctrine of Domat is that the postulates of society are divisible into (1) Laws immutable, (2) Laws arbitrary. He refers the principle of prescription to the first, the ascertainment of its limits to the second. Civil Law in its Natural Order, bk. iii. tit. 7, sec. 4. Burke was perhaps thinking of Cicero, who repeats the ordinary notions as to the end of society being security of property: "Hanc ob causam maxime, ut sua tenerent, respublicae civitatesque constitutae sunt." De Off. lib. II. c. 21, sec. 73 (see also c. 23).

L. 27. *If prescription be once shaken,* &c. Burke's fears were needless. The principle was never shaken, nor has it ever been seriously threatened.

P. 257, L. 6. *Anabaptists of Münster.* Originally organised in the Netherlands, these fanatics were admitted by the citizens of Münster after the expulsion of their bishop. Münster saw the community of goods and wives carried out, and a tailor who took to himself seventeen wives, proclaimed King of the Universe.

L. 10. *just cause of alarm.* The policy of Luther, which steadily maintained the cause of the Reformation free from political revolutions, kept them in isolation.

P. 258, L. 4. *best governed.* Regarded from the point of view of the *bourgeois* oligarchy, not of the peasant.

L. 16. *standards consecrated,* &c. Two of the members of the Patriotic Society at Nantes had been despatched to the Revolution Society, to deliver to them the picture of a banner used in the festival of the former Society in the month of August, bearing the motto "Pacte Universel," and a representation of the flags of England and France bound together with a ribbon on which was written: "A l'union de la France et d'Angleterre." At the bottom was written, "To the Revolution Society in London." The messengers were respectfully received and entertained by the committee of the society. These facts were submitted to the society in the report of the committee presented at the meeting of Nov. 4, 1790.

L. 20. *expedient to make war upon them.* Anticipating the policy afterwards so strenuously advocated by Burke.

REFLECTIONS ON THE REVOLUTION IN FRANCE

[372] **P. 260, L. 8.** *general earthquake in the political world.* Cp. ante note to p. 149, l. 10. Burke almost repeats the vaticinations of Hartley.

L. 9. *confederacies and correspondences.* It would be too long to recapitulate the unimportant history of the secret society of the *Illuminati,* and of the exaggerated panic which the detection of it produced. The *Illuminati,* no small body, and composed of members of some standing in society, arose in Bavaria, under Dr. Adam (Spartacus) Weishaupt and Baron (Philon) Knigge. Their tenets were a political version of the harmless social amusement of Freemasonry, not ill-adapted to the spirit of the age, and possessing, except for themselves, no real significance. They were betrayed by four malcontents for infringing the Electoral decree of 1781 against secret societies, which was prompted by the same suspicion which still prohibits Roman Catholics from being members of similar fraternities. Weishaupt was deprived of his Professorship of Law at Ingoldstadt, and the Lodges of the *Illuminaten-Orden* were closed in 1785. The best account of the Illuminati and their constitution, doctrines, and ceremonies, is to be found in the Abbé Barruel's Mémoires pour servir à l'histoire de Jacobinisme, Part 3. Many books were published to expose the supposed conspiracy, among which that first mentioned by Burke was the first. The title is: "Einige Originalschriften des Illuminate-nordens, welche bey dem gewesenem Regierungsrath Zwack, durch vorgenommene Hausvisitation zu Landshut den 11 und 12 Octob. 1786, vorgefunden worden." See also in English, Robinson's "Proofs of a Conspiracy formed by Freemasons, &c., against all the Religions and all the Governments of Europe." The groundlessness of the panic was shown by Mounier, "De l'influence attribuée aux philosophes, aux francs-maçons et aux illuminés sur la Royaume de France," Tübingen 1801.

L. 22. *Justice . . . the great standing policy.* A good adaptation of the not very lofty maxim that "Honesty is the best policy."

L. 26. *When men are encouraged,* &c. The abstract principle is admitted by Mackintosh, with a just censure on its false application: "The State is the proprietor of the Church Revenues, but its faith, it may be said, is pledged to those who have entered into the Church, for the continuance of those incomes, for which they have abandoned all other pursuits. The right of the State to arrange at its pleasure the revenues of any future priests may be confessed, while a doubt may be entertained whether it is competent to change the fortune of those to whom it has promised a certain income for life. But these distinct subjects have been confounded, that sympathy with suffering individuals might influence opinion in a general question—that feeling for the degradation of the hierarchy might supply the place of argument to establish the property of the Church."

P. 261, L. 23. *such as sophisters represent it,* i. e. as a case of leaving an abuse to grow and flourish, or of cutting it up by the roots. The "middle" spoken of by Burke would be to trim its exuberances, and to graft better scions upon it.

[373] **L. 26.** *Spartam nactus es; hanc exorna.* The version of Erasmus (Adag. 2501) of the quotation, familiar in Roman Literature, of the first of two lines of Euripides, preserved by Stobaeus:

Σπάρτην ἔλαχες, κείνην κόσμει·
Τὰς δὲ Μυκήνας ἡμεῖς ἰδίᾳ.

They are from the *Telephus* (Dind. Frag. 695), and are apparently the words of Agamemnon to Menelaus. See Cic. Ep. Att. I. 20, IV. 6, and Plut. Περὶ τῆς εὐθυμίας. The passage is mistranslated by Erasmus, and the wrong meaning is kept up in Burke's allusion. Κοσμεῖν means to *rule*, not to *improve* or *decorate*. The original is equivalent to "Mind your own business."

P. 262, L. 10. *purchase* = leverage.

L. 22. *The winds blow,* &c., St. John, iii. 8. Burke alludes to the case of the sailor, who cannot control the motive forces on which he depends, and means that the politician must similarly regard his motive power and material as produced by some force out of his control.

P. 263, L. 8. *steam . . . electricity.* The forecast in these lines, written long before steam was successfully applied to navigation, is most remarkable. Electricity had been discovered by the English philosopher Gilbert two centuries before, but was as yet unapplied to any practical purpose.

L. 31. *You derive benefits,* &c. Burke alludes to the Passions, as described by his favourite moralist:

The surest virtues thus from passions shoot,
Wild nature's vigour working at the root.
                              Essay on Man, II. 183.

Pope proceeds to derive all the virtues from the two sources of pride and shame.

P. 264, L. 4. *Superstition is the religion,* &c. So Lord Chesterfield in the "World": "Ceremony is the superstition of good-breeding, as well as of religion; but yet, being an outwork of both, should not be absolutely demolished."

L. 13. *Munera Terrae.* The Homeric expression used by Horace, Bk. II, Ode 14, l. 10, to express the conditions of mortal existence. Burke means by *munera terrae* the mundane as opposed to the imperishable elements of life.

L. 14. *Wisdom is not the most severe corrector of folly. They are the rival follies,* &c. Cp. Young, Satire II:

> He scorns Florello, and Florello him;
> This hates the *filthy* creature, that the *prim:*
> Thus in each other both these fools despise
> Their own dear selves, with undiscerning eyes;
> Their methods various, but alike their aim,
> The sloven and the fopling are the same.
> Ye Whigs and Tories! thus it fares with you,
> When party-rage too warmly you pursue;
> [374] Then both club nonsense and impetuous pride,
> And folly joins whom sentiments divide.
> You vent your spleen, as monkies when they pass
> Scratch at the mimic monkey in the glass,
> While both are one; and henceforth be it known,
> Fools of both sides shall stand for fools alone.

Mackintosh, alluding apparently to this passage of Burke, agrees with Montesquieu that under bad governments one abuse often limits another. "But when the abuse is destroyed, why preserve the remedial evil? Superstition certainly alleviates the despotism of Turkey; but if a rational government could be erected in that empire, it might with confidence disclaim the aid of the Koran, and despise the remonstrances of the Mufti."

P. 265, L. 5. *In every prosperous community,* &c. The well-known doctrines of the French economists of the physiocratic school, popularised some years before by Adam Smith. The arguments here based on them by Burke will be differently estimated by different people. They have no immediate bearing on the main point of the work, and certainly are opposed to, and form a standing censure upon, the deliberate policy of England at the Reformation.

L. 34. *as usefully employed,* &c. A surprising turn is given to the argument. Burke compares the monastery and the monks with the factory and its then overtasked and degraded "hands." Public attention was just becoming attracted to the condition of the factory workers, and in 1802 the first Sir Robert Peel succeeded in passing the first of the Factory Acts.

P. 268, L. 6. *whether sole,* &c. The phrase is technical. A bishop is an example of a "corporation sole."

L. 7. *susceptible of a public direction,* &c. This was done, in a remarkable way, at the disestablishment of the Alien Priories by Henry V, when their revenues were largely applied to purposes of education. It was also done to a smaller extent at the English Reformation. The Church and Education, however, on this occasion, were benefited to a less degree than the nobility.

L. 15. *commendatory abbots.* Those who held inferior benefices *in commendam,* by way of plurality, an abuse which grew up with many others out of the claims of the Holy See in the twelfth century. Cp. note to p. 250, l. 8.

L. 17. *Can any philosophic spoiler,* &c. Bishop Berkeley, Guizot, and Dr. Arnold have brought forward the substance of this excellent argument, which rests on the popular and accessible nature of Church preferment.

P. 269, L. 13. Here commences the Second Part of the work, which seems to have been resumed after an interval of some months, corresponding with the Parliamentary Session of 1790. Early in the Session, several liberal measures were introduced; but thwarted by the consideration of the prevalence of Jacobinism, Fox's Resolution in favour of the Dissenters, against the Test and Corporation Acts, was opposed by Burke, who cited [375] passages from Price and Priestley, and proved that the dissenters cared not "the nip of a straw" for the repeal of these Acts (which he said he would have advocated ten years ago), but that their open object was the abolition of Tithes, and State Public Worship. Hood was also defeated in his motion for a Parliamentary Reform Bill.

L. 32. *I have taken a review,* &c. Burke proceeds to criticise the positive work of the Assembly, and in the first place, after some general remarks, to deal with the nature of the bodies into which the citizens were to be formed for the discharge of their political functions (p. 277). "In this important part of the subject," says Mackintosh, "Mr. Burke has committed some fundamental errors. It is more amply, more dexterously, and more correctly treated by M. de Calonne, of whose work this discussion forms the most interesting part."

P. 270, L. 16. *they have assumed another,* &c. As the Long Parliament did in England, and as the present Assembly (1874) have done in France. Such assumptions are, under justifying circumstances, in the strictest sense political necessities. Cp. p. 270, l. 35.

L. 23. *The most considerable of their acts,* &c. This introduces casually the interesting question of the competence of majorities, which Burke so philosophically considers in connexion with the doctrine of Natural Aristocracy, in the Appeal from the New to the Old Whigs. He argues that (1) an incorporation produced by unanimity, and (2) an unanimous agreement, that the act of a mere majority, say of one, shall pass as the act of the whole, are necessary to give authority to majorities. Nature, out of civil society, knows nothing of such a "constructive whole": and in many cases, as in an English jury, and formerly in a Polish national council, absolute unanimity was required. "This mode of decision (by majorities), where wills may be so nearly equal, where, according to circumstances, the smaller number may be the stronger force, and where apparent reason may be all upon one side, and on the other little less than impetuous appetite—all this must be the result of a very particular and special convention, confirmed afterwards by long habits of obedience, by a sort of discipline in society, and by a strong hand, vested with stationary, permanent power, to enforce this sort of constructive general will."

P. 271, L. 9. *To make a revolution,* &c. Burke did not know that the Revolution had been foreseen and demanded, ever since the middle of the century. The failures of Turgot stimulated expectation; but reformers had for some years been now dejected and weary of waiting. "Men no longer," says Michelet, "believed in its near approach. Far from Mont Blanc, you see it; when at its foot you see it no more." Mably, in 1784, thought public spirit too weak to bring it about. No reasons for a revolution were ever asked in France; the only question was, who ought to suffer by that which was inevitable.

L. 27. *a pleader,* i. e. not a speaker, but one who draws the *pleas,* or formal documents used in an action at law, according to set precedents.

[376] **P. 272, L. 18.** *eloquence in their speeches.* There was plenty of fluent speaking, but more of dismal lecturing, in the Assembly. Set speeches were the fashion. Mirabeau is said on more than one occasion to have delivered speeches taken entirely from those of Burke.

L. 20. *eloquence may exist,* &c. The well-known sentence of Sallust on Catiline: "Satis eloquentiae; sapientiae parum."

NOTES

L. 23. *no ordinary men.* Burke elsewhere compliments the vigilance, ingenuity, and activity of the Jacobins.

P. 273, L. 6. *Pater ipse colendi,* &c. Virg. Georg. i. 121.

L. 20. *The difficulties,* &c. Cp. vol. i. p. 170, l. 20.

P. 274, L. 2. Your *mob.* "Your" is expletive.

L. 4. *Rage and phrenzy will pull down,* &c. So in Preface to Motion, June 14, 1784: "Its demolition (an independent House of Commons) was accomplished in a moment; and it was the work of ordinary hands. But to construct, is a matter of skill: to demolish, force and fury are sufficient." The tendencies of the age often prompted similar warnings. "A fool or a madman, with a farthing candle, may cause a conflagration in a city that the wisest of its inhabitants may be unable to extinguish." S. Jenyns, Reflections.

L. 6. *The errors,* &c. This paragraph is in Burke's most striking tone, that of an experienced political philosopher, contemptuously exposing the shallowness of the sciolist.

L. 11. *loves sloth and hates quiet.* The epigram belongs to Tacitus, Germ. 15: "Mira diversitate naturae, cum iidem homines sic ament inertiam et oderint quietem."

L. 18. *expatiate.* In the now almost disused sense = roam at will. Milton, Par. Lost, I. 774. So Pope, Essay on Man:

The soul, uneasy, and confined from home,
Rests, and *expatiates,* in a life to come.

P. 275, L. 15. *the true lawgiver,* &c. Aimed at the cold and mathematical Sieyès.

L. 16. *to love and respect his kind, and to fear himself.* Echoed by Shelley, Hymn to Intellectual Beauty:

Whom, Spirit fair, thy spells did bind
To fear himself, and love all human kind.

L. 19. *Political arrangement,* &c. Burke here brings to the question the results of his personal experience. These pages contain fundamental axioms of practical politics.

L. 28. *have never yet seen,* &c. So South: "God has filled no man's intellectuals so full but he has left some vacuities in them that may send him sometimes for supplies to minds of a lower pitch. . . . Nay, the greatest abilities are sometimes beholding to the very meanest."

P. 276, L. 7. *composition,* i. e. combined multiplicity.

L. 11. *the work itself requires the aid of more minds than one age can furnish.* The common notion being that we should complete something [377] for which posterity will thank our foresight. We do better by so arranging our labours, that posterity may enter into them, and enlarge and complete what we have attained.

L. 15. *some of the philosophers.* The Schoolmen. "Plastic nature" or "plastic virtue" is a phrase intended by them to express the generative or vegetative faculty.

L. 30. *take their opinions,* &c. Chiefly the comedians, e. g. the ridicule of Molière against medicine, of Steele against law.

P. 277, L. 2. *those who are habitually employed,* &c. "By continually looking upwards, our minds will themselves grow upwards; and, as a man by indulging in habits of scorn and contempt for others is sure to descend to the level of what he despises, so the opposite habits of admiration and enthusiastic reverence for excellence impart to ourselves a portion of the qualities which we admire." Dr. Arnold, Preface to Poetry of Common Life.

L. 10. *complexional* = constitutional, as at p. 364, l. 2.

L. 12. quadrimanous *activity,* i. e. monkey-like, wantonly destructive. Helvetius had remarked, in his peculiar way, on the monkey-like necessity for perpetual activity in children, even after their wants are satisfied. "Les singes ne sont pas susceptible de *l'ennui* qu'on doit regarder comme un des principes de la perfectibilité de l'esprit humain."

L. 13. *paradoxes of eloquent writers.* Burke follows Bishop Warburton in treating all writers who had hinted at revolutionary ideas as mere paradox-mongers. Cardan seems to have been the first: after him comes Bayle, whose opinion that neither religion nor civil society were necessary to the human race is treated as a pleasant paradox by Warburton, Divine Legation, vol. i. p. 76. The immediate allusion is to Rousseau, whose "misbegotten Paradoxes" had been long ago exposed by Warburton in the 2nd Book of the "Alliance between Church and State." Burke here maintains the opinion expressed thirty years before in the Annual Register, in reviewing Rousseau's letter to D'Alembert. He thought the paradoxes it contained were, like his own Vindication of Natural Society, intended as satire. He charges him with "a tendency to paradox, which is always the bane of solid learning. . . . A satire upon civilized society, a satire upon learning, may make a tolerable sport for an ingenious fancy; but if carried farther it can do no more (and that in such a way surely is too much), than to unsettle our notions of right and wrong, and lead by degrees to universal scepticism." Mr. Lecky says of Rousseau, "He was one of those writers who are eminently destitute of the judgment that enables men without exaggeration to discriminate between truth and falsehood, and yet eminently endowed with that logical faculty which enables them to defend the opinions they have embraced. No one plunged more recklessly into paradox, or supported those paradoxes with more consummate skill." Hist. of Rationalism, vol. ii. p. 242.

L. 20. *Cicero ludicrously describes Cato, &c.* In the Preface to the *Paradoxa*. See also the Oration Pro Muraena.

[378] **L. 25.** *"pede nudo Catonem."* Hor. Ep. i. 19. 12–14:

Quid? si quis vultu torvo ferus, et pede nudo,
Exiguaeque togae simulet textore Catonem,
Virtutemne repraesentet moresque Catonis?

i. e. the apparel does not make the philosopher, as the cowl does not make the monk. "Video barbam et pallium—philosophum nondum video." The bearing of the allusion on the matter is more recondite than is usual with Burke.

IBID. *Mr. Hume told me, &c.* Burke seems to err in taking this statement of Rousseau to Hume, whatever its exact purport may have been, as a serious disclaimer of the ostensible ends of his writings. If ever a man was the serious dupe of his own errors, it was surely Rousseau. "It is not improbable," says Mackintosh, "that when rallied on the eccentricity of his paradoxes, he might, in a moment of gay effusion, have spoken of them as a sort of fancy, and an experiment on the credulity of mankind."

P. 278, L. 3. *I believe, that were Rousseau alive, &c.* This is likely enough from some passages in his writings. The following, for instance, on the metaphysical reformers, might have been written by Burke himself: "Du reste, renversant, détruisant, foulant aux pieds tout ce que les hommes respectent, ils ôtent aux affligés la dernière consolation de leur misère, aux puissants et aux riches le seul frein de leurs passions; ils arrachent du fond des coeurs le remords du crime, l'espoir de la vertu, et se vantent encore d'être les bienfaiteurs du genre humain. Jamais, disent ils, la vérité n'est nuisible aux hommes.[1]

---

1. The allusion is to the maxim of the Abbé de Fleury: "Les lumières philosophiques ne peuvent jamais nuire."

Je le crois comme eux; et c'est, à mon avis, une grande preuve que ce qu'ils enseignent n'est pas la vérité."

P. 279, L. 8. *correctives . . . aberrations.* The allusion is to the use of the compass in navigation, as is implied in the next page.

L. 12. *In them we often see,* &c. Often repeated by Burke, after Aristotle.

L. 29. *like their ornamental gardeners.* The Jardin Anglais, with its mounds, shrubs, and winding walks, had by this time scarcely become popular on the continent, though the model of Kent was not unknown. The French mechanical style to which Burke alludes was the invention of Le Nôtre, who laid out the gardens of Versailles.

P. 280, L. 2. *regularly square,* &c. Burke errs in stating that such a geometrical division and subdivision ever took place. Such plans were discussed, but all the new divisions were limited by natural boundaries. Burke did not see fit to correct the error when pointed out, not considering it material.

L. 20. *on the system of Empedocles.* The allusion seems to be to this philosopher's obscure notion of four successive stages of generation. See Ritter and Preller, Hist. Philos. No. 175.

[379] **IBID.** *and Buffon.* Alluding to the subordination of orders, genera, and species, applied to the animal world by Buffon, e.g. the order of carnivorous animals includes several genera, e.g. the genus *felis,* which includes several species, e.g. the lion, the tiger, and the cat. The application of such a principle in politics is directly contrary to Burke's conception of a state, which regarded the political division as *lateral,* and running as it were in strata over the whole extent of the land.

P. 281, L. 2. *dividing their political and civil representation into three parts.* It is right to notice that Mr. Pitt, in arranging the new representation of Ireland, in 1800, adopted two of these bases, those of population and of contribution, considering that these, taken together, formed a better ground of calculation than either separately, though he did not pretend that the result of the combination could be considered accurate.

L. 8. *third for her dower.* Alluding to the legal dower, of a third of the husband's real property, to which a widow is entitled.

L. 21. *But soft, by regular degrees, not yet* (by regular *approach*). Pope, Moral Essays, Ep. iv. l. 129.

NOTES

P. 285, L. 4. *as historians represent Servius Tullius*, &c. Burke had probably read the sceptical comments of Beaufort, which were developed by Niebuhr, on the early Roman History.

P. 290, L. 11. *Hominem non sapiunt.* Martial, x. 4. 10:

. . . . . . hominem pagina nostra sapit.

L. 27. *such governments do exist*, &c. Burke alludes to America, Holland, and Switzerland.

L. 31. *the effect of necessity.* In escaping in each case from external tyranny.

P. 291, L. 3. *treat France exactly like a country of conquest.* This bold and original observation is true enough. A conquest had been achieved, and it was intended to be consolidated.

P. 292, L. 9. *facies Hippocratica.* The old medical term for the appearance produced in the countenance by phthisis, as described by Hippocrates—the nostrils sharp, eyes hollow, temples low, tips of ears contracted, forehead dry and wrinkled, complexion pale or livid. It was held a sure prognostic of death. So in Armstrong's Satire "Taste":

Pray, on the first throng'd evening of a play
That wears the *facies Hippocratica*, &c.

L. 11. *the legislators*, &c. I suspect that this paragraph was written by the younger Burke. See footnote, p. 209.

L. 13. *metaphysics of an undergraduate.* It must be noticed that in 1790 this implied in Oxford (apparently alluded to) something very different to what it does at the present time. See an amusing account of the progress formerly necessary to a degree: "doing generals," "answering under-bachelor," "determining," "doing quodlibets," "doing austins," &c., in Vicesimus Knox's Essays, No. 77. See also a metaphysical Parody, by Porson, in Watson's Life of Porson.

[380] **L. 18.** *they were sensible*, &c. These views are summed up in the opinions of Aristotle.

P. 293, L. 32. *troll of their categorical table.* The French politicians, however, set small store by the Aristotelian logic. I cannot think that Burke would have penned this trivial repartee.

P. 294, L. 19. *if monarchy should ever again*, &c. How accurately these remarkable presages were to be fulfilled, was soon understood under Bonaparte.

REFLECTIONS ON THE REVOLUTION IN FRANCE

P. 296, L. 21. *a trustee for the whole, and not for the parts.* In its domestic policy, however, the unreformed House of Commons acted like a trustee for the agricultural interest.

L. 23. *several and joint securities.* Cp. the extract, p. 386, ll. 21–29.

L. 34. *Few trouble their heads,* &c. Cp., however, note to p. 281, l. 2, ante.

P. 297, L. 2. *on different ideas.* Referring rather to the means by which candidates were returned, than to the basis on which representation was distributed. Burke always attacked the corrupt sale and purchase of the constituencies, which was so thoroughly established in general opinion that Pitt's Reform Bill was based on the principle that the nation should buy from the boroughs the right to redistribute the seats.

P. 298, L. 17. *Limbus Patrum.* The border or outside ground between paradise and purgatory, as defined by Thomas Aquinas. Cp. Mr. Hales' note to Milton's Areopagitica, p. 13, l. 6.

L. 20. *like chimney-sweepers.* Chimneys were cleansed by sending a child up them. As the child grew to be a man, of course he became disqualified for his trade. See Sydney Smith's Essay on the subject, 1819.

P. 301, L. 3. *They have reversed the Latonian kindness,* &c. *Oras et littora circum.* Alluding to the Greek legend that Delos was a wandering island, fixed in its place at the instant when Latona gave birth to Apollo and Diana. Virg. Aen. iii. 75:

Quam pius arcitenens, *oras et littora circum*
Errantem, Gyaro celsa Myconoque revinxit.

L. 10. *holy bishop.* Talleyrand, Bishop of Autun.

L. 13. *not a good,* &c. Burke, however, was certainly both a good and an old farmer. He was devoted to agriculture, and farmed his own lands at Beaconsfield up to the time of his death.

L. 19. *encouragement*—in the objective sense = hope.

IBID. *Diis immortalibus sero.* Burke follows the track of Bolingbroke in alluding to the beautiful sentiment of Cicero, de Senect. vii. 25. Death holding a handle of the plough is an embellishment of Burke's.

P. 302, L. 3. *Beatus ille.* The well-known Epode of Horace, with its humorous conclusion, thus happily imitated by Somervile (1692–1742):

NOTES

Thus spoke old Gripe, when bottles three
Of Burton ale, and sea-coal fire,
[381] Unlock'd his breast; resolved to be
A gen'rous, honest country 'squire.
That very night his money lent
On bond, or mortgage, he called in,
With lawful use of six per cent;
Next morn—he put it out at ten.

L. 29. *In the Mississippi and the South Sea.* See post, p. 358.

P. 304, L. 33. *falls* = makes to fall.

P. 305, L. 22. *Serbonian bog.* Par. Lost, ii. 592. Cp. vol. i. p. 254, l. 28.

P. 306, L. 28. *hackled* = cut small. Dutch, *hakkelen.*

P. 307, L. 7. *instead of being all Frenchmen,* &c. Burke's surmise has not been justified. The French certainly glory in the unity implied in their national name, and the Savoyard and Alsatian share the enthusiasm.

L. 12. *We begin our public affections,* &c. Cp. ante, p. 136, and vol. i. p. 148, l. 1. There is here also an allusion to the beautiful lines of Pope, cited before.

P. 308, L. 22. *Never, before this time,* &c. I do not know whether the δῆμος ἔσχατος of Aristotle was ever realized, but the idea was certainly formed by him.

P. 312, L. 11. *your supreme government,* &c. Cp. vol. i. p. 100, l. 27.

P. 313, L. 14. *attack them in the vital parts.* Cp. p. 99, l. 21.

P. 316, L. 24. *sed multae urbes,* &c. Juv. x. 284.

L. 25. *He is now sitting,* &c. In October, 1790, when this pamphlet was published, Necker was no longer sitting on the ruins of the French monarchy, having resigned office on the 9th of September.

P. 318, L. 23. *were not wholly free,* &c. See this amply illustrated in Voltaire's amusing "Histoire du Parlement de Paris," published in 1769.

P. 319, L. 6. *the vice of the antient democracies,* &c. See footnote, p. 225.

L. 9. *it abated the respect,* &c. The difference between French and English political sentiment has been epigrammatically stated as follows: the French respect authority and despise law: the English respect law and despise authority.

P. 322, L. 6. *on good appointments,* i. e. if well supplied with all necessary equipment.

L. 9. *wolf by the ears.* The famous expression of Tiberius, "lupum se auribus tenere," Suet. Tib. 25. The image was more than once used by Burke with striking effect in a Parliamentary debate.

L. 14. *M. de la Tour du Pin.* He was a man of moderate views, and strongly attached to the monarchy. Necker had appointed him war minister about the middle of 1789. He resigned, together with all the rest of the ministry, except Montmorin, shortly after Burke's book was published.

L. 28. *Addressing himself,* &c. The allusions to the extract which follows are to the mutinies of the regiments of Metz and Nancy. See Carlyle's Hist. of the Rev., book ii.

[382] **P. 326, L. 16.** *comitia.* The filiation of the term *comices* is introduced to show what it involves.

P. 328, L. 23. *grand compounders—shorten the road to their degrees.* Alluding to an obsolete practice in the universities.

L. 33. *stiff and peremptory.* The expression is from Browne's Christian Morals.

P. 329, L. 1. *grand climacteric.* The sixty-third year ($7 \times 9 = 63$) of human life.

L. 3. *Si isti mihi largiantur,* &c. Slightly altered from Cic. de Senect. xxiii. 83. The original sentiment occurs in a favourite book of Burke's, Browne's Christian Morals, Part III, § 25, and was adopted by Prior as a motto for his poem "Solomon."

P. 332, L. 27. *until some popular general,* &c. A similar prediction was made by Schiller, who thought that some popular general of the Republic would make himself master not only of France but of a great part of Europe. It was accurately fulfilled in Bonaparte.

P. 335, L. 4. *The colonies assert,* &c. Burke's presages on the colonies were accurately fulfilled in the terrible history of the Revolution of St. Domingo.

P. 337, L. 8. *image and superscription.* St. Luke xx. 24.

L. 29. *unfeathered two-legged things.* The famous Greek definition of

Notes

a man, in the words used by Dryden in his celebrated description of Achitophel.

P. 340, L. 18. *systasis of Crete.* See an account of it in Plutarch's Treatise De Fraterno Amore. The Cretan cities quitted their internal feuds and united for defence when attacked by a common enemy. This was called συγκρητίζειν, whence our word "Syncretism."

P. 341, L. 9. *The revenue of the state,* &c. This admirable exposition of the nature of public revenues, and their relation to national action, should not be passed over as part of the merely critical section of the work. It possesses a real historical significance, for Pitt's great reforms in the revenue were just coming into operation.

P. 343, L. 14. *Cedo quî vestram,* &c. Naevius, quoted in Cic. de Senect. c. vi. 20. It is necessary to refer to the context: "Quod si legere aut audire voletis externa, maximas respublicas ab adolescentibus labefactas, a senibus sustentatas et restitutas reperietis.

Cedo, quî vestram rempúblicam tantam ámisistis tám cito?

Sic enim percontantur, ut est in Naevii ludo: respondentur et alia, et haec in primis:

Proveniebant orátores noví, stulti, adolescéntuli."

P. 345, L. 12. *John Doe, Richard Roe.* Cp. vol. i. p. 129, l. 16.

L. 20. *took an old huge full-bottomed perriwig,* &c. The allusion is to the offerings of silver plate made to Louis XIV by the court and city of Paris at the financial crisis, produced by the long war, of 1709. See Saint Simon, Mémoires, vol. vii. p. 208. "Cet expédient," says Saint Simon, "avait [383] déjà été proposé et rejeté par Pontchartrain, lorsqu'il était contrôleur-général, qui, devenu chancelier, n'y fut pas plus favorable." Notwithstanding the fact that the king expected every one to send their plate, the list of donors amounted to less than a hundred names: and the result was far below the king's expectation. "Au bout de trois mois, le roi sentit la honte et la faiblesse de cette belle ressource, et avoua qu'il se repentait d'y avoir consenti." Saint Simon confesses that he sent a portion only of his own, and concealed the rest.

L. 27. *tried in my memory by Louis XV.* In 1762, towards the close of the calamitous Seven Years' War. "La France alors était plus malheureuse. Toutes les ressources étaient épuisées: presque tous les citoyens, à l'exemple du roi, avaient porté leur vaisselle à la monnaie." Voltaire, Siècle de Louis XV, ch. 35.

REFLECTIONS ON THE REVOLUTION IN FRANCE

P. 349, L. 25. *Mais si maladia*, &c. From the comical interlude in Molière's Malade Imaginaire, in which the examination of a Bachelor for the doctor's degree is conducted in dog-latin. The candidate has already given the famous answer to the question, "Quare opium facit dormire?" "Quia est in eo virtus dormitiva," &c. On being interrogated as to the remedy for several diseases in succession, he makes the same answer:

Clysterium donare,
Postea segnare,
Ensuita purgare.

Which is repeated after the final question in the text. Burke happily compares the ignorance which made the assignat the panacea of the state, to this gross barbarism in the art of medicine.

P. 350, L. 4. *pious and venerable prelate.* Bitter irony, on Talleyrand.

P. 355, L. 24. *club at Dundee.* The Dundee "Friends of Liberty," whose proceedings acquired some notoriety a year or two later. In 1793 the Unitarian minister Palmer was transported for seven years for writing and publishing a seditious address bearing the name of this society.

P. 357, L. 8. *Credat who will.* Horace, Sat. lib. i. v. 100.

L. 31. *nuzzling* = following blindly by the *nose*. So Pope:

The blessed Benefit, not there confin'd,
Drops to the third, who nuzzles close behind.

P. 358, L. 4. *glimmerings of reason—solid darkness.* Pope, Dunciad iii. 226:

. . . a ray of reason stole
Half through the solid darkness of his soul.

So Dryden, Macflecknoe:

"Some beams of wit on other souls may fall,
Strike through, and make a lucid interval," &c.

P. 359, L. 18. *his atlantic regions.* The allusion is to Bailly's Letters on the subject of the fabled island of Atlantis.

L. 20. *smitten with the cold, dry, petrifick mace.* Par. Lost, x. 293:

The aggregated Soyle
[384] Death with his Mace petrific, cold, and dry,
As with a Trident smote.

NOTES

P. 361, L. 7. *tontines.* Lotteries on groups of lives, so called from their inventor. They had been adopted in England, and in the session which preceded the publication of this work, a batch of them had been converted into ordinary annuities.

L. 21. *all-atoning name.* Dryden, in the famous character of Achitophel, says that he

Assumed a patriot's all-atoning name.

L. 28. *Grand, swelling sentiments,* &c. See especially, Lucan, Book VII. This poet was excluded from the collection of classics edited "for the use of the Dauphin," on account of his tyrannicide principles: Corneille records his preference of Lucan before Virgil.

L. 31. *Old as I am,* &c. Perhaps an allusion to Addison's Cato, Act II:

You have not read mankind; your youth admires
The throes and swellings of a Roman soul,
Cato's bold flights, th' extravagance of virtue.

L. 32. *Corneille.* See "Cinna" (Clarendon Press Series).

P. 362, L. 3. *severe brow,* &c. Perhaps a reminiscence of Thompson's "Liberty," Book III:

The passing clouds
That often hang on Freedom's jealous brow.

P. 364, L. 21. *one of our poets.* Addison, in the celebrated Soliloquy of Cato, Act v. sc. 1:

Eternity! thou pleasing dreadful Thought!
Through what Variety of untry'd Being,
Through what new Scenes and Changes must we pass!

L. 32. *snatches from his share,* &c. The allusion is to the proceeding against Hastings.

The typeface used for this book is ITC New Baskerville, which was created for the International Typeface Corporation and is based on the types of the English type founder and printer John Baskerville (1706–75). Baskerville is the quintessential transitional face: it retains the bracketed and oblique serifs of old style faces such as Caslon and Garamond, but in its increased lowercase height, lighter color, and enhanced contrast between thick and thin strokes, it presages modern faces.

Printed on paper that is acid-free and meets the requirements of the American National Standard for Permanence of Paper for Printed Library Materials, z39.48-1992. ∞

Book design by Martin Lubin, New York, New York
Composition by Tseng Information Systems, Inc., Durham, North Carolina

Printed and bound by Sheridan Books, Inc., Chelsea, Michigan